D0707325

MOUNTAIN MEASURES

A COLLECTION OF WEST VIRGINIA RECIPES

"The purpose of the Junior League is exclusively educational and charitable and is to promote voluntarism, to develop the potential of its members for voluntary participation in community affairs, and to demonstrate the effectiveness of trained volunteers."

Published by

Junior League of Charleston, West Virginia, Inc.

© Copyright 1974

Junior League of Charleston, West Virginia, Inc.

ISBN No. 0-9606232-0-5
Library of Congress Catalog No. 75-316544

All rights reserved, including the right to reproduce this book, or parts thereof, in any form, except for the inclusion of brief quotations in review.

First Printing, 1974—10,000 copies
Second Printing, 1975—10,000 copies
Third Printing, 1976—10,000 copies
Fourth Printing, 1977—10,000 copies
Fifth Printing, 1979—15,000 copies
Sixth Printing, 1981—20,000 copies
Seventh Printing, 1983—20,000 copies

While the recipes in this book may not all be original, they were donated as favorites by the contributors.

Proceeds from the sale of **MOUNTAIN MEASURES** will go to all community projects of the Junior League of Charleston, West Virginia.

Art work by Mrs. Robert M. Chilton.

THE COVER
"Sunshine and Shadows," the quilt pattern chosen for the cover, is a variation of the traditional log cabin design. It was created by Cabin Creek Quilts.
Cover design by J. Michael Meador.
Cover photograph by Roger Hughes.

Copies may be obtained by addressing MOUNTAIN MEASURES, The Junior League of Charleston, P.O. Box 1924, Charleston, West Virginia, 25327. Price $9.95 per copy plus $1.50 mailing costs. West Virginia residents please add 50¢ sales tax. Order blanks in back of book.

**KANSAS CITY
PRESS, INC.**

1012 Locust
Kansas City, Missouri 64106

CONTENTS

Each section is keyed by a traditional quilt pattern. When this quilt pattern appears in the margin by the title of a recipe, it indicates a regional dish.

METRIC CONVERSION TABLE

The meter (M.) is the unit of length, the liter (L.) of volume and the gram (Gm.) of weight. Measurements are made in multiples of 10 or are divided by 10. The following are common equivalents of the metric system.

1 liter (L.)	= 1000 milliliters (Ml.)
1 meter (M.)	= 1000 millimeters (mm.)
1 gram (Gm.)	= 1000 milligrams (mg.)

1 Gm. = 1 ml. = 1 cc. (cubic centimeters)

20 drops	= 1 ml.	
5 ml.	= 1 teaspoonful	
10 ml.	= 1 dessertspoonful	
15 ml.	= 1 tablespoonful	
30 ml.	= 2 tablespoonsful	= 1 fluid ounce
240 ml.	= 1 cup	= 8 fluid ounces
480 ml.	= 1 pint	= 16 fluid ounces
960 ml.	= 1 quart	= 32 fluid ounces

28 Gm.	= 1 ounce
454 Gm.	= 1 pound
1 Kg. (1000 Gm.)	= 2.2 pounds

1 meter (M.)	39.37 inches
1 inch	2.54 centimeters (cm.)

ACKNOWLEDGEMENTS

COOKBOOK COMMITTEE

Mrs. Ronald A. McKenney, Chairman

Mrs. Robert M. Chilton

Mrs. John P. Killoran

Mrs. John C. Thomas, Assistant Chairman

Mrs. Charles G. Moyers, Jr.

Mrs. E. Charles Brod

TYPISTS

Mrs. John G. McGarty

Mrs. David H. Wallace

With special thanks to Mrs. William Wykle, Mrs. C.K. Payne, III, Mrs. K. Paul Davis, Mrs. Peter White, and to all those Junior League members and their families who researched, tested, evaluated, and provided invaluable assistance.

5

KATCHIE VERNER'S HARVEST

It pleasures her to gather
A hoard when autumn comes:
Of grapes in scroll-worked silver
Red-streaked-with-amber plums,
Winesaps and seek-no-farthers,
Green peppers, russet pears,
White roastin'-ears for drying
On frames above the stairs,
Queer handled gourds for dishes
And dippers at the spring,
Long butternuts, fat pumpkins,
Cream-colored beans to string,
Wild meats to jerk and pickle,
Brown chestnuts tipped with cold,
Cranberries from the marshes,
Tree honey dripping gold.

In barrels and crocks and suggins,
In pokes upon the floor
And hanging from the rafters
Is Katchie Verner's store
Against the mountain winter
When sleet-hard drifts will freeze
The deep loam of her garden
And gird her orchard trees.

Reprinted by permission of Louise McNeill, from **Gauley Mountain;** Harcourt, Brace and Company; New York, New York; 1939; Page 24.

Louise McNeill, a poet whose family has lived in West Virginia since the 1700's, is the author of several volumes of poetry including **Gauley Mountain** and **Paradox Hill: From Appalachia to Lunar Shore.** She has a doctorate in history and has published in many respected national literary magazines such as **Saturday Review, Atlantic Monthly** and **Harper's.**

Photo by Gerald S. Ratliff.

PREFACE

The Junior League of Charleston, West Virginia, invites you to enjoy *Mountain Measures,* a harvest of kitchen-tested recipes from the Appalachian region of the United States.

Our theme is the pioneer woman, her recipes, arts, and crafts. As an introduction, we have selected "Katchie Verner's Harvest" by Louise McNeill. To give a regional flavor, we have chosen fifteen photographs representative of the natural beauty of West Virginia and the native skills of its people. With these photographs are selected excerpts from the prose and poetry of Appalachian men and women.

Each section of the book is designated by a traditional quilt pattern, which is repeated with the recipes that are distinctively regional. One may find many favorites from local cooks and restaurants as well as famous West Virginians. The range extends from simple family fare to elegant dinner recipes.

Let us explore briefly the nature of our heritage. The early pioneers came across the rugged mountains of western Virginia or through the long valleys from Pennsylvania on foot or horseback, by wagon or boat. First they cleared the land and planted the garden, which contained the all-important corn as well as other vegetables the Indian had grown long before the European came to North America: beans, squash, cabbage, pumpkins, melons, cucumbers, sweet potatoes, and turnips. Occasionally there were a few precious herbs.

After provisions were made for a supply of food, the settlers built sturdy log houses with big fireplaces around which centered many family activities. Utensils included heavy iron pots hanging on a crane, a Dutch oven set in the coals for baking, skillets for frying, a carved wood mortar and pestle for pounding corn into meal, and a variety of baskets, gourds, and earthenware vessels made from the native clay.

Apple, pear, peach, and plum trees were set out and, while they matured, many wild fruits and berries were gathered; "sarvice" berries, mulberries, grapes, quinces, papaws, and persimmons. Those not eaten in season were dried, pickled, or otherwise preserved for use in the winter.

Following the precedent of the Indians, the settlers hunted the wild game that was initially so plentiful. Deer, bear, squirrel, rabbit, and wild turkey were found on many early tables, as well as fish from rivers and streams. Before the corn crop produced edible grain for corn bread, pone, hominy, and mush, it was not uncommon to use the turkey breast as a substitute for bread!

There were no recipe books on the frontier. Most knowledge

9

was passed down from generation to generation. A young wife learned from her mother how to pick a "mess of sallet greens," usually a mixture of three or four greens selected from lamb's quarter, plantain, poke, wild lettuce, mustard, dandelion, watercress, and others. These were then cooked with bacon grease or a slice of pork to produce an important part of the meal.

The pig was the primary meat animal in this area, as it was farther south. The animal required little care, running wild and feeding in the forest. As corn became abundant, it was fed to the pigs, which produced a tastier and more tender meat. Hog killing and preparation have remained basically unchanged from the earliest times to the present. Hard work was involved, but it meant ham for frying and roasting, sausages, souse meat, liver pudding, head cheese, bacon for eating and seasoning, and lard for cooking, soap, and candle-making. The settlers also had beef, mutton, and an occasional chicken, but pork remained the region's favorite meat. If the family were fortunate enough to have a cow, then milk, cream, butter, buttermilk, and sometimes cheese became important staples.

Adopting an Indian practice, the pioneer dried, salted, cured, smoked, and preserved many of the vegetables, fruits, and meats for the long, cold winters. Dried corn was a favorite, as were fodder beans, dried in the hulls, often while still hanging on the corn stalks on which they had grown. These are still popular in the hills.

As salt was plentiful at the Malden salt mines and fruits were available to make vinegar, the housewife could pickle and preserve a wide variety of foodstuffs. Jars and crocks of sauerkraut, beans, pickled meats, cucumber pickles, and relishes filled the pantry shelves and cellars.

Cane sugar was scarce, unless one lived on a major waterway. So, for sweetening the wife relied on maple syrup, maple sugar, and honey from wild bees. During the Civil War there was introduced into the region a variety of sorghum from which a sweet syrup was obtained by boiling the juice. When an inhabitant of the Appalachian highlands says "molasses," he means this sorghum syrup, rather than the molasses which was a by-product of cane sugar.

Spices, too, were scarce, but the settler used native herbs, as well as those raised from treasured seeds brought from the old country. Herbs, such as sassafras, dittany, and mint, not only served as flavorings and bases for tea, but also for medicine. It was not unusual for the pioneer to make stronger drink from the surplus crop of corn and fruit. The distillation of whiskey from grain was a Scotch-Irish custom continued in this new land, where there was an abundance of the necessary ingredients: grains, pure water, and food for the fire.

Undoubtedly there were lean times and hungry times in those early days. Although virtually isolated by the heavily forested mountains, the pioneer woman and her family combined courage and ingenuity with their European heritage and the practical wisdom of the native Indian to produce a unique food tradition. It is an inheritance which we present to you with pride and with the joy of sharing the bounty of our harvest.

Mary Helen Cutlip
and
The Cookbook Committee

COVERED BRIDGE AT MILTON

The Milton Bridge, built in 1821, is located on the East Mud River Road in Cabell County.

"It was made from timber that grew nearby. The material was hewed with the broadax and adz, hauled to the site by ox teams, and put in place by strong and sturdy hands. The bridge was first covered with boards made from white oak and split to shape with a froe. Wooden nails and pegs were used to fasten the boards and the timbers.

"Soon after the bridge was completed, a stagecoach stop and inn was opened in a log structure on the west side of the river . . .

"It is believed that the Marquis de Lafayette, Henry Clay, Andrew Jackson, and John Breckenridge made use of this route, as did Abraham Lincoln in 1847 when on his way to Washington to take his seat in Congress.

"When the Civil War broke out in 1861, Union troops occupied a church nearby as a garrison to protect the covered bridge which was guarded twenty-four hours a day. On April 5, 1861, a group of Confederates attempted to take the bridge, but were repulsed by Union troops.

"Out of the thousands of covered bridges built throughout the United States, only a few hundred remain from the romantic past. Of the fifty-four bridges still standing in West Virginia in 1953, only a few are extant."

Reprinted by permission from Caldwell Dudley, Editor and Owner of the *Cabell Record*, Milton, West Virginia.

Photo by James Rust

APPETIZERS

Rising Star

ALMOND-BLUE CHEESE BALLS

½ pound cream cheese
½ pound blue cheese
A little cream
1½ tablespoons grated onion
1½ tablespoons chopped
  parsley

1½ tablespoons chopped chives
1½ tablespoons drained chutney,
  chopped
Salt and pepper
Chopped almonds

Blend and form in little individual balls. Roll in chopped almonds and chill.

Mrs. C. K. Payne, III

APPETIZER SAUSAGE BALLS IN BLANKET

1½ cups flour
2 teaspoons curry powder
1 teaspoon paprika
¼ teaspoon salt

2 cups (8 ounces) shredded
  Cheddar cheese
½ cup butter or margarine
1 pound sausage (mild or hot)

Mix flour, curry, paprika, salt, and cheese. With pastry blender, cut in butter until mixture resembles coarse crumbs. Shape pastry mixture into ball with hands. Cover and refrigerate at least an hour. Shape sausage into small balls. Fry until browned. Drain on towels. Divide dough into as many pieces as there are sausage balls. Shape dough around balls. (Dough may be crumbly but will form.) Wrap and freeze. Preheat oven to 400° and bake on cookie sheet 12 minutes. (Careful with baking time since they burn easily.) Makes about 3 dozen.

Mrs. Charles G. Moyers, Jr.

ASPARAGUS ROLL-UPS

4 ounces blue cheese
4 ounces Roquefort cheese
8 ounces cream cheese
1 egg
1 tablespoon mayonnaise

2 (14½ ounces each) cans long
   spear asparagus
40 pieces sandwich bread, crust
   removed
1 stick margarine
Paprika

Mix cheeses, egg, and mayonnaise with an electric mixer. Flatten each piece of bread with a rolling pin until almost paper thin. Spread cheese mixture on each side, lay one spear of asparagus on each piece, and roll up. Melt the margarine and add paprika for color. Dip each roll in the margarine, and place on an ungreased cookie sheet. Bake at 350° for 15 minutes. Serves 10 to 12 as an hors d'oeuvre. Can be frozen and reheated.

Mrs. Charles Q. Gage

BOILED SHRIMP

⅔ cup chopped onion
⅔ cup chopped celery
2 teaspoons seasoned pepper
2 teaspoons salt

5 dashes Tabasco
Pinch of bay leaf
1 tablespoon lemon juice
3 pounds large or medium
   shrimp in shell

In a six quart pan, bring 4 quarts water to a boil. Add everything except the shrimp, and boil for a few minutes. Add shrimp, bring liquid to a boil and boil for 11 minutes. Pour liquid and shrimp into colander and drain. Celery, onions and seasoning will mix with the shrimp. Let stand and cool. Serve at room temperature with seafood sauce. Will serve 6 shrimp eaters or 8 dainty eaters.

Mrs. H. Jarrett Walker

BRACIOLA

Meat:
     Eye of the round of beef,   Lard or butter
       sliced paper thin
       across the grain

Spread each piece of meat with lard or butter.

Stuffing:
2 cups bread crumbs
1 cup Parmesan cheese
2 or 3 tablespoons parsley

Olive oil, to moisten
1 teaspoon garlic salt
Dash pepper
½ pound mozzarella cheese

Mix bread crumbs, Parmesan cheese, parsley, olive oil, garlic salt, and pepper for stuffing. Place small amount of stuffing on each slice of meat. Put small strip of mozzarella cheese on top. Roll up and place on small skewer. When skewer is full, spread lard on each side and dip in bread crumb mixture. Broil on each side until brown; do not overcook. Makes 150 to 200 depending on size of meat.

Mrs. William C. Payne

BRAISED CHICKEN WINGS

¼ cup soy sauce
½ cup water
½ cup brown sugar, packed

¼ cup sherry
1 teaspoon dry mustard
2 green onions cut in 1" pieces

10 chicken wings, separated at joints
(Discard tips or use to make broth for
another dish.)

Combine all ingredients in medium-sized saucepan. Cover; heat to boiling; simmer 30 minutes. Uncover; simmer 15 minutes longer, basting frequently. Serve hot or cold. Serves 4.

Good for a Chinese meal or for outdoor eating. Use big napkins to catch the drips or follow with a steamed hand towel.

Mrs. Charles G. Moyers, Jr.

BUTTERED PARMESAN TOAST FINGERS

Bread slices   Parmesan cheese, grated
                    Melted butter

Remove crusts and make 4 lengthwise strips of several slices of bread. Roll strips of bread in melted butter and then in cheese. Place in shallow pan and broil until brown on both sides.

Mrs. Robert C. Payne

CEVICHE ACAPULCO STYLE

2 pounds firm fresh fish
4 ounces lemon juice
1 (16 ounce) can whole
    tomatoes with juice
2½ tablespoons olive oil
½ teaspoon finely ground
    oregano
½ teaspoon freshly ground
    black pepper

¼ teaspoon Tabasco sauce
¼ cup orange juice
¼ cup catsup
1 preserved Jalapeño chile
    pepper or any other
    Mexican style chile pepper,
    chopped finely
½ cup finely chopped onion
Salt to taste

Place the fish, cut in ¼ inch squares, in the lemon juice for 20 minutes, stirring gently to be sure all fish is well coated. Cut the whole tomatoes in ¼ inch cubes. Remove the fish and rinse with fresh water. Mix the prepared fish with the remainder of the ingredients. Leave the Ceviche in the refrigerator for at least 6 hours before serving. Serve chilled. Serves 8.

Mrs. Ronald A. McKenney

CHARLESTON PRESS CLUB MEAT BALLS

Meat Balls:

1 pound finely ground beef	Salt and pepper
1 egg	¼ cup catsup
½ cup cracker meal	1 onion, finely chopped

1 small green pepper, chopped finely

Combine all ingredients thoroughly. Roll into 20 small balls. Place on slightly greased baking sheet, allowing enough space between balls so they will not stick. Bake 20 minutes in a 350° oven. Add to the barbecue sauce.

Sauce:

1 small onion, finely chopped	1 teaspoon brown sugar
2 tablespoons olive oil	1 tablespoon Worcestershire
¼ cup vinegar	sauce
1 cup water	½ teaspoon chili powder
2 or 3 tablespoons prepared	½ teaspoon salt
mustard	Pinch garlic powder
1¼ cups tomato purée	½ teaspoon Tabasco sauce

Sauté onion in olive oil until golden brown. Combine remaining ingredients except Tabasco sauce, and add to cooked onion. Simmer one hour, stirring occasionally. Add Tabasco sauce 15 minutes before serving. If time is scarce, a bottled barbecue sauce can be used. Can be frozen, but place in a large flat container so as not to disturb the meat balls. Serve in a chafing dish.

CHEDDAR CHEESE CRISPIES

¾ cup softened butter	½ teaspoon salt
9 ounces sharp Cheddar	Tabasco sauce to taste
cheese, grated	(approximately 1 teaspoon)
1½ cups sifted flour	3 cups Rice Krispies

Cream butter and cheese together until well blended. Add flour, salt and Tabasco and knead until well blended. Knead in the Rice Krispies.

Make tiny balls out of teaspoon amounts of dough. Place on an ungreased cookie sheet and press down with fork until each teaspoon of dough is round and approximately ¼ inch thick.

Bake in pre-heated oven at 400° for 10 to 12 minutes. Remove to rack to cool. Store in airtight container. This recipe makes 50 Crispies.

Mrs. Isaac N. Smith, Jr.

CHEESE BISCUITS

1 (10 ounce) roll sharp process cheese
1 stick margarine or butter
1 cup flour
¼ teaspoon red pepper
¼ teaspoon Worcestershire sauce
1 package whole pecans, for garnish

Soften and blend cheese and butter; add flour, pepper, and Worcestershire. Knead together until well mixed. Roll in a long roll the size of a silver dollar. Freeze. When ready to use, let soften 5 minutes. Slice ¼ inch thick, place on cookie sheet. Add pecan on top. Bake at 350° for 10 minutes. Remainder of roll can be re-frozen. Serves 15. Serve as an appetizer or with luncheon salads.

Mrs. Meredith K. Rice

CREAM CHEESE BISCUITS

¼ pound butter
1 cup flour
1 (8 ounce) package cream cheese
½ teaspoon salt

Mix all ingredients and pat out on floured board. Cut bite-size pieces, and place on cookie sheet. Bake at 450° about 12 minutes or until lightly browned. Makes about 60.

These biscuits are nice for cocktails when filled with ham, turkey, or cocktail spreads. Also, good for lunch when made a little larger.

Mrs. Richard Repaire

CHEESE-DATE BISCUITS

Dough:
½ cup butter or margarine
2 cups N.Y. State cheese, grated
1½ cups flour
Dash cayenne pepper
1 teaspoon sugar

Mix first 3 ingredients thoroughly. Add cayenne pepper and sugar. Mix well.

Filling:
1 (8 ounce) package dates, cut   2 tablespoons water
    into small pieces   1 tablespoon sugar

Mix these ingredients well and cook 3 minutes.

Roll cheese dough thinly; cut with biscuit cutter. Spread date mixture on each round; fold over and press edges to seal. Bake at 375° for 15 to 20 minutes. Makes about 40 biscuits. Good for parties, coffees, teas, receptions, etc.

CHEESE PUFF HORS D'OEUVRES

½ pound margarine (2 sticks)   1 (8 ounce) package sharp
1 (8 ounce) package cream   Cheddar cheese, grated
    cheese   2 egg whites, beaten stiff
                1 loaf unsliced bread

Melt cheeses and butter together in top of double boiler over hot water. Beat till smooth and completely blended. Cool to lukewarm. Fold in 2 stiffly beaten egg whites. Cut unsliced loaf into 9-10 slices (½" - ¾" thick); cut slices into cubes. Dip cubes into cheese mixture to coat completely. Put on cookie sheet and freeze immediately. When frozen, store in plastic bags in freezer. (Will keep for weeks.) To serve, place frozen cubes on greased cookie sheet and bake at 450° for 8 minutes, or until golden brown. Serve hot. Makes several dozen.

Mrs. Edward W. Rugeley, Jr.

CHEESE STRAWS

1 (10 ounce) package pie crust   1 teaspoon dry mustard
    mix   Dash cayenne pepper
1 cup (8 ounce package) grated   1 teaspoon Worcestershire
    sharp Cheddar cheese   sauce
                ¼ cup water

Combine all ingredients, except Worcestershire and water. Add Worcestershire sauce to water and gradually add to first mixture, until pastry leaves side of bowl. Shape into a ball. Divide into 4 pieces and refrigerate until firm. On a lightly floured surface, roll 1 piece of dough into 7" × 8" rectangle. Cut into 10 strips and twist each strip 4 times. Refrigerate strips 30 minutes. Bake in a preheated oven of 425° for 10 minutes or until golden brown. Makes 40 straws.

Mrs. Betty Scott Cowden

CHEESE-STUFFED MUSHROOMS

18 medium-sized mushrooms
   Melted butter
1 (3 ounce) package cream
   cheese

¼ cup grated Parmesan cheese
2 tablespoons milk
⅛ teaspoon onion juice
   Sliced almonds

Wipe mushrooms with a damp cloth; remove the stems for another use; roll caps in melted butter. Beat softened cream cheese until light; beat in Parmesan cheese, milk and onion juice. Fill the mushroom caps with the cheese mixture; top each cap with a sliced almond; arrange them on a buttered baking sheet. Bake in a moderate oven (350°) for 15 minutes, or until the tops are lightly browned, and serve immediately. Serves 6.

Mrs. Marsha Pushkin

CHICKEN LIVERS WITH PINEAPPLE

1 pound (or more) chicken
   livers
2 tablespoons cornstarch
½ teaspoon salt
2 tablespoons salad oil
½ cup water

1 large or 2 medium onions,
   chopped
1 chicken bouillon cube
1 (8 to 12 ounce) can pineapple
   tidbits in heavy syrup
1 tablespoon soy sauce

Hot cooked rice

Mix the chicken livers with cornstarch and salt. In a large skillet, brown the livers well in hot salad oil. Stir in water, onions, chicken bouillon cube, pineapple tidbits with syrup, and soy sauce. Reduce heat to low; cover and simmer 5 minutes, or until livers are tender, stirring occasionally. Serve as an hors d'oeuvre in a chafing dish or over hot rice as a main dish. Serves 4.

Mrs. E. Charles Brod

CRAB-STUFFED MUSHROOMS

1 pound (or more) large, fresh
   mushrooms
1 (7 ounce) can crabmeat
1 cup grated sharp Cheddar
   cheese

½ cup mayonnaise
½ cup crushed Ritz
   crackers
   Parmesan cheese

Remove stems from mushrooms and wash carefully. Save stems for another dish.
Combine drained crabmeat and grated sharp cheese. Add mayonnaise and mix well with a fork. Stuff this mixture into each mushroom cap. Sprinkle each with crushed crackers. Bake for 10 min-

utes in 350° oven. Then sprinkle with Parmesan cheese and run under the broiler until they bubble. Serves 8 as an appetizer; or 4 as a first course, in individual seafood shells.

Mrs. James L. Surface

CREAM CHEESE AND HAM BALLS

2 (8 ounce) packages cream
    cheese
½ grated onion (to taste)
2 tablespoons mayonnaise
½ pound shaved ham

Soften cream cheese and mix well with onion and mayonnaise. Roll into bite size balls and wrap with shaved ham. Chill well before serving. Makes approximately 4 dozen bite-sized canapés.

EDAM CHEESE-BEER BALLS

1 (1¾ pound) Edam cheese
    sphere in red wax (at
    room temperature)
1 cup beer
¼ cup softened butter
1 teaspoon dry mustard
1½ teaspoons caraway seeds
½ teaspoon sesame seeds
½ teaspoon celery salt

Cut top off cheese sphere and discard. Scoop cheese out with spoon, leaving ¼ inch cheese "wall" in red wax shell. Refrigerate shell. Grate cheese finely. Mix all ingredients well with electric mixer. Stuff cheese mixture into shell, over-running the top. Wrap in plastic wrap and foil and refrigerate several days before serving with crackers.

Mrs. W. Gaston Caperton, III

ERNIE'S HOT COQUILLE

Ernie's Esquire provides luxurious club-type dining. The speciality of the house, seafood coquille, is served at both the Wheeling and Charleston, West Virginia, restaurants.

12 tablespoons butter, divided
 6 tablespoons flour
 2 teaspoons salt
¼ teaspoon white pepper
 4 cups light cream
 1 pound scallops
½ cup finely chopped onion
1 cup sliced mushrooms
1 pound small shrimp, cooked
½ pound crabmeat
¼ cup sherry
6 tablespoons fine
    bread crumbs
Pimiento

Melt 9 tablespoons butter in a saucepan; blend flour in smoothly and cook the roux over low heat for several minutes, stirring frequently. Season roux with salt and white pepper. Gradually stir in light cream, and cook sauce, stirring constantly until it begins to bubble. Simmer it over low heat for 5 minutes. In a skillet, sauté scallops and onions in 3 tablespoons butter until the onions are golden. Remove the scallops and onions and in the same skillet sauté sliced mushrooms for 3 minutes. Combine the mushrooms with the scallops and onions and the cream sauce, and stir in shrimp, crabmeat, and sherry. Spoon the mixture into a casserole or individual scallop shells and sprinkle with bread crumbs. Bake the coquille at 400 degrees for 10 minutes or until bread crumbs are slightly browned. Then garnish the dish with bits of pimiento and serve at once as a first course or an entree. Serves 10 to 12. This is an extremely rich dish. It was printed in *Gourmet* magazine on September 30, 1971.

Ernie's Esquire Supper Club

GARLIC CHEESE LOG

1 pound mild Cheddar
　cheese
13¼ ounces extra sharp
　Cheddar cheese
1 (8 ounce) package cream
　cheese
Olives

1 (5 ounce) jar of pimiento
　cheese spread
Salt and pepper
2 dashes Tabasco sauce
2 garlic cloves
Paprika

Grate finely the first two cheeses. Add other two, a little black pepper, salt, Tabasco, and grated or pressed garlic cloves. Mix all until smooth and well blended; form into 2 long rolls 1½" x 6". Roll logs in paprika. Wrap in waxed paper and foil and store in refrigerator. To serve, slice rolls, placing each slice on cracker and garnish with stuffed olive.

Mrs. James Cabell

GARLIC-PICKLE RELISH CHEESE BALL

1 (8 ounce) package cream
　cheese
4 ounces blue cheese
1 teaspoon Worcestershire
　sauce

2 heaping tablespoons sweet
　pickle relish
½ to ¾ teaspoon garlic salt
½ cup chopped parsley
¾ cup chopped nuts

Combine all ingredients except nuts. Form into one large or two small balls and roll in nuts. Can be frozen.

Mrs. Kenneth Kleeman

GOUGERE

¾ cup diced ham
½ cup diced Swiss cheese
½ cup water

¼ cup butter or margarine (½ stick)
½ cup flour
Salt and pepper

3 eggs

Dice ham and cheese in ¼ inch cubes. Bring water to a boil in a small pan. Add butter. When butter has melted, add flour all at once. Keep stirring and cooking until it forms a ball which leaves the sides of the pan — this takes just a few minutes.

Cool the dough a little and turn it into a large bowl. Add the eggs one a a time, beating well until each one is absorbed before adding the next one. Season with salt and pepper and fold in the cheese and ham.

With a spoon, form the dough into puffs, about the size of a pecan, and place on a well-greased cookie sheet. Place in a preheated 425° oven for 7 minutes. Reduce heat to 375°, but don't open the oven. Bake for 15 additional minutes. Serve hot for an appetizer. Keep warm in a chafing dish.

Note:

This may be made in a well-greased ring mold and served with chicken salad or another type of salad in the middle. If using a ring, bake at 425° for 20 minutes, reduce heat to 375° and bake 25 minutes longer.

This may be baked and frozen, but reheat immediately before serving.

Mrs. James McCain

HAM-STUFFED MUSHROOMS

2 dozen large fresh mushrooms, whole
1 cup fresh mushrooms, chopped
½ cup minced onions
1 tablespoon olive oil

1 cup diced country ham, cooked
1 cup bread crumbs
Additional olive oil
2 garlic cloves
6 teaspoons brandy

Remove stems from mushroom caps; wipe caps with a damp cloth and set aside. Sauté onion in 1 tablespoon olive oil until transparent. Add ham and chopped mushrooms and heat. Mix onion, mushroom, and ham mixture in a bowl with bread crumbs. Fill mushroom caps with this mixture. Put ⅛ inch olive oil in a skillet, brown garlic cloves and remove. Put mushroom caps in (filled side up) and cook very slowly for 5 minutes. Remove mushrooms with a slotted spoon and place in a baking dish. Pour ¼ teaspoon of brandy over each mushroom and dust with bread crumbs. Place under broiler, 4 inches from heat, and brown tops. Serve immediately.

Mrs. John D. Amos

HOT DOG CANAPE

2 to 3 cans cocktail hot dogs   ½ cup brown sugar
1 small bottle catsup   ½ cup bourbon

Parboil the hot dogs for a few minutes. Make a sauce of the catsup, brown sugar and bourbon. Heat. Mix the sauce and hot dogs and serve in a chafing dish.

Mrs. Kenneth Kleeman

HOT SHRIMP TEMPTER

Cyrus R. Vance, a one-time Secretary of the Army and Under-Secretary of Defense, is currently President of the Association of the Bar of the City of New York. A native of Clarksburg, West Virginia, Mr. Vance performed as a special representative of the President at Cyprus in 1967 and Korea in 1968 and as a negotiator at the Paris Peace Conference on Vietnam in 1968 and 1969. He was awarded the Medal of Freedom in 1969.

¼ cup butter   ¼ cup Madeira or sherry
½ cup thinly sliced green   1 teaspoon salt
   onions   Dash of pepper
½ pound mushrooms,   1½ pounds cooked and cleaned
   washed and sliced   shrimp
3 tablespoons flour   2 tablespoons chopped
1 cup half and half cream   parsley

Sauté onions in butter until limp; add mushrooms and cook until tender (about 5 minutes). Add flour and mix. Add half and half and wine and cook until thickened, stirring constantly. Season with salt and pepper. Fold in shrimp and heat, stirring often. Put in small pastry shells and sprinkle with parsley.

Cyrus Vance

HOT SWISS CHEESE BALLS

3 cups grated Swiss cheese   Salt, pepper and paprika to
2 tablespoons flour   taste
4 tablespoons sherry   6 egg whites
                  Cracker crumbs

Mix the cheese and flour and add sherry and seasonings. Beat egg whites as stiff as possible and fold in. Form into 1" balls and roll in cracker crumbs. Fry in deep hot fat in a frying basket until golden brown. Drain. Serve with wooden picks to facilitate handling.

Miss Elizabeth Beury

LEMONS STUFFED WITH SARDINES

4 to 6 lemons
1½ tablespoons butter
1 tin sardines, drained, reserving oil
1 small onion, chopped

1 inch strip green pepper, chopped
1 rib celery, chopped
¼ to ⅓ cup mayonnaise, divided
1 hard boiled egg, chopped

4 to 6 sprigs parsley

Cut tops off lemons and scoop out well. See that lemons stand on plate by cutting off bottom. Place butter and sardine oil in sauce pan. Cook with onion and green pepper. When cool, add celery, mayonnaise, cut up sardines and hard boiled egg. Mix well and stuff individual lemons. Place enough mayonnaise on top to round off lemon. Place a sprig of parsley on top. Chill. Serves 4 to 6 as first course with melba toast.

Mrs. Robert W. Lawson, Jr.

LIVER STRUDEL - HORS D'OEUVRE

Rabbi Samuel Cooper was the rabbi of B'nai Jacob Synagogue of Charlestown, West Virginia, from 1932 to 1974. Concerned with human rights, Rabbi Cooper has performed as chairman of the West Virginia Human Rights Commission. Mrs. Cooper, a well-known gourmet cook who has published several cookbooks, comments that she always practices her dishes on the Rabbi first.

Crust:
1¼ cups sifted flour
½ teaspoon salt

⅓ cup shortening
3 tablespoons water (approx.)

Sift flour and salt together. Cut in shortening until mixture is like coarse sand. Add water a little at a time until all is moistened and pieces cling together.

Filling:
2 minced onions
3 tablespoons fat
½ pound sliced beef liver

4 hard boiled eggs
½ teaspoon salt
Dash of pepper

1 egg, beaten

Sauté onions in fat until light yellow. Add liver and sauté 4 minutes on each side. Put onions, livers, and eggs through food chopper. Mix with remaining fat left in skillet and salt and pepper.

Divide dough into thirds and roll very thin into strips 4 inches by 12 inches. Lay a bar of liver mixture down the middle of each strip. Roll half the pastry over it; brush with eggs and cover with other side of pastry. Brush all over with egg and seal ends. Place on baking sheets and bake in 400° oven for 20 minutes. Cool slightly and cut into ½ inch slices. Makes 50 pieces.

Note:
The filling (chopped liver) for this recipe may be purchased at a delicatessen.

Rabbi Samuel Cooper

MARINATED MUSHROOMS

⅓ cup red wine vinegar
⅓ cup salad oil
1 onion, thinly sliced
   (preferably red)
1 teaspoon salt
2 teaspoons dried parsley
   flakes

1 tablespoon brown sugar
1 teaspoon prepared mustard
3 cans mushroom caps,
   drained, or 3 cups of fresh
   mushrooms, peeled, stems
   removed, cooked one
   minute, and drained

Simmer all except mushrooms for five minutes. Drain mushrooms and add to marinade. Store in refrigerator at least 24 hours and as long as 2 weeks. Remove from refrigerator at least 1 hour before serving; they are best at room temperature. Serve in bowl with toothpicks. You may add canned artichokes to marinade for a variation.

Mrs. T. H. Edelblute, Jr.

MINIATURE MEAT BALLS

4 to 6 slices dry bread
2 pounds ground beef
3 eggs
½ cup grated mozzarella or
   Romano cheese
2 tablespoons chopped parsley
½ teaspoon garlic salt

½ teaspoon crushed oregano
1 teaspoon salt
Dash of pepper
1 (16 ounce) jar spaghetti sauce
   or favorite home-made
   sauce
Olive oil

Soak bread in water 2 or 3 minutes, then squeeze out moisture. Combine bread with remaining ingredients, except spaghetti sauce. Mix well. Form into about 40 small balls. Brown slowly at medium heat in olive oil or margarine. Add spaghetti sauce. Cook in sauce 30 minutes over low heat. Serves 20.

Mrs. Otis O'Conner

MUSHROOMS A L'ESCARGOT

1 (6 ounce) package fresh
   medium mushrooms
4 tablespoons butter, divided
1 small onion, finely chopped
6 garlic cloves, finely minced
1 tablespoon parsley
Salt and pepper to taste

Wipe mushrooms with damp cloth and remove stems; save stems for another use. Cook onion and garlic until tender in 2 tablespoons butter; cool and mix with remaining butter. Stuff and bake caps for 30 minutes at medium temperature (350°). Serve in the same manner as snails with French bread to help absorb the garlicky butter. Serves 4 to 6.

Mrs. Ronald A. McKenney

MUSHROOM TURNOVERS

Dough:
   9 ounces cream cheese,
      softened
1 stick butter, softened
1½ cups flour

Cream thoroughly and chill.

Filling:
   1 large onion, minced
   ½ pound mushrooms, minced
   3 tablespoons butter
1 teaspoon salt
¼ teaspoon thyme
2 tablespoons flour
¼ cup sour cream

Sauté onion and mushrooms in butter; add remaining ingredients, except sour cream, and cook until thickened. Stir in sour cream.

Divide dough in half and roll each half thinly. Cut in rounds and place as much of the mixture on each as possible; fold over to make half-round and seal. May be frozen at this point. Preheat oven to 450°. Remove desired quantity from freezer; pierce each top with knife point and brush each with a mixture of one egg yolk, beaten with 1 teaspoon water. Bake 12 to 15 minutes until golden. Makes at least 4 dozen. You may have some mushroom mixture left over.

Mrs. George W. Higginbotham

OLIVE BALLS

2 cups (½ pound) finely
   grated Cheddar cheese
½ cup softened butter
1 cup sifted flour
1 teaspoon paprika
Medium size olives

Blend cheese, butter, flour, and paprika. Roll in balls the size of walnuts, enclosing an olive in each one. Bake at 400° for 15 minutes. Makes 4 to 5 dozen.

Mrs. Robert F. Goldsmith

OLIVE-BLUE CHEESE BALL

8 ounces cream cheese
4 ounces blue cheese, crumbled
4 ounces chive cream cheese

¼ cup soft butter
⅔ cup chopped stuffed green olives
⅓ cup chopped walnuts
Parsley, nuts or olives, optional

Soften cheeses, and butter; blend. Drain olives and stir with walnuts into the mixture. Divide into 3 one-cup cheese balls or 1 large three cup cheese ball. Trim with parsley, nuts, or olives. Serve with crackers or raw vegetables, such as celery.

Mrs. Daniel O. Martin

ONION BITS

White bread rounds
Mayonnaise

Paper-thin onion slices
Parmesan cheese

Cut small (1½" to 2" diameter) rounds of white bread. Spread top with mayonnaise (not salad dressing) ¼ inch thick. Place slice of onion about the same diameter as the bread on each round. Sprinkle liberally with Parmesan cheese. Broil until golden brown (2-3 minutes). Best prepared early in the day and refrigerated until ready to brown them. Serve hot as an hors d'oeuvre or with a soup.

Mrs. Richard R. Meckfessel

OYSTER LOAF

4 to 6 slices of bacon
4 tablespoons butter, divided
½ cup flour
1 pint to 1 quart oysters
1 loaf French bread

2 garlic cloves
2 medium firm tomatoes
1 cup mayonnaise
Horseradish to taste
Lemon wedges

Fry bacon in 1 tablespoon butter. When crisp, drain and crumble, Flour oysters and fry in bacon drippings. Drain and cool slightly. Cut thick slice lengthwise from top of French bread and save it to use as a lid. Hollow out inside of loaf and rub with mashed garlic cloves. Discard garlic. Drizzle 3 tablespoons melted butter inside loaf and add oysters and crumbled bacon. Barely sauté thick tomato slices and arrange on top of oysters. Put top of loaf on, wrap in foil and bake at 350° for 10 to 15 minutes, depending on amount of oysters. Slice as you would a loaf of bread, spoon mayonnaise and horseradish mixed to taste on each serving, and garnish with lemon wedges. Serves 8 to 10 as a first course.

Mrs. John Casto

PARMESAN-ON-RYE CANAPES

⅓ cup grated Parmesan cheese
¾ cup mayonnaise
½ cup diced onion
1 teaspoon Worcestershire sauce
Dash of salt and pepper
Party rye bread, toasted

Combine all ingredients but bread. Spread topping on small slices of bread. Put under broiler till bubbly and beginning to brown. Serve hot. Makes about 2 dozen.

Mrs. Edward W. Rugeley, Jr.

PARTY PIZZAS

2 loaves Rubel's Tangy French Rye Bread
Cooking oil
1 (10½ ounce) can tomato soup
1 (6 ounce) can tomato paste
1 teaspoon onion salt
1½ teaspoons oregano
1 teaspoon curry powder
1 package sharp Cheddar cheese, grated
Pepperoni slices
Oregano
Parsley flakes
Parmesan cheese
Tomato sauce

Place slices of party rye on baking sheets and brush bread with cooking oil to edges. Mix tomato soup, tomato paste, onion salt, oregano and curry powder. Brush this mixture on bread almost to edge. Sprinkle with grated Cheddar cheese; place pepperoni slice in center of each pizza. Add a dash of oregano to each one, then sprinkle with parsley flakes and then with Parmesan cheese. Put an additional ½ teaspoon tomato sauce on top. Bake in 350° oven 7 to 10 minutes until bubbly. Serves 12 generously. May be made ahead and frozen on baking sheets.

Mrs. Seigle W. Parks

PICKLED SHRIMP

¾ cup oil, divided
3 garlic cloves
2 onions, chopped
2½ pounds shrimp
2 onions, thinly sliced

½ cup vinegar
1½ teaspoons salt
¼ teaspoon dry mustard
½ teaspoon pepper
¼ teaspoon dried ground
   chili peppers

Heat ¼ cup oil. Add garlic and chopped onion. Sauté 10 minutes, stirring. Add shrimp. Sauté 7 minutes, stirring. Let cool 15 minutes. Shell. Combine sliced onions, remaining oil, vinegar, salt, mustard, pepper, and chili peppers. Add shrimp and stir. (For a more potent flavor, 1 cup of vinegar may be used instead of ½ cup.) Marinate at least 24 hours.

Mrs. Soul Snyder

ROQUEFORT CHEESE BALL

Ball:
2 (3 ounce) wedges Roquefort
   or blue cheese
1 (10 ounce) container Cheddar
   cheese spread
4 (3 ounce) packages cream
   cheese

2 tablespoons minced onion
1 teaspoon Worcestershire
   sauce
¼ cup dried parsley
½ cup ground pecans

Day before: Let cheeses soften at room temperature. In a medium bowl, combine cheeses, onion, and Worcestershire; blend well. Stir in parsley and pecans. Shape into one large ball. Place in bowl lined with wax paper; regrigerate overnight or place in freezer. Best aged several days.

Topping:
½ cup ground pecans

¼ cup parsley

To serve: About 1 hour before serving, remove ball from refrigerator and roll in mixture of ground pecans and parsley. Serve with crisp crackers. Makes 4½ cups.

Mrs. Thomas H. Edelblute, Jr.

SAUSAGE-CHEESE BALLS

1 pound sausage (mild or hot)

1 pound sharp Cheddar cheese,
   grated
3 cups Bisquick

For ease in handling, mix one half of all ingredients at a time. Roll in balls the size of large marbles. Bake at 350° for 15 minutes (until golden). These freeze beautifully after baking. Reheat in aluminum foil. Makes 100 balls.

Mrs. J. Eldon Rucker, Jr.

SHAD ROE HORS D'OEUVRES

1 can shad roe	Worcestershire sauce to taste
1 (8 ounce) package cream cheese	Cayenne pepper
	Mayonnaise or sour cream
Chopped onion to taste	Red cabbage shell

Mix all ingredients but the cabbage, using enough mayonnaise or sour cream to make a good spreading consistency. Stuff into a red cabbage shell with outer leaves peeled back. Serves 12.

Mrs. Robert W. Lawson, Jr.

SHRIMP-CHEESE BALLS

6 ounces cream cheese	Cayenne pepper
1½ teaspoons prepared mustard	Salt
1 teaspoon grated onion	¾ cup fresh cooked shrimp, or
1 teaspoon lemon juice	1 (4½ ounce) can
⅔ cup mixed nuts or pecans	

Soften the cream cheese. Blend in the mustard, onion, lemon juice, cayenne pepper and salt to taste. Drain the shrimp. Break into pieces, stir into cheese mixture and chill. Form into ½ inch balls and roll in the chopped nuts. Makes 3½ dozen balls. Crabmeat or lobster may also be used in place of the shrimp.

Mrs. William R. McDavid

SUPER RAMAKI

12 chicken livers	12 water chestnuts
¼ cup soy sauce	Brown sugar
¼ cup bourbon	12 strips bacon

Cut raw livers in half and soak for 4 hours in a mixture of soy sauce and bourbon. Drain on paper towels. Cut water chestnuts in half. Slit chicken liver and slide water chestnut into cavity. Roll in brown sugar and pack the sugar on the chicken liver.

Lay each liver on ½ strip of uncooked bacon. Roll and put a toothpick through it. Lay on a jelly roll pan, then add a little more brown sugar. Bake at 400° for 20 to 30 minutes, turning occasionally (once or twice).

These can be made the day before and covered tightly. Bake immediately before serving.

Mrs. Kenneth Underwood

BEER AND CHEESE DIP

1 pound sharp Cheddar cheese   Beer
                               Catsup

Put cheese through a meat grinder or grate into a large bowl. Mix cheese with catsup and beer until mixture is right for a dip. Refrigerate. Take out an hour before the party so it will be ready to serve. Serves 20 to 25.

Mrs. James Cabell

CHILI CON QUESO

1 small onion, minced
1 tablespoon butter
1 cup tomatoes, chopped
Salt and pepper to taste

1 cup hot green chilies, chopped
8 ounces cream cheese, cubed
1 cup half and half, or milk

Sauté onion in butter. Add tomatoes, green chilies, salt and pepper. Simmer 15 minutes. Add cubed cream cheese and stir to melt the cheese. After the cheese has melted, add enough milk or cream to make it dip consistency. Serve hot with tortilla chips.

Mrs. William Mullett

CLAM-CREAM CHEESE DIP

1 (7½ ounce) can minced clams, drained
1 (8 ounce) package cream cheese, softened
1 tablespoon lemon juice
1 teaspoon Worcestershire sauce

⅛ teaspoon pepper
1 tablespoon mayonnaise
½ tablespoon chopped parsley
¼ teaspoon prepared mustard
½ tablespoon chopped chives (or onions)

Mix all ingredients with softened cream cheese. Heat through before serving. Good with club crackers or potato chips. May be served cold, but delicious hot. Serves 6 to 8.

Mrs. J. Charles Thomas

CLAM DIP

2 onions, minced
6 tablespoons butter
1 green pepper, minced
1 red pepper, minced
3 cans minced clams, drained
¼ to ½ pound sharp Cheddar
    cheese, cut into small
    pieces

8 tablespoons catsup
2 tablespoons Worcestershire
    sauce
2 tablespoons sherry
½ teaspoon pepper

In large saucepan or Dutch oven, sauté onion in melted butter. Add peppers and sauté until soft. Add remainder of ingredients, except sherry, and cook gently over low heat until cheese melts. Add sherry last. This can be made two or three days before serving. Store in covered containers. To serve, keep warm in a chafing dish surrounded by Melba rounds. Serves 20 to 25.

Mrs. Thomas H. Edelblute, Jr.

COCKTAIL DIP

1 teaspoon chili sauce
1 small onion, grated
1 teaspoon water
1 teaspoon tarragon vinegar
½ teaspoon garlic powder
1 teaspoon prepared
    horseradish

1 package Ranch Salad
    Dressing Mix
1 cup sour cream
1 cup mayonnaise
1 teaspoon mustard, cream
    or dry
¼ teaspoon Worcestershire
    sauce

Combine chili sauce, onion, water, vinegar, garlic powder, and horseradish in blender and purée at low speed. Add all remaining ingredients and blend well. Allow to set a few hours. Makes 2 to 3 cups. Serve with potato chips or raw vegetables. It may be served as a dressing on tossed salad.

Mrs. Thomas J. Blair, III

COCKTAIL FONDUE

1 (10½ ounce) can Cheddar
   cheese soup, undiluted
1 tin of Jalapeña dip
   (preferred) or 1 (4 ounce)
   tin of French onion dip
   plus dash of Tabasco sauce

1 teaspoon dry mustard
4 ounces grated sharp
   Cheddar cheese
¼ cup dry sherry
French or Italian bread,
   cut in large cubes

Mix ingredients in order listed, except bread. Heat slowly over low heat in saucepan. When hot, put in fondue pot and use bread cubes for dipping.

Mrs. Frederick H. Auld

CRABMEAT DIP

1 (3 ounce) package and 2 (8
   ounce) packages cream
   cheese
1 large can crabmeat, drained
¼ to ½ cup milk
½ cup mayonnaise

½ teaspoon garlic powder
¼ teaspoon lemon juice
¼ teaspoon Worcestershire
   sauce
2 teaspoons minced onion
2 drops Tabasco sauce

In top of double boiler, heat the cream cheese until soft; add remaining ingredients, mixing well. Make the day before serving, and refrigerate to blend flavors. To serve, heat in double boiler and keep hot in chafing dish. Serves 20 to 25.

Mrs. Frederick L. Thomas, Jr.

CRYSTALLIZED GINGER-CREAM CHEESE DIP

3 to 4 pieces crystallized ginger
1 (8 ounce) package cream
   cheese or Neufchatel
   cheese
6 to 8 drops Tabasco sauce

1 teaspoon Worcestershire
   sauce
Dash of garlic powder (⅛
   teaspoon)
⅛ teaspoon paprika
Sour cream

Chop ginger so that it is easily seen in the dip. Thin cream cheese with sour cream to the consistency of your own liking. Mix with remaining ingredients. Refrigerate for several hours to blend flavors; bring to room temperature before serving. Serve with thin wheat crackers.

Mrs. Charles M. Love, III

GREEN BLENDER DIP

½ bunch parsley
½ bunch green onions
2 tablespoons anchovy paste

1 tablespoon lemon juice
1 teaspoon liquid garlic
1 pint mayonnaise

Chop the parsley and onions coarsely. Combine all the ingredients together in blender at a low speed so the mayonnaise won't separate. Makes one pint. Especially good with raw vegetables.

Mrs. Andrew V. Roderick

BAKED CRAB DIP OR SPREAD

1 (8 ounce) package cream
   cheese
1 tablespoon milk
2 teaspoons Worcestershire
   sauce

1 (7½ ounce) can crabmeat
2 tablespoons chopped onion
2 tablespoons toasted almonds

In mixing bowl, combine cream cheese, milk, and Worcestershire sauce. Drain, pick and flake crabmeat. Add to cream cheese mixture along with onions. Turn into small, greased, shallow baking dish or an 8 inch pie plate. Sprinkle almonds on top. Bake in 350° oven for 20 minutes. Serve warm with crackers or melba toast rounds. Serves 4.

Mrs. Latelle M. LaFollette, III

BRANDIED BLUE CHEESE POT

8 ounces blue cheese,
   crumbled
6 ounces cream cheese
8 ounces Cheddar cheese,
   finely grated

1 to 2 tablespoons
   mayonnaise
2 tablespoons (or more) brandy
1 teaspoon caraway seed
½ teaspoon garlic salt

Bring cheeses to room temperature. Combine all ingredients and mix well. Pack in cheese crock, or other container, and seal with paraffin. Will keep at least a month under refrigeration.

This makes a lovely Christmas gift when put in a pretty coffee mug or an individual casserole pot. Makes about 2½ crocks.

Mrs. Charles G. Moyers, Jr.

CHICKEN LIVER SPREAD

½ pound chicken livers
Salt and pepper to taste
Flour
Margarine

2 hard boiled eggs
¼ medium onion
Mayonnaise
Generous splash red wine

Salt and pepper the chicken livers, and dredge in flour. Sauté in margarine till done and crisp — 20 to 30 minutes. Chill thoroughly. Put chilled chicken livers, one hard cooked egg, and onion through food grinder. Add a splash of red wine or sherry and moisten with enough mayonnaise for spreading consistency. Grate yolk of second egg over top, chill overnight, and serve with melba toast or crackers. Serves 8 to 10.

Mrs. H. H. Smallridge

CHILE PEPPER BAKE

3 (4 ounces each) cans
green mild chile peppers,
chopped

10 ounces sharp Cheddar
cheese, grated
3 eggs
3 tablespoons milk

Lightly grease an 8 inch ovenproof pie plate, spread peppers on the bottom and place the cheese on top. Beat the eggs and milk well and pour egg mixture over the cheese. Bake at 325° for 45 minutes. Serve on mild crackers.

Mrs. David Huffman

CRAB FONDUE

½ pound butter
3 onions, chopped
1 scallion, chopped
1 cup cubed Cheddar cheese
¾ cup catsup

4 tablespoons Worcestershire
sauce
¾ cup medium dry sherry
Cayenne pepper
4 cups prepared crabmeat

Melt butter and add chopped onions and chopped scallion. Add cheese, catsup, Worcestershire, sherry and cayenne pepper to taste. When the cheese is melted and sauce is smooth, blend in crabmeat. Refrigerate if serving later. Serve with melba rounds or small party shells. Dry sherry is excellent sipping with this. Makes enough for 25 at cocktail party or 8 for a luncheon dish in party shells.

Mrs. D. Stephen Walker

CRABMEAT MOLD

1 (8 ounce) can crabmeat
1 package (1 tablespoon)
   gelatin
1 (10½ ounce) can undiluted
   cream of mushroom soup
2 (3 ounces each) packages
   cream cheese, at room
   temperature

1 cup finely chopped celery
1 cup finely chopped onion
1 cup mayonnaise
2 tablespoons lemon juice
Salt to taste

Drain and pick crabmeat, reserving juice. Measure juice and if necessary, add water to make 3 tablespoons liquid. Dissolve the gelatin in this liquid. Heat the undiluted soup; then add the gelatin mixture and the cream cheese (cut into several pieces). Remove from heat and stir until cheese is melted. Beat smooth.

Add the celery, onion, crabmeat, mayonnaise, lemon juice, and salt to taste. Blend well. Pour into a ring mold (about 4 cup size) and refrigerate for several hours or until firm. Unmold onto a plate and serve with crackers for an hors d'oeuvre. If there is any leftover, the remaining crabmeat mixture can be frozen. When thawed, stir and serve as a dip. (The shape may be gone, but the flavor is just as good!)

Mrs. Lawrence Conques

CRABMEAT SPREAD

1 cup finely flaked canned
   crabmeat
2 tablespoons parsley

3 tablespoons mayonnaise
¼ teaspoon curry powder
1 teaspoon lemon juice

1 tablespoon minced onion

Blend all ingredients and chill for 1 hour. Serve with crackers or as a dip.

Mrs. Joseph R. Goodwin

LIVER PATE MOLD

1 envelope unflavored gelatin
¼ cup cold water or sherry
1 (10½ ounce) can consommé
1 (3 ounce) package cream
   cheese, softened

1 (4¾ ounce) can Sell's liver
   paste or liverwurst
Several drops red food
   coloring

Soften gelatin in water or sherry and stir into heated consommé. Pour ½ cup of heated mixture into 4-cup mold and chill. Add cheese and liver paste to remaining soup; pour over set consommé in mold. Return to refrigerator until competely firm. Serve with crackers. Serves 12.

Mrs. Stanley H. Rose

PARTY EGG SALAD

12 medium-size eggs,
    hard-cooked
1 stalk celery, finely chopped
Grated onion, to taste
Salt and pepper

2 tablespoons sweet piccalilli
2 tablespoons or more
    mayonnaise
Black caviar
Cherry tomatoes

Cool hard-cooked eggs, peel, and mash with a fork or potato masher. Add celery, onion, salt and pepper, piccalilli, and mayonnaise. Place in a greased mold and refrigerate. Unmold on lettuce or endive; ice with a sharp knife, and place black caviar on top. Trim sides with cherry tomatoes. Serve with party rye or crackers.

Icing:
1 (3 ounce) package cream
    cheese, softened

½ cup sour cream

Blend icing ingredients until smooth.

Mrs. William E. Hamb

PECAN SPREAD

1 (8 ounce) package cream
    cheese, softened
2 tablespoons milk
1 (2½ ounce) jar sliced dried
    beef
¼ cup finely chopped green
    pepper, (optional)
2 tablespoons dehydrated
    onion flakes

½ teaspoon garlic salt
¼ teaspoon pepper
½ cup sour cream
½ cup coarsely chopped pecans
2 tablespoons butter or
    margarine
½ teaspoon salt

Combine softened cream cheese and milk, mixing until well blended. Stir in dried beef, green pepper, onion flakes, and seasonings; mix well. Fold in sour cream. Spoon into 8" pie plate. Heat and crisp pecans in melted butter or margarine and salt; sprinkle over cream cheese mixture. Bake at 350° for 20 minutes. Serve hot with crackers.

Mrs. Robert J. Singleton

SHRIMP MOLD

1 (10¾ ounce) can tomato soup
1 (8 ounce) package cream cheese
2 tablespoons gelatin dissolved in ½ cup water
1 to 1½ cups chopped (fresh or frozen) shrimp (crab meat may also be used)
1 cup chopped onion
1 cup chopped celery
1½ tablespoons horseradish
3 tablespoons lemon juice
⅛ teaspoon cayenne pepper or dash of Tabasco
Salt to taste
1 cup mayonnaise

Heat soup, add cream cheese till melted. Stir with wisk until smooth. Add dissolved gelatin and stir until blended. Remove from heat and add remaining ingredients. Mix well and pour into large fish shape mold. Serve with flaky crackers.

This recipe may be made ahead of time and frozen until you wish to use it. Allow ample time for it to thaw before serving. May also be served as a luncheon salad.

Mrs. William R. McDavid

SHRIMP SPREAD

2 (8 ounce) packages cream cheese
4 tablespoons mayonnaise
4 tablespoons catsup
1 teaspoon Worcestershire sauce
1½ teaspoons lemon juice
2 cups shredded shrimp (10-12 ounces)
½ medium onion, grated

Beat cheese until fluffy, add liquid ingredients and beat until smooth. Fold in shrimp and onion. Makes about 4 cups. Goes well with crackers and raw vegetables. Freezes well with just a few stirs to revive it.

Mrs. Martin Cohen

STEAK TARTARE

2 pounds tenderloin steak, ground just before using
10 anchovy fillets, mashed
½ cup finely chopped onions
2 egg yolks
1 teaspoon salt
Black pepper (from mill)
Dash Tabasco sauce
1 tablespoon Dijon mustard
2 tablespoons cognac

Blend ingredients into tenderloin one at a time. Keep chilled until ready to serve. Serve in a mound or loaf, to be spread on crackers or small slices of bread.

Mrs. F. Thomas Graff, Jr.

STATE CAPITOL

"During the year that I spent in Washington, and for some little time before this there had been considerable agitation in the state of West Virginia over the question of moving the capital of the state from Wheeling to some other central point. As a result of this, the Legislature designated three cities to be voted upon by the citizens of the state as the permanent seat of government. Among these cities was Charleston, only five miles from Malden, my home. At the close of my school year in Washington I was very pleasantly surprised to receive, from a committee of white people in Charleston, an invitation to canvass the state in the interests of that city. This invitation I accepted, and spent nearly three months in speaking in various parts of the state. Charleston was successful in winning the prize and is now the permanent seat of government."

Reprinted from **Up From Slavery**, An Autobiography by Booker T. Washington; Houghton Mifflin Company, The Riverside Press; Cambridge, Massachusetts; 1928; Page 92.

Photo by Commerce Photography

SOUPS, SALADS AND DRESSINGS

Duck Paddle

CREME D'ARTICHAUX AUX HUITRES
(A New Orleans Creation)

3 green onions, finely chopped
2 tablespoons butter
1 dozen large oysters
1 quart rich chicken stock
1 (14 to 16 ounce) can artichoke hearts

Pinch of tarragon
Pinch of chervil
Salt and pepper to taste
1 cup light cream
4 tablespoons chopped parsley for garnish

Cook onions in butter in a large skillet until wilted. Add the oysters and their liquid and simmer very gently, just until the oysters plump a little on the edges. Do not overcook. Remove oysters immediately with a slotted spoon and set aside. Add the chicken stock to the skillet.

Drain the artichokes and add their juices to the stock and pan juices. Put in the tarragon, chervil, salt, and pepper, and simmer mixture uncovered until it is reduced to about 3 cups. Place 1 cup of the stock in a blender with the artichoke hearts and blend to a fine purée. (If a blender is not available, chop the artichokes finely.) Return the artichoke mixture to the skillet with the rest of ingredients, and simmer about 10 minutes to blend flavors. At this point the soup may be set aside or refrigerated.

Just before serving, heat the soup to boiling. Reduce heat, and add the cream and poached oysters. Correct salt and pepper seasoning. Return the soup to a simmer. Sprinkle with parsley and serve. Serves approximately 6 as an appetizer.

Mrs. Charles G. Moyers, Jr.

BEAN SOUP

1 pound navy beans
Ham pieces
2 small onions, chopped
½ carrot, diced
2 stalks celery, diced
1 potato, diced

1 teaspoon celery salt
Dash garlic salt
½ teaspoon pepper
2 tablespoons salt
½ teaspoon celery seed
½ teaspoon parsley flakes

1 cup tomato juice

Wash beans. Cover with water and bring to a boil. Add ham, vegetables, and seasonings. When mixture begins to thicken, add tomato juice. Cook until thick and well done, at least 3 hours. Use low heat. Add water, if necessary. Serves 8.

Mrs. Fred L. Kellemeyer

SENATE BEAN SOUP

2 cups dried white beans, washed and drained
1 large smoked ham hock
3 potatoes, cooked and mashed with milk and butter

2 medium-size yellow onions, chopped
1 cup diced celery
½ teaspoon garlic salt
Salt and pepper, to taste

Cover beans with water; bring to a boil and boil for 2 minutes. Remove from heat and cover pan; let it stand for 1 hour. Drain beans and measure liquid. Add enough water to beans and liquid to make 3 quarts. Bring to a boil again and simmer, covered, for 2 hours or until beans begin to mush. Add remaining ingredients, except salt and pepper, and simmer, covered, for 1 more hour. Remove ham hock. Season to taste. Makes about 2½ quarts.

Mrs. Joseph R. Goodwin

BOUILLON

Recipe of Mrs. Auretus Brooks Fleming, wife of Governor Fleming and Brooks McCabe's great-grandmother

1 beef bone
1 veal bone

1 lamb or mutton bone
1 chicken

Cover with cold water and let simmer all day. Then strain, and when cold, skim the grease. Yields 3 quarts of solid stock.

1 pint tomatoes
1 stalk celery
3 small onions, size of a walnut
2 bay leaves
6 or 8 cloves
1 small piece of mace about an inch square
½ teacupful of dried corn or ½ can of corn

½ teacup of barley
1 green pepper
1 potato
A sprig of parsley
2 or 3 apples, if small
3 medium-sized turnips
1 stalk of asparagus
Juice of 1 orange, strained

Boil all of the above ingredients except orange juice in clear water and strain. There should be a pint of this vegetable stock after it is strained

Allow a small teacup of beef stock to every person and add the vegetable stock to it. Let is come to a boil and skim. Add salt and red pepper (should be rather peppery), and when ready to serve, add the strained juice of one orange to this quantity. Sweeten the orange juice until it is palatable. The soup may require a touch of sugar as some of the vegetables are acidic.

This is only an outline; ingredients may be varied according to taste. Serves 6.

Mrs. Brooks F. McCabe

HOMESTYLE CHILI

1 pound bacon, sliced	2 (16 ounces each) cans red
10 medium onions, chopped	kidney beans
1 pound ground beef	1 tablespoon chili powder
2 (16 ounces each) cans	Salt and pepper to taste
whole tomatoes	

Cook bacon, keeping drippings. Crumble bacon and place in large tall pot. Cook onions until soft in bacon grease. Place in pot. Brown ground beef and add beans, tomatoes, and seasonings. Bring all to a boil over medium heat; reduce heat and simmer for 4 hours. Keep pot covered.

For less thick chili and more juice, cook faster and for shorter time. For less grease, use only ½ pound bacon.

Freezes well and tastes even better after frozen and reheated. Serves 6.

Mrs. John R. Fowler

COMPANY CHILI

3 pounds ground chuck	1 (10½ ounce) can tomato soup
5 tablespoons bacon grease	8 cloves garlic, pressed
3 tablespoons olive oil	3 bay leaves, crushed
1½ cups chopped green peppers	3 teaspoons cumin
1½ cups chopped onions	1 tablespoon sugar
1½ cups chopped celery	2 teaspoons salt
3 (20 ounces each) cans	1 teaspoon oregano
tomatoes	1 teaspoon black pepper
3 (6 ounces each) cans tomato	3 teaspoons parsley flakes
paste	1 tablespoon paprika
3 (20 ounces each) cans kidney	6 tablespoons chili powder
or chili beans	(more later, if desired)

Tomato juice for thinning

Brown ground chuck in bacon grease and olive oil in a large pot. Add green pepper, onion, and celery to the pan and sauté. Add the remaining ingredients in the order listed, and cook slowly until the mixture is well blended. Thin with tomato juice while cooking, if necessary. Makes 4 to 5 quarts. Serves 12 generously.

Mrs. Carl B. Hall, Jr.

CLAM CHOWDER

2 cubic inches chopped salt
    pork
¼ cup chopped green pepper
½ cup chopped onions
2 cups diced potatoes
1½ cups water
½ cup diced carrots
½ cup sliced celery
2 tablespoons chopped
    parsley

1 teaspoon salt
¼ teaspoon black pepper
¼ teaspoon thyme
2 cups milk
1 tablespoon butter
1 (10 ounce) can minced
    clams
6 to 8 crackers, broken
⅛ cup sherry

Fry out salt pork; remove cooked meat. Sauté green peppers and onions in remaining fat. Boil together potatoes, water, carrots, celery, chopped parsley, salt, black pepper, and thyme. Combine and cook for a few minutes. Then add milk, butter, minced clams, and crackers. Simmer for several minutes over low heat. Add sherry. Makes scant 2 quarts. Serves 6 to 8.

Mrs. Carl B. Hall, Jr.

COLD CUCUMBER SOUP

2 cucumbers, peeled
¼ cup chopped green pepper
1 teaspoon dry mustard
2 tablespoons parsley
¼ teaspoon Worcestershire
    sauce

1 cup skim milk
½ cup sour cream
1 small onion, optional
Lemon and parsley
    for garnish

Combine all ingredients a little at a time in blender, and blend to purée consistency. While still in blender container, store overnight in refrigerator. Before serving, blend again slightly. Serve chilled with lemon and parsley to garnish. Serves 4.

Mrs. Stephen Thomas, III

COLD CURRY CUCUMBER SOUP

1 (10½ ounce) can tomato
    soup
1 cup buttermilk
1 teaspoon curry powder

1 teaspoon Worcestershire
    sauce
1 chopped, peeled cucumber
Tabasco sauce, to taste

Blend buttermilk into tomato soup. Add curry powder and Worcestershire sauce. Stir in Tabasco sauce and chopped cucumber. Serve chilled. Serves 4.

Mrs. Edward C. Armbrecht, Jr.

LENTIL SOUP

1 pound dried lentils
6 cups cold water
    Ham bone
2 stalks celery, sliced thinly

1 medium onion, chopped
2 small carrots, grated
    Salt to taste
    Pepper to taste
Sherry, optional

Place lentils in cold water with ham bone and simmer 1 hour. Add vegetables to soup, and simmer 1 hour more. Add sherry, salt and pepper to taste. Serves 6 to 8.

Mrs. Ronald A. McKenney

LOBSTER-SHRIMP CHOWDER

¼ cup chopped celery
2 tablespoons finely chopped
    onion
2 tablespoons butter
1 (10¾ ounce) can frozen
    condensed cream of
    shrimp soup

1 (10¾ ounce) can
    condensed cream of
    mushroom soup
1 soup can milk
1 cup half and half
1 (5 ounce) can lobster
¼ cup dry sherry
1 tablespoon snipped parsley

Cook celery and onion in butter until tender. Add soups, milk, and cream. Stir in lobster, sherry, and parsley. Heat until very hot. Do not boil. Serves 8.

Mrs. Phyllis Dusic

MISS BESS'S CREAM OF MUSHROOM SOUP

3 tablespoons butter
2 tablespoons flour
1 pint half-and-half
1 pint chicken stock

1 (8 ounce) can mushrooms,
  finely chopped
Salt and pepper
Juice of 1 lemon

Melt the butter and add flour. When bubbling, add the cream and stock slowly. Add all the mushroom liquid, seasoning, and mushrooms. Remove from heat and add juice of 1 lemon. (Stock best made a day before in order to remove fat.) Serves 4 to 6.

Mrs. Frederick W. Prichard

SOUPE A L'OIGNON

1 heaping teaspoon butter
2 small onions, thinly sliced
1 teaspoon flour

3 cups beef broth or water
Salt and pepper
2 thin slices of toast

1 tablespoon grated Parmesan or Swiss cheese

Melt the butter in a saucepan and add the onions. Cook very slowly, stirring occasionally with a wooden spoon. The secret of a perfect onion soup lies in how the onions are cooked. They must be thoroughly cooked and still be soft and of a light golden color before any liquid is added. Then, stir in the flour and cook a little. Pour in the beef broth, add salt and freshly ground pepper to taste, and simmer for 10 to 15 minutes. Correct the seasoning, if needed. Place slices of toast in soup tureen, sprinkle with cheese, and pour the soup over it. Gratin in a moderately hot oven or under the broiler. Serves 4 to 6.

The Greenbrier

CREAM OF PEA SOUP

1½ cups green peas
1 slice onion
1 cup chicken broth

1 tablespoon butter
1 tablespoon flour
2½ cups half and half (or
  diluted evaporated milk)

Cook peas with onion. Drain and purée in blender with chicken broth. In saucepan, melt butter; stir in flour and the purée. Cook to boiling point and add milk. This is good served hot, and delicious cold. Makes about 4 cups.

Mrs. John M. Slack, III

SPLIT PEA SOUP

1½ cups dried split peas
8 cups cold water, divided
1 medium onion, chopped
2 tablespoons margarine, divided
1 ham bone or small shank end

½ teaspoon celery salt
½ teaspoon salt
1 teaspoon pepper
1 tablespoon flour
2 cups milk

Soak dried peas overnight in 2 cups of the cold water, then drain. Sauté onion until tender in one tablespoon of the margarine. Add ham bone, drained peas, celery salt, pepper, salt, and remaining 6 cups of cold water. Cover, bring to boil, and simmer gently for 3 hours. Remove ham bone and all surface fat. Make a thin white sauce by adding flour to remaining 1 tablespoon margarine in the top of a double boiler. Add milk and cook, stirring until thick. Combine with soup and heat well. Serves 6 to 8.

Mrs. William T. Ziebold

GARTH'S GAZPACHO

1 (16 ounce) can stewed tomatoes
1 (10½ ounce) can condensed beef broth
1 cup peeled, chopped cucumber

1 cup chopped celery
1 cup sliced onions
2 tablespoons lemon juice
1 small garlic clove, minced
Dash of pepper

Combine all ingredients. Simmer gently until onions and celery are tender (about 12 minutes). Chill before serving. Serves 4 to 6.

Mrs. E. Garfield Atkins

SALAD SOUP

1 garlic clove
3 tomatoes, finely diced
½ unpeeled cucumber, thinly sliced
6 scallions or green onions with tops, thinly sliced (or 1 tablespoon finely chopped chives)
½ cup thinly sliced celery

3 tablespoons salad oil
2 tablespoons white vinegar (or lemon juice)
½ teaspoon salt
¼ teaspoon pepper
1 teaspoon monosodium glutamate
2¼ cups tomato juice
4 tablespoons sour cream

Rub tureen or large bowl with garlic clove. Spear garlic with toothpick and leave in bowl. Add tomatoes and cucumbers. Add onions and celery. Add oil and vinegar. Sprinkle with salt, freshly ground pepper and monosodium glutamate. Mix well. Add tomato juice. Chill at least three hours or overnight. Remove garlic and serve with a spoonful of sour cream in the center. Serves 4.

Mrs. William C. Payne

SUMMER SQUASH SOUP

3 medium yellow squash	¼ teaspoon pepper
2 tablespoons butter	¼ teaspoon dried rosemary
1½ teaspoons garlic salt	½ cup chicken broth
½ teaspoon salt	½ cup water

1 (6 ounce) can boned chicken, cut up

Scrub squash; do not peel. Cut 12 paper-thin slices from the narrow ends and place slices in cold water to crisp. Reserve these slices for garnish. Cut remainder of squash (seeded, if necessary) into small chunks to make 5 to 6 cups. Sauté very slowly in butter, seasoned with garlic salt, salt, pepper, and rosemary. Keep pan tightly covered and do not allow squash to brown. Add 1 or 2 tablespoons water if necessary when squash is softened. Purée in electric blender. Return purée to pan and add chicken broth, water, and boned chicken. Heat until flavors are well blended. Pour into serving dish or soup bowls and garnish with crisp squash slices. Makes 1 quart.

Mrs. Alexander S. Giltinan

NEW YEAR'S TOMATO BOUILLON

3 cups canned tomato juice	4 whole cloves
1 thick slice of onion	1 (10½ ounce) can consommé
1 stalk celery, sliced	½ cup red wine
1 bay leaf	Salt and pepper

6 lemon slices

Combine tomato juice, onion, celery, bay leaf, and cloves in a saucepan. Bring to boil; cover and simmer for 20 minutes. Strain. Add consommé, wine, and salt and pepper. To serve, float a slice of lemon in each cup. Serves 6.

Mrs. Andrew A. Payne, Jr.

WHOLE TOMATO SOUP

2 beef bouillon cubes	2 celery stalks with leaves,
½ cup boiling water	cut to convenient lengths
1 tablespoon butter	Salt, pepper, cayenne,
1 fresh tomato, peeled	marjoram or basil

Combine bouillon cubes and water to make bouillon. Melt butter in saucepan. Add whole tomato, bouillon, and celery. Sprinkle with salt, pepper, cayenne, marjoram or basil, to taste. Cover and simmer 30 minutes. Remove celery. Serve in large soup plate. Serves 1.

Mrs. Neil Robinson, II

VEGETABLE SOUP

1½ pounds lean stew meat
1 quart water
3 medium onions, diced
2 or 3 carrots, sliced
½ small cabbage, shredded
3 stalks celery, sliced
1 (8 ounce) can tomato sauce
Salt and pepper

Monosodium glutamate
2 tablespoons sugar
2 tablespoons Worcestershire sauce
1 tablespoon soy sauce
2 beef bouillon cubes
½ cup macaroni
1 cup creamed corn, optional

1 cup cooked green lima beans, optional

Cut meat into bite-size pieces and put in the water to simmer for 1 hour. Add onions, carrots, cabbage, celery, tomato sauce, salt, pepper, monosodium glutamate, sugar, Worcestershire sauce, soy sauce, and bouillon cubes. Additional water may be required. Simmer until meat and vegetables are tender. Add the macaroni, corn, and limas, and cook until the macaroni is tender.

Mrs. Frederick L. Thomas, Jr.

VICHYSSOISE
(Cold Leek and Potato Soup)

3 cups (3½ medium) peeled, sliced potatoes
3 cups sliced white of leek (Use two large leeks and make up the difference, if any, in sliced yellow onions.)

1½ quarts chicken stock or 6 tablespoons instant chicken bouillon dissolved in 6 cups hot water
Salt to taste
1 cup whipping cream
Minced chives, fresh or freeze-dried

Simmer the vegetables in the chicken stock until tender (about 45 minutes). Use an electric blender to purée the cooled vegetables and the liquid to a smooth soup. Stir whipping cream into the soup. Chill. Serve in chilled bowls, and decorate with minced chives.

This keeps well and can be thinned to the desired consistency with cold milk. Serves 6 to 8.

Mrs. Joseph Goodwin

EMERALD VICHYSSOISE

3 tablespoons butter
1½ cups chopped green
 onions with tops
1 (10 ounce) package frozen
 chopped spinach, thawed
2 (10½ ounces each) cans
 frozen potato soup,
 thawed

1 cup light cream or
 coffee cream substitute
2½ cups boiling chicken broth
2 tablespoons lemon juice
½ teaspoon salt (or to taste)
¼ teaspoon pepper
 Chives as garnish

Melt butter in double boiler until frothy. Sauté onions in butter 2 to 3 minutes. Add spinach, potato soup, cream, and chicken broth. Mix well and stir for 15 minutes. Purée in blender, adding lemon juice, salt and pepper. Chill several hours or overnight. Serve with sprinkle of chives on top. May be thinned with milk, if desired. Makes approximately 2½ quarts.

CREAM OF POTATO SOUP

5 medium potatoes, peeled
 and sliced (about 5 cups)
1 medium onion, minced
2 teaspoons salt
 Dash pepper

4 tablespoons butter
1 tablespoon parsley
2 to 3 cups milk (or your
 discretion, depending on
 how thick you like soup)

Cook potatoes and onion in salted cold water to cover barely in a covered pot until quite tender. Mash in liquid. Add butter, parsley, and milk. Heat to boiling. Serve at once. Serves 4 to 6.

Mrs. John C. Thomas

CINNAMON APPLE SALAD

½ cup water
1 cup sugar

¼ cup red-hot cinnamon gems
4 apples, peeled and cored

Melt together the water, sugar, and cinnamon gems. Add the apples and simmer them in the cinnamon mixture, turning them upside down when the bottoms become red and soft. Continue simmering, adding more water if necessary, until the apples are uniformly tender and red. Chill and serve on a lettuce leaf. Serves 4. These apples would also be excellent as a garnish for a pork roast or ham, or as a dessert with some of the cinnamon syrup spooned over each one.

Mrs. E. Charles Brod

SCANDINAVIAN APPLE SALAD

2 cups diced unpeeled
  red apples
1 cup diced celery
2 cups shredded cabbage
½ cup sour cream
  Juice of 1 lemon
Salt and sugar to taste
½ cup halved and seeded
  grapes
½ cup chopped nuts
  (optional)

Combine apples, celery, and cabbage. Combine remaining ingredients except grapes. Add to apple mixture. Toss to mix. Garnish with grapes. Serves 8.

Mrs. V. Courtlandt Smith, II

ARTICHOKE PEPPER SALAD

1 (12 ounce) jar pepper salad
1 (6 ounce) can black olives,
  drained
1 (10 ounce) can green olives,
  drained
1 can artichokes, drained

Place pepper salad with liquid in bowl. Cut olives in pieces and add to pepper salad. Add sliced artichokes and mix gently. Serves 6. Good with Italian food.

Mrs. J. Douglas Machesney

MARINATED ARTICHOKE SALAD

2 large cans artichoke hearts
½ cup vinegar
1 cup vegetable oil
2 tablespoons sugar
1½ teaspoons salt
½ teaspoon pepper
1½ teaspoons dill weed
2 medium onions, sliced
  (or more if desired)
Pimiento

Drain artichoke hearts. In a large bowl mix vinegar, oil, sugar, salt, pepper, and dill weed. Add artichoke hearts and sliced onions; marinate overnight. Just before serving, add chopped pimiento. Serve on a lettuce leaf. Serves 4 to 6.

Mrs. Kenneth Kleeman

ASPARAGUS SALAD

Lettuce, either head or
  other kind
Asparagus, canned cut
  variety
Avocado, peeled and cubed
Blue cheese
Croutons
Italian dressing
Salt
Pepper

No amounts are given because it depends on the number you wish to serve. One avocado and one can of cut asparagus with reasonable amounts of the other ingredients will feed 6 to 8 people. Use dressing sparingly; put a little in the bottom of the salad bowl and toss from the bottom up. Add more dressing if leaves are not lightly coated. Season to taste with salt and pepper and add croutons before serving.

Mrs. Edward L. Sherwood

SWEET AND SOUR ASPARAGUS SALAD

1 pound fresh asparagus spears	Dash salt
6 slices bacon	Pepper to taste
¼ cup wine vinegar	2 green onions (chopped)
2 teaspoons sugar	Shredded lettuce

2 hard boiled eggs, sliced

Cook asparagus in boiling water until tender. Drain. Cook bacon until crisp. Drain, crumble and set aside. Combine vinegar, sugar, salt, pepper and onion with bacon drippings in skillet. Add asparagus and heat through. Arrange a bed of lettuce on each of 6 salad plates. Remove asparagus from skillet and arrange on lettuce. Top with egg slices. Pour hot bacon dressing over each salad. Sprinkle with bacon and serve. Serves 6.

Mrs. John Nesius

GREEN BEAN SALAD

1 (16 ounce) can cut green beans, drained	1 green pepper, cut in thin rings
1 (16 ounce) can cut waxed beans, drained	⅔ cup vinegar
1 (16 ounce) can kidney beans, drained	⅓ cup cooking oil
	½ cup sugar
1 medium onion, cut in thin rings	Salt
	Pepper

Combine beans, onion, and green pepper. Mix rest of ingredients and pour over the vegetables. Marinate for 24 hours before serving, stirring several times. Serves 8 to 10.

Mrs. Angus E. Peyton

MARINATED SLAW

1 large head cabbage   1 large green pepper, chopped
1 large sweet onion, chopped   1 cup sugar

Shred the cabbage and arrange it in layers with the onion and green pepper. Pour the sugar on top.

DRESSING

1 cup vinegar   1 tablespoon sugar
¾ cup oil   1 tablespoon salt
1 tablespoon celery seed   1 teaspoon dry mustard

Bring the dressing ingredients to a rolling boil and pour over the slaw. Do not stir. Refrigerate for at least 12 hours. Toss before serving. Serves 10 to 12.

Mrs. Carol Fletcher

CAESAR SALAD

2 heads romaine lettuce   Juice of 1 lemon
Grated Parmesan cheese   ⅓ cup garlic olive oil
Salt and pepper to taste   Dash Worcestershire sauce
2 tablespoons wine vinegar   2 (1 minute) coddled eggs
Garlic croutons

Wash lettuce and break into 2 to 3 inch pieces. Refrigerate for several hours. Just before serving, sprinkle generously with grated Parmesan cheese, and salt and pepper. Make dressing by combining wine vinegar, lemon juice, garlic olive oil, Worcestershire sauce, and coddled eggs. Beat until well blended. Pour over lettuce and toss to coat. Toss in croutons and serve. Serves 6.

To coddle eggs, just have them at room temperature and simmer 1 minute.

Mrs. John G. McGarty

CRUNCHY SALAD

½ cup sunflower seeds, roasted meats
½ cup nuts or 1 cup small shrimp
2 tablespoons raw wheat germ
1 teaspoon dried parsley or 1 tablespoon chopped fresh

2½ cups shredded lettuce
1 cup diced mild cheese
½ cup bean sprouts, fresh or canned
1 cup diced cucumber
2 tablespoons crumbled bacon

Mix seeds, nuts, wheat germ and parsley. Combine with remaining ingredients in medium salad bowl. Divide into two equal parts and serve with dressing. Makes 2 servings.

Mrs. Leigh Shepherd

CUCUMBERS IN SOUR CREAM WITH FRESH DILL

2 cucumbers, pared or unpared and sliced
1 cup thinly sliced onion rings
1 tablespoon cider vinegar
1 tablespoon water

½ teaspoon salt
¼ teaspoon ground black pepper
¼ cup sour cream
2 tablespoons finely chopped fresh dill

Marinate cucumber slices and onion rings in vinegar, water, salt and pepper in the refrigerator. Drain after a few hours. Mix cucumbers and onions with sour cream and dill. Serve as a salad or appetizer. Serves 4 to 6.

Mrs. Connie Carrico

WILTED LETTUCE

5 cups Bibb lettuce, torn into bite-size pieces
2 to 3 onions, chopped
5 slices bacon, crumbled
¼ teaspoon dry mustard

2 tablespoons brown sugar
3 tablespoons vinegar
1 tablespoon water
½ teaspoon salt

Put lettuce and onions in salad bowl. Fry bacon crisp and cool on paper towel. Cool bacon grease slightly; add sugar, vinegar, water, salt, and mustard. Pour over lettuce and onion. Sprinkle bacon on top and serve immediately. Serves 6.

MANDARIN AND LETTUCE SALAD

¼ head iceberg lettuce
2 small heads Bibb lettuce
½ bunch endive
2 (16 ounces each) cans
   mandarin oranges,
   drained well

1 (3 ounce) can French
   fried onions
Italian dressing

Wash lettuce, dry, and tear into bite-sized pieces. Toss with drained oranges. When ready to serve, toss lightly with Italian dressing. Add French fried onions and toss lightly again. Serves 6 to 8.

Mrs. Craig M. Wilson

ELEGANT MUSHROOM AND OLIVE SALAD

Bibb lettuce
Romaine lettuce
1 cup black olives, pitted
½ pound fresh mushrooms
Roquefort cheese, 2 to
   4 ounces

Juice of 1 lemon
1 tablespoon olive oil
Salt
Coarsely ground black
   pepper

Break up enough lettuce into bite-size pieces to make 2 quarts. Slice the olives and mushrooms. Crumble the cheese and toss lightly. Add lemon juice and olive oil. Do not substitute other oils. Add salt and cracked pepper to taste, and toss again.

Mrs. David Haden

ITALIAN MUSHROOM AND LIMA BEAN
SALAD WITH CLASSIC GARLIC DRESSING

1 (10 ounce) package frozen
   lima beans
8 fresh mushrooms, sliced, or
   1 (4 ounce) can sliced
   mushrooms, drained

4 green onions, sliced (3 to
   4 tablespoons)
1 tablespoon chopped fresh
   parsley, or 1 teaspoon
   dry parsley flakes

½ teaspoon oregano

Cook beans until tender; drain and rinse under cold water; then drain thoroughly. Toss with remaining ingredients. Chill 1 to 2 hours. Add classic garlic dressing. Serves 6 to 8.

CLASSIC GARLIC DRESSING

2 tablespoons vegetable oil
1 tablespoon vinegar
1 small clove garlic, crushed
¾ teaspoon salt
Dash of ground black pepper
Dash of monosodium glutamate

Shake all ingredients together in small jar. Chill.

Mrs. J. Vann Carroll

RAMP SALAD

"Didn't believe ramps were so good..."

Ramps, cut fine
Salt to taste
Hard-cooked egg slices
Ham pieces
Vinegar

Cook West Virginia mountain ramps until tender, but do not parboil. Season with salt, ham fryings, and vinegar. Garnish with sliced, hard-cooked eggs. Serve warm as a salad.

Mrs. Carl B. Hall, Jr.

SPINACH SALAD

1 garlic clove
1½ to 2 bags fresh spinach
2 small onions, chopped
¼ pound Roquefort cheese, crumbled
4 hard-boiled eggs

Rub large salad bowl well with garlic. Wash and dry spinach and break into small pieces. Place a layer of spinach, onion, and cheese in the bowl; repeat until bowl is filled. Put a large clove of garlic on a toothpick and place in center of salad. Refrigerate all day or overnight. When ready to serve, remove garlic and add 4 finely chopped hard-boiled eggs. Toss with the following dressing:

DRESSING

1 cup cooking oil
⅓ cup white wine tarragon vinegar
1 garlic clove
1 teaspoon salt
Coarsely ground pepper
Paprika
½ teaspoon dry mustard

Combine above ingredients.

Mrs. John L. Sullivan, Jr.

SPINACH AND LETTUCE SALAD

½ pound fresh spinach   ½ head lettuce
1 (3½ ounce) can French fried onions

Wash the spinach and drain. Place in a plastic bag and put into refrigerator vegetable bin to crisp. Break lettuce into pieces. Some spinach leaves may need to be broken if they are large. Heat onions in oven until they are crisp, and drain on paper towels. Add onions to greens immediately before serving. Toss with blue cheese dressing; all of dressing probably will not be required; save it for another salad. Serves 6.

BLUE CHEESE DRESSING

½ cup cooking oil
3 tablespoons blue cheese, crumbled
1 tablespoon vinegar

2 tablespoons sugar
1 teaspoon celery seed
1 teaspoon salt
⅛ teaspoon pepper

Blend the ingredients together in a blender, or mix with an electric mixer. Vinegar, sugar, and blue cheese may be adjusted according to taste.

Mrs. Charles G. Moyers, Jr.

FRENCH TOMATO SALAD

4 to 6 medium tomatoes, chopped   1 bunch scallions, sliced
1 bunch fresh parsley, chopped

Mix with a favorite French dressing and chill for one hour. Serves 6 to 8.

Mrs. Robert C. Payne

STUFFED TOMATOES

6 hard-cooked eggs, chopped
¼ cup chopped green pepper
¼ cup chopped ripe olives
¼ cup chopped green onions

⅓ cup mayonnaise
1 teaspoon salt
¼ teaspoon black pepper
6 medium tomatoes, peeled
6 large ripe olives

Combine eggs, green pepper, olives, and onions. Blend mayonnaise, salt, and black pepper; add to egg mixture. Chill at least 1 hour.

Cut peeled tomatoes into three sections like petals; do not cut all the way through. Fill tomatoes with chilled filling. Top with a ripe olive on a toothpick. Serves 6. Looks pretty on a tray along with cucumber wedges, garden spring onions, carrot curls, and floweret of cauliflower.

Mrs. Thomas J. Blair, III

VEGETABLE SALAD RUSSE

2 boxes frozen mixed
   vegetables
¼ cup sliced green onions
½ cup chopped celery
½ cup chopped cucumber

½ cup sharp French dressing
2 tablespoons mayonnaise
2 tablespoons chili sauce
Dash Tabasco sauce

Cook the frozen vegetables; drain and cool. Add and mix gently all the other ingredients. Cover and refrigerate overnight to blend the flavors. Serves 6.

Mrs. Bernard C. Board

LAYERED VEGETABLE SALAD

1 head lettuce, shredded
½ cup chopped onion, red if
   possible
½ cup chopped celery
½ cup chopped green pepper
   (optional)

1 (10 ounce) package frozen
   peas, cooked, drained, and
   cooled
1 pint good mayonnaise
1 tablespoon sugar
¾ cup grated Swiss or sharp
   Cheddar cheese

10 slices bacon, cooked and crumbled

Layer the lettuce, onion, celery, pepper, and peas in a bowl. Cover with a layer of mayonnaise, sealing the edges. Sprinkle with sugar, grated cheese, and crumbled bacon. Cover tightly and refrigerate for up to 24 hours. Toss and serve. Serves 8.

Mrs. L. Douglas Curnutte

OVERNIGHT VEGETABLE SALAD

1 head lettuce, washed and
   dried
1 small head cauliflower, in
   bite-size pieces

1 pound bacon, fried crisp and
   crumbled
1 medium onion, minced

Layer these ingredients in salad bowl. Spread the following salad dressing over top. Cover with plastic wrap, sealing edges. Serve next day. Serves 8 to 10.

SALAD DRESSING

¼ cup sugar
⅓ cup grated Parmesan cheese
2 cups mayonnaise
1 teaspoon salt
¼ teaspoon pepper

Mrs. Kenneth E. Underwood

RAW VEGETABLE SALAD AND DRESSING

½ cup bean sprouts, drained
1 head Boston lettuce
½ cup sliced raw mushrooms
½ cup raw cauliflower buds
½ cup frozen green beans,
slightly undercooked and
drained
½ cup sliced water chestnuts
½ cup sliced radishes

Mix all ingredients and serve with the dressing that follows. Serves 4.

DRESSING

½ cup wine vinegar
4 tablespoons cooking oil
1 tablespoon chili sauce
½ teaspoon paprika
1 teaspoon *fines herbes*
1 clove garlic, crushed
1 teaspoon cracked pepper

Shake all ingredients in a covered jar and toss with salad.

SCANDINAVIAN VEGETABLE SALAD

1 (16 ounce) can French cut
green beans
1 (2 ounce) jar chopped
pimiento
1 (16 ounce) can small peas
1 cup chopped celery
2 onions, chopped
½ cup sugar (scant)
1 cup vinegar
½ cup cooking oil
Salt and pepper to taste

Mix all the vegetable ingredients. Mix the sugar, vinegar, oil, and salt and pepper. Pour the dressing over the vegetables and toss lightly. Best if made ahead and allowed to marinate overnight in the refrigerator. Serves 8.

Mrs. Robert W. Lawson, Jr.

CORNED BEEF SALAD

2 (3 ounces each) packages
    lemon gelatin
2 cups hot water
3 tablespoons vinegar
1 cup mayonnaise
1 can corned beef, shredded

3 tablespoons finely chopped
    onion
2 tablespoons finely chopped
    green pepper
2 cups celery
Spicy mustard (optional)

Dissolve the gelatin in the hot water and vinegar. Cool and add the remaining ingredients. Pour into a 6 cup mold and chill until firm. Mustard may be added to the ingredients for those who like a spicy salad. Serves 8 to 10.

Variation: Two tablespoons horseradish may be substituted for the mustard.

Mrs. Seigle W. Parks

CONGEALED BEET RELISH SALAD

2½ cups canned beets, drain
    and reserve juice
1 tablespoon unflavored
    gelatin
¼ cup sugar
½ teaspoon salt

⅓ cup vinegar
1 tablespoon prepared horse-
    radish (optional)
⅛ cup chopped onion
½ cup chopped celery
¼ cup chopped green pepper

Dissolve gelatin in ¼ cup cold reserved beet juice. Mix ½ cup hot reserved beet juice, sugar, salt, vinegar, horseradish, onion, celery, and green pepper. Add to gelatin mixture. Chop beets and add to gelatin. Fill a 3 cup mold or individual molds and chill until firm. Serves 6.

Mrs. J. Vann Carroll

BROCCOLI SALAD MOLD

2 packages frozen broccoli
    spears or 1 bunch fresh
    broccoli, cooked lightly
    and chopped
4 hard boiled eggs, chopped
1 tablespoon gelatin
¼ cup cold water

1 cup condensed consomme'
¾ cup mayonnaise
4 tablespoons Worcestershire
    sauce (optional)
2 tablespoons lemon juice
Dash of Tabasco
1 scant tablespoon salt

Mix the broccoli and eggs. Soften the gelatin in cold water and add heated consommé. Stir until the consommé dissolves the gelatin; then add the rest of the ingredients and pour over the broccoli and eggs. Mix well. Pour into a ring mold or 12 individual molds.

Refrigerate until firm. Serves 12. Serve with fresh garden lettuce and homemade mayonnaise.

Mrs. Henry Battle

CUCUMBER MOUSSE

1½ cups boiling water
3 (3 ounces each) packages lemon gelatin
1 package unflavored gelatin, softened in ¼ cup water
1 teaspoon salt

⅓ cup white vinegar
1½ cups sour cream
¾ cup mayonnaise
3 cups grated peeled cucumber
2 tablespoons chopped green onion

Pour boiling water over the lemon gelatin and stir until dissolved. Add unflavored gelatin which has been softened, salt, and white vinegar. Place in refrigerator until gelatin mixture begins to thicken. Beat with electric mixer until gelatin mixture is foamy, 2 to 3 minutes. Fold in, or beat in at low speed with mixer, sour cream and mayonnaise. Add cucumber and onion, mixing thoroughly.

Place in a well greased 2 quart mold and chill until set, about 2 hours. To unmold place a warm cloth around the mold to loosen it. Garnish with cucumber slices so your guests will not mistake this for a lime dessert mold. Serves 8 to 10.

Mrs. M. M. Alexander

JAXON SALAD

1 (3 ounce) package lemon gelatin

1 cup boiling water
1 (pint) jar of Jaxon Relish

Use one scant cup of boiling water to dissolve jello. Add the relish. Mold, refrigerate, and serve when desired. Serves 4 to 6. This keeps for days and is great for a buffet.

Miss Virginia Kelly

SWEET AND SOUR RELISH ASPIC

1 cup cold water, divided
2 tablespoons gelatin
1 cup hot water
2 cups sugar
½ cup cider vinegar
½ teaspoon salt
Green food coloring

1 cup slivered blanched almonds
1 cup sliced sweet pickle
1 cup crushed pineapple, drained
1 cup stuffed green olives, sliced

Soften gelatin in ½ cup cold water. Dissolve in hot water and add rest of the cold water. Add sugar, vinegar, and salt and mix well. Add green food coloring, one drop at a time, until desired color. Let cool and refrigerate. When mixture begins to thicken, add remaining ingredients and stir to blend. Turn into wet ring mold or 9″ square pan and chill until set. Serve plain or with mayonnaise. Serves 8.

Mrs. Edward W. Rugeley, Jr.

TOMATO ASPIC WITH ARTICHOKES

Miss Hallanan is a Charleston lawyer who has been particularly interested in young people and their problems, serving as the judge of the first full-time Juvenile Court in West Virginia. She was the first woman to be elected president of the Great Lakes Conference of Public Utilities Commissioners.

2 cups tomato juice	1 teaspoon Worcestershire
1 (3 ounce) package lemon	sauce
gelatin	1 tablespoon onion juice
1 tablespoon vinegar	1 teaspoon celery salt
1 (6 ounce) can artichokes, drained	

Heat 1 cup tomato juice, add gelatin, and dissolve. Add remaining ingredients. Chill until firm. Serves 4 to 6.

Miss Elizabeth V. Hallanan

TOMATO ASPIC — CREAM CHEESE SALAD

Cheese Layer:

6 ounces cream cheese	4 teaspoons lemon juice
½ cup mayonnaise	4 tablespoons boiling water
½ teaspoon salt	½ cup finely chopped celery
1 teaspoon unflavored gelatin	2 tablespoons chopped chives or onion

Blend softened cream cheese with mayonnaise and salt. Soften the gelatin in lemon juice and dissolve in boiling water. Combine all ingredients and put in bottom of oiled individual molds or one large mold. Chill until firm before adding aspic layer.

Aspic:

2 envelopes unflavored gelatin (from which the above 1 teaspoon gelatin has already been used)	1 cup boiling water
	1 (15 ounce) can seasoned tomato sauce
¼ cup cold water	2 tablespoons lemon juice
	1 teaspoon salt

Soften remaining gelatin in cold water; dissolve in boiling water. Add remaining ingredients and pour over cream cheese layer. Chill until firm.

Depending on the size of the mold used, there may be some of the tomato sauce mixture leftover which can be used molded alone.

Mrs. John Charles Thomas

CREAMED TOMATO ASPIC RING

3 cups tomato juice
Salt
2 (3 ounces each) packages
   lemon gelatin

2 (3 ounces each) packages
   cream cheese
1 cup mayonnaise

Salt tomato juice to taste and heat. Dissolve gelatin in heated juice, stir well, and cool. When cool, stir in softened cream cheese and mayonnaise. Pour into a greased 5 or 6 cup ring mold and chill until firm. Unmold and fill center with a favorite tossed salad mixed with a favorite dressing. Serves 6.

Mrs. W. O. McMillan, Sr.

JELLED TOMATO SALAD

Bottom Layer:
2½ cups tomato juice
2 tablespoons unflavored
   gelatin
½ cup cold water

½ cup lemon juice
2 tablespoons grated onion
1½ cups chopped celery
½ cup catsup
½ teaspoon salt

Heat tomato juice to boiling. Soften gelatin in cold water; dissolve in hot tomato juice. Add lemon juice, onion, celery, catsup, and salt. Pour in a mold and refrigerate. Add top layer when bottom layer is firm.

Top Layer:
1 tablespoon unflavored
   gelatin
½ cup cold water

1 cup hot water
1 cup cottage cheese
1 cup mayonnaise

Soften gelatin in cold water; dissolve it in hot water. Add cottage cheese and mayonnaise. Pour this over congealed first layer. Chill until set. Serves 10.

Mrs. Charles Q. Gage

SIMPLE TOMATO ASPIC

1 (3 ounce) package lemon
   gelatin
1 cup boiling water

1 cup tomato juice
3 tablespoons vinegar
1 teaspoon Worcestershire
   sauce

Chopped onion, green pepper or celery, optional

Dissolve gelatin in boiling water. Add rest of ingredients and chill until set. Chopped onion, green pepper, or celery may be added in equal amounts, not to exceed 1 cup total. Serves 6.

Mrs. William C. Weaver

JELLIED VEGETABLE SALAD

2 (3 ounces each) packages
   lemon gelatin
1 cup hot water
1 cup cold water
1 cup sweet pickle juice (cold)
⅛ cup lemon juice

½ teaspoon salt
2 tablespoons grated onion
1 cup sour cream
3 cups finely chopped raw
   cabbage, carrots, and green
   pepper

Dissolve gelatin in hot water. Add cold water, pickle juice, lemon juice, salt, onion, and sour cream. Use the electric mixer at low speed to blend in the sour cream. Chill until the mixture begins to congeal. Fold in vegetables and chill until firm. Makes 24 individual molds.

Mrs. Andrew R. Quenon

TART COTTAGE CHEESE VEGETABLE SALAD RING

1 (3 ounce) package lime
   gelatin
1 cup boiling water
½ cup carrots
1 green pepper

1 medium onion
2 tablespoons sugar
½ cup mayonnaise
½ cup cream (or whole milk)
¼ teaspoon salt

1 (16 ounce) carton cottage cheese

Dissolve gelatin in water; set aside.
Put carrots, pepper, and onion through the food grinder or coarse blender speed. Combine the rest of the ingredients, add grated vegetables, and pour into an oiled salad ring. Chill until set. Serves 8. Especially good served with ham or sliced cold turkey.

Mrs. Mary Floyd Auld

JELLIED APPLESAUCE

1 tablespoon unflavored
   gelatin
3 tablespoons cold water

2 cups hot applesauce
Sugar to taste
1 teaspoon grated orange or
   lemon rind

Soften gelatin in cold water. Stir in applesauce, sugar and rind.
Pour into mold ring or individual molds and chill until firm.

Mrs. Donald Ellsworth

CHERRY SALAD SUPREME

1 (3 ounce) package raspberry
   gelatin
2 cups boiling water, divided
1 (21 ounce) can cherry pie
   filling
1 (3 ounce) package lemon
   gelatin

1 (3 ounce) package cream
   cheese
⅓ cup mayonnaise or salad
   dressing
1 (8¾ ounce) can crushed pineapple, undrained (1 cup)
½ cup whipping cream
1 cup miniature marshmallows
2 tablespoons chopped nuts

Dissolve the raspberry gelatin in 1 cup boiling water; stir in
the pie filling. Turn into a 9" x 9" x 2" baking dish; chill until partially set. Dissolve lemon gelatin in 1 cup boiling water. Beat together the softened cream cheese and mayonnaise. Gradually add
lemon gelatin; then stir in undrained pineapple. Whip whipping
cream; fold into lemon mixture with miniature marshmallows.
Spread on top of cherry layer; sprinkle with chopped nuts. Chill
until set. Serves 12. This salad can also be served for dessert.

Mrs. Frederick H. Morgan

BLACK CHERRY SALAD

1 can dark cherries, pitted
1 cup cherry juice
1 (3 ounce) package lemon
   gelatin

1 cup port wine
1 tablespoon lemon juice
Pinch of salt
Cottage cheese

Drain the cherries and put around a 4 cup mold. Heat juice and
add gelatin. Stir until dissolved. Add wine, lemon juice, and pinch
of salt. Pour on top of the cherries. Chill in refrigerator. Unmold
and fill center with cottage cheese. Serves 6.

Mrs. Frederick H. Belden, Jr.

CHRISTMAS SALAD

3 (3 ounces each) packages
    raspberry gelatin
9½ cups boiling water, divided
2 (3 ounces each) packages
    lemon gelatin
5 ounces cream cheese,
    softened
½ pint whipping cream
2 (3 ounces each) packages
    lime gelatin
2 (13½ ounces each) cans crushed pineapple

Dissolve raspberry gelatin in 4½ cups boiling water. Pour into a 9" x 13" pan. Chill. After the red layer has congealed, dissolve the lemon gelatin in 3 cups boiling water. Add cream cheese. Cool completely. Beat whipping cream and fold into mixture. Pour on top of the red layer. Chill. When the white layer has set, dissolve the lime gelatin in 2 cups of boiling water. Add pineapple and pour over the white layer. Chill.

Serve on a lettuce leaf and garnish with whipping cream, mayonnaise, or a cherry cut into a flower. Serves 12 generously.

Mrs. Carl B. Hall, Jr.

CRANBERRY SALAD

1 (6 ounce) package cherry
    gelatin
1 cup hot water
1 cup sugar
1 tablespoon lemon juice
1 cup pineapple syrup
1 cup ground cranberries
1 whole orange, grated with
    peel included
1 cup crushed and drained
    pineapple
1 cup English walnuts

Dissolve gelatin in hot water. Add sugar, lemon juice, and pineapple syrup. Stir and chill until thickened. Add the remaining ingredients before the gelatin sets. Pour into mold and refrigerate until firm. Serves 10.

Mrs. Leslie Hawker

FRUIT SALAD

1 cup pineapple chunks,
    drained
1 cup fruit cocktail, drained
1 cup sour cream
1 cup small curd cottage cheese
1 cup miniature marshmallows
1 cup grated or flaked coconut
1 cup slivered almonds
    (optional)
Lettuce leaves

Mix all ingredients and serve chilled on lettuce. Serves 10 to 12.

Mrs. John R. Fowler

FROZEN FRUIT SALAD

4 egg yolks
4 tablespoons tarragon
vinegar or 2 tablespoons
cider vinegar plus 2 tablespoons pineapple juice
4 tablespoons sugar
½ pound marshmallows
1 pint whipping cream,
whipped
1 (3 ounce) package cream
cheese
¼ teaspoon salt
1 small bottle maraschino
cherries, cut in half
1 (13½ ounce) can pine-
apple chunks
1 cup pecan halves

Mix first three ingredients and cook in top of double boiler until thick. Add marshmallows. Chill. Add whipped cream and softened cream cheese. Add remaining ingredients. Put in a double
ice cube tray and freeze. Cut in squares to serve. Serves 12.

Mrs. Alexander J. Ross

GELATIN FRUIT SALAD

2 (3 ounce) packages lemon
gelatin
1¾ cups hot water
1¾ cups cold water
4 large bananas, diced
2½ cups crushed pineapple,
drained (reserve juice)
1½ cups small marshmallows

Make gelatin and fold in fruit. Chill until firm in an 8 x 12 inch
pan.

TOPPING

1 cup pineapple juice
(or reserved pineapple juice
plus enough water to make
1 cup)
½ cup sugar
2 tablespoons flour
1 egg, beaten
2 teaspoons butter
1 tablespoon lemon juice
1 package whipped topping
mix
Grated sharp cheese

Mix pineapple juice, sugar, flour, egg, butter and lemon juice.
Cook topping until thick. Chill. Prepare whipped topping mix and
fold into topping. Spread on firm gelatin. Top with grated sharp
Cheddar cheese. Serves 15-18.

Mrs. Fred L. Kellmeyer

GUMDROP FRUIT SALAD

1 cup whipping cream
2½ cups pineapple tidbits, drained
2 cups seeded grapes
2 cups miniature marshmallows

¾ cup gumdrop candy, cut fine (omit black candy)
1 (4 ounce) jar maraschino cherries, cut and drained
½ cup chopped pecan meats

Whip cream and stir all ingredients together. Add cooled dressing, and refrigerate overnight. Serves 8 to 10 generously.

DRESSING

½ cup pineapple juice
¼ cup sugar
2 tablespoons flour

¼ teaspoon salt
3 tablespoons lemon juice
1½ teaspoons vinegar

Blend all ingredients in a saucepan and cook until thick, stirring constantly. Cool before adding to the salad.

Mrs. Estil Monk

MOLDED FRUIT SALAD WITH DRESSING

1 (6 ounce) package lime gelatin
2 cups boiling water
½ cup cold water

2 tablespoons lemon juice
Pinch of monosodium glutamate
1 (8 ounce) can crushed pineapple, drained

Mix these ingredients and let set to the jelly stage.

1 large avocado, diced
1 to 2 cups small seedless green grapes

1 cantaloupe, diced or in balls
1 tablespoon lemon juice
Dash of monosodium glutamate

Mix all of these ingredients together and fold into gelatin mixture. Turn into a flat glass dish or mold.

DRESSING

1 (8 ounce) package cream cheese
3 heaping tablespoons mayonnaise

½ cup strained honey
½ cup sour cream

Mix all of these ingredients and serve with the salad. Serves 12.

Mrs. C. K. Payne, III

LEMON CHEESE RING

1 envelope (1 tablespoon)
   gelatin
¼ cup cold water
2 (3 ounces each) packages
   cream cheese
3 tablespoons sugar

1 cup milk
½ cup boiling water
1 (6 ounce) can frozen
   lemonade
Fruit (cranberries, blue-
   berries, strawberries, or a
   mixture)

Soften the gelatin in cold water. Blend the softened cream cheese and sugar, gradually adding milk. Dissolve the gelatin in boiling water and add to the cheese mixture along with the lemonade. Pour in a one quart mold; chill for 3 hours. Add fruit at serving time to the center of ring. Serves 4 to 6. To use as a dessert, substitute ¾ cup of sugar for 3 tablespoons sugar.

Mrs. Robert Swiger

MANDARIN ORANGE SALAD

Mrs. Benfield is the wife of the minister of First Presbyterian Church in Charleston. Dr. Benfield served as Moderator of the General Assembly of the Presbyterian Church, U. S. in 1970 and 1971.

1 (3 ounce) package orange
   gelatin
1 cup boiling water
1 (6 ounce) can frozen orange
   juice, undiluted

1 (16 ounce) can crushed pineapple
1 (11 ounce) can mandarin
   oranges, drained

Stir gelatin into boiling water; add orange juice and mix until orange juice has blended. Drain and reserve liquid from pineapple. Combine pineapple, mandarin oranges and the gelatin mixture. Place in refrigerator.

DRESSING

Juice from drained pineapple
½ cup sugar
1 teaspoon flour
1 egg, beaten

2 cups miniature
   marshmallows
Grated Cheddar cheese,
   (optional)

Cook pineapple juice with sugar and flour until thickened. Remove from heat. Slowly add beaten egg and cook about a minute longer. Add marshmallows and stir until dissolved. Cool. Mix refrigerated mixture with this and pour into a greased large mold. Before serving grated Cheddar cheese may be sprinkled on top. Serves 8 to 10.

Mrs. William Benfield, Jr.

UNDERSEA PEAR SALAD

1 (16 ounce) can pear halves
Water
1 tablespoon vinegar
1 tablespoon sugar
¼ teaspoon salt

1 (3 ounce) package lime
gelatin
1 (3 ounce) package cream
cheese, softened

Drain juice from the pears. Add enough water to the juice to make 2 cups. Heat this liquid and add vinegar, sugar, and salt to it. Stir heated liquid into gelatin; cut pears into pieces, and place them in the bottom of a 1 quart mold. Pour 1 cup gelatin mixture over the pears. Congeal. Gradually beat the other cup of gelatin mixture into the cream cheese and pour it over the congealed pear-gelatin mixture. Serves 6.

Mrs. Charles G. Moyers, Jr.

SPICED GELATIN

2 quarts water
5 cinnamon sticks
1 tablespoon whole cloves
Rind of 1 orange
Rind of 1 lemon
2 (3 ounces each) packages
orange gelatin
2 (3 ounces each) packages
lemon gelatin

3½ cups sugar
1 envelope (1 tablespoon)
unflavored gelatin
¼ cup cold water
⅛ teaspoon salt
2 teaspoons vanilla
1 tablespoon vinegar
Juice of 6 oranges
Juice of 4 lemons

Simmer 2 quarts water, cinnamon sticks, cloves, and orange and lemon rinds in stainless steel pan for two hours, covered. Strain. Mix flavored gelatins with sugar; pour strained liquid over this. Soak unflavored gelatin in cold water and add to hot mixture. Stir in salt, vanilla, vinegar, and juices. Pour into mold. Chill. Serves 12.

Mrs. Robert W. Lawson, Jr.

STRAWBERRY SALAD

2 (3 ounces each) boxes
strawberry gelatin
1½ cups boiling water
2 (10 ounces each) packages
frozen strawberries,
unthawed

2 to 3 bananas, mashed
1 (20 ounce) can crushed
pineapple, drained
1 cup chopped nuts
1 cup sour cream or
whipping cream, whipped

Mix gelatin and boiling water until the gelatin is dissolved. Add the frozen strawberries and stir until thick. Add the bananas, pineapple, and nuts. Pour half of the mixture in a 13″ x 9″ x 2″ pan; refrigerate until set. Spread with sour cream or whipped cream; then cover with the remaining gelatin mixture. Refrigerate. Serves 10 to 12. This salad is good also as a dessert.

Mrs. Harry Wise

STRAWBERRY AND RHUBARB MOLD

2 (3 ounces each) packages
   lemon gelatin
2 cups boiling water
2 tablespoons unflavored
   gelatin

½ cup cold water
2 (10 ounces each) packages
   frozen rhubarb
2 (10 ounces each) packages
   frozen strawberries

1 tablespoon lemon juice

Dissolve lemon gelatin in boiling water. Soften unflavored gelatin in cold water, add to first mixture. Cool. Cook rhubarb for 5 minutes. Defrost strawberries. When gelatin mixture is slightly thickened, add fruit and lemon juice. Pour into a 2 quart mold and chill until firm. Unmold and serve with salad greens and mayonnaise. Serves 8 to 12.

Mrs. L. M. LaFollette, III

CAESAR SALAD DRESSING

1 garlic clove, minced
½ cup salad oil
1 egg, beaten

½ cup grated Parmesan cheese
¼ cup lemon juice
½ teaspoon salt

½ teaspoon pepper

Combine all ingredients in a shaker and shake well. Serve on any lettuce salad.

Mrs. Craig M. Wilson

COUNTRY INN SALAD DRESSING

½ cup sugar
1 teaspoon salt
¼ teaspoon red pepper
1 cup cooking oil

½ cup catsup
½ cup vinegar
Small chunks of blue cheese,
   optional

Grated onion, optional

Combine ingredients in a quart jar and shake vigorously until well mixed. May also be blended in an electric blender, adding blue cheese after blending. Makes about 1 pint.

Mrs. Betty Scott Cowden

DIXIE'S HOMEMADE SALAD DRESSING

1 egg, beaten
1 tablespoon dry mustard
2 teaspoons salt
2 teaspoons paprika
½ teaspoon black pepper

1 (14 ounce) can sweetened
   condensed milk
¾ cup vinegar
¼ cup melted butter or
   margarine

Add dry mustard, salt, paprika, and pepper to beaten egg and blend well. Add sweetened condensed milk, vinegar, and melted butter and beat thoroughly until thick and smooth. Makes about 2 cups.

Serve on tossed salad for those who like a tart, zippy dressing. For those who prefer a milder flavor, combine equal parts home-made dressing with prepared salad dressing or mayonnaise.

Mrs. Edward W. Rugeley, Jr.

FRENCH DRESSING

Originally built in 1894 during the oil boom days, the Wells Inn at Sistersville, West Virginia, has the Victorian charm reminiscent of that time. In addition to its lovely decor, the Wells Inn is recognized for its fine food.

2 cups catsup
1 cup vinegar
1½ cups sugar
½ teaspoon salt

1 tablespoon Worcestershire
   sauce
1 garlic clove, minced
¾ cup salad oil

Blend all ingredients except the oil; then beat in oil last. Makes 1 quart.

Wells Inn

GREEN GODDESS DRESSING

1 to 3 garlic cloves, crushed	½ bunch fresh parsley
3 green onions, with tops minced	¼ teaspoon white pepper
	¼ teaspoon or more salt
1 tablespoon lemon juice	3 tablespoons vinegar
1 cup sour cream	½ tube anchovy paste, or less
½ cup mayonnaise	to taste

Combine in blender. Makes 1 pint.

Mrs Philip Angel, Jr.

GUAVA DRESSING

1 (8 ounce) package cream   ½ jar guava jelly
cheese, softened

Place cream cheese and jelly in a blender. Blend until smooth.
Serve on grapefruit and avocado slices arranged on lettuce.

Mrs. A. S. Thomas, Jr.

KAIKAN SALAD DRESSING

6½ ounces cooking oil	½ cup lemon juice or vinegar
1 clove garlic	1 teaspoon thyme
1 small onion, chopped	7 drops Tabasco sauce
½ green pepper, chopped	1 teaspoon parsley
2 stalks celery, chopped	1 teaspoon salt
½ bottle chili sauce	Pepper to taste

Slice garlic and soak in oil for one day; strain out garlic. Place onion, green pepper, and celery in jar. Add oil, chili sauce, lemon juice, thyme, Tabasco, parsley, salt, and pepper. Let stand for 2 hours. Stir before serving. Makes 1 quart.

Mrs. W. O. McMillan, Sr.
from Peer Club in Tokyo, Japan

PARMESAN CHEESE DRESSING

⅔ cup mayonnaise   ⅓ cup milk
⅓ cup grated Parmesan cheese   1 teaspoon white wine vinegar
         ¼ teaspoon Worcestershire sauce

Mix all ingredients well. Makes 1 cup.

Miss Julia Newhouse

PAUL AND ALFRED'S FAMOUS DRESSING

8 teaspoons cooking oil   1 tablespoon chili sauce
4 to 6 garlic cloves   1 tablespoon catsup
1 tablespoon mayonnaise   2 teaspoons vinegar
      1 teaspoon Worcestershire sauce

Peel garlic and put in cooking oil for 3 to 4 days. Remove garlic cloves, add remaining ingredients, and refrigerate. Must be refrigerated to blend flavors well. Makes about ½ cup. Use dressing on a salad of lettuce, tomato, sliced hard-boiled egg, and cubed American cheese. Sprinkle liberally with Parmesan cheese.

Mrs. Sydney P. Davis, Jr.

ROQUEFORT CHEESE DRESSING

1 pound Roquefort cheese,   ½ cup mayonnaise
   crumbled   ½ cup salad oil
1 cup buttermilk   1 teaspoon salt
         Juice of 1 lemon

Mix the ingredients by hand. Place in a 1 quart jar, cover and refrigerate. Delicious served on salads and baked potatoes.

Mrs. Jon M. Gaston

SALAD DRESSING

1½ or 2 cups sugar
1 tablespoon salt
2 teaspoons pepper
1 tablespoon oregano
1 teaspoon garlic powder
1 quart cider vinegar
1 quart salad oil

Stir dry ingredients and vinegar in a large container. Add oil and shake well. Makes 2 quarts.

Mrs. Jerry Hyatt

SWEDISH DRESSING

⅓ cup sugar
¼ cup hot water
¼ cup vinegar
1 hard-boiled egg, chopped
1 cucumber, sliced
1 carrot, diced
½ cup catsup
½ cup cooking oil
1 teaspoon salt
1 small onion, chopped

Dissolve sugar in hot water. Add vinegar, egg, cucumber, carrot, catsup, oil, salt, and onion. Shake in a jar and keep as long as a month or more in the refrigerator. Makes about 2½ cups.

Mrs. Marsha Pushkin

EASY THOUSAND ISLAND SALAD DRESSING

1 teaspoon grated onion
½ cup mayonnaise
3 tablespoons catsup
2 tablespoons sweet pickle relish
¼ teaspoon seasoned salt
½ hard-cooked egg, sieved

Combine all ingredients and chill at least 1 hour before serving on tossed salad. Makes ¾ cup.

Mrs. Thomas J. Blair, III

DRESSING FOR TOMATO ASPIC

1 teaspoon horseradish   ½ teaspoon sugar
¼ teaspoon salt   1 pint sour cream

Mix all ingredients and serve over tomato aspic.

Mrs. E. Garfield Atkins

CUCUMBER DRESSING FOR TOMATO ASPIC

½ cup grated cucumber   ½ cup mayonnaise
                Salt and pepper to taste

Mix all ingredients; fill center of tomato aspic ring.

Mrs. John M. Slack, III

WHIPPED CREAM MAYONNAISE

4 tablespoons sugar   3½ tablespoons vinegar
1 tablespoon flour   1 teaspoon water
⅛ teaspoon salt   1 egg, beaten
¼ teaspoon dry mustard   1 tablespoon butter
                ½ pint heavy cream, whipped

Combine all ingredients except whipped cream. Stir together until egg is well mixed with everything. Cook until bubbly. Cool completely. Fold in whipped cream. Makes 2 cups.

Mrs. Craig M. Wilson

VINAIGRETTE DRESSING

1 teaspoon dry mustard   Salt and pepper to taste
2 cloves garlic, pressed   ½ cup wine or tarragon vinegar
1 teaspoon sugar (optional)   1 cup oil, fine olive oil
Several shakes monosodium   preferred
   glutamate

Add mustard, garlic, sugar, monosodium glutamate, salt, and pepper to vinegar. Mix well. Add oil to vinegar and shake well. Store in refrigerator. Use as a salad dressing, or as a marinade for cooked chilled vegetables.

Mrs. Richard D. Kitching

GRIST MILL

" . . . There was a damp, cool smell about the millpond, even in the heat of July, partly because, in the narrowing hollow, the big wooden mill itself took the place in the sun and cast a shadowed reflection over it for most of the day. Its glass windows shone in the water, breathed where the ducks dived. Its wheel turned and groaned, dragging always its dark damp passengers of moss . . . "

Reprinted by permission of Mary Lee Settle, from **Know Nothing;** The Viking Press; New York, New York; 1960. Copyright by Mary Lee Settle. Page 45.

Photo by Gerald S. Ratliff

BREADS

Triple Sunflower

CHEESE BREAD

1 stick butter
⅓ cup Romano cheese
¼ cup Parmesan cheese
1 teaspoon paprika

2 (6 ounces each) packages
  mozzarella cheese
1 loaf French bread
Garlic salt

Melt butter, let cool; add Romano cheese, Parmesan cheese, and paprika. Stir to blend but do not let cheeses melt. Place mozzarella cheese slices on cut sides of 1 loaf French bread halved lengthwise, and spread with butter mixture. Sprinkle with garlic salt. Broil 2 to 5 minutes until lightly browned. Makes 8 to 10 servings.

Mrs. James Harvey Hammons

DILLY BREAD

1 package active dry yeast or
  1 cake yeast
¼ cup warm water
1 cup creamed cottage cheese
1 tablespoon butter
2 tablespoons sugar

1 tablespoon instant minced
  onion
2 teaspoons dill seed
1 teaspoon salt
¼ teaspoon soda
1 egg, unbeaten

2¼ to 2½ cups flour

Soften yeast in water. Heat cottage cheese and butter together until lukewarm. Combine sugar, onion, dill seed, salt, soda, and egg in bowl. Beat with spoon. Add cottage cheese and butter. Beat well. Add yeast and beat well, then add flour gradually to form stiff dough. Cover and let rise until double in size. Punch down and turn into well-greased 1 pound coffee can, 1 loaf pan or 12 muffin pans. Let rise until light, 30 minutes. Bake in 350° oven for 25 minutes for cans, 40 to 50 minutes for loaf pan, 15 minutes for muffin tins.

Mrs. William Gravely

QUICK FRENCH BREAD

½ cup milk
1 cup water
1 package yeast dissolved
   in ¼ cup warm water

1½ tablespoons sugar
2 teaspoons salt
1½ tablespoons shortening
4 cups flour

Warm milk with water. Add the dissolved yeast. Add sugar, salt, flour, and shortening (you may dissolve shortening in warmed liquids). Mix just enough to put together; do not knead; dough will be soft. Let rise in warm place for approximately 2 hours, or until about double in bulk. Shape dough into 2 oblong loaves and put into greased pans. Let rise again. Bake 15 minutes at 400° — or 30 minutes at 350°. 400° generally gives a crustier top.

Mrs. Joe C. Hereford

EASY HERB BREAD

3 cups warm water
3 cakes or packages yeast
¼ cup sugar
9 or 10 cups flour
5 teaspoons salt

½ teaspoon each savory,
   marjoram, sage, and
   minced parsley
5 tablespoons salad oil

Combine the water, yeast, and sugar. Stir until yeast dissolves. Add half of the flour, and all the salt and herbs. Beat hard with a spoon (preferably wooden) until batter is smooth. Add as much flour as the dough will absorb, and blend well. Pour the oil over the dough and knead, in the bowl, until the oil is absorbed, 2 or 3 minutes. Cover the bowl and let dough rise in warm place about 45 minutes, until doubled. Punch down, turn out on floured board and knead lightly. Shape into two loaves and place in buttered 9" x 5" loaf pans, or, shape into three loaves and place in three buttered 8" x 4" glass pans or 1½ quart casserole dishes. Let rise to top of pans. Bake in a 400° oven for 30 minutes, or until very brown and bread comes loose from pan when pan is shaken up and down, and loaf sounds hollow when thumped with knuckles on top surface. Remove from pans to cool.

Mrs. Jon M. Gaston

KENTUCKY BREAD

6 cups flour
1½ teaspoons salt
¼ cup sugar
½ teaspoon soda
1½ teaspoons baking powder

½ cup shortening (lard is better)
1 yeast cake or 1 package dry
   yeast
½ cup lukewarm water
1¾ cups buttermilk

Mix all dry ingredients. Add shortening and blend well with pastry blender. Add yeast dissolved in water. Add buttermilk and knead thoroughly with hands, until all ingredients are mixed. Cover tightly and let rest in refrigerator overnight or until chilled. Shape into two loaves and put into 8" x 4" bread pans. Grease tops and put in warm place to rise until loaves double in size. Bake at 375° for 40 minutes. Let cool for 5 minutes and remove from pans to cooling racks. Makes 2 loaves.

Mrs. Mack L. Johnson

GRANDMA'S OATMEAL BREAD

2 packages active dry yeast	1 tablespoon salt
½ cup warm water	6 to 6¼ cups all-purpose flour
1¼ cups boiling water	2 eggs, beaten
1 cup quick-cooking rolled oats	4 tablespoons rolled oats
½ cup molasses	1 egg white
⅓ cup shortening	1 tablespoon water

Soften yeast in ½ cup warm water. Combine 1¼ cups boiling water, quick-cooking rolled oats, molasses (dark), shortening, and salt; cool to lukewarm. Sift 6 to 6¼ cups all-purpose flour. Stir in 2 cups sifted flour; beat well. Add beaten eggs and the yeast; beat well. Add enough remaining flour to make a soft dough. Turn out on lightly floured surface; cover and let rest 10 minutes. Knead till smooth. Place in a lightly greased bowl, turning dough once. Cover, let rise till double (about 1½ hours).

Punch down. Coat 2 well-greased 8½" x 4½" x 2½" loaf pans with 2 tablespoons rolled oats each. Divide dough in half. Shape in loaves and place in pans. Cover, let double (45 to 60 minutes). Brush with mixture of 1 egg white and 1 tablespoon water; sprinkle lightly with rolled oats. Bake at 375° for 40 minutes. Cover with foil after baking 15 minutes if tops are getting too brown. Makes 2 loaves.

Mrs. J. Vann Carroll

ONION-CHEESE BREAD

½ cup chopped onion	1½ cups Bisquick
1 tablespoon shortening	1 cup grated sharp Cheddar
1 egg, slightly beaten	cheese
½ cup milk	1 tablespoon poppy seeds
2 tablespoons melted butter	

Sauté onion in shortening until soft, but not browned. Mix egg and milk; blend in Bisquick. Add sautéed onion and ½ cup of the grated cheese. Blend thoroughly. Spread dough in a greased baking dish (6" x 8" or 8" square). Sprinkle remaining ½ cup cheese and poppy seeds over top. Drizzle melted butter over all. Bake for 20 to 25 minutes in a pre-heated 400° oven. Cut in squares to serve. Serves 6 to 8.

Mrs. Edward W. Rugeley, Jr.

PUMPERNICKEL BREAD

3 packages active dry yeast or
   3 cakes compressed yeast
1½ cups water
½ cup dark molasses
1 to 2 tablespoons caraway
   seed

1 tablespoon salt
2 tablespoons soft shortening
2¾ cups stirred rye flour
2¼ to 2¾ cups sifted all-purpose
   white flour

Soften active dry yeast in warm water or compressed yeast in lukewarm water. Combine molasses, caraway seed, salt, shortening, the rye flour, about 1 cup of the white flour, and the softened yeast. Beat until smooth. Add enough flour to make a stiff dough. Turn out on a lightly floured surface and knead till smooth and elastic (8 to 10 minutes). Place dough in a greased bowl, turning once to grease surface. Cover and let rise in a warm place until double (about 1½ hours).

Punch down and divide dough into 2 parts. Cover and let rest 10 minutes. Round each part into a smooth ball. Place on opposite corners of a corn meal sprinkled baking sheet. Cover and let rise until double (about 30 minutes). Bake loaves in a moderate oven (375°) for about 30 to 35 minutes or until well browned. For a chewy crust, brush tops of the loaves with warm water several times during the baking, after the first 20 minutes. Makes 2 round loaves.

Mrs. J. Vann Carroll

SWEDISH RYE BREAD

1 package active dry yeast
¼ cup warm water
¼ cup dark brown sugar
¼ to ½ cup dark molasses
1 tablespoon salt

2 tablespoons shortening
1½ cups hot water
2½ cups medium rye flour
3 tablespoons caraway seeds
3½ cups sifted white flour

1 tablespoon orange rind (optional)

Soften the yeast in the warm water. In a bowl, combine the brown sugar, molasses, salt, shortening, and hot water. Stir until dissolved and cool to lukewarm. Stir in the rye flour and beat well. Add the yeast and the caraway seeds and mix well. Add the sifted white flour a little at a time until the dough can be handled with floured hands. Then allow the dough to rest, covered, for 10 minutes. Knead about 10 minutes on a floured board, and then place the dough in a lightly greased bowl, turning once to grease the top. Cover, and let rise in a warm place until doubled in bulk, about 1½ hours.

Punch down the dough, cover, and let rest for 10 minutes. Again knead well and divide into two portions. Shape into loaves and place in two lightly greased loaf pans. Let rise until doubled in bulk, about 30 minutes. Bake in a 375° oven for 25 to 35 minutes. Cool on a rack. Makes 2 loaves. For an interesting taste, ½ cup of orange juice may be substituted for an equal amount of the water and 1 tablespoon of orange rind added.

Miss Julia Newhouse

NO RISING WHOLE WHEAT BREAD

1 cup unbleached white flour	2 teaspoons soda
2 cups unbleached whole wheat flour	½ cup honey
	¼ cup blackstrap molasses
1 teaspoon salt	2 cups buttermilk

Blend all dry ingredients well. In a separate bowl mix buttermilk, honey, and molasses. Add dry ingredients gradually, beating well. Pour into two well-greased 4½" x 8½" loaf pans. (Batter will be stiff.) Place in preheated 400° oven, and immediately reduce heat to 350°. Bake approximately 1 hour. Turn out onto rack to cool.

Delicious toasted with butter, or with cream cheese-nut spread for sandwiches.

Mrs. Edward D. Spilman

WHOLE WHEAT BREAD —
LIKE YOUR MOTHER NEVER MADE

Two important points in making bread are (1) don't kill the yeast by using water that is too hot, (2) knead the dough for at least 15 minutes.

2 cakes of yeast	2 tablespoons salt
4½ cups water at 85°	2½ tablespoons vegetable oil
2½ tablespoons honey	1⅓ cups instant non-fat dry milk
8 to 9 cups whole wheat flour	4 cups white flour
½ cup wheat germ	

Put yeast in a large mixing bowl, and let it come to room temperature. Stir in 1 cup of water, honey, and 1 cup of wheat flour. Let stand for 10 minutes. Add rest of water, salt, and vegetable oil. Gradually blend in dry milk, white flour, wheat germ, and 6 cups wheat flour. Add more flour if necessary until dough is formed. Knead dough and add flour until dough no longer sticks to the board. Make certain you knead for at least 15 minutes.

Grease a large bowl and place dough in it. Grease exposed surface of dough. Cover with a damp cloth and let rise in a warm place (about 2 hours) until doubled.

Separate the dough into 3 equal balls. Knead each ball 2 minutes. Form loaves and place into metal loaf pans that have been heavily greased. Cover with a damp cloth and let rise again in a warm place. In 1½ to 2 hours the dough will fill the pan. Place the pans in an oven preheated to 400° and bake for 20 minutes. Reduce the oven temperature to 350° and cover the loaves with an aluminum foil tent. Bake another 30 minutes. Makes 3 loaves.

Mrs. John C. Steven

DOUBLE CORN CORN BREAD

1 cup self-rising cornmeal mix	2 eggs
1 cup sour cream	¼ cup oil
1 cup cream-style corn	1 teaspoon salt
½ teaspoon sugar	

Combine all ingredients. Pour into a hot, well-greased skillet or 8" x 8" cake pan. Bake at 400° for 30 minutes or until it pulls away from side of pan. Serves 8.

Mrs. Daniel O. Martin

GRANDMOTHER KISER'S CORN BREAD

2 cups white cornmeal	½ teaspoon soda
1½ cups flour	3 tablespoons baking powder
1 teaspoon salt	1 egg
2½ cups buttermilk	

Mix all ingredients in order given. Bake at 400° for 20 minutes or brown as you like. This is better baked in a well-greased 12" iron skillet but can be baked in a 13" x 9" pan 30 to 40 minutes. Serves 8 to 10.

Note: Corn cakes can be made by using ½ of this recipe. Drop the batter by tablespoonfuls onto a well-greased hot 12" skillet. Turn cakes when bubbly. Serve hot with butter and syrup.

Mrs. Robert F. Goldsmith

CORN PONE

2½ cups white or yellow
    cornmeal
1⅓ cups boiling water
½ cup molasses
½ cup bacon drippings
1 cup sour milk or buttermilk

½ cup cold water
¼ teaspoon soda
2 eggs, beaten
1¼ cups flour
2 teaspoons baking powder
1 teaspoon salt

Place cornmeal in a bowl and over it pour boiling water. Add the molasses and drippings, and cool. Combine milk, cold water, and soda; stir in. Add beaten eggs, flour, baking powder, and salt. Beat thoroughly. Pour into a well-greased 9" x 13" hot baking pan. Bake at 400° for 25 to 30 minutes. Cut in squares and serve hot. Serves 8.

Mrs. Carl B. Hall, Jr.

HUSH PUPPIES

1 cup yellow cornmeal
1 cup flour
1 tablespoon salt
3 teaspoons baking powder

1 medium onion, finely minced
1 egg mixed with ½ cup cold
    water
Cooking oil

Mix well cornmeal, flour, salt and baking powder. Stir in egg, water, and onion. Add enough more cold water (about ½ cup) so that batter will drop, not pour from spoon. Drop into about 1 inch of oil and fry until brown. Good with fish. Makes about 1 dozen.

Mrs. David Haden

JOHNNY CAKE

1 rounded teaspoon soda
1 cup cornmeal
1 teaspoon salt

1 teaspoon sugar
2 eggs, well beaten
2 cups sour milk

1 tablespoon butter, melted

Sift soda with a cup of cornmeal; mix with salt and sugar. Mix eggs with the sour milk; then mix in the dry ingredients, adding more cornmeal to make a batter as for layer cake. Stir in melted butter and turn into greased 7" or 8" pan. Bake at 425° for 25 or 30 minutes. Serves 6.

Mrs. Carl B. Hall, Jr.

CHEESE SPOON BREAD

2 cups milk
1 cup cornmeal
1 teaspoon salt

4 tablespoons butter
4 eggs, separated
½ cup grated mild Cheddar
cheese

Heat milk in double boiler. When hot, add cornmeal. Stir until thick. Add salt, butter, egg yolks and cheese. Beat egg whites and fold into cornmeal mixture. Bake in two quart casserole at 350° for 35 minutes. Serves 8.

Mrs. Phyllis Dusic

DR. MAGGIE'S OLD FASHIONED SPOON BREAD

Dr. Margaret B. Ballard was in private medical practice in Baltimore, Maryland, for nearly forty years and taught obstetrics and gynecology at the University of Maryland School of Medicine. Now retired from medical practice, Dr. Ballard has returned to her native Monroe County, West Virginia, where she is engaged in genealogical and historical research. In addition to her research activities, Dr. Ballard markets in considerable quantity her home-made soap which she makes in a cast iron kettle.

1 pint sweet milk
1 cup sifted cornmeal
1½ tablespoons sugar

½ teaspoon salt
1 heaping tablespoon butter
(do not use margarine)

3 eggs, separated

Scald the milk and slowly add the cornmeal, sugar and salt. Cook until it "puffs," stirring constantly. Set off the stove and add the butter. Allow to cool for 3 minutes. Stir in well-beaten egg yolks. Fold in the stiffly beaten egg whites. Bake in a dish heavily greased with cooking oil until it is brown and cracks near the edges, about 50 minutes at 350°. The bread will "fall" when removed from the oven, so eat immediately with plenty of butter. Serves 4.

Margaret B. Ballard, M.D.

DRESSING

1 long loaf Vienna or Grecian
bread
6 medium onions
1 bunch celery
1 teaspoon salt
2 sticks butter

1 teaspoon sage
1 teaspoon pepper
2 (13 ounces each) cans chicken
broth
Yellow coloring
3 eggs, beaten

Break bread in small pieces. Chop onions and celery and sauté with salt and butter until soft. Spread on top of bread. Sprinkle sage and pepper on top. Heat chicken broth and spoon it over this. Lightly stir this so all will be moistened — not too wet. Cover. Let stand about 4 hours. Adjust seasoning. Add eggs with fork just before you bake it. Do not stir it anymore than you have to. Bake at 450° until brown. Cut in squares to serve.

Mrs. Estil Monk

CORNBREAD DRESSING

½ to ¾ cup chopped onion
½ cup chopped green pepper
½ cup chopped celery
4 tablespoons butter
1 pan cornbread, crumbled
½ package herb-seasoned stuffing

Giblets, optional
3 hard cooked eggs
1 (10½ ounce) can chicken or turkey stock or broth
Salt and pepper to taste
2 teaspoons or more poultry seasoning

Sauté onion, green pepper and celery in butter until tender. Mix cornbread and stuffing. Add all this to cornbread and stuffing mixture. Mix well. Add giblets and eggs to mixture. Add stock or soup until moist. Season with salt and pepper (must use salt and pepper liberally; keep tasting). Add more poultry seasoning if necessary. Bake at 350° for 30 minutes in a casserole, or use to stuff a turkey.

Mrs. Chester P. Smith, Jr.

STUFFING BALLS

4 cups chopped celery
2 large onions, chopped
2 teaspoons sage
1 teaspoon celery salt
2 teaspoons salt
½ teaspoon pepper
¾ cup margarine or butter

1¼ cups chicken broth or water (may use beef broth if serving with beef)
2 small packages Pepperidge Farm Dressing Mix
1 cup coarsely chopped fresh cranberries, optional

Sauté celery, onions, and seasonings in the margarine in a skillet for 5 minutes. Add remaining ingredients and mix well. Shape in 12 balls and put one in each of 12 well-greased muffin pan sections. Bake in moderate oven at 350° for 30 minutes.

Variation: Add chopped cranberries for flavor and color. Serves 10 to 12.

Mrs. Richard Repaire

ANGEL BISCUIT

2 cups buttermilk
1 cup vegetable shortening
1 package active dry yeast
¼ cup warm water

4 tablespoons sugar
5 cups flour
1 teaspoon salt
1 tablespoon baking powder

Melted butter

Warm buttermilk and add shortening, stirring to melt, and cool. Add the yeast which has been softened in ¼ cup warm water. Add sugar. Sift together and add flour, salt, and baking powder. Stir to mix and cover with a damp cloth and an inverted plate. Chill overnight. At this point, the dough will keep about 5 days to be used as needed. The 6th and 7th days, use the dough as cobbler topping or for fried pies.

When ready to use dough, roll out ¼" thick, cut into 1½" rounds, brush each round with melted butter and stack two together. Place in greased pan, almost touching. Let rise 1 hour, then bake at 400° for 10 minutes or until done, depending on size of biscuits.

A good use for Angel Biscuit Dough on the 6th and 7th days is Fried Apple Pies.

FRIED APPLE PIES

Applesauce, seasoned   Water

Oil

Roll Angel Biscuit dough thinly; cut into squares or circles. Fill with seasoned homemade or commercial applesauce, fold over and seal the edges by moistening with water, and pressing with fork tines. Pierce top once. Fry in a little oil until brown, turning once and piercing other side. Do not deep fry.

Mrs. Miller C. Porterfield

BATTER BISCUITS

This is an Appalachian recipe from Eastern Kentucky.

1 tablespoon salt
½ tablespoon baking powder
¼ (or less) baking soda (use
    this to your own taste)

2⅓ cups flour
1 quart (or more) buttermilk
2 eggs
½ pound butter

Preheat oven to 425°. Mix dry ingredients. Add buttermilk until about the consistency of pancake batter. Beat eggs and add to batter. Batter must be slightly thinner than pancake batter and beaten very smooth. Melt butter. Put ½ teaspoon in each hole of small muffin tins. Heat on surface until butter is very hot. Spoon

1 tablespoon of batter into each hole and bake for 20 minutes. Turn out and serve immediately with your favorite jam or preserves. Makes 5 dozen biscuits.

Mrs. Don R. Richardson

BUTTERMILK BISCUITS

2 cups flour	1 teaspoon salt
2¼ teaspoons baking powder	⅓ cup plus 2 teaspoons
¼ teaspoon soda	shortening
¾ cup buttermilk	

Measure dry ingredients into mixing bowl. Sift and cut in shortening. Stir in buttermilk. When thoroughly mixed, turn onto a lightly-floured board, knead, and roll to about ½ inch thickness. Put on greased baking pan and brush tops with melted butter. Bake at 450° for 12 to 15 minutes. Serve hot. Makes 14 to 16 biscuits.

Miss Kathy Potterfield

ONION BISCUITS

¼ cup finely chopped onion	½ teaspoon salt
1 tablespoon shortening	½ teaspoon celery seed
1½ cups sifted all-purpose flour	¼ cup shortening
	1 slightly beaten egg
1½ teaspoons baking powder	⅓ cup milk

Cook onion in 1 tablespoon shortening till tender but not brown. Sift together the sifted flour, baking powder, and salt; stir in celery seed. Cut in shortening till mixture resembles coarse crumbs. Add onion, egg, and milk all at once and stir just till dough follows fork around bowl.

Turn out on lightly floured surface and knead gently ½ minute. Pat or roll ½ inch thick. Cut with floured 1¾ inch cutter. Bake on ungreased baking sheet in hot oven (425°) for 12 minutes or till done. Makes 12 medium-sized biscuits. (These are a delicious change of pace biscuit).

Mrs. J. Vann Carroll

SOPAIPILLAS

1¾ cups flour
2 teaspoons baking powder
1 teaspoon salt

2 tablespoons shortening
⅔ cup cold water
Fat for deep frying

Sift flour, baking powder, and salt into bowl. Cut in shortening and stir in about ⅔ cup cold water. Knead lightly until smooth. Cover with a cloth and an inverted bowl, allowing 10 minutes to rest. Meanwhile, heat fat to 385° in deep pan. Roll dough about ⅛″ thick and cut in 3 inch squares. Drop in a few at a time, and turn several times so that they will puff evenly. Drain on paper. Makes about 20.

To eat, break off a corner and fill with honey — a delightful contrast to the hot Mexican foods with which they are traditionally served.

Mrs. Ronald A. McKenney

HOT ROLLS WITH CORNMEAL

⅓ cup cornmeal
½ cup sugar
1 teaspoon salt
½ cup melted shortening

2 cups milk
1 cake or package yeast
¼ cup warm water
2 eggs, beaten

4 cups flour

Cook cornmeal, sugar, salt, shortening, and milk until thick over medium heat; cool to lukewarm. Dissolve yeast in warm water. Add to mixture with two beaten eggs. Let mixture rise for 2 hours, covered, in a warm place. Then add flour to form soft dough. Knead well and let rise 1 hour, until doubled. Knead again and roll out about ½″ thick. Cut with biscuit cutter, brush with melted butter, crease and fold over like Parker House rolls. Let rise 1 hour. Bake at 375° for 15 minutes on greased cookie sheet. Makes 4 dozen.

Mrs. Bernard Miller

REFRIGERATOR POTATO ROLLS

1 medium-sized baking potato
½ cup solid shortening
½ cup sugar
1 beaten egg

1 package dry yeast
¼ cup warm water
1 cup potato water
1 teaspoon salt

5½ cups sifted flour

Cook baking potato until well done in 2 to 3 cups water. Cool when done and reserve 1 cup of the liquid. If you don't have 1 cup liquid left, add enough water to make 1 cup.

Cream shortening and sugar in a large mixing bowl. Use an electric mixer for best results. Add beaten egg and mix well with electric mixer. In a separate dish or cup add dry yeast to ¼ cup warm water and allow to stand for 5 minutes. Use the electric mixer to cream the potato with as few lumps as possible. Add the creamed potato and potato water to the shortening, sugar, egg mixture, and beat with the electric mixer until well mixed. Stir in the yeast-water mixture and run electric mixer just long enough for yeast to disperse evenly. Add flour and salt to the mixture, using your hands if needed. The dough will be very stiff.

Use ¼ cup flour to flour a board and your hands. Make a large ball of the dough and move to board. Knead for 10 minutes. In about 8 to 9 minutes the dough will be smooth and will feel cold and clammy. At the end of 10 minutes of kneading, grease a large mixing bowl and form dough into a ball. Place dough in bowl, turning once so all sides are greased. Set in a warm place, cover with a light cotton tea towel, and allow to rise until double, about two hours.

This dough can now be rolled and cut into rolls or placed in the refrigerator in a tightly covered container and used when needed for up to a week.

When ready to use, roll dough out on floured board with rolling pin and cut with biscuit cutter. Fold over for Parker House rolls. Place in greased biscuit pans and allow to rise until double or for 2 hours. Bake at 425° for 10 minutes. Spread melted butter on top before baking if desired.

To make cinnamon buns, roll dough in rectangle, fill with favorite filling, roll up, slice, allow to rise, bake as directed, and ice.

Mrs. James L. Surface

ANTIQUE MUFFINS

2 cups sifted enriched
    self-rising flour
⅓ cup sugar
1 teaspoon cinnamon
1 cup chopped peeled apple
    (1 medium apple)

½ cup chopped nuts
1 cup sour cream
1 egg, beaten
½ cup milk
¼ cup sugar for topping

Sift together flour, sugar, and cinnamon. Stir in apple and nuts. Reserve ¼ cup sour cream. Blend egg and milk with remaining sour cream. Add liquid all at once to flour mixture, stirring only until flour is moistened. Fill large greased muffin cups ⅔ full. Drop 1 teaspoon reserved sour cream in center of each muffin and cover sour cream with 1 teaspoon sugar. Bake in hot oven 425° 20 to 25 minutes or until edges are golden brown. Makes 12 large muffins.

Mrs. C. K. Payne, III

DROP DONUT BALLS

⅓ cup sugar
½ cup milk
1 egg
2 tablespoons cooking oil
1½ cups flour

2 teaspoons baking powder
½ teaspoon cinnamon
½ teaspoon salt
½ teaspoon nutmeg
Powdered sugar

Mix sugar, milk, and egg. Add oil and sifted dry ingredients except powdered sugar. Drop from teaspoon into deep fat at 365° and cook until browned. Roll in powdered sugar and serve warm. Makes 3 dozen balls.

Mrs. Ronald A. McKenney

RAISED DOUGHNUTS (FASTNACHTS)

Part I:
1 cup milk
1 tablespoon sugar
¼ teaspoon salt

1 cake yeast
½ cup warm water
2 cups flour

Scald milk, add sugar and salt, cool. Dissolve yeast in warm water and stir into milk. Beat in flour. Mix well, cover, let rise in a warm place overnight or until it has doubled in bulk.

Part II:
3 tablespoons butter
¼ cup sugar

2 eggs, beaten
½ teaspoon nutmeg
Flour

Cream butter and sugar. Add this to risen sponge with the beaten eggs and nutmeg. Stir in as much flour as mixture will take up to make a soft dough. Let rise again until doubled in bulk. Turn out on a well-floured board and roll to ½" thick. Cut with doughnut cutter. Let rise again; then fry in deep, hot fat.

Miss Ann Hunter

NEW ORLEANS DOUGHNUTS

1 cup milk
¼ cup sugar
2 tablespoons margarine or butter

½ teaspoon salt
1 teaspoon dry yeast
¼ cup warm water
1 egg
3½ cups flour

Scald milk in saucepan. Remove from heat and dissolve sugar in the milk. Add butter and salt and stir until dissolved. Cool mixture to lukewarm. Dissolve dry yeast in warm water. Beat egg well and combine all ingredients. Beat well until flour is blended and smooth. No kneading should be necessary. Refrigerate dough until chilled and easy to handle. Roll dough to ¼ inch in square shape. Do not allow dough to rise. Cut dough into 2″ square shapes using scissors. Fry immediately in deep fat at 370°. Drain on paper towels and glaze or roll in sugar while still warm. If recipe is cut in half, the measure of 1 teaspoon dry yeast should still be used. Makes 3½ dozen.

Mrs. Ladd M. Kochman

ORANGE MUFFINS

1 stick butter
1 cup sugar
2 eggs, separated
2 cups flour
1 teaspoon baking powder
⅔ cup milk

1 teaspoon vanilla or lemon
  extract
1 orange and 1 lemon (juice
  and rind)
  Juice of another orange
1¼ cups sugar

Cream together the butter and sugar. Add the egg yolks and mix until lemon-colored. Sift together the flour and baking powder, and add this alternately with the milk to the first mixture. Add the flavoring, either vanilla or lemon extract. Beat the egg whites until stiff and fold in. Drop by spoonfuls into greased small muffin tins, filling ⅔ full. Bake at 350° for 20 minutes.

Grate the rind of 1 orange and 1 lemon and mix with the juice of 2 oranges and 1 lemon. While the muffins are still hot, dip them first in the juice and then in the sugar. Put on wax paper to cool. Makes 2 or 3 dozen small muffins.

Mrs. Chapman Revercomb

APRICOT BREAD

¾ cup dried apricots
¾ cup cold water
2 tablespoons lemon juice
¼ cup shortening

½ cup sugar
1 egg
2 cups flour
¾ teaspoon soda

Wash and finely cut apricots. Put in water and add lemon juice. Cream shortening with sugar. Beat and add egg. Mix well. Add flour sifted with soda to shortening and egg mixture. Now mix all together and put in greased loaf pan. Bake at 325° for 1 hour. Makes 1 loaf.

Mrs. Helen Townsend Ziebold

BANANA NUT BREAD

⅓ cup shortening
½ cup sugar
2 eggs
1¾ cups sifted flour

1 teaspoon baking powder
½ teaspoon salt
½ teaspoon soda
1 cup mashed ripe banana

½ cup chopped walnuts

Cream shortening and sugar; add eggs and beat well. Sift together dry ingredients. Add to creamed mixture alternately with banana, blending well after each addition. Stir in nuts. Pour into well-greased 9½" x 5" x 3" pan. Bake in 350° oven 40 to 45 minutes. Test for doneness by inserting toothpick in center. If pick comes out clean, bread is done. Remove from pan and cool on rack.

Mrs. Robert W. Lawson, III

DATE NUT BREAD

1 cup finely cut dates
1 tablespoon butter
1 teaspoon soda
1 cup boiling water
1 egg, beaten

1 cup sugar
1½ cups flour
2 teaspoons baking powder
½ teaspoon salt
½ cup chopped nuts

2 teaspoons vanilla

Combine dates, butter, soda and water. Cool. Add remaining ingredients and bake in 9" x 5" x 3" pan for 1½ hours at 300°. Serves 8.

BISHOP'S BREAD

Shortening
1 cup milk
1 tablespoon vinegar
1 cup sifted flour
⅓ cup sugar
1 teaspoon soda
¾ teaspoon salt
1 cup quick oats
⅓ cup semi-sweet chocolate
  pieces

1 cup golden seedless
  raisins
¾ cup candied cherries,
  chopped
¾ cup blanched almonds,
  chopped
1 egg
¼ cup vegetable oil
1 teaspoon vanilla

Grease an 8" x 4" x 2" loaf pan with shortening; line with wax paper and grease the paper. Combine the milk and vinegar and set aside. Sift together flour, sugar, soda and salt. Stir oats, chocolate pieces, raisins, cherries and almonds into dry ingredients. Beat egg slightly; stir in oil, vanilla and the soured milk. Add flour mixture to egg mixture and stir until dry ingredients are moistened.

Pour batter into prepared pan and bake at 325° 60 to 65 minutes, or until a cake tester inserted in center of the bread comes out clean. Remove bread from oven and cool on a wire rack for 10 minutes. Remove bread from pan and cool completely. When cool, wrap in plastic or aluminum wrap and store overnight before slicing. Makes one loaf.

PERSIMMON — HICKORY NUT BREAD

Euell Gibbons is widely known as a forager of wild foods and herbs which he expertly uses in camp meals and the home kitchen. He is the author of **Stalking the Good Life, Stalking the Wild asparagus, Stalking the Blue-Eyed Scallop,** *and* **Stalking the Healthful Herbs.** *Each year he conducts a nature weekend at West Virginia's North Bend State Park.*

2 cups flour	1½ sticks margarine
1 teaspoon soda	2 eggs
1 cup sugar	1 cup persimmon pulp
½ cup hickory nuts or black walnuts	

Sift flour and soda together. In a separate bowl cream sugar with margarine and add well-beaten eggs. Add soda-flour mixture, persimmon pulp and chopped nuts. Stir mixture up into a very stiff batter. Line 2 small loaf pans with waxed paper and place half of the batter in each. Bake 1 hour at 325°.

Euell Gibbons

PUMPKIN BREAD

6 eggs	3 teaspoons cinnamon
3 cups sugar	2 cups and 4 teaspoons cooking
4½ cups flour	oil
3 teaspoons baking powder	3½ to 4 cups pumpkin
3 teaspoons soda	3 teaspoons vanilla
3 teaspoons salt	1 cup or more chopped nuts (optional)

Mix eggs and sugar. Sift remaining dry ingredients together. Add oil and dry ingredients alternately with pumpkin. Add vanilla and fold in nuts. Grease 5 (1 pound each) coffee cans and fill about half full. Bake at 350° for 50 to 60 minutes.

Mrs. Richard Repaire

DOUGHNUT COFFEE CAKE

4 rolls doughnuts (found in
   dairy case)
1 (6 ounce) can frozen
   orange juice, undiluted
2 cups brown sugar

1 teaspoon nutmeg
1 tablespoon cinnamon
1 teaspoon ground cardamom
2 cups chopped pecans
½ pound margarine

Fresh orange slices

Line bottom of 13" spring tube pan with foil and then grease. Divide each doughnut piece in half. Roll each half into a small ball. Arrange balls in the bottom of the pan so they are just touching. Drip ⅓ orange juice over balls. Mix brown sugar with spices. Sprinkle ⅓ brown sugar mixture and ⅓ pecans over balls. Dot with ⅓ of margarine. Repeat this layer twice more, making 3 layers. To garnish top layer, add fresh sliced orange pieces, then the nuts, brown sugar and butter. Cover with damp cloth and allow to rise about 3 hours in a warm place. Bake in 400° oven about 35 to 40 minutes. Serves 20 to 25.

Mrs. Steven Thomas, III

HUNGARIAN COFFEE CAKE

1 cup milk, scalded
1 teaspoon salt
¼ cup sugar
¼ cup butter
1 package dry yeast (or 1 cake)
¼ cup warm water

1 egg
3½ cups flour
1 cup granulated sugar
2 tablespoons cinnamon
1 cup chopped nut meats
6 tablespoons melted butter

Add salt, sugar, and butter to scalded milk. Dissolve yeast in warm water. When milk mixture has cooled to lukewarm, add dissolved yeast to it. Add egg and small portions of flour at a time, beating well after each addition. Do not knead. Place dough in greased bowl and let rise until double in bulk. Combine sugar with cinnamon and chopped nuts. Pinch off pieces of dough slightly larger than a walnut; roll each piece in melted butter, then in sugar-cinnamon-nut mixture. Place balls of dough in layers in greased tube pan. Cover and let stand until dough rises again, double in bulk. Bake at 375° for 30 minutes. Remove from oven; let stand 2 or 3 minutes, then turn upside-down on large cake plate.

Mrs. Seigle W. Parks

SOUR CREAM COFFEE CAKE

½ cup margarine or butter
1 cup sugar
2 eggs
1 teaspoon vanilla
½ cup raisins (soaked in hot
    water, then drained) or
    dates quartered

¼ cup maraschino cherries
    (quartered)
2 cups all-purpose flour
1 teaspoon baking powder
1 teaspoon baking soda
½ teaspoon salt
1 cup sour cream

Cream butter until soft and add sugar. Add eggs 1 at a time and beat well. Add vanilla, raisins, and cherries. Sift together flour and dry ingredients. Add dry ingredients and sour cream alternately. Mix topping together well. Pour half of batter into 9" x 9" cake pan; cover with half of nut topping; repeat. Bake at 325° for 40 to 50 minutes or until done when tested with toothpick. If prepared ahead, heat to serve. This may be cut in two, which makes 2 loaf-size cakes.

NUT TOPPING

Nut Topping:
½ cup chopped walnuts
    or pecans
⅓ cup brown sugar

¼ cup white sugar
1 teaspoon cinnamon

Mix well.

Mrs. Garth E. Neville

SUSAN'S STOLLEN

2 cups flour
½ cup sugar
1¼ teaspoons salt
2 packages dry yeast
¾ cup milk
½ cup water

⅔ cup butter or margarine
3 eggs, at room temperature
4½ cups flour
¾ cup chopped almonds
¾ cup candied fruit
½ cup golden raisins

Powdered sugar icing

Mix flour, sugar, salt and yeast. Heat milk, water and butter until warm and add liquid mixture to dry mixture. Beat 2 minutes at medium speed with electric mixer. Add eggs and ½ cup flour. Beat 2 minutes at high speed. Add 3½ to 4 cups flour. Knead 8 to 10 minutes on floured board. Cover and allow to rise 1½ hours in greased bowl. Punch down, turn out onto floured board, and knead· in chopped almonds, candied fruit and raisins. Divide dough into 3 equal balls. Pat each piece into a 12" x 7" oval. Fold over lengthwise. Place on greased baking sheets. Cover, let rise 45 minutes. Bake at 350° for 20 to 25 minutes.

While warm, frost with powdered sugar icing and trim with whole almonds and candied fruit. Makes 3 loaves.

Mrs. E. Garfield Atkins

SWEDISH TEA RING

1 package active dry yeast	½ teaspoon salt
¼ cup warm water (105° to 115°)	1 egg
¼ cup lukewarm milk (scalded, then cooled)	¼ cup shortening or butter or margarine
¼ cup sugar	2¼ to 2¾ cups flour, divided

Filling:

2 tablespoons butter or margarine, softened	½ cup brown sugar
	2 teaspoons cinnamon
½ cup raisins	

Dissolve yeast in warm water. Stir in milk, sugar, salt, egg, shortening, and 1½ cups of flour. Beat until smooth. Mix in enough remaining flour to make dough easy to handle. Turn dough onto lightly floured board; knead until smooth and elastic, about 5 minutes. Place in greased bowl; turn greased side up, cover; let rise in warm place until double, about 1½ hours.

Roll dough into rectangle, 15" x 9". Spread with butter or margarine, softened, and sprinkle with brown sugar, cinnamon, and raisins. Roll up beginning at wide side. Pinch edge of dough into roll to seal well. Stretch roll to make even. With sealed edge down, shape into ring on lightly greased baking sheet. Pinch ends together. With scissors, make cuts ⅔ of the way through ring at 1-inch intervals. Turn each section on its side. Let rise until double (45 minutes). Bake 25 to 30 minutes at 375°. Frost while warm with sweet icing. Decorate with nuts and cherries. Serve warm.

SWEET ICING

1 cup powdered sugar, sifted	½ teaspoon vanilla
1 tablespoon milk	Cherries and nuts for garnish

Mix sugar, milk, and vanilla until smooth. Garnish.

Mrs. V. Courtlandt Smith, II

BASIC TASTY EGG BREAD RECIPE

1½ cups scalded milk	3 packages active dry yeast
½ cup butter or margarine	½ cup lukewarm water
1¾ teaspoons salt	2 beaten eggs
½ cup sugar	8 to 9 cups flour

Pour scalded milk over butter, salt, and sugar. Cool. Dissolve the yeast in warm water and let stand 4 to 5 minutes. Add yeast and beaten eggs to cooled milk. Gradually add flour, beating well. Add only enough flour to make an easily handled dough, as this makes a light bread. Knead on a floured board until smooth and shiny, 5 to

8 minutes. Place in a greased bowl, cover, and let rise until doubled in size, about 1 to 1½ hours. Punch down and turn out onto a lightly floured board. Shape into 3 loaves and place in greased 8″ loaf pans. Cover and let rise until not quite double, about 1 hour. Bake at 425° for 10 minutes, lower heat to 350° and bake 30 to 35 minutes longer. Makes 3 loaves.

This bread recipe makes a delicious sweet roll.

SWEET ROLL

Melted butter
Confectioners sugar
Brown sugar

Cinnamon
Chopped nuts
Raisins

Roll out the Tasty Egg Bread dough to 1 inch thick instead of shaping it into loaves. Spread it with butter, sprinkle liberally with confectioners sugar, brown sugar and cinnamon. Chopped nuts and raisins may also be added. Roll up as for a jelly roll and slice into 1 inch slices and place in a well-greased pan. Rise and bake as for Tasty Egg Bread, only less time, 425° for 10 minutes and then lower to 350° for 15 to 20 minutes. May be iced if desired.

A sweet cake may also be made from this bread recipe.

SWEET CAKE

⅓ of Tasty Egg Bread Dough
¼ cup sugar

⅓ cup soft butter
¾ cup raisins and nuts, mixed
1 beaten egg

Knead the sugar, butter and raisins and nuts into the bread dough. Shape into a round loaf and place in a buttered pie tin or round cake pan. Cover and let rise until doubled, about 30 to 40 minutes. Brush with a beaten egg and sprinkle with lots of sugar. Bake at 425° for 10 minutes, then lower to 350° for 25 to 30 minutes more. Cut into wedges. A sugar glaze may be put on top after baking instead of sprinkling with sugar before baking.

Mrs. Edwin M. Bartrug, Jr.

BUTTERSCOTCH BUNS

1 (3 ounce) package butter-
    scotch pudding mix (not
    instant)
1½ cups milk
8 tablespoons margarine

1 package active dry yeast
¼ cup warm water
2 large eggs, beaten (or 3 small)
1 teaspoon salt
4½ cups flour

Prepare pudding mix according to package directions, except use 1½ cups of milk. Add margarine; cool. Soften yeast in water; add to cooled pudding. Add the eggs, salt and flour, beating well.

Cover with a damp cloth and an inverted plate and refrigerate overnight. (Should rise in refrigerator.)

On a floured board roll dough out to about 10" x 36".

Filling:

| 6 to 8 tablespoons butter | ¾ cup coconut |
| ¾ cup brown sugar | ¼ cup finely chopped nuts |

Brush rolled dough with melted butter. Sprinkle with sugar, coconut and nuts. Roll dough lengthwise and cut into 36 1-inch slices. Place almost touching in greased pans, cut side down, and let double in size, about 1 hour. Bake at 375° for 10 to 12 minutes. Drizzle glaze over each bun while hot.

Glaze:

| ¼ cup brown sugar | 3 tablespoons butter |
| 3 tablespoons milk | 1 cup confectioners sugar |

Boil together sugar, milk and butter for 1 minute. Add confectioners sugar and stir. Makes 3 dozen buns.

Mrs. Ronald A. McKenney

GLAZED ORANGE ROLLS

1 cup milk	1 cake or 1 package active dry
3 tablespoons margarine	yeast
½ cup sugar	3 eggs
½ teaspoon salt	4 to 4½ cups flour

Scald milk; add margarine, sugar and salt. Cool to lukewarm and add yeast. Let stand for 3 minutes, then add eggs and 1 cup flour. Beat well. Add 3 to 3½ cups flour and knead on floured board for 10 minutes. Place in a greased bowl, turning once to coat the top; cover, and let double about 2 hours. Divide into two balls. Roll each one out to 12" x 8", spread with filling, roll each up as for jelly roll, and cut 18 slices from each. Place in greased pans and let double for about 1½ hours. Bake at 375° for 15 minutes. Cool slightly. Glaze with the mixed orange juice and powdered sugar.

Filling:

| 6 tablespoons margarine | ½ cup sugar |
| | Grated peel of 1 orange |

Glaze:

| 4 to 5 tablespoons orange juice | 2 cups powdered sugar |

Mrs. Paul Saylor

PECAN ROLLS

½ cup butter
½ cup margarine
1½ cups milk
½ cup warm water
2 packages active dry yeast
1 tablespoon sugar
7 cups flour

½ cup sugar
2 teaspoons salt
2 eggs, room temperature
Rind of 1 lemon, grated
Brown sugar
Chopped nuts
Butter

Melt butter and margarine in small saucepan; add milk. Cool to lukewarm.
To water add yeast and sugar. Do not stir. Let this double in volume.
Put flour into a large bowl (4-quart). Make a well in flour; add yeast mixture. Cover with flour. Add sugar, salt, eggs and lemon rind. Add melted butter and milk mixture as you work it in with fingers. Knead until dough slides off fingers — about 5 minutes. Cover with wet cloth and let rise until double in volume.
On floured surface roll out about ⅓ to ¼ inch thickness. Spread with brown sugar and chopped nuts and dot with butter. Roll jelly roll fashion and cut with floured knife. Place in greased pan with sides just touching. Let rise again 30 minutes. Bake at 375° for 30 minutes.

Mrs. Robert F. Goldsmith

QUICK CREPE RECIPE

1 cup Bisquick
2 eggs

⅔ cup milk
⅓ cup water

Put all ingredients in blender. Heat griddle as for pancakes. Pour enough mixture for 1 regular size pancake (1 large tablespoon or so). Immediately roll griddle (or skillet) around to cause pancake to spread as far as it will, to about 5 inches. Cook on one side until done and turn out on bread board. When first one cools (after next pancake is poured and spread), put it between pieces of waxed paper. Continue until all are made. These can be frozen or will keep in refrigerator for several days. Makes 14 to 16 five-inch crêpes.

Mrs. John M. Slack, III

BREAKFAST CREPES AND APPLES

¾ cup flour
1 teaspoon baking powder
2 tablespoons powdered sugar
½ teaspoon salt

2 eggs, beaten
⅔ cup milk
⅓ cup water
¾ teaspoon vanilla or grated
  lemon rind

Sift together the flour, baking powder, sugar, and salt. Beat together the eggs, milk, water, and vanilla. Pour the liquid into the dry ingredients and combine with a few stirs. Do not try to get rid of lumps as they will take care of themselves as they cook. Grease a small skillet and heat till drops of water dance on it. Add a small quantity of batter and tip the skillet to coat. When one side is brown, turn the crêpe and brown the other side. Stack the crêpes between layers of waxed paper. They may be refrigerated overnight or frozen until needed.

Apple Filling:

12 cooking apples	4 tablespoons butter
1 cup sugar	

In a skillet, cook about a dozen peeled, cored, and thinly sliced cooking apples in butter. After about five minutes, add sugar and cook the apples, covered, stirring often until they are soft. Fill each crêpe with a spoonful of the hot apples and roll up. Place two on each breakfast plate with sausage and top each crêpe with a dab of butter. Makes about 14 five-inch cakes.

Mrs. Robert M. Chilton

SOY-WHOLEWHEAT CREPES

Brian Van Nostrand, an essentially self-taught potter, began working with ceramics in 1965 after having earned a degree in philosophy. Seeking the repose of rural life, he and his wife, Montie, settled on a farm at Hacker Valley in Webster County, West Virginia. Here Van Nostrand finds a variety of clays to use for his pottery which is made primarily by hand. He writes about his crêpes recipe that those concerned with nutrition will appreciate "the high protein, low saturated fat content of these pancakes as well as the nutlike flavor the healthful flours impart."

1 cup soybean flour	4 eggs
1 cup wholewheat flour	2 tablespoons oil
½ teaspoon salt	2 cups milk

Mix dry ingredients. Add eggs, oil, and milk. Beat until smooth. Coat bottom of oiled, pre-heated skillet (preferably one with sloping sides) with about 3 tablespoons of batter, tilting the pan quickly for an even coating. When edges curl and crêpe slides freely, flip over and brown other side. Slide gently onto platter and keep warm in hot oven with door open. Makes about 2 dozen.

Breakfast variation: Serve 4 or 5 flat or folded in half and topped with an egg, sunny side up. If desired, drizzle with molasses, honey or syrup.

Main dish variation: Spread with spiced meat filling; roll and serve hot with cheese or tomato sauce. Two or three per serving.

Dessert variation: Spread with cream cheese and/or fruit preserves. Roll and serve warm with more preserves heated and thinned as a sauce. Top with whipped cream if desired. One crêpe per serving.

Brian and Montie Van Nostrand

BLINTZ PANCAKES

1 cup flour	1 cup sour cream
1 tablespoon sugar	1 cup cottage cheese
½ teaspoon salt	4 beaten eggs

Sift dry ingredients into bowl. Add sour cream, cheese, and eggs. Fold only till flour is barely moistened. Cook on a hot, lightly-greased skillet. Makes about 16 pancakes. Serve with strawberry preserves.

Mrs. Leigh Shepherd

HEALTHY PANCAKES

½ cup warm water	2 eggs
1 to 3 tablespoons of package or cake baker's yeast	2 tablespoons vegetable oil
	½ cup wheat germ
1 tablespoon honey, molasses, or sugar	1 cup whole wheat flour or 1 cup regular flour
1 cup sweet or sour milk, buttermilk, or yogurt	minus 1 tablespoon
	½ cup powdered milk
1 teaspoon salt	

Stir the warm water, yeast, and honey or molasses together in a bowl. Allow to stand for 5 minutes. Add milk, eggs, oil, and wheat germ. Sift into the liquid the flour, powdered milk, and salt. Stir and bake on a slow griddle immediately if 3 tablespoons of yeast were used. Let rise in a warm place for 30 minutes if 2 tablespoons of yeast were used. Let rise overnight if 1 tablespoon of yeast was used. Serves 6.

Mrs. Henry W. Battle

TERRA ALTA BUCKWHEAT CAKES

1 cake of yeast
½ cup warm water
2 cups warm water
1½ to 2 cups buckwheat
    flour

Pinch of baking soda
¼ cup warm water
1 to 2 tablespoons flour
2 teaspoons baking powder
1 tablespoon sugar

½ teaspoon salt

The night before serving, dissolve yeast in about ½ cup warm water. Put 2 cups warm water in a large warm mixing bowl and mix into it 1½ to 2 cups buckwheat flour; use enough flour to make the mixture of a consistency which will rise. Then mix the softened yeast into the mixture, beating it hard and thoroughly. Do not refrigerate.

The next morning, put a pinch of baking soda in about ¼ cup warm water; stir this gently into the mixture in the large bowl. Add 1 to 2 tablespoons of flour, baking powder, sugar and salt in the batter and stir well, but do not beat.

Make cakes (the batter will be thin). Be sure to save some batter as a starter for the next batch. Refrigerate the remaining batter, covered, until the night before you wish to serve the cakes (should not be more than 2 weeks).

The night before serving, add to the batter which has been saved, 2 cups warm water, and from 1½ to 2 cups buckwheat flour, beating it thoroughly and allowing it to sit out overnight as before. The next morning, mix in the baking soda, water, flour, baking powder, sugar, and salt as stated above.

Mrs. G. Clayton Rex

CORNMEAL GRIDDLE CAKES

2 cups water ground cornmeal
1 teaspoon salt

1 teaspoon soda
2 eggs

3 cups buttermilk

Using a wire wisk, combine all the ingredients in the order given and bake on a hot griddle well greased with bacon fat. Grease griddle as needed. Makes 36 cakes.

Mrs. Henry Payne, Jr.

QUILTING

"Quilting parties were often followed by a dance. At the beginning of the dance, the circle of partners gathered around the quilt holding the edges in their hands. The quilt was stretched out smoothly as the circle danced round and round.

"Suddenly the house cat was tossed into the middle of the quilt, which was shaken vigorously, tossing the cat this way and that. When the cat finally made its escape, it was noted which partners the cat jumped towards. This couple was marked for the earliest marriage of the group. For the young people, it was hilarious fun, but probably much less fun for the cat."

Reprinted by permission of William B. Price, from "Pioneer Life" in **Tales and Lore of the Mountaineers;** Quest Publishing Company; Salem, West Virginia; 1963. Copyright by William B. Price. Page 145.

Photo by Mountain Artisans

PICKLES AND PRESERVES

Delectable Mountains

CRANBERRY JELLY

4 cups cranberries (1 pound)　　2 cups water
2 cups sugar

Boil cranberries and water for 20 minutes, or until berries are tender. Put through a strainer or food mill. Add sugar to berry purée. Cook rapidly for 5 minutes, stirring constantly. Pour into mold and chill.

Mrs. Frederick M. Staunton

MINT JELLY

Green and red crab apples　　Fresh mint
Sugar　　Green food coloring

Wash well equal quantities of green and red crab apples (the large variety that turn a deep almost purple color). Put whole apples into very large pot, and add water to about ⅓ the depth of the apples. Bring to a boil and cook until the apples are soft and fall apart. Strain through a jelly bag — do not squeeze if you desire a clear jelly.

Measure juice and place equal amounts of juice and sugar in a large pot. (Pot must be very deep for small amount of juice or it will boil over.) Place pot over high heat and bring to a full rolling boil. Continue to boil until juice reaches jelly stage. (Either two drops come together and form one as dropped from spoon, or drop forms a soft ball when dropped into a dish of cold water.

Remove from heat and skim foam from top of jelly. Swirl several sprigs of fresh mint in the hot jelly and leave for a few minutes. Remove mint sprigs and add several drops of green food coloring. Ladle into clean jelly glasses and seal with self-sealing lids or melt paraffin and pour a thin layer over hot jelly, tipping glass to coat edges.

Fresh mint jelly may be used as a garnish for lamb.

Mrs. Cynthia Chilton Quattrochi

VIOLET JELLY

Violets
Boiling water

1 lemon
1 package Sure-Jell
4 cups sugar

Fill any size glass jar with violet blossoms. Cover with boiling water, put lid on jar, and let blossoms infuse for 24 hours. The next day, open the jar and strain the blue infusion, discarding the spent violets. Measure out 2 cups of the infusion and add the juice of 1 lemon and 1 package Sure-Jell. Bring this just to a boil and immediately add sugar. Bring back to a boil and boil hard for one minute. Pour into glasses or jars and seal.

Mrs. Mack L. Johnson

EASY GRAPE JAM

8 cups grapes

6 cups sugar

Mash grapes. Add sugar. Bring mixture to boil, and boil for 25 minutes. Put through a sieve and pour into sterilized jars. Seal. Makes 4 pints.

Mrs. Si Galperin

STRAWBERRY JAM

1 quart strawberries

3 cups sugar

To berries add 1½ cups sugar; boil 5 minutes and then add other 1½ cups sugar. Boil 15 minutes. If soft and watery, boil longer. Pour into mixing bowl; stir, then cover with plate. Let stand 24 hours or longer. Ladle into jars and add paraffin.

Mrs. Thomas H. Edelblute, Jr.

CITRUS MARMALADE

3 whole lemons, ground
3 whole oranges, ground
Water

1 whole grapefruit, ground
Sugar, approx. 5½ to 6
pounds

Using 3 times as much water as fruit, cover and soak overnight. Next day, cook until tender, about 45 minutes. Combine equal amounts of sugar and fruit. Cook for 45 minutes over medium-high

heat. Remove from heat and when cool, ladle into sterile jars and seal with paraffin.
Yield: 6 to 7 pints.

Mrs. Leigh Shepherd

WILD PLUM MARMALADE

Wild plums (6½ cups cooked)   8 cups sugar
1 box Sure-Jell   Paraffin

Wash ripe or semi-ripe wild pink plums and just cover with water in large kettle. Boil until skins begin to come off and inside is soft. (About 15 minutes). When cool, remove seeds by hand, leaving both skins and pulp for the preserves. (This is best done while wearing clean rubber gloves.)
Measure 6½ cups of fruit and juice into tall kettle. Stir in box of Sure-Jell and bring to boil, stirring occasionally. In the meantime, measure 8 cups of sugar and add all at once, stirring thoroughly so it will not burn. After it comes to a full, hard boil, continue cooking 1 minute. Let cool, stir and put in sterilized jars and top with paraffin. This is tart and has a pretty color and a wonderful wild, fresh flavor.

Mrs. Tinsley A. Galyean

APPLE BUTTER

2 pecks apples   2 tablespoons cinnamon (or
1 gallon sweet cider   to taste
12 cups sugar   ½ tablespoon ground cloves

Quarter and core apples. Cook with cider to soften; they will make their own juices. Stir often. Put through a sieve. Place in an iron kettle or large pot. Add rest of ingredients. Cook over outdoor fire (or inside) 3 or more hours to taste, stirring often. Seal in jars.

Mrs. Si Galperin

OLD-FASHIONED TOMATO BUTTER

5 quarts ripe tomatoes, peeled   2 cups white sugar
  and ground   3 cups brown sugar
3 medium onions, peeled and   1 teaspoon ground cloves
  ground   1 teaspoon allspice
1 pint white vinegar   1 teaspoon cinnamon
            1 tablespoon salt

Combine vinegar, sugars, spices, and salt in heavy enameled saucepan. Bring to a boil. Add peeled and ground vegetables and simmer over low heat until thickened. Stir frequently to prevent sticking. Ladle hot mixture into hot sterilized jars and seal at once. May also be cooked in a 350° oven to avoid having to stir the butter. Yield: about 5 pints.

Excellent with biscuits and butter or spooned over a cake of softened cream cheese and served with crackers as a spread.

Mrs. Donald Ellsworth

JANE'S CUCUMBER PICKLE

4 quarts sliced cucumbers	4 cups sugar
1½ cups sliced white onion	1½ teaspoons turmeric
2 large garlic cloves	1½ teaspoons mustard seed
½ cup salt	3 cups white vinegar
2 trays ice, crushed	

Wash, drain, and slice cucumbers. Add onion, garlic, and salt. Mix thoroughly. Cover with ice and allow to stand 3 hours in a crock.

Remove garlic. Combine remaining ingredients and heat to boiling; add cucumber and onion to this mixture. Return to boil, lower heat, and heat 5 minutes. Fill sterilized jars ½ inch from top. Process 5 minutes in boiling water. Makes about 5 to 6 pints.

Mrs. G. Thomas Battle

ROBERTA'S DILL PICKLES

¼ bushel young cucumbers	12 tablespoons canning salt
6 cups water	Garlic
6 cups white vinegar	Dill
Mustard seed	

Select medium to small sized cucumbers, scrub with vegetable brush, and pack in sterilized canning jars. Combine and boil the water, vinegar, and canning salt; pour mixture over the packed cucumbers (within 1 inch of top). Add to **each** jar: 2 cloves garlic, 1 teaspoon dill and 1 teaspoon mustard seed. Seal jars.

Place jars in a water bath canner, and fill with enough water to reach the neck of the jars. Cover and bring to a boil. Boil for 5 minutes. Turn heat off, and let stand in water 5 more minutes. Remove jars from canner and let them seal. Makes 7 to 8 quarts.

These dill pickles must age 3 to 4 weeks before they are ready to eat.

Mrs. Latelle M. La Follette III

GREEN TOMATO PICKLE

3 cups slacked lime*	3 teaspoons whole cloves
2 gallons water	2 teaspoons allspice
7 pounds thinly sliced green tomato, unpeeled	2 teaspoons celery seed
	2 sticks cinnamon, halved
5 pounds sugar, divided	1 teaspoon powdered mace
2 quarts vinegar	1 teaspoon ground ginger

Mix lime and water; soak tomatoes in lime water for 24 hours. Put tomatoes in fresh cold water for 24 hours.

Put tomatoes in fresh cold water for 4 hours changing water every hour. Drain well.

Place 3½ pounds sugar and vinegar in kettle. Make 4 small cloth bags for spices; divide spices among bags. Bring syrup to boil (with bags in it) and pour over drained tomatoes. Let stand overnight. (A stone crock is the thing to use.)

Next morning, boil 1 hour. Take some of the hot syrup, add 1½ pounds sugar and bring to boiling point, pour over pickle and let stand 24 hours. The next morning, heat the pickle, put in jars and seal. Makes 8 pints.

* Slacked lime from drugstore.

Mrs. Robert W. Lawson, Jr.

PEACH PICKLE

7 pounds peaches	4 pounds sugar
21 to 28 whole cloves, dark tops removed	1 pint vinegar
	1 ounce stick cinnamon

Peel peaches. Stick three or four cloves in each one. Put peaches in stone jar. Boil sugar and vinegar to a thick syrup. Pour over peaches and weight down. Let stand overnight. The first morning, pour off juice, add cinnamon, and bring to boiling. Pour hot syrup back over peaches. The second morning, pour off juice and bring to boiling. Pour hot syrup back over peaches. The third morning, heat syrup and add peaches a few at a time. Cook slowly until tender. Do not overcook. Add more peaches to the same syrup until all are cooked. As peaches are cooked, pack in canning jars. Boil syrup until thick. Pour over peaches packed in jars. Seal jars.

Miss Mary J. Wilson
Valley View Farm
Lewisburg, W. Va.

WATERMELON PICKLE

3½ pounds watermelon rind
   (about ½ watermelon)
3½ pounds sugar
½ cup water

1½ cups cider vinegar
¼ teaspoon oil of cloves
¼ teaspoon oil of cinnamon
2 teaspoons alum

Trim off dark green rind and most of the pink pulp. Cut rind into strips 1 inch by ½ inch wide. Parboil rind until tender (about 1 hour) but not soft or mushy. Drain well in colander. Place in crock, glass, or enamel bowl and cover with enough ice cubes so that when ice melts it will provide ice water to cover rind. When ice has melted, sprinkle 2 teaspoons alum over rind. Leave in ice water 4 hours. Combine sugar, vinegar, oil of clove, and oil of cinnamon and bring to a boil in saucepan. Drain ice water from rind in colander. Drain well. Return rind to bowl and pour heated mixture over rind. Cover with lid, plate, or heavy towel and allow to stand at room temperature for 4 nights. During the four day standing period, drain off syrup mixture and heat to boiling point each morning; pour syrup back over rind and cover. On the fourth day place rind in clean jars with tight fitting lids; add the heated syrup and one cinnamon stick and several whole cloves per jar. Seal with wax paper and lids and refrigerate. Pickles should be allowed to mellow several weeks before use. Makes 4 pints.
Serve with beef, pork and fowl.

Mrs. Ladd M. Kochman

CORN RELISH

1 quart cabbage, chopped
12 onions (medium), chopped
3 green peppers, chopped
3 red peppers, chopped
   (or 1 can small pimento)
5 (10 ounces each) boxes frozen whole grain corn, thawed

3 tablespoons salt
3 cups cider vinegar
1 cup red wine vinegar
2 cups sugar
1 tablespoon ground mustard
1 tablespoon celery seed
¼ teaspoon turmeric

Combine ingredients and cook 25 minutes, stirring often. Pour into sterilized jars and seal.

Mrs. W. H. Gardner

CRANBERRY CHUTNEY

1 cup water
1 cup sugar
½ cup chopped onion
½ clove garlic, minced
   Dash cayenne pepper

4 whole cloves
1 teaspoon cinnamon
½ teaspoon salt
¼ cup cider vinegar

Simmer the above together for 5 minutes in a saucepan.

2 cups fresh cranberries   ½ cup chopped dates
½ cup seedless raisins   ½ cup diced preserved ginger
            ¼ cup light brown sugar

Add the above to the mixture in the saucepan. Simmer, stirring occasionally, 12 more minutes. Cool and store covered in refrigerator. Serve chilled. Makes 3½ pints.

Mrs. Jon Michael Gaston

GREEN PEPPER RELISH

4 (16 ounces each) cans tomato   36 green peppers, cut in ¼"
    sauce   strips
5 cups vegetable oil   12 onions, sliced
         3 tablespoons salt, or to taste

Mix tomato sauce in turkey roasting pan. Add green peppers, onions, and salt, and mix well. Bake at 275° for 2 hours, stirring occasionally. Can in airtight jars or freeze.

Mrs. A. S. Thomas, Jr.

PASTISHE (ANTIPASTO RELISH)

2 green peppers, chopped   1 (2 ounce) tin anchovies,
1 pound fresh mushrooms,   finely diced
    wiped off and chopped   2 cups tomato juice
1 clove garlic, minced   1 cup catsup
½ cup cooking oil   1 (6½ ounce) can tuna
1 cup chopped celery   1 (7 ounce) jar stuffed olives,
1 cup chopped carrot   drained
1 small head cauliflower,   1 teaspoon salt
    divided into florets   Dash Tabasco sauce
1 cup chopped sweet pickles   1 can small onions (pearl),
1 cup chopped dill pickles   drained
         1 cup cooked green beans

Cook peppers, mushrooms, and garlic in oil in skillet. Do not drain. Cook celery, carrot and cauliflower in small amount of boiling water until tender. Drain and reserve. To skillet, add all remaining ingredients except reserved cooked vegetables and green beans. Simmer 1 hour after bringing to boil. Add cooked vegetables and green beans. Boil two minutes. Cool, put in covered jars and store in refrigerator, or pack in hot jars and seal. Makes about 2½ quarts. Serve thoroughly chilled.

Mrs. Jon Michael Gaston

CHILI SAUCE

7 pounds tomatoes, peeled and chopped
2 hot banana peppers, ground
5 sweet red peppers, ground
1½ cups ground onion
3 tablespoons salt

⅔ cup brown sugar
⅓ cup white sugar
1½ cups vinegar
½ cup water
1 teaspoon cloves
1 teaspoon allspice

2 sticks cinnamon

Place tomatoes, peppers, onions, salt, sugar, vinegar, and water in large kettle or roaster. Tie spices in clean white cloth and add to kettle. Cook, stirring occasionally, until thick — 3 to 4 hours.

Mrs. Robert F. Goldsmith

GREEN CATSUP

"This recipe was given to us by our neighbor, Neva Anderson, who was born and raised in the hills of Webster County. The recipe dates back to the times before Mason jars when 'souring' and 'pickling' were favorite ways of preserving vegetables for winter use. This vegetable, similar to sauerkraut, was heated in a skillet with lard or bacon grease and served with a country-style dinner of brown beans and corn bread. We enjoy it the same way. Those of you who share our interest in nutrition will note the high vitamins A and C content of the 'catsup', made from fresh garden vegetables and soured raw. The water bath method is a modern addition to the recipe, for the original method left the catsup in the crock to be removed as needed during the winter."

Brian Van Nostrand

10 quarts cabbage, chopped
2 to 3 gallons green tomatoes, coarsely chopped
1 cup salt

½ gallon onion, chopped
24 sweet green peppers, chopped
4 or 5 hot peppers, chopped (if desired)

Mix all ingredients; press down firmly into stoneware crock until juice covers the vegetables. Sprinkle top with salt. Cover with a cloth and inverted plate. Place a weight on the plate so that the juice will keep vegetables covered. Let ferment for three weeks. Skim mold from top, remove coverings, and place in clean quart jars. Process in water bath for 15 minutes. Store in dark place.

Brian and Montie Van Nostrand

MUSTARD

½ cup wine vinegar
½ cup Burgundy wine
1 cup dried mustard

2 eggs
1 cup sugar
½ teaspoon salt

Stir vinegar, wine, and mustard and let stand overnight. The next day, beat the eggs and sugar until creamy. Combine all ingredients in a double boiler and cook until thick, about 30 minutes. Stir in the salt. Use as you would any mustard.

Mrs. Joseph R. Goodwin

CORN SALAD RELISH

12 ears tender yellow corn, cut from cob
1 quart chopped cabbage
6 onions, chopped
3 green peppers, chopped
3 red sweet peppers, chopped

1 tablespoon ground mustard
1 teaspoon celery seed (optional)
1 teaspoon turmeric
1 quart vinegar
Salt to taste

Mix chopped vegetables together. Make solution of remaining ingredients and bring to full boil. Add vegetables and bring to full boil again. Pack in sterilized jars and seal. Makes about 6 pints. Use as a relish or as a salad.

Mrs. O. Karr Faber

HIGHLAND FENCES

" . . . To raise a fence took more
Than human skill; they went at night,
Used a heavy-handed moon for light,
Blocked the landscape with their thumbs,
Wrestled the load stones into place,
And set up the slew line. The rails
Could wait, be added any time,
Day or night, whenever they were split
From standing chestnut trees a blight
Had held too long . . . "

Reprinted by permission of Joseph Garrison, from "Highland Fences," in **Poems From The Hills;** Copyright © (MHC); Edited by William Plumley; Morris Harvey College Publications; Charleston, West Virginia; 1971; Page 50.

Photo by Gerald S. Ratliff

DAIRY

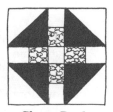

Churn Dash

CHEESE FONDUE

16 ounces (4 cups) grated
  Cheddar cheese
½ cup beer
2 teaspoons Worcestershire
  sauce

½ teaspoon dry mustard
⅛ teaspoon garlic powder
  Dash Tabasco
1 tablespoon cornstarch
2 tablespoons water

Beat cheese with mixer. Gradually add beer. Mix until fluffy. Add Worcestershire sauce, mustard, garlic and Tabasco. Beat well. Melt mixture in fondue pot on stove. Blend cornstarch and water; stir into cheese mixture. Cook and stir until thick and bubbly. Serve with bread sticks or French bread cubes. May be prepared in the morning and reheated before serving. Serves 4.

Mrs. Rosemary Galperin

HAM RAREBIT

1 cup cubed processed
  cheese
1½ cups milk
4 to 6 tablespoons flour
3 tablespoons margarine

¼ teaspoon freshly ground
  pepper
1½ teaspoons Worcestershire
  sauce
¼ teaspoon dry mustard

2 cups cubed ham

Combine all ingredients except ham, in blender, and blend thoroughly. Transfer to saucepan; cook until thickened, stirring constantly. Remove from heat; add ham, and let stand a few minutes to mellow. Serve over dry toast, rice or Holland Rusk. Serves 6.

Mrs. G.T. Weaks

RING-TUM-DIDDY

1 tablespoon butter or
   margarine
1 small onion, chopped
   finely
1 cup or more Cheddar
   cheese, shredded or
   chopped

1 (10¾ ounces) can
   cream of tomato soup
1 cup milk
2 eggs beaten
1 cup bread, cut in
   small cubes
1 tablespoon Worcestershire
   sauce

Melt butter or margarine in 10″ skillet, add onion and cook until just tender. Add cheese and soup, stirring until cheese is melted. Add milk and gradually add beaten eggs, stirring all the time. Add bread cubes and Worcestershire sauce. Serve over crackers or toast. This may be made in a chafing dish and used as a hot dip.

Mrs. W. O. McMillan

BLENDER CHEESE SOUFFLE

8 ounces sharp Cheddar cheese
10 slices buttered bread, crust
   removed

4 eggs
2 cups milk
1 teaspoon salt
½ teaspoon dry mustard

Cube cheese. Put half of cheese, bread, eggs and milk in blender. Turn on high speed until thoroughly mixed. Add remaining cheese, salt and mustard. Blend. Cook in greased uncovered casserole (1½ quart) for 1 hour at 350°. Serves 6 to 8. Can be made ahead or at the last minute.

Mrs. John G. McGarty

CHEESE SOUFFLE

3 tablespoons butter
3 tablespoons flour
1 cup milk

½ cup grated Cheddar cheese
3 eggs, separated
¼ teaspoon salt
⅛ teaspoon paprika

In saucepan, melt butter, gradually stir in flour. Allow butter-flour mixture to cook for a few minutes. Slowly stir in milk and cook until thickened. Reduce heat and stir in grated cheese. When cheese is melted, add 3 beaten egg yolks, salt and paprika. Cook and stir for 1 minute. Cool. Whip egg whites until fairly stiff, fold into cheese mixture. Place soufflé in an ungreased 7 inch pan, in a 325° oven. After 10 minutes increase heat to 350°. Bake until firm, about 30 minutes.

Dr. Ruth Ann Musick

MOCK CHEESE SOUFFLE

Senator Jennings Randolph, Democrat, has continuously represented West Virginia in the United States Senate since 1958. One of his outstanding contributions to the Senate is his long tenure as chairman of the Committee on Public Works.

5 slices bread, buttered	3 eggs
½ pound grated Cheddar	1 teaspoon salt
cheese	1 teaspoon dry mustard
2 cups milk	¼ teaspoon thyme

Remove crust from bread and place layers of cheese between slices of bread in a casserole. Mix milk, eggs, salt, mustard, and thyme. Pour over bread and let stand several hours or overnight in refrigerator. Place casserole in pan of water and bake 1 hour in a 350° oven. This can be reheated. Serves 4.

Mrs. Jennings Randolph

BREAKFAST CASSEROLE

2 cups plain or garlic croutons	½ teaspoon prepared mustard
1 cup shredded cheese	⅛ teaspoon onion powder
4 eggs, slightly beaten	Pepper
2 cups milk	½ can green chilies, chopped
½ teaspoon salt	4 slices bacon, cooked crisp

Grease 10" x 6" x 1¾" baking dish. Combine croutons and cheese and pour into baking dish. Mix eggs, milk, salt, mustard, onion powder, pepper, and chilies. Blend well and pour over croutons. Crumble bacon and sprinkle over casserole. Bake at 325° for 55 to 60 minutes or until set. Cut into squares. Serves 6.

Mrs. Sidney P. Davis, Jr.

CURRIED SOUR CREAM EGGS

Eggs	Curry powder
Sour cream	Salt
Mayonnaise	Pepper

Break 2 eggs per person into a well-buttered, flat baking dish and cover loosely with foil. Place baking dish in a larger pan containing a little boiling water. Bake at 350° for 15 minutes. Remove from oven and cover eggs with equal parts of mayonnaise and sour cream mixed together and seasoned to taste with curry powder. Broil for 2 to 5 minutes.

Good for lunch, a first course for dinner, or a late-evening supper. Optional: for a different flavor, omit the curry powder and use sherry.

Mrs. H. H. Smallridge

EGGS CREOLE AND SAUSAGE

½ pound sausage links (cut
   in 1" pieces)
2 (8 ounces each) cans
   tomato sauce
½ cup finely chopped
   green pepper

2 tablespoons instant
   minced onion
8 eggs
⅓ cup milk
½ teaspoon salt
   Dash of pepper

Sour cream

Brown sausage in saucepan; pour off excess fat. Add tomato sauce, green pepper, and onion. Simmer 5 minutes. Beat together eggs, milk, salt, and pepper. Scramble in buttered skillet. Place servings of scrambled eggs on buttered toast. Spoon on sausage-tomato sauce mixture. Top with dollops of sour cream. Serves 4.

Mrs. Andrew R. Quenon

EGG FU YUNG

6 eggs
2 teaspoons salt, divided
½ cup soup stock
8 tablespoons peanut oil,
   divided
½ cup canned crab meat or
   shrimp
4 ounces Chinese ham or
   barbecued pork, shredded

3 dry black mushrooms,
   soaked and shredded or 3
   tablespoons chopped
   canned mushrooms,
   drained
1 cup bean sprouts or
   shredded bamboo shoots
⅓ cup shredded green
   onion

1 tablespoon soy sauce

Beat eggs until frothy. Add 1 teaspoon salt and soup stock (or cold water) and mix again. Heat 6 tablespoons oil in frying pan, stir crab (or shrimp), ham (or pork), mushrooms, bean sprouts (or bamboo shoots) and green onion. Add soy sauce and 1 teaspoon salt. Stir about ½ minute over high heat. Splash 2 tablespoons oil down side of pan and add egg mixture. Fry on both sides until golden. Remove to plate and serve with or without sauce.

SAUCE

1 cup chicken stock
1 teaspoon salt

1 tablespoon cornstarch
1 tablespoon cold water

Bring stock and salt to a boil. Mix cornstarch and water. Gradually stir cornstarch paste into stock and cook until thickened. Serves 4.

Joe Sestito

EGGS MEUNIERE

3 slices bacon
1 tablespoon butter
1 small onion, chopped
1 tablespoon flour
¾ cup bouillon
¾ cup red wine

Salt, pepper, and garlic salt
to taste
1 bay leaf
1 sprig each thyme and parsley
4 eggs
4 English muffins or 4 slices
French bread, toasted

Sauté 3 slices of bacon until crisp. Remove bacon and pour out most of the grease. Add butter to pan and sauté onion in this until soft but not browned. Sprinkle flour over onion and butter and blend over heat. Add bouillon and red wine and bring to simmer. Add salt, pepper, garlic salt, bay leaf, thyme, and parsley. Simmer, covered, for 20 minutes. Strain sauce, return to pan, and poach eggs, one by one, in boiling sauce. Serve eggs on toasted French bread or English muffins. Pour sauce over and top with crumbled bacon. Serves 2 to 4.

Mrs. Charles B. Stacy

GOUGERE

¾ cup water
6 tablespoons margarine
¾ cup flour
5 eggs

¾ cup diced cooked ham
8 ounces Gruyère cheese,
shredded
Salt and pepper to taste

Bring water and margarine to a boil. Add flour all at once, and stir to a ball. Beat in eggs one at a time. Add ham, cheese, and seasoning. Grease well an angel food cake pan, or use a Teflon angel food pan. Bake in preheated oven at 425° for 20 minutes. Reduce heat to 350° and bake 10 minutes longer.

Gougère will fall when it is taken from oven. Can be served immediately, or can be refrigerated (overnight if desired) and reheated to serve later. Cut into thin slices. Do not double recipe.

Mrs. James McCain

CHEESE BISCUITS

1 can Pillsbury Butterflake Biscuits
½ stick margarine or butter
5 ounces sharp Cheddar cheese

Melt margarine and cheese in top of double boiler. Put biscuits in pan, pour on melted cheese mixture, and bake according to instructions on biscuit package.

Mrs. Richard D. Kitching

HOT CHEESE PUFF OPEN SANDWICH

6 slices bread
6 slices boiled ham
6 slices American processed cheese
18 to 24 hot cooked asparagus spears
3 egg yolks
¼ cup salad dressing
¼ teaspoon salt
Dash pepper
3 stiffly beaten egg whites

Toast bread on one side. Place slices of ham and cheese on untoasted side. Broil to partially melt cheese. Place 3 or 4 spears of asparagus on top of cheese. Beat egg yolks until lemon-colored. Stir in salad dressing, salt, and pepper. Fold in egg whites. Pile mixture on top of asparagus. Bake in 350° oven for 13 minutes or until mixture sets. Serves 6.

Mrs. Richard Repaire

QUICHE JORDINE

¾ cup chopped onion
¾ cup chopped green pepper
½ stick margarine
½ teaspoon thyme
2- 9" pie crusts
2 packages cherry tomatoes, 20 to 25
½ cup flour
2 cups grated Swiss cheese
2 eggs
½ pint whipping cream
½ teaspoon cayenne pepper

Sauté onion and pepper in butter until soft. Add thyme, set aside, save butter. Pierce pie crusts. Partially bake in 450° oven until brown. Cut cherry tomatoes in half. Coat tomatoes with just enough flour to stick. Add flour and tomatoes to butter and sauté until tomatoes are soft. Sprinkle green pepper and onion mixture on bottom of pie, place tomatoes on top, then cheese.

Blend eggs, cream, and cayenne pepper. Pour on top of pies. Garnish with strips of green pepper and cherry tomatoes. Bake 20 to 25 minutes at 375°. Let pie settle before cutting. Makes 2 pies.

Each pie serves 6 to 8 or makes 12 to 14 canapés.
Freezing method: freeze after cooked, half thaw, then bake.

Mrs. Charles Bibbee

SHIRRED EGGS

Having first come to West Virginia in the 1960's as a field worker in the Action for Appalachian Youth program, John D. Rockefeller, IV has remained and has become one of the leading citizens of the state. A member of the West Virginia House of Delegates in 1966 and Secretary of State from 1968 to 1972, Rockefeller was a gubernatorial candidate in 1972. Currently he is the president of West Virginia Wesleyan College at Buckhannon, West Virginia. Sharon Rockefeller tells us that Jay's "favorite Sunday morning breakfast is shirred eggs with the many variations."

6 tablespoons cream	½ teaspoon salt
6 eggs	⅛ teaspoon pepper
1 tablespoon melted butter	

Put a tablespoon of cream in each of 6 individual ovenproof ramekins. Slip an egg (without breaking the yolk) into each; sprinkle with salt and pepper, and add a little melted butter. Bake in a 350° oven until eggs are just set. If you wish to serve more than one egg per person, use a shirred egg dish or shallow casserole. One tablespoon of butter per egg may be substituted for the cream. Serves 3 to 6.

Variations: The eggs may be sprinkled with a few drops of Worcestershire sauce or sherry, or a few *fines herbes*. Try adding cooked chicken livers or ham to the eggs when almost done.

Jay Rockefeller

ASPARAGUS OMELET

2 packages frozen asparagus	½ cup butter
6 eggs, beaten	1 onion, grated
2 cups milk	2 cups soft bread crumbs
½ pound sharp cheese, cubed	(3 slices)
1 teaspoon salt	2 cups cubed ham or chicken

Cut asparagus spears in small pieces and cook until tender-crisp. Combine remaining ingredients, mix with asparagus and pour into greased 2 quart baking dish. Bake 1¼ hours in moderate oven (300° to 325°) or until firm.

Mrs. Frederick H. Belden, Jr.

CHINESE OMELET

5 eggs
¾ teaspoon salt
½ cup thinly sliced scallions,
    green tops included
1 medium size green pepper,
    chopped finely

1 (4 to 5 ounces) can water
    chestnuts, drained and
    thinly sliced
1 cup bean sprouts, drained
½ cup diced cooked chicken,
    packed
¼ cup vegetable oil

Beat eggs with salt just until yolks and whites are combined and eggs are slightly foamy. Add scallions, pepper, water chestnuts, bean sprouts and chicken. Mix. Heat oil in 10″ skillet over low heat until very hot. Add egg mixture and spread vegetables evenly. Cover tightly and do not stir; oil should bubble gently so bottom will be golden brown and top set in about 15 minutes. With sharp knife, cut into 4 portions in skillet. With wide spatula, remove to several thicknesses of paper towels to drain. Serve brown side up at once with thin Chinese gravy and cooked rice. Serves 4.

CHINESE GRAVY

½ to ¾ cup chicken broth
2 tablespoons soy sauce

2 tablespoons cornstarch

Mix cornstarch and broth (2 tablespoons) to make a paste. Heat the remainder of broth. Gradually stir in cornstarch paste to broth. Add soy sauce and cook until gravy looks clear.

Mrs. W. O. McMillan

HARVEST OMELET

12 slices bacon
2 cups cubed, cooked potatoes
¼ cup finely chopped onion
¼ cup chopped fresh parsley

8 eggs
¾ teaspoon salt
2 tablespoons milk
½ cup shredded American or
    Cheddar cheese

Cut bacon into 1″ pieces and fry until crisp. Remove from pan, drain, and reserve. Brown potatoes and onions in bacon drippings. Sprinkle with parsley, add bacon bits, and reduce heat to low. Beat eggs slightly; add salt and milk. Pour egg mixture over bacon and potatoes. Cover and cook over low heat until eggs are almost set, slipping spatula around edge of pan occasionally to allow uncooked egg to run down. (Takes about 10 minutes). Sprinkle with shredded cheese, cover again, and cook until cheese melts. Cut in wedges to serve. Serves 6 to 8.

Mrs. Edward W. Rugeley, Jr.

SAUCE FOR SPANISH OMELET

1 cup tomatoes   1 medium sized onion,
½ cup peas   chopped

Mix all ingredients together in pan and heat through. Pour over 3-egg omelet.

Dr. Ruth Ann Musick

HOMEMADE YOGHURT

1 gallon whole or skimmed   2 cups commercial or
     milk   homemade unflavored
Nonfat dry milk   yoghurt, as a "starter"

In a double boiler, heat milk (do not boil) for 45 minutes to 1 hour. Cool milk to above blood temperature (i.e. hot on your wrist). Put 2 inches nonfat dry milk in bottom of a sterile gallon jar. Add hot milk and 2 cups "starter" yoghurt, and stir. Close the jar tightly, and let it sit for 6 to 14 hours at room temperature or until thick. Do not stir. Be sure to leave out long enough to thicken. Put in the refrigerator for several hours before stirring or using. Save 2 cups as a "starter" for your next gallon. Makes one gallon.

Mrs. William E. Chilton, II

APPALACHIANS

"The mountain lifts its humped back and its bare gray shoulders into the dull blue haze of the Appalachians. The river is a wild ripsnorter that carries sweet upland water to the deep brown soil of the plain. The town squats under the cliffs beside the river . . . "

Reprinted by permission of Louise McNeill, from **Gauley Mountain;** Harcourt, Brace and Company; New York, New York; 1939; Page 1.

Photo by Gerald S. Ratliff

FISH

Lobster

FRESH CRAB CAKES

½ stick butter, melted
1 pound fresh crabmeat,
  carefully picked
1 egg, well-beaten
2 slices bread, cut in small
  pieces

¼ teaspoon salt
Dash pepper
1 tablespoon mustard
1 small onion, minced
2 sprigs parsley, chopped
1 teaspoon Tabasco
Deep fat

Mix all ingredients well. Shape into patties and fry in deep fat. Serve immediately. Serves 4.

Mrs. John Charles Thomas

CRAB DELIGHT

1 (7 ounce) can tuna or
  crabmeat

2 tablespoons lemon juice
3 hard cooked eggs, sliced
1 can cooked peas

In a 1½ quart greased casserole, layer crab or tuna sprinkled with lemon juice, peas, and eggs. Repeat layers. Make sauce.

SAUCE

4 tablespoons butter or
  margarine
4 tablespoons flour
2 cups milk
1 cup grated medium sharp
  cheese
½ teaspoon salt

½ teaspoon dry mustard
⅛ teaspoon pepper
1 teaspoon Worcestershire
  sauce
1 cup fresh bread crumbs,
  buttered
Parsley
Garlic salt

Melt butter and flour and cook for 2 minutes over low heat making a roux. Add milk, cheese, and seasonings. Gently simmer until thick. Pour cheese sauce over layered fish, eggs, and peas. Put butter-soaked crumbs on top. Sprinkle with parsley and a little garlic salt. Bake at 350° for 20 to 30 minutes. May serve in pastry shells.

Mrs. Robert C. Payne

CRAB IN DEVILED SAUCE

2 tablespoons chopped onion
2 tablespoons chopped green
   pepper
¼ cup butter or margarine
¼ cup flour
1⅓ cups milk
1 tablespoon chopped chives
1 tablespoon prepared
   mustard

2 teaspoons Worcestershire
   sauce
Few grains cayenne pepper
1 teaspoon salt
1 pound flaked and boned fresh
   crabmeat
2 tablespoons melted
   margarine
1 cup soft bread crumbs

Sauté onion and green pepper in butter. Add flour; mix until blended. Add milk gradually. Cook, stirring constantly, until thickened; simmer 2 minutes. Remove from heat; add chives, mustard, Worcestershire, cayenne, and salt. Mix well and add crab. Turn into 1 quart casserole, or 4 to 6 individual ramekins, custard cups, or shells. Combine 2 tablespoons melted margarine and bread crumbs. Sprinkle on crab mixture. Cover and refrigerate. One half hour before serving, uncover, and bake at 375° for 30 minutes or until crab mixture is bubbly and crumbs are browned. Serves 6 for lunch and 4 for dinner. If 1 quart casserole is used, bake for approximately 45 minutes.

Mrs. Charles G. Moyers, Jr.

CRAB GOURMET

2 cups canned crabmeat or
   frozen crabmeat, thawed,
   picked over and flaked
½ cup toasted walnuts,
   broken up coarsely
2 hard-boiled eggs, chopped
½ cup mayonnaise
2 teaspoons lemon juice

1 teaspoon Worcestershire
   sauce
¼ teaspoon dry mustard
¼ teaspoon salt
Dash cayenne pepper
1 cup soft bread crumbs
¼ cup melted butter or
   margarine

Chopped parsley

Mix the crabmeat lightly with the walnuts and eggs. Mix the mayonnaise with lemon juice, Worcestershire, mustard, salt, and cayenne. Stir into crab mixture. Pour gently into a small shallow casserole. Top with fresh bread crumbs mixed with melted butter and parsley, and bake at 400° about 20 minutes, or until the top is well-browned. Serves 4.

Mrs. Ralph Jones

CRAB AND MUSHROOM STUFFED POTATOES

4 medium potatoes, baked
¼ cup butter or margarine, melted
¼ cup heavy cream, heated
1 teaspoon salt
⅛ teaspoon pepper

1 (3 ounce) can mushrooms chopped and boiled
1 tablespoon onion, grated
1 cup sharp Cheddar cheese, grated and divided
1 can (6½ ounce) crabmeat, drained and flaked

Cut potatoes in half lengthwise. Scoop out all pulp without breaking the skin. Mash or whip pulp and add butter, cream, salt and pepper. Beat until light and fluffy. Drain mushrooms. Add mushrooms, onions, ⅔ cup grated cheese and crabmeat. Top with remaining cheese. Bake at 350° for 20 minutes. Makes 8 stuffed potatoes.

Mrs. Donald Ellsworth

GOURMET CRAB RING

1 teaspoon unflavored gelatin
¼ cup cold water
2 (8 ounces each) packages cream cheese, softened
2 tablespoons sherry
¾ teaspoon seasoned salt
½ teaspoon dry minced onion

1 (2 ounce) jar pimientos, chopped, or 2 ounces chopped green peppers
1 (6 ounce) package king crabmeat, thawed and cut up
⅛ teaspoon pepper
2 tablespoons chopped parsley

Parsley sprigs for garnish

Sprinkle gelatin in water to soften. Stir over hot water until dissolved. Mix into cream cheese. Stir in next 6 ingredients and 2 tablespoons parsley. Pour into 3 - cup ring mold. Refrigerate at least 4 hours. Turn on platter and serve with crackers, as a spread. Trim platter with parsley sprigs. Makes 3 cups.

Mrs. Stanley H. Rose, Jr.

CRABMEAT SUPREME

1 cup chopped celery
8 slices buttered white bread
2 cups canned or frozen crabmeat (if frozen, thaw)
1 medium onion, chopped
½ cup chopped green pepper

½ cup mayonnaise
4 eggs, beaten
3 cups milk
1 (10¾ ounce) cream of mushroom soup
¼ cup grated American or Cheddar cheese

Cook celery slowly in a little water until soft, about 10 minutes. Drain. Dice ½ of bread (4 slices) to cover bottom of oblong baking pan. Combine crabmeat, onion, celery, green pepper and mayonnaise. Spread this mixture over diced bread. Dice remaining bread and layer over crabmeat mixture. Mix beaten eggs with milk and pour over all. Refrigerate, covered, several hours or overnight. Bake for 15 minutes in a pre-heated 325° oven. Then spoon the mushroom soup over top and sprinkle with cheese to cover. Bake one hour longer until golden brown. Serves 8.

Mrs. Edward W. Rugeley, Jr.

FILET FARCIS A LA CREME

6 filets of sole or flounder	2 cans tiny shrimp, or 2½ cups
Salt and pepper	fresh crabmeat
2 tablespoons butter	2 tablespoons flour
2 small onions, chopped	1 cup light cream
½ pound mushrooms, sliced	½ cup dry white wine
2 tablespoons snipped parsley	2 tablespoons cognac, optional

½ cup grated Swiss cheese

Sprinkle filets with salt and pepper. Sauté onions and mushrooms in butter until golden. Stir in parsley and shrimp and heat thoroughly. Place part of this mixture by teaspoonfuls on large end of each filet. Roll up and place side by side in shallow baking dish. Into remaining onion - shrimp mixture, stir flour, then cream, wine, and cognac. Season with salt and pepper. Bring to boil while stirring and pour over filets. Sprinkle with cheese. Bake at 400° about 25 minutes or until golden. Serves 3 to 4.

Mrs. Neil Robinson, II

FILET OF SOLE OR FLOUNDER

¾ cup chopped green onions	1 bay leaf
3 tablespoons butter	⅛ teaspoon celery salt
1 cup chopped mushrooms	Salt and pepper to taste
4 ounces white wine	1 pound frozen sole or flounder
Pinch thyme	½ cup cream

2 tablespoons Parmesan cheese

Sauté onions in butter about 5 minutes. Add mushrooms and cook about 5 minutes. Add wine and cook 5 minutes more. Add herbs. Strain mixture. Save liquid in another saucepan. Put mushroom-onion mixture in a buttered casserole and place fish in a single layer on top. Add about ½ cup cream to liquid and pour over fish. Sprinkle with Parmesan cheese. Bake at 350° for about 45 minutes or until lightly browned. Serves 2 to 4.

BAKED FILLET OF SOLE OR FLOUNDER

1 stick butter
2 pounds fish fillets
Salt and pepper to taste
Paprika
Lemon juice
1 tablespoon dry white wine
Parmesan cheese

Put butter in shallow baking dish in 450° oven and cook until sizzling and quite brown. Season fish fillets with salt and pepper. Put fillets in hot browned butter, flesh side down, and bake 10 to 15 minutes depending on the thickness of fillets. Turn with spatula, baste with juice, and sprinkle with lemon juice and wine. Return to oven for 5 minutes. Sprinkle with cheese and paprika and run under broiler for 1 to 2 minutes. Serves 4 to 6.

Mrs. H. H. Smallridge

BAKED FILLETS WITH SHRIMP SAUCE

2 pounds frozen fish fillet, thawed (cod, sole, or flounder)
2 tablespoons butter, melted
2 tablespoons dry white wine, optional
1 teaspoon salt
1 (10 ounce) can cream of shrimp soup
1 teaspoon lemon juice
1 package frozen peas, cooked and drained

Divide fish into 6 servings. Arrange in a single layer in well-greased 12" x 8" baking dish. Spoon butter and wine over fish; season with salt. Cover dish tightly with foil. Bake in a 350° oven about 25 minutes, or until fish flakes easily with a fork. Remove fillets to warm serving dish; blend soup and lemon juice into pan juices. Stir in peas and heat a minute longer. Pour sauce over fish. Serves 6.

Mrs. Frederick H. Morgan

FILLETS OF SOLE OR TURBOT DELUXE

3 pounds fillet of sole
1 quart milk
¼ to ½ cup minced onion
¼ to ½ cup diced green pepper
2 tablespoons butter
¼ to ½ cup diced pimientos
½ cup butter
¼ to ½ cup flour
2 cups light cream
Salt and pepper to taste
Buttered bread crumbs

Cover fillets with milk and poach until fish separates easily. Drain, but reserve liquid. Separate fish into flakes and arrange in a shallow baking dish. Sauté onion and pepper in butter for three minutes. Add pimientos. Make roux with butter and flour; add milk from poaching and as much light cream as needed. Cook, stirring until thickened. Add green pepper, onion, and seasonings. Pour over fish. Sprinkle with bread crumbs and heat in 375° oven until crumbs are brown and fish is hot. (If you prefer, the fillets may be left whole after poaching). Serves 8.

Mrs. Ralph Jones

HADDOCK BAKED IN CREAM

2 pounds haddock or flounder	4 or more tablespoons butter
Flour	1 cup cream
Salt and pepper	2 tablespoons chopped onion
10 flat anchovy filets	2 tablespoons chopped parsley

Cut haddock into serving pieces. Dry thoroughly. Dredge in seasoned flour. Sauté anchovy filets in butter until they melt. Brown fish quickly in anchovy butter. Place fish in casserole, pour in cream, and sprinkle with onion and parsley. Cover and bake at 350° for 30 minutes. Serves 4.

Mrs. Neil Robinson, II

STEIKT SKARKOLAFICK

A fish recipe from Iceland in which the fish is fried in a beer batter.

¾ cup unsifted flour	¾ cup beer
1 egg	2 pounds fresh fish fillets
½ teaspoon salt	Cooking oil

Place flour in deep bowl. In another bowl beat egg until frothy. Add salt and beer. Combine liquids with flour. Beat until free of lumps. Coat each fish fillet separately when ready to fry. Deep fry until light brown in deep heated oil. Serve with lemon slices and a glass of cold beer. Serves 6.

Alternate method of cooking. Fry fish in frying pan with ¼ inch of heated oil. Turn once when fish is browned on first side.

Mrs. Andrew V. Roderick

CIOPPINO (SEAFOOD STEW)

½ cup olive or salad oil
3 cloves garlic, finely
  chopped
1¼ cups chopped green onion
¾ cup chopped green pepper
1 (11½ ounce) jar whole clams
1 (1 pound, 12 ounce) can
  tomatoes, drained
1 (6 ounce) can tomato paste
1¾ cups Burgundy

⅓ cup chopped parsley
2 teaspoons dried oregano
  leaves
½ teaspoon dried basil leaves
2 teaspoons salt
¼ teaspoon pepper
¾ cup water
1½ pounds halibut steaks
½ pound raw shrimp, shelled
  and deveined

3 (6 ounces each) packages frozen crabmeat,
  thawed and undrained

Slowly heat oil in 6 quart kettle. In hot oil, sauté garlic, onions, and green pepper until tender, about 10 minutes. Meanwhile, drain clams, reserving ¼ cup liquid. Set clams aside. Add reserved clam liquid, tomatoes, tomato paste, Burgundy, parsley, oregano, basil, salt, pepper, and ¾ cup water to sautéed vegetables, mixing well. Bring to boiling, reduce heat, and simmer uncovered for 10 minutes. Meanwhile, cut halibut in 1″ pieces; discard skin and bones. Add halibut, shrimp, crabmeat, and clams to tomato mixture; simmer covered for 15 minutes. Then simmer uncovered 15 minutes longer. Serves 6 to 8.

To freeze: Let Cioppino cool completely. Line a large bowl with foil, letting foil extend about 6 inches above the top of the bowl. Turn cooled mixture into bowl; fold foil over top. Freeze until firm. Remove foil-wrapped Cioppino from bowl, cover tightly with foil, label, and freeze until ready to use. To serve, remove foil and place Cioppino in large kettle. Cook covered over boiling water 40 minutes or until heated through, or thaw in pot and then reheat slowly. Makes 4 quarts or 6 to 8 servings.

Mrs. Edward L. Sherwood

OYSTERS DUNBAR

1 stick butter
¼ cup flour
1 medium onion, minced
1 garlic bud, pressed
1 teaspoon Bouquet Garni
½ teaspoon thyme
  Salt and pepper to taste

¼ cup juice from oysters
¼ cup white wine (or ½ cup
  oyster juice only)
2 packages artichoke hearts,
  cooked
2 pints oysters, drained
½ teaspoon parsley, chopped

½ cup buttered bread crumbs

Melt butter, add flour. Add onion and garlic and cook until onion is transparent. Add seasonings and salt and pepper to taste. Add juices; ¼ cup oyster juice, ¼ cup wine; vary according to your taste.

Wine can be optional. Add oysters and cook slowly until oysters are done and sauce has thickened.

Butter casserole 12"x7" x2". Put precooked artichokes in casserole. Put oysters on top. Top with parsley and buttered bread crumbs. Cook in 350° oven until bubbly, 15 to 20 minutes. Can be prepared ahead and refrigerated, except add bread crumbs before baking. Serves 6.

Mrs. William O. McMillan, Jr.

SCALLOPED OYSTERS

2 dozen oysters, drained (save liquor)
2 cups coarse bread crumbs
¼ cup melted butter
2 tablespoons cream
1 teaspoon Worcestershire sauce

2 tablespoons sherry
¼ cup oyster liquor
1 teaspoon pepper
½ teaspoon salt
Dash cayenne

Combine butter and crumbs. Cover bottom of buttered shallow casserole with ⅓ of crumb and butter mixture. Mix together the cream, Worcestershire, sherry, oyster liquor, salt, pepper, and cayenne to make sauce. Arrange ½ oysters on crumbs in casserole. Alternate crumbs, oysters, and sauce, ending with crumbs on top. Bake at 425° for 30 minutes. Serves 8 to 10.

Mrs. William T. Ziebold

SALMON CASSEROLE

1 pound can red salmon
1 cup clam chowder
1 egg

½ teaspoon salt
Dash of pepper
1 cup corn flakes

Remove skin and bones from salmon. Mix ingredients. Sprinkle additional buttered corn flakes on top. Bake in buttered casserole for 30 minutes at 400°.

Mrs. Frederick L. Thomas, Jr.

SALMON TIMBALES

½ cup ripe or stuffed green olives
1 (16 ounce) can salmon
3 tablespoons butter
3 tablespoons flour
½ teaspoon onion salt

⅛ teaspoon pepper
⅛ teaspoon tarragon, crumbled
Milk (about 1 cup)
2 tablespoons tomato paste, optional
½ cup soft, fine bread crumbs

3 eggs, beaten

Cut olives into wedges and set aside. Drain salmon and save the liquid. Remove and discard skin and large bones from salmon. Flake fish. Melt butter and stir in flour, salt, pepper, and tarragon. Add enough milk to liquid from drained salmon to make 1⅓ cups. Gradually add this to butter-flour mixture and cook, stirring constantly, until mixture boils and sauce thickens. Stir in tomato paste. Mix together salmon, olives, and bread crumbs. Beat eggs until bubbly and stir into salmon mixture. Add the thickened, seasoned sauce and mix well. Spoon into five (6 ounces each) custard cups which have been well greased. Place cups in pan holding about 1 inch of hot water. Bake at 350° for about 50 minutes or until knife inserted in center of mixture comes out clean. Remove from water and let stand 5 minutes. Unmold and serve with Mornay sauce. Serves 5.

MORNAY SAUCE

2 tablespoons butter	¾ teaspoon salt
3 tablespoons flour	⅛ teaspoon pepper
1⅔ cups milk	⅓ cup grated Parmesan cheese

Melt butter. Add flour. Gradually add milk and cook, stirring constantly, until mixture boils and has thickened. Add salt, pepper, and cheese. Continue to stir until cheese melts. Makes 1¾ cups sauce.

Mrs. Charles G. Moyers, Jr.

SALMON MOUSSE

Mrs. Brotherton's husband has served in the West Virginia Legislature continuously since 1952 and was elected President of the Senate in 1973. Senator Brotherton was named West Virginian of the Year in 1970.

½ cup water	½ cup mayonnaise
1 envelope unflavored gelatin	¼ teaspoon paprika
3 tablespoons lemon juice	1 pound can salmon
1 small onion	1 teaspoon dried dill
1 cup sour cream	

Bring water to a boil. Empty gelatin into blender. Add lemon juice, onion, and boiling water. Place top on blender and blend 40 seconds. Turn off blender and add mayonnaise, paprika, salmon, and dill. Cover blender and turn to high speed. Uncover and slowly add cream. Blend for 30 seconds; then pour into mold. Chill until firm. Serves 6.

Mrs. William T. Brotherton, Jr.

SEAFOOD MOUSSE

2 envelopes unflavored
    gelatin
½ cup cold water
1½ cups mayonnaise
⅓ cup lemon juice
2 teaspoons dry mustard
2 teaspoons sugar

¼ teaspoon liquid hot pepper
    sauce
¾ cup sliced celery
2 pounds sea scallops, cooked
    and quartered
1 pound shrimp, cooked and
    diced

1 cup whipping cream

Sprinkle gelatin on cold water and dissolve over boiling water. Combine mayonnaise, lemon juice, mustard, sugar, and hot pepper sauce. Add dissolved gelatin and mix well. Stir in celery, scallops, and shrimp. Whip cream and fold in. Spoon into an 8-cup mold. Chill until set. Serves 12.

Mrs. Andrew R. Quenon

SHRIMP JAMBALAYA

3 cups cooked rice
¼ cup salad oil
1 large onion, chopped
½ green pepper, cut in thin
    strips
2 stalks celery, thinly sliced

2 fresh tomatoes, peeled and
    cut up
½ teaspoon salt
1 teaspoon paprika
⅛ teaspoon pepper
1 pound fresh clean shrimp,
    boiled

Heat oil in skillet; add onion, pepper, and celery. Cook until tender, but not browned. Add tomatoes and seasonings and cook 10 minutes. Add shrimp and heat through. Remove from heat and mix in cooked rice. Turn into a greased casserole. Set casserole in a pan of hot water. Cover and bake at 375° for 30 minutes. Serves 4.

Mrs. J. Crawford Goldman

JAMBALAYA

1 tablespoon shortening
1 pound sausage or left-over
    ham or chicken, cut into
    ½ inch cubes
½ green pepper, chopped
1 tablespoon flour
3 cups cooked shrimp
3 cups diced tomatoes, fresh
    or canned
2½ cups water

1 large onion, sliced
1 clove garlic, minced
2 tablespoons chopped parsley
2 cups uncooked rice
1¼ teaspoons salt
2 tablespoons Worcestershire
    sauce
½ teaspoon thyme
¼ teaspoon red pepper

Melt shortening in large electric skillet; add sausage or other meat and green pepper. Cook 5 minutes, stirring frequently. Stir in flour until smooth and cook 1 minute longer. Add shrimp, tomatoes, water, onion, garlic, and parsley. Heat to boiling point; then stir in rice and all remaining ingredients. Cover and cook over low heat for 30 minutes or until rice is tender and most of liquid is absorbed. Water can be added to make more liquid, if desired. Sprinkle with chopped parsley and serve hot. Serves 8.

Note: Polish sausage or smoked ham may be used, if you prefer that flavor.

Mrs. Charles B. Watkins

SHRIMP OR LOBSTER ASPIC

2 tablespoons unflavored gelatin	½ cup chili sauce
	Salt to taste
¾ cup cold chicken broth	1 cup diced celery
1 cup hot chicken broth	2 chopped dill or sweet pickles,
Juice of 1 large lemon	optional

1 pound fresh boiled shrimp or lobster, diced

Soak gelatin in cold broth a few minutes, add hot broth, and stir until dissolved. Let cool slightly; add lemon juice, chili sauce, and salt to taste. Set aside in cool place. Just when it begins to thicken, add chopped and diced ingredients. Place in mold and chill until firm. Serve on cold lettuce leaves with mayonnaise. Serves 6.

Mrs. F. G. Bannerot, Jr.

SHRIMP SALAD

1 cup cold cooked rice	1 tablespoon chopped olives
1 cup cooked shrimp	½ teaspoon salt
¼ cup diced green pepper	1 tablespoon lemon juice
¾ cup diced celery	2 tablespoons French dressing
1 tablespoon chopped onion	⅓ cup mayonnaise

Mix rice, shrimp, and vegetables. Mix salt, lemon juice, French dressing, and mayonnaise and pour over the shrimp and vegetables. Mix lightly and chill at least 1 hour. Serves 4.

Mrs. Richard R. Meckfessel

SHRIMP TEMPURA

Sauce:

1½ cups chicken stock	6 tablespoons sherry
1 tablespoon soy sauce	⅛ teaspoon ginger
Horseradish	

Cook 5 minutes until well-blended and heated through. Serve in individual bowls for dipping. May add ginger and/or horseradish to taste.

Shrimp:

6 large shrimp per person	1 egg yolk
6½ tablespoons flour	⅔ cup plus 3 tablespoons water
Peanut oil	

Shell shrimp; slit lengthwise not clear through to butterfly. Cut across lightly in three places to prevent shrinking. Wipe dry to prevent oil splatters. Mix flour, egg yolk, and water gently. Batter will be lumpy. Heat oil 2 inches deep to 250°. Dip shrimp in batter and drop in oil. They will float when done. Drain on paper; serve immediately with sauce. Leftover sauce is excellent baking medium for pork steaks.

Don Piper

SHRIMP AND SCALLOP NEWBURG

1½ pounds frozen shrimp	Dash cayenne pepper
1 package frozen scallops	1 cup milk
1 stick margarine, divided	1 cup whipping cream
4 tablespoons flour	2 egg yolks
1 teaspoon salt	¼ cup sherry
Paprika	

Combine frozen shrimp and scallops with 4 tablespoons butter in large frying pan. Cover. Cook slowly for 15 minutes. Drain. As seafood cooks, melt the remaining 4 tablespoons butter in a large saucepan; stir in flour, salt, and cayenne. Cook, stirring just until bubbly. Stir in milk and cream, and continue cooking until the sauce thickens and boils for one minute. Beat egg yolks in a small bowl, and stir in about ½ cup of the hot mixture; then stir back into remainder in saucepan. Cook for one minute. Stir in sherry and fold in cooked seafood. Spoon into heated chafing dish, and sprinkle with paprika. Serve over patty shells. Serves 8.

Mrs. Andrew R. Quenon

SHRIMP AND LOBSTER IN WHITE WINE ROWLEY

4 (8 ounces each) frozen rock lobster tails
2 pounds raw shrimp, shelled and deveined
2 (7½ ounces each) cans king crabmeat, drained
10 tablespoons butter
⅔ cup flour
2 teaspoons salt
1 teaspoon paprika
¼ teaspoon white pepper
3 cups light cream
1¼ cups dry white wine
Parsley, as garnish

In large kettle, bring 2½ quarts water to a boil. Add lobster. Return to boiling, reduce heat, and simmer, covered, for 8 minutes. Remove lobster to colander to cool. Return water to a boil. Add shrimp. Return to boiling, reduce heat, and simmer, covered, for 5 minutes. Drain. Remove crabmeat from cans in large pieces. Drain. Cut lobster in bite-size pieces. Set all seafood aside.

Melt butter in Dutch oven. Remove from heat. Stir in flour, salt, paprika, and pepper. Gradually stir in cream until smooth. Bring to a boil, stirring. Reduce heat and simmer 5 minutes. Add wine and seafood and stir until combined. Cook over low heat until hot. **Do not boil.** Serve with rice. Garnish with parsley. Serves 12.

Mrs. W. Gaston Caperton, III

SEAFOOD CASSEROLE

¼ cup chopped green onions
3 tablespoons butter
3 tablespoons flour
1 cup milk
Salt
Pepper
Cayenne pepper
1 tablespoon Worcestershire sauce
Tabasco sauce
1 cup sharp grated cheese
1 cup shrimp
1 cup crabmeat
3 hardboiled eggs, chopped
½ cup chopped pecans
1 cup stuffing mix, divided

Sauté green onions in butter. Add flour and milk. Season with salt, pepper, cayenne pepper, Worcestershire sauce, and a few drops of Tabasco sauce. Add to sauce ¾ cup of the cheese, shrimp, crabmeat, and chopped eggs. Use remaining ¼ cup cheese to mix with chopped pecans and ½ cup stuffing mix. Layer in casserole, the fish mixture, then crumb mixture. Use rest of crumbs on top. Bake at 375° for 20 to 25 minutes. Serves 6.

Mrs. John M. Slack, III

SHRIMP CREOLE

1 to 1½ pounds fresh, de-
    veined, shelled shrimp
2 medium onions, minced
1 green pepper, minced
4 stalks celery, cut fine
4 tablespoons butter or
    margarine

2 tablespoons flour
½ teaspoon sage
1 teaspoon salt
⅛ teaspoon pepper
2 cups tomatoes and 1 (8 ounce)
    can tomato sauce OR 3 cups
    tomato sauce
1 tablespoon vinegar

Cook shrimp in salted water until they begin to turn pink, about 5 minutes. Drain and cut in bite-size pieces. Brown onions, green pepper, and celery in butter. Blend in flour, sage, salt, and pepper. Add tomatoes, tomato sauce, and vinegar. Cover and simmer 10 minutes. Add shrimp; bring to a boil again. Cover; simmer 5 more minutes. Serve over rice. Serves 6. May be made ahead and reheated before serving.

Mrs. John Charles Thomas

SWEET AND SOUR SHRIMP OR PORK

1 tablespoon shortening
1 medium onion, chopped
1 medium green pepper,
    diced
1 cup catsup
2 tablespoons vinegar

2 tablespoons soy sauce
⅓ cup sugar
1 (8 ounce) can pineapple
    chunks
1½ tablespoons cornstarch
2 cups cooked shrimp or
    pork

Cook onion and green pepper in shortening in skillet until crisp-tender. Add catsup, vinegar, soy sauce, and sugar. Heat through. Drain pineapple chunks, reserving liquid. Add water to liquid to make 1 cup. Mix small amount with cornstarch to make a thin paste. Add liquid to skillet, then add paste. Cook about 3 minutes, until clear and thickened. Add pineapple chunks and pork or shrimp and heat through. Serves 4.

Mrs. Jon Michael Gaston

BAKED TUNA SOUFFLE SANDWICH

Buns, halved
¼ cup butter
1 cup sliced fresh mush-
    rooms
¼ cup chopped onion

1 (7 ounce) can tuna, drained
    and flaked
¼ cup mayonnaise
2 eggs, separated
2 cups grated Swiss cheese
Cayenne and black pepper to taste

Separate bun halves and brush each cut surface with butter; broil until brown, about 3 to 4 minutes. Sauté mushrooms and onion in butter until golden, about 5 minutes. Add sautéed mushrooms and onion to tuna; stir in mayonnaise and spread mixture on buns. Mix egg yolks, grated Swiss cheese, cayenne, and black pepper to taste. Beat egg whites until stiff, fold into cheese, and spoon over tuna. Bake at 375° for 12 to 15 minutes until puffed and firm. Serves 4 to 8.

Mrs. Ronald A. McKenney

FIESTA CASSEROLE

1 cup chopped onion
2 tablespoons cooking oil
3 (6½ ounces each) cans chunk light tuna, drained and flaked
2 (1 pound each) cans stewed tomatoes
2 teaspoons chili powder
1½ teaspoons salt
¼ teaspoon pepper
2 eggs, beaten
½ cup milk
5 ounces tortilla chips
3 cups shredded jack cheese
1 cup sour cream
Chopped parsley and black olives

Brown onion in hot oil until tender. Add tuna. Stir in tomatoes and seasonings. Blend eggs and milk. Stir into tuna mixture. Place half of chips in bottom of 3 quart casserole. Top with half of cheese, then half of tuna mixture. Repeat layers. Spread sour cream on top. Bake at 325° for 45 minutes. Garnish with parsley and black olives. Serves 6.

Mrs. William H. Knight

TUNA - NOODLE CASSEROLE

2 cups noodles
1 (7 ounce) can tuna fish
¼ cup water or milk
1 (10¾ ounce) can cream of mushroom soup
Bread crumbs or potato chips

Cook noodles 5 minutes and drain. Drain and flake tuna fish. Grease a glass baking dish. Mix tuna and noodles. Add water to can of mushroom soup and pour over tuna and noodles. Sprinkle with bread crumbs or crushed potato chips and bake for 10 to 15 minutes at 450°. Serves 4.

Mrs. John G. McGarty

TUNA - RICE CASSEROLE

¼ cup minced onion
1 tablespoon butter
1 (13 ounce) can evaporated
    milk
½ teaspoon salt
1½ teaspoons dry mustard
1½ cups grated American
    cheese, divided

1 (10 ounce) can tuna fish
⅓ cup sliced olives stuffed
    with pimiento
⅛ teaspoon pepper
1 egg, slightly beaten
½ cup water
1¼ cups minute rice

Sauté onion in butter until tender. Add milk, salt, mustard, and 1 cup cheese. Heat until cheese melts. Add tuna, olives, pepper, egg, water, and rice. Blend well. Place in a 2 quart casserole and sprinkle remaining ½ cup cheese on top. Bake at 350°, covered, for 20 to 25 minutes. Serve immediately. Serves 4 to 6.

Mrs. John C. Thomas

TUNA - SHRIMP CASSEROLE

1 (12 ounce) can tuna fish
1 (10¾ ounce) can cream of
    shrimp soup

1 soup can of milk
1 cup minute rice
1 tablespoon mayonnaise

Cracker crumbs, optional

Combine all ingredients in casserole. Bake at 350° about 20 to 30 minutes. Cracker crumb topping is optional.

Mrs. Otis L. O'Conner

TUNA SPINACH AU GRATIN

1 (7 ounce) can tuna,
    drained and flaked
⅓ cup fine dry bread
    crumbs
1 (10 ounce) package frozen
    chopped spinach, cooked
    and drained

1 tablespoon lemon juice
2 tablespoons grated
    Parmesan cheese
¼ teaspoon salt
⅛ teaspoon pepper
½ cup mayonnaise

Blend first seven ingredients and fold in mayonnaise. Spoon into individual shells or a 1 quart casserole dish. Bake at 350° for 20 minutes. Serves 6.

Mrs. I. N. Smith, Jr.

FISH SAUCE

1 cup mayonnaise	2 tablespoons chopped chives
2 cups sour cream	Juice from 2 lemons
1 teaspoon minced onion	Salt and pepper
½ stick butter, melted	

Combine all ingredients and heat over hot water. Serve warm over baked or broiled fish fillets. Serves 6.

Mrs. Robert M. Chilton

HORSERADISH SAUCE FOR FISH

½ cup tomato juice	1 teaspoon parsley
2 teaspoons horseradish	Pepper to taste

Combine all ingredients. Spread over fish while broiling.

Mrs. K. Paul Davis

NEWBURG SAUCE FOR SHELLFISH

¼ cup butter	Salt, to taste
4 egg yolks	Paprika (for color)
1½ cups heavy cream or	¾ pound cooked and shelled
half & half	crab, lobster, or shrimp
Dry sherry, to taste	Prepared patty shells

Combine butter, egg yolks, cream, sherry, salt, and paprika in top of double boiler. Stir until thick, fold in fish. Serve in patty shells. Serves 4.

153

THE FLAME

Where limestone water cleft a time-worn ledge
To spread its moving silver as a fan
And rim the bluegrass with a curve of foam,
He paced a five-yard square between the edge
Of jagged gulch and where the wild began
And drove four hickory stakes into the loam.

He rolled four gray, unpolished blocks
Unto the corners, tamped them there
And squinted till he got them plumb.
Of hand-hewn logs and hand-dressed rocks
He built his cabin strong to bear
The unleashed force of winds to come.

The evening when he hung the puncheon door
He tried the leather hinges, raised the latch,
And thankful of his labor near at end,
Passed through, scraped up dry shavings from the floor,
Struck flint against his knife, and watched flame catch
Upon the rugged hearth his sons would tend.

Reprinted by permission of Louise McNeill, from **Gauley Mountain;** Harcourt, Brace, and Company; New York, New York; 1939; Page 10.

Photo by Commerce Photography

MEATS AND MARINADES

Flying Geese

BEEFSTEAK EN ROQUEFORT EN CHAMPIGNONS

Overlooking historic Blennerhassett Island in the Ohio River at Parkersburg, West Virginia, is the Point of View Restaurant where the diner delights in succulent steaks and other prime cuts.

5 (16 ounce) porterhouse or T-bone steaks or
7 (12 ounce) delmonicos or N.Y. strip steaks or
10 (8 ounce) filets

MARINADE

1 pint sour cream with chives	1 teaspoon vinegar
1 pint mayonnaise	¼ teaspoon celery salt
¼ cup red wine	¼ teaspoon garlic salt
¾ cup buttermilk	¼ teaspoon onion salt
¼ pound Roquefort cheese	Few drops Tabasco sauce
1 tablespoon Worcestershire sauce	Salt to taste
1 tablespoon lemon juice	Freshly ground black pepper to taste

Mix ingredients in order listed. In a suitable pan, (13″ x 9″ x 2½″ loaf pan is adequate) arrange a layer of steaks; pour over half the marinade. Arrange a second layer of steaks and add the remaining marinade. Cover and let stand in the refrigerator 4 to 24 hours. Remove the steaks from the marinade, while being careful to keep as much of the mixture clinging to the steaks as possible, and grill to desired doneness over a hot charcoal fire.

MUSHROOMS

1 pound fresh mushrooms   1 stick butter

Wash and clean mushrooms. Split lengthwise and sauté in butter until just tender. Serve over steaks.

Point of View Restaurant

FILET OF BEEF WELLINGTON

DUXELLES

1 pound mushrooms, very finely chopped	8 tablespoons butter
	¼ cup parsley
6 to 8 shallots, finely chopped	

Cook the mushrooms and shallots in the butter very slowly, stirring now and then, until all the moisture has disappeared and the mushrooms have become almost a paste. Stir in the parsley and cool. Duxelles may be prepared the day before and refrigerated.

PASTRY

3 cups flour	1 cup butter, at room temperature
	½ cup cold water

Blend flour and butter with the fingers until they are well amalgamated and the mixture resembles coarse salt. Add enough cold water, about ½ cup, to hold the dough together. If not enough water is added, the pastry may be too tender. Chill. This dough can also be made the day before it is needed.

TENDERLOIN

1 beef tenderloin, 3 to 3½ pounds	3 tablespoons butter
	1 cup Madeira

Fold the small end of the tenderloin back and tie it well. Melt the butter in a long oval pan and braise the meat in it, turning frequently. As it cooks, baste it with Madeira, using up to a cup in all. Remove the meat after ½ hour and cool, but do not refrigerate. Save the butter-Madeira mixture in the bottom of the pan.

SAUCE

1 cup beef broth	Approximately 1 cup Madeira
1 tablespoon arrowroot	
Salt and pepper	

Pour the reserved butter-Madeira mixture from the braising pan into a saucepan, and add the beef broth. Dissolve the arrowroot in ½ cup Madeira. Add to the saucepan and heat over low fire, stirring until the sauce has thickened. Add more Madeira if needed. Season to taste with salt and pepper.

PUTTING IT ALL TOGETHER

3 or 4 ounces pâté de foie gras	1 egg yolk
	1 tablespoon water

Roll the pastry between 2 sheets of waxed paper into a rectangular shape large enough to envelop the tenderloin, and between ⅛ and ¼" thick. Mix the pâté de fois gras with the duxelles and spread the mixture over the pastry, leaving uncovered a strip 1 inch wide on one side and on the ends. Center the tenderloin on the pastry and wrap a side over it, using uncovered side last, so the seam is on the bottom. Tuck in the ends, trimming as necessary, and seal the edges with water. Put the tenderloin, seam side down, on a baking pan or cookie sheet; slash or prick the dough in a pretty pattern; and decorate with fancy shapes (roses, leaves, etc.) cut from the scraps of dough and pasted on with water. Brush the top with a mixture of 1 egg yolk and 1 tablespoon of water, beaten together. Place in a 400° oven and cook for 20 to 30 minutes, until the pastry is nicely browned. Serve with the sauce in a separate dish. Each rare slice will be encased in a frame of pastry with a darker inner border of the duxelles. Serves 8.

Mrs. F. Thomas Graff, Jr.

FLANK STEAK

Unseasoned meat tenderizer
1 flank steak
1 clove garlic

Freshly ground pepper
½ cup soy sauce
¼ cup vermouth
Dash of Tabasco sauce

Use tenderizer according to directions on label. Put garlic clove through a press, and rub steak with garlic and freshly ground pepper. Mix together soy sauce, vermouth, and Tabasco and pour over steak. Marinate for 2 hours or longer. Broil under very high heat for 3 to 4 minutes on each side. Serve rare and carve diagonally. Flank steak must be rare to be tender. Serves 4.

Mrs. Harry N. Casto

ORIENTAL CHI CHOW

1 pound sirloin steak, about
   1 inch thick, cut into
   narrow strips
½ cup chopped green onion
1 medium onion, cut in wedges
1 (5 ounce) can bamboo shoots,
   drained
1 (5 ounce) can water
   chestnuts, drained

1 (3 ounce) can sliced mushrooms, drained
1 tablespoon sugar
1 beef bouillon cube dissolved
   in ½ cup hot water
2 teaspoons cornstarch
1 tablespoon cold water
¼ cup soy sauce

Brown meat, half at a time, in hot fat. Add next seven ingredients. Cover and simmer for 5 minutes. Blend cornstarch, 1 tablespoon cold water, and soy sauce; add to meat. Cook and stir until thick. Serves 4. Serve on rice or over hot noodles.

Mrs. Paul F. Saylor

PEPPERED STEAK

6 filets of beef, 1 to 2 inch thickness	¼ cup olive oil
Fresh pepper, ground	1 chicken bouillon cube
Salt	3 ounces water
¼ cup butter	3 ounces dry white wine
	2 ounces brandy

Press freshly ground pepper into both sides of filets. (Use a mortar & pestle to coarsely grind pepper.) Salt the beef to taste.

Heat butter and olive oil in a large skillet. Dissolve bouillon cube in water. When butter and oil are at frying temperature, sear filets on both sides; then cook for about 5 minutes on each side. Put meat on heated platter. Add the wine and bouillon to skillet. Stir and scrape to deglaze the pan. Add brandy. Pour sauce over filets and serve immediately.

Ronald A. McKenney

POLYNESIAN BEEF AND PEPPERS

2 pounds round, sirloin, or flank steak	2 teaspoons sugar
Cooking oil	1 teaspoon cornstarch
2 tablespoons soy sauce	1 large onion
1½ tablespoons sherry	1 large green pepper
	2 medium tomatoes
¼ cup water	

Slice meat 1" wide by ⅛" thick. Brown in oil in skillet. Make sauce of soy sauce, sherry, sugar, and cornstarch; add to meat and marinate 10 minutes. Coarsely chop onion and add to meat. Cut pepper into large chunks and add to meat. Cook for 5 minutes. Slice tomatoes and add to meat with water. Cook for 3 minutes. Less expensive cuts of meat may need longer cooking time. Serves 4.

Mrs. Richard R. Meckfessel

STEAK AU POIVRE

Sirloin steak, 2 or 3 inches thick	Oil
½ cup whole peppercorns	Salt
	Melted butter
Lemon juice	

Trim fat from steak. Crush two handfuls of whole peppercorns by spreading evenly on a board, covering with a dish towel, and crushing with a rolling pin. Pound pepper into each surface of steak, which has been lightly brushed with oil. Wrap steak loosely in waxed paper; refrigerate several hours or overnight. Before cooking, brush off loose pepper. **Do not salt.** Allow steak to stand at room temperature before cooking. Heat heavy skillet red hot; coat with a little oil. Sear steak on each side for 3 minutes. Remove skillet from heat. Salt steak; place in a moderate oven (350°). Bake 20 to 25 minutes for rare; 30 to 35 minutes for medium rare. Spread with lemon butter, made by blending melted butter and lemon juice to taste. Slice very thinly. Serves 8.

Mrs. Connie Carrico

SUKIYAKI

1½ pounds sirloin steak, or flank steak, sliced thin, on diagonal (easiest to slice frozen with electric knife)	1 tablespoon sake, vermouth, or dry sherry
¼ cup peanut oil with 3 to 4 drops sesame oil added	3 medium onions, thinly sliced
½ cup beef broth or bouillon	½ cup diced celery
½ cup soy sauce	1 (5 ounce) can bamboo shoots
1 tablespoon sugar	½ pound mushrooms, sliced
1 to 2 cloves garlic, minced	1 cup shredded raw spinach
	4 green onions, sliced
	1 pound vermicelli, cooked and drained, or folded fettucine, or rice

Brown steak in hot oil in large skillet (electric skillet is perfect). Combine broth, soy sauce, sugar, garlic, and sake. Add half to the meat. Push meat to side of pan. Add onions and celery and cook over low heat for 3 minutes. Add remaining broth mixture, bamboo shoots, mushrooms, and spinach, and cook for 3 minutes. Add green onions and cook for 1 minute. Place hot cooked vermicelli on one side of platter, sukiyaki on other, or serve directly from skillet. Serve at once. Serves 4 to 6. (Allow 25 minutes for preparation, 10 minutes to cook.)

Mrs. Philip Angel, Jr.

TERIYAKI STEAK

½ cup soy sauce
¼ cup brown sugar
2 tablespoons salad oil
1 teaspoon ginger

¼ teaspoon pepper
2 cloves garlic, crushed
1 ounce or more sherry
1 to 1½ pounds sirloin steak

Mix the first 7 ingredients for marinade. Cut the sirloin steak in 1" width strips. Marinate at least 2 hours. Broil or grill; best cooked over charcoal. Serves 2.

Mrs. Charles Q. Gage

HERBED BEEF ROAST

5 to 6 pound beef roast (eye of round)
½ cup flour
3 teaspoons salt

1 teaspoon paprika
1 teaspoon basil
1 teaspoon marjoram
Watercress

Place roast on a sheet of waxed paper. Mix remaining ingredients, except watercress. Pat well into roast. Place on a rack in a shallow baking pan. Do not add water or cover pan. Roast in slow oven (325°) for 2¼ hours, or if using a meat thermometer, until thermometer registers 140° for rare. Cover pan loosely with a sheet of foil, and let stand at room temperature until serving time. Place on platter and garnish with watercress. Serve with Mustard Cream. Serves 25 for cocktail buffet.

MUSTARD CREAM

1 cup mayonnaise
½ cup prepared mustard

½ cup canned condensed beef consommé

¼ cup cream

Combine all ingredients in a bowl. Beat with electric mixer until well blended. Chill. Makes 2 cups.

Mrs. Andrew R. Quenon

BEEF ROLL UPS

6 slices sirloin tip, or round steak, cut in wedges ¼" thick
Flour
Salt and pepper

2 carrots
1 onion
1 green pepper
2 or 3 slices uncooked bacon
3 tablespoons bacon fat

Coat meat well with a mixture of flour, salt, and pepper. Cut each carrot into 3 pieces. Cut onion into 6 wedges and green pepper into 6 strips. Slice bacon strips into 3 pieces each. Place a piece of uncooked bacon, carrot, onion, and green pepper on each piece of meat, and roll up. Tuck under ends to keep vegetables inside the roll. Insert wooden picks through folded ends and through center of each roll. Melt fat in skillet. Slowly brown meat rolls on all sides. Place meat rolls in casserole.

SAUCE

2 tablespoons butter	2 cups milk
2 tablespoons flour	½ cup mushrooms, drained
¼ teaspoon salt	1 tablespoon minced parsley
Dash pepper	1 teaspoon Worcestershire sauce

Melt butter; blend in flour, salt, and pepper. Heat until it bubbles. Remove from heat and gradually stir in milk. Return to heat and cook rapidly, stirring constantly, until sauce thickens. Add mushrooms, parsley and Worcestershire sauce. Pour over meat. Cover casserole and bake at 350° for 1 to 1½ hours or until meat is tender when pierced with a fork. Serves 6.

Mrs. Leslie Hawker

PAPRIKA BEEF ROLL

2 round steaks, 3 pounds total	½ cup melted butter or bacon drippings
Salt	
Pepper	1 tablespoon boiling water
Paprika	1 egg
¼ pound mushrooms, sliced	Stuffed olives
1 onion, sliced	¼ cup butter or bacon drippings
Pimiento	6 whole mushrooms
Bread crumbs	3 small whole onions
1 cup red wine	

Pound steaks until thin, rub in salt, pepper, plenty of paprika. Overlap steaks on meat board, making one large steak. Spread with a layer of sliced mushrooms and a layer of thinly sliced onions. Add pimiento. Cover with finely rolled bread crumbs.

With beater, combine: ½ cup melted butter or bacon drippings, boiling water, and egg. Immediately dribble this mixture over bread crumbs.

Arrange stuffed olives in a row on long side of steak. Roll the meat around olives. Tie roll firmly. Salt and pepper the outside. Brown in ¼ cup butter or drippings in roaster or deep earthenware baker.

Place whole mushrooms and onions into roaster, and sprinkle

all lightly with salt, pepper, and paprika. Add 1 cup of red wine. Roast meat in 350° oven for about two hours. Serve hot or cold. Serves 6.

Mrs. Henry E. Payne, III

BEEF ARLESIENNE

3 pounds boneless pot roast in ½" slices
2 tablespoons oil
6 tomatoes, peeled and quartered
1 (4 ounce) can sliced mushrooms and juice

½ cup pitted black olives
1 clove garlic, crushed
½ teaspoon salt
¼ teaspoon pepper
Pinch of dried sweet basil
1 bay leaf

Heat oil in Dutch oven or electric frying pan. Add meat and brown well on both sides. Pour off fat and add the rest of the ingredients to the pan. Cover tightly and simmer 2½ to 3 hours. Serves 6.

Mrs. Hugh G. Thompson, Jr.

BEEF BURGUNDY

3 pounds cubed beef, chuck or round
2 (10¾ ounces each) cans cream of mushroom soup
1 envelope dry onion soup mix
½ cup Burgundy wine

Mix all ingredients in a large casserole. Cover tightly with lid or foil. Bake 5 hours at 250°. Serve over rice or noodles. Serves 8. Keeps well in refrigerator overnight and also freezes well.

Mrs. W. H. E. Marshall

DEVILED STEAK CUBES

Dr. John G. Barker is past president of Marshall University at Huntington, W. Va.

1 tablespoon flour
1 teaspoon salt
Dash pepper
1 pound stew beef, round steak, or sirloin cut in bite-size cubes
2 tablespoons cooking oil

1 medium onion, thinly sliced
1 (8 ounce) can tomato sauce
¼ cup water
½ teaspoon dry mustard
1½ teaspoons Worcestershire sauce

Combine flour, salt, and pepper. Coat meat and brown slowly in oil. Add remaining ingredients; cover and simmer 1½ to 2 hours, or until tender. Serve over rice or noodles. Serves 4.

Dr. John G. Barker

FLANK STEAK DELUXE

1½ pounds flank steak
¼ cup flour
1 teaspoon salt
¼ teaspoon black pepper
1 tablespoon cooking oil
2 tablespoons Worcester-
  shire sauce
Dash of Tabasco
2 tablespoons lemon juice
1½ cups water

½ cup catsup
1½ teaspoons prepared
  mustard
1 teaspoon grated lemon
  rind
¼ cup minced onion
1 clove garlic
Mushroom slices,
  optional
Parsley for garnish

Score meat. Mix flour, salt, and pepper; thoroughly pound into meat. Brown in hot oil. Combine remaining ingredients; pour over meat and cover. Cook over low heat until tender, 1½ to 2 hours. (Do not cook in electric skillet.) Serve surrounded by border of cooked rice. Garnish with parsley. Serves 4.

Mrs. Carl B. Hall, Jr.

RED WINE STEW

2 pounds boneless chuck, cut
  in 2″ cubes
¼ cup flour
½ teaspoon salt
½ teaspoon garlic salt
⅛ teaspoon pepper
½ cup butter or margarine
2 (4 ounces each) cans sliced
  mushrooms, drained

1 onion, chopped
2 stalks celery, cut in ½″
  pieces
3 carrots, cut in ½″ pieces
1 cup water
1 cup red wine
1 (10½ ounce) can beef
  consommé
2 tablespoons flour

¼ cup water

Combine the ¼ cup flour, salt, garlic salt, and pepper. Dredge meat in flour mixture. Brown meat in butter. Add mushrooms and onion. Cook over low heat until onion is tender. Add next five ingredients. Cover. Simmer, stirring occasionally, for 2 hours or until tender. Combine the 2 tablespoons flour and ¼ cup water to make a paste. Stir into stew. Cook until slightly thickened. Flavor improves by keeping until second day. Serve over rice. Serves 8.

Mrs. John C. Thomas

SPICY MEAT CURRY AND RICE

2 pounds beef or pork, cubed	1 clove garlic, minced
1 large onion, chopped	2 large potatoes, cubed
1 tablespoon cooking oil	3 tablespoons shredded
Water	coconut
4 tablespoons curry powder	Pinch red pepper
2 teaspoons chili powder	2 cups cooked rice
Large pinch powdered cloves	Spanish peanuts
2 tablespoons salt	Sliced bananas
Indian chutney	

Brown meat and onion in oil. Cover meat and onion with water. Bring to a rapid boil and add curry powder, chili powder, cloves, salt, and garlic. Boil 20 minutes and add water to cover; then add potatoes, coconut, and red pepper and simmer until vegetables are tender. Prepare rice for 6. Serve curry on top of rice with these side dishes for a topping on curry: Spanish peanuts, sliced bananas, and Indian chutney.

Mrs. J. Crawford Goldman

BEEF STROGANOFF

Senator Robert C. Byrd, Democrat, first began serving as a United States Senator from West Virginia in 1959. Among Senator Byrd's credits in the Senate can be listed his role as Majority Whip.

1½ pounds round steak	1 clove garlic, minced
¼ cup butter	½ cup chopped onion
1 cup sliced mushrooms	1 (10½ ounce) can tomato soup
or 1 (3 ounce) can,	1 cup sour cream
drained	Salt and pepper

Cut beef into long, thin strips. Brown well in ¼ cup butter in a heavy skillet. Add mushrooms, chopped onion, and garlic. Cook until lightly browned. Blend in tomato soup, sour cream, and salt and pepper. Cover and simmer about 1 hour, or until beef is tender. Stir occasionally. Serve with hot cooked rice. Serves 4 to 6.

Senator Robert Byrd

MOCK STROGANOFF

2 pounds beef stew meat	1 cup dry vermouth
2 (10½ ounces each) cans cream	1 package dehydrated
of mushroom soup	onion soup
1 (6 ounce) can or 1 pound fresh mushrooms	

Mix ingredients together. Put into covered casserole and bake at 350° for 3½ to 4 hours. Serve over rice or buttered parsleyed noodles. Serves 4 generously.

Mrs. William E. McClellan

BAKED SWISS STEAK

2 pounds round steak, 1" thick
Flour
1 large onion
1 green pepper
4 stalks celery
3 large carrots

1 (28 ounce) can tomatoes
⅓ cup catsup
1 (8 ounce) can tomato sauce
2 teaspoons horseradish
1 tablespoon Worcestershire sauce
Salt and pepper to taste

Roll meat in flour and brown in fat in skillet. Place in a large, deep baking dish. Cut onion, pepper, celery, and carrots in large pieces and add to the meat. Mix remaining ingredients and pour over the meat. Bake, covered, for 2 to 2½ hours, at 325°, until tender. Serves 6 to 8.

Mrs. Ronald A. McKenney

ROUND STEAK WITH TOMATO SAUCE

2½ pounds top round steak, cut in 6 serving pieces
¾ cup catsup
¼ cup flour
1 cup chili sauce

¼ cup water
6 thin slices onion
6 thin slices lemon (¼ cup lemon juice may be substituted for lemon slices)

Mix catsup, flour, chili sauce, and water. Pour just enough catsup mixture to cover bottom of greased 3-quart flat casserole. Place steak in casserole. On each piece of meat, place a slice of onion and a slice of lemon (or pour lemon juice over all). Cover with remaining catsup mixture. Seal tightly with aluminum foil. Bake at 400° for 1½ to 2 hours. Serves 6.

Mrs. William C. Payne

CORN BREAD — WEINER — BEAN CASSEROLE

6 weiners, cut into bite-size pieces
1 (20 ounce) can pork and beans

¾ cup catsup
½ cup water
1 tablespoon mustard

Mix these ingredients well and put into a casserole.

CORNBREAD TOPPING

¾ cup flour
1 tablespoon sugar
1½ teaspoons baking powder
1 teaspoon salt
⅔ cup cornmeal
1 beaten egg
⅔ cup milk
¼ cup cooking oil
⅓ cup minced onion

Sift flour, sugar, baking powder and salt. Stir in cornmeal. Add all at once to the dry ingredients the egg, milk, oil and onion. Stir and spoon over bean mixture. Bake at 400° for 35 minutes. Serves 4.

CABBAGE ROLLS

1 medium head cabbage
3 tablespoons olive oil
1 pound ground beef or ¾ pound ground beef and ¼ pound ground pork
1 onion
½ cup raw rice
¼ to ½ cup parsley
1 (6 ounce) can tomato paste, divided
1½ teaspoons salt and pepper, to taste
1 pint tomatoes
1 teaspoon sugar, or less
Cornstarch, optional

Sauté meat and onion in olive oil. Add the raw rice, parsley, 3 tablespoons tomato paste, salt, and pepper, and mix well. Meanwhile, cook the cabbage in rapidly boiling water until the leaves can be loosened (about 8 minutes). Drain. Do not overcook. Place a large spoonful of the hamburger mixture in the middle of each cabbage leaf. Roll and secure with a pick, if necessary. Place in a heavy pot and cover with the tomatoes and the remainder of the tomato paste, mixed with a little water. Add sugar. Simmer, covered, for 1 to 2 hours. Just before serving, if desired, add a little cornstarch to the sauce to thicken. Serves 6.

Mrs. Carol Fletcher

SENATOR BYRD'S CABBAGE ROLLS

1 pound lean ground beef
1 cup cooked rice
Small onion, chopped
1 teaspoon salt
¼ teaspoon pepper
1 egg
Cabbage leaves
Cooking oil
2 (8 ounces each) cans tomato sauce
¼ cup water

Mix ground beef, cooked rice, chopped onion, salt, pepper, and egg. Boil cabbage for 8 to 10 minutes. Trim off thickest part of stem from cabbage leaves. Divide meat into equal portions; wrap each in a leaf; fasten with wooden picks. Brown cabbage rolls slightly in cooking oil. Add the tomato sauce and water. Cover and cook slowly for about 40 minutes.

Senator Robert Byrd

CHILI CASSEROLE

1 medium onion, chopped
2 tablespoons butter
2 pounds ground beef
1 or 2 (1 pound) cans tomatoes
1 (12 ounce) can corn
1 can pitted black olives, drained

¼ cup cornmeal
4 teaspoons or more chili powder
1½ to 2 teaspoons salt
Pepper
1 cup grated Cheddar cheese

Brown onion in butter in skillet. Add meat and brown. Drain off fat. Add remaining ingredients except cheese and mix. Season. Put in a 3 quart baking dish and sprinkle with cheese. Bake at 350° for 40 to 50 minutes. Serves 6 to 8.

Mrs. Kenneth Kleeman

EASY HAMBURGER QUICHE

½ pound ground beef
½ cup mayonnaise
½ cup milk
2 eggs
1 tablespoon cornstarch

1½ cups (½ pound) Cheddar or Swiss cheese, chopped
⅓ cup green onions, sliced
Dash of pepper
1 unbaked 9-inch pastry shell

Brown meat in skillet over medium heat. Drain fat and set meat aside. Blend next 4 ingredients until smooth. Stir in meat, cheese, onion, and pepper. Turn into pastry shell. Bake at 350° for 35 to 40 minutes until brown on top. Serves 6 to 8. Can be frozen.

Mrs. K. Paul Davis

FIVE SOUP HOT DISH

2 pounds ground beef
2 medium onions, chopped
1 (10½ ounce) can cream of celery soup
1 (10½ ounce) can cream of mushroom soup
1 (10½ ounce) can cream of chicken soup
1 (10½ ounce) can beef with barley soup
1 (10½ ounce) can chicken and rice soup
1 (8 ounce) can chow mein noodles

Brown beef and onions. Add soups and mix well. Fold in ⅔ of the noodles. Place in a large casserole and top with remaining noodles. Bake at 350° for 45 minutes. Serves 6 to 8.

Mrs. William H. Knight

GROUND MEAT CASSEROLE

Governor Arch A. Moore, Jr., Republican, was first elected governor of West Virginia in 1968 and was reelected for a second term in 1972. Prior to the governorship, Governor Moore served in the United States House of Representatives from 1956 to 1968. He writes that this casserole is served frequently at the Mansion.

1 pound ground round beef	1 (8 ounce) package cream
1 tablespoon butter	cheese, softened
2 (8 ounces each) cans tomato	¼ cup thick sour cream
sauce	⅓ cup chopped green onion
1 (8 ounce) package thin	1 tablespoon chopped green
noodles	pepper
1 cup cottage cheese	3 tablespoons butter, melted

Brown meat in butter in heavy skillet and add tomato sauce. Cook noodles according to directions on package. Butter a 2½ quart casserole and spread half of the noodles on the bottom. Layer cottage cheese, soft cream cheese, sour cream, and chopped mixtures. Spread remainder of the noodles over this, and then add the browned meat and tomato sauce mixture. Pour melted butter over the top and bake for 45 minutes at 350°. Serves 6 to 8.

Governor Arch Moore

GROUND BEEF — ONION — BEAN CASSEROLE

3 tablespoons cooking oil	2 (16 ounces each) cans kidney
2 pounds ground beef	beans, undrained
1 cup chopped green pepper	2 cups cooked rice or macaroni
1 (2¾ ounce) package onion	1 (16 ounce) can tomatoes
soup mix	1 (10½ ounce) can condensed
1 tablespoon chili powder	tomato soup
¼ teaspoon pepper	1½ cups grated American cheese

Lightly grease 1 large or 2 medium casseroles. In a large skillet, heat the oil and sauté the ground beef until it loses its red color. Drain off the fat, and stir in the green pepper, onion soup mix, chili powder, and pepper. Turn this mixture into the beans, rice, tomatoes, and tomato soup. Mix well. Pour into the casserole and bake for 45 minutes at 400°, uncovered. Sprinkle the surface with grated cheese and bake 10 minutes longer.

GROUND BEEF — NOODLE SUPPER

2 tablespoons cooking oil
1 large onion, chopped
1 green pepper, chopped
1 pound ground beef
¼ pound wide noodles
1 (16 ounce) can cream style
   corn

1 (16 ounce) can tomatoes
1 (6 ounce) can tomato paste
Salt and pepper
1 teaspoon chili powder
1 tablespoon Worcestershire
   sauce
1 pound grated sharp cheese

In a skillet, brown the onion and green pepper in oil. Add ground beef and cook until browned. Cook the noodles according to package directions for 7 minutes. In a large bowl, mix the creamed corn, tomatoes, and tomato paste. Add the beef mixture to this and then the noodles. Season to taste with salt and pepper, chili powder, and Worcestershire sauce. Pour half the mixture in a 3-quart casserole, and cover with half the grated cheese. Repeat another layer of beef mixture and top with the rest of the cheese. Bake for 45 minutes to 1 hour at 350°. This recipe can be divided into 2 casseroles and one placed in the freezer. Adjust baking time for smaller casseroles.

Mrs. William C. Payne

HAMBURGER RICE CREOLE

2 small onions, sliced
2 tablespoons butter
½ pound ground beef
⅓ cup raw rice (not minute)
½ green pepper, chopped
¼ cup chopped celery
1 (8 ounce) can tomato sauce
1 cup water

2 tablespoons parsley (fresh) or
   2 teaspoons, dried
½ bay leaf, crushed
Pinch thyme
Pinch marjoram
1 teaspoon salt
½ teaspoon sugar
¼ teaspoon pepper

Sauté onions in butter. Brown the ground beef. Place in a covered casserole with remaining ingredients. Bake covered at 350° for 1 hour. Serves 4.

Mrs. David J. Christensen

ITALIAN LASAGNA

½ pound lasagna noodles
2 tablespoons oil
2 cloves garlic, minced
1 medium onion, chopped
1 pound ground beef
2½ teaspoons salt
¼ teaspoon pepper
½ teaspoon rosemary

1 tablespoon minced parsley
2 (6 ounces each) cans tomato
  paste
1½ cups hot water
2 eggs, beaten
1 pint cottage cheese
½ pound mozzarella cheese,
  sliced

¼ cup grated Parmesan cheese

Cook noodles in salted water for 15 minutes. Drain. Heat oil in skillet, and cook garlic and onion until soft. Add beef and seasonings and cook until crumbly. Drain off the fat. Add tomato paste and hot water. Simmer for 5 minutes and set aside. Blend beaten eggs with cottage cheese in a bowl. In a baking dish 9" x 13" x 2", put a thin layer of the meat sauce, half the noodles, all of the cottage cheese-egg mixture, and half of the mozzarella cheese. Repeat with half the remaining meat sauce, the rest of the noodles, remainder of the sauce, and mozzarella cheese. Sprinkle with Parmesan cheese. Bake at 350° for 30 minutes. Let cool 10 minutes before serving. Serves 8.

Mrs. George V. Hamrick

LASAGNA

⅔ pound lasagna noodles
1½ pounds ground beef
1 onion, chopped
6 ounces cream cheese
1⅓ cups sour cream
1⅓ cups cottage cheese

3 (6 ounces each) cans tomato
  sauce
½ teaspoon sweet basil
½ teaspoon oregano
¼ teaspoon pepper
¼ teaspoon paprika

Cook lasagna noodles according to directions on package. Brown beef and chopped onion and add salt. With a mixer, combine cream cheese, sour cream, and cottage cheese. In saucepan warm tomato sauce with seasonings. (You may substitute 1½ teaspoons pre-mixed Italian seasonings for those listed.) Grease 9" x 12" casserole. Layer noodles, cheese, meat, and sauce. Repeat. Then top with noodles and sauce. Heat in 350° oven for 40 minutes. Serves 6.

Mrs. Seigle W. Parks

EASY MEAT LOAF

2 pounds ground lean beef
1 box (2 envelopes) onion soup
  mix

1 (13 ounce) can evaporated
  milk

Mix ingredients together and place in an ungreased shallow baking pan. With wet hands, shape into a loaf. Bake 1 hour at 350°. Serves 8 to 10.

Mrs. William T. Brotherton, Jr.

ITALIAN MEATLOAF

2 slices rye bread
2 slices white bread
½ cup water
1 pound ground beef
1 medium onion, chopped
1 tablespoon chopped parsley
3 tablespoons grated
  Parmesan cheese

1 cup cottage cheese
1 egg
1 teaspoon salt
¼ teaspoon pepper
2 tablespoons butter
1 (8 ounce) can tomato sauce
1 teaspoon oregano

Break bread into small pieces and soak in water. Combine beef with moistened bread, onion, parsley, cheeses, egg, salt and pepper. Mix. Place in 8¾" x 5 x 2½" greased loaf pan. Dot with butter. Bake at 375° for 30 minutes. Pour tomato sauce over meat and sprinkle with oregano. Bake 20 more minutes. Serve hot. Serves 6 to 8.

Mrs. Robert N. Hart

MEAT LOAF

1 pound meat loaf mix (beef,
  pork, and veal)
1 (16 ounce) can stewed
  tomatoes (drain; save juice)
1 egg

½ teaspoon salt
½ teaspoon celery salt
½ teaspoon onion salt
1 teaspoon Worcestershire
  sauce
¾ cup Special K cereal

Mix all ingredients together except tomato juice. Form into large egg-shaped loaf, and put in greased square pyrex baking dish, leaving air space around. Let stand several hours in refrigerator. Pour juice from canned tomatoes over loaf and bake, uncovered, at 400° for 30 minutes. Reduce heat to 350° and bake 30 minutes more. Baste. Serves 4.

Mrs. John Prince Harris

SWEDISH MEAT BALLS IN BURGUNDY

¾ pound ground beef
¾ cup dry bread crumbs
1 small onion, minced
¾ teaspoon cornstarch
  Dash allspice
1 egg, beaten
¾ cup milk (or light cream)
1¼ teaspoons salt, divided

¼ cup cooking oil
3 tablespoons flour
2 cups water
1 cup Burgundy (don't use
  other wine)
2 beef bouillon cubes
⅛ teaspoon pepper
1½ teaspoons sugar

Bottled sauce for gravy

Combine meat, crumbs, onion, cornstarch, allspice, egg, milk, and ¾ teaspoon salt; shape into 24 or 26 balls. Drop a few at a time into hot fat; brown well on all sides; transfer to plate. For sauce, stir flour into remaining fat in skillet; stir in water, Burgundy, bouillon cubes, ½ teaspoon salt, pepper, sugar, and enough bottled sauce to make a light brown gravy. (Make gravy as light or dark as desired.) Cook, stirring until smooth. Put meat balls in sauce; simmer, covered, for 30 minutes. Serve on hot mashed potatoes, buttered noodles, wild rice, fluffy instant rice, or a mixture of white and wild rice; or use for canapés.

Mrs. Paul F. Saylor

MOUSSAKA

4 pounds eggplant
  Salt
2 pounds lean ground beef
1½ cups chopped onion
1 stick margarine or butter,
  divided
½ cup Burgundy wine
2 teaspoons salt
¼ teaspoon freshly ground
  pepper
1½ teaspoons oregano or
  thyme

1 tablespoon parsley
2 eggs, beaten
1 cup grated sharp Cheddar
  cheese, divided
½ cup bread crumbs, divided
  Olive oil
2 (1 pound each) cans plum
  tomatoes, drained
⅓ cup flour
3 cups milk
  Salt, pepper, nutmeg, to taste
4 egg yolks, lightly beaten

Peel eggplant and slice crosswise thinly. Sprinkle with salt; place in colander and weight with a plate to drain (to remove bitterness). Let stand ½ hour. Sauté beef and onions until browned and cooked. Drain to remove excess fat, and add 2 tablespoons margarine, seasonings, and wine. Stir to melt butter and blend in seasonings. Simmer until no liquid remains. Stir in 2 eggs, ¾ cup of the cheese, and half the bread crumbs. Lightly dip eggplant in oil; place on cookie sheets and broil until brown on both sides. Grease

4-quart casserole well, and sprinkle with remaining crumbs. Fill with layers of eggplant, meat, tomatoes — ending with eggplant, and leaving room for expansion at the top. Melt rest of butter; blend in flour, egg yolks, and remainder of seasonings mixed with milk. Cook until thickened, stirring constantly. Pour sauce over casserole; sprinkle on remaining cheese. Bake at 350° for 45 to 60 minutes, until top is golden. Serves 10 to 12.

May be frozen before adding the white sauce and finished at serving time.

Mrs. Laurance Morrison

ITALIAN TOMATO SAUCE AND MEAT BALLS
ITALIAN TOMATO SAUCE

Olive oil	1 (12 ounce) can tomato paste
1 large onion, chopped	1 (29 ounce) can tomatoes
2 cloves garlic, minced	Pinch basil
1 strip green pepper, chopped	1 teaspoon chopped parsley
Salt and pepper, to taste	

Generously cover a large heavy pan (an electric skillet at 200° is good) with ¼ inch or more olive oil. Chop onion, garlic, and green pepper; sauté these in olive oil until tender. Add tomato paste and cook until it begins to separate, stirring constantly. Add the can of tomatoes by pressing them through a strainer. Discard pulp. Add basil, parsley, salt, and pepper. Cook gently for 1 hour or more in a covered pot. Stir frequently and add water, if necessary. (Meatballs, chicken cooked in olive oil, or beef cubes of round or sirloin may be added during the simmering phase.)

ITALIAN MEATBALLS

2 pounds ground beef	2 eggs
2 cloves garlic, minced	4 slices bread
1 small onion, minced	Salt and pepper
Olive oil	

Mix meat, garlic, onion and eggs. Soak bread in water and squeeze out water. Add the bread to the meat mixture with the seasonings to taste and mix all with the hands. Cover bottom of skillet with ¼" of olive oil. Gently form meatballs into 1½" diameter for dinner or 1" diameter for cocktails. Fry in olive oil until lightly browned. Drop into tomato sauce when sauce starts to simmer, and cook for 1½ to 2 hours. The secret of good meatballs is to handle them as little as possible when mixing and forming. Serves 8.

Mrs. Alexander J. Ross

MRS. WISE'S SPAGHETTI SAUCE

1 or 2 slices bacon, diced
1 pound ground beef
1 onion, chopped
½ green pepper, chopped
1 (6 ounce) can tomato paste
2 cups tomato juice

1 (10½ ounce) can tomato soup
1 tablespoon Worcestershire
  sauce
2 cloves garlic, minced
2 tablespoons sugar
Spaghetti

Fry bacon. Add ground meat, onion, and green pepper. Fry until meat is brown. Put tomato paste, tomato juice, soup, Worcestershire sauce, garlic, and sugar in pan and add meat mixture. Cook very slowly for 3 hours. Ladle over cooked spaghetti. Serves 8.

Mix leftover sauce with a can of chili and water and serve as chili. Also good over hot dogs.

Mrs. Charles B. Watkins

SPAGHETTI SAUCE

1 pound ground beef
¼ pound ground veal
¼ pound pork sausage
6 to 8 garlic cloves, chopped
⅓ cup olive oil
2 (15 ounces each) cans tomato
  sauce
1 (6 ounce) can mushrooms,
  undrained
½ cup chopped parsley
1 medium onion, chopped
1 stalk celery, chopped
2 pimientos, chopped
¼ cup chopped green peppers

1 tablespoon salt
1 teaspoon pepper
1½ teaspoons chili powder
1 tablespoon paprika
2 teaspoons sugar
1 teaspoon monosodium
  glutamate
½ teaspoon oregano
½ teaspoon rosemary
Dash allspice
2 or 3 drops hot sauce
1 teaspoon Worcestershire
  sauce
Sliced stuffed olives

Mix beef, veal, and pork well. Work garlic cloves in meat, and cook in natural juices until done. Add remaining ingredients and cook slowly for 4 to 6 hours. Add tomato juice, if necessary, to thin. Put sliced stuffed olives on top when serving. Makes ½ gallon of sauce. Serves 8.

Mrs. Carl B. Hall, Jr.

TACO SALAD

1 pound ground chuck	5 ounces sharp Cheddar cheese cubed
1 onion, chopped	
2 tablespoons cooking oil	1 (about 6 ounces) bag taco chips or tortilla chips, broken
1 cup taco sauce	
1 head iceberg lettuce	
1 bunch green onions, coarsely chopped	Hot peppers, optional

Sauté onion in oil until soft; add chuck and brown. Drain off all grease. Add taco sauce; heat and simmer for 5 to 10 minutes. Make tossed salad of other ingredients. Add heated meat mixture; toss and serve. Hot peppers may be served as a sidedish. Serves 8.

Mrs. David J. Christensen

TONY MINZETTI

1 pound ground beef	½ pound mushrooms
Chopped onion, to taste	½ pound Velvetta cheese
½ pound wide noodles	Cornflakes
1 (10½ ounce) can tomato soup	Butter

Brown meat with onion. Cook noodles. Add all ingredients, except cornflakes and butter, together with a small amount of water, and fill casserole. Top with cornflakes browned in melted butter. Bake at 350° for about 40 minutes. Serves 4.

Mrs. Herbert Meckfessel

HAM BALLS

1 egg	2 cups ground ham
1 cup bread crumbs	¼ cup milk
	Salad oil

Form the first 4 ingredients into balls. Brown in small amount of oil. Cover with the following sauce.

SAUCE

¾ cup brown sugar	¼ cup vinegar
¼ cup water	½ teaspoon dry mustard

Combine all ingredients for the sauce and pour over the ham balls. Bake at 350° or simmer in covered skillet until hot and bubbly, about 15 minutes.

Mrs. Carol Fletcher

HAM AND CHEESE CREPES

5 tablespoons butter, melted
6 tablespoons flour
2 cups scalded milk
  Salt and pepper to taste
1 dash Tabasco (or more
  to taste)

¾ cup finely chopped ham
¾ cup coarsely grated Swiss
  cheese
Parmesan cheese

Make thick white sauce by stirring flour into melted butter; add milk, and cook, stirring, until thick. Add seasonings, ham, and Swiss cheese. Divide filling among crêpes; roll up and place on heat-proof platter. Brush tops with melted butter; sprinkle with Parmesan cheese and broil until lightly browned. Serves 6 to 10. For crêpes see Breads.

Mrs. Ronald A. McKenney

HAM ROLLS WITH CHEESE SAUCE

1 recipe biscuit dough
  (2 cups)
3 cups cooked ground ham

3 tablespoons prepared
  mustard
3 tablespoons butter, melted
Cheese sauce

Make 1 biscuit recipe. Roll out ¾ inch thick in a 14 inch square. Combine ham, mustard and butter and spread over dough. Roll up jelly-roll fashion and cut in 1 inch slices. Place cut side down in greased pan. Bake at 450 degrees until brown; 15 to 20 minutes. Serve hot with cheese sauce.

SAUCE

2 tablespoons butter
2 tablespoons flour
1 to 1½ cups scalded milk

¾ cup grated Cheddar cheese
Salt and pepper to taste
Dash cayenne pepper

Melt butter, stir in flour and cook 2 to 3 minutes. Stir in milk and seasonings. Remove from heat and stir in cheese. Sauce need not be smooth.

Mrs. Estil Monk

SWEET 'N' SOUR HAM LOAF

½ cup brown sugar
2 tablespoons prepared
  mustard
¼ cup vinegar
1½ pounds ham, ground

½ pound fresh ground pork
½ cup cracker crumbs
Dash pepper
2 slightly beaten eggs
½ cup milk

Blend brown sugar, mustard and vinegar; set aside. Combine remaining ingredients. Add half of brown sugar mixture; mix well. Shape into a loaf in 10" x 6" x 1½" baking dish. Pour remaining brown sugar mixture over loaf. Bake at 350° for 1¼ hours. Serves 6 to 8.

Mrs. Peter S. White

VIRGINIA HAM

Ham
Water

Vinegar
Brown sugar
Bread crumbs

Soak a Virginia ham in cold water to cover for 24 hours. Remove and drain. Scrub with a mixture of vinegar and water. Place in a ham boiler or roasting pan, fat side up, cover with water, and simmer about 20 minutes per pound, until small bone in hock comes out easily or until ham pierces easily with a sharp point. Remove from water and skin it. Pat a mixture of equal parts brown sugar and bread crumbs over it and brown in the oven.

Mrs. Robert Lawson, Jr.

LAMB CASSEROLE

2 cups cooked and cubed lamb
1 (4 ounce) can mushrooms
2 cups meat stock
1 (16 ounce) can tomatoes
2 cups chopped onions

Salt and pepper
3 tablespoons butter
½ cup raw rice
2 tablespoons Worcestershire
  sauce

Heat lamb, mushrooms, stock, tomatoes, and onions for 15 minutes over low heat. Do not boil. Season with salt and pepper. Brown rice in frying pan with butter. Combine rice and lamb mixture in buttered casserole. Bake, covered, at 350° for 40 minutes or more. Serves 4 to 5.

LAMB SHOULDER WITH HERBS

1 lamb shoulder
2 tablespoons chervil
1 teaspoon basil
½ teaspoon ginger

2 tablespoons marjoram
2 tablespoons lemon juice
1 tablespoon prepared mustard
1 tablespoon flour

Place lamb in oven at 450° for about 30 minutes. Reduce heat to 350°. Combine remaining ingredients and pat over roast. Cover tightly and roast for 3 hours. Serves 4 to 5.

Mrs. James Harvey Hammons

LEG OF LAMB

Leg of lamb
Salt and pepper
Worcestershire sauce

Flour
2 cups water
1 medium yellow onion, sliced

Trim lamb and sprinkle with Worcestershire sauce, salt, pepper, and flour. Pour water in roasting pan and put the lamb in it. Cover pan. Place in 500° oven for 30 minutes. Reduce the heat to 350° and put the onion over the lamb. Continue baking for 3½ hours. Baste and/or add water as needed.

Miss Sallie Jefferds

LEG OF LAMB A LA PROVENCE

1 pound dried navy pea beans
2 cloves garlic
¼ cup butter
2 pounds onions, sliced
2 teaspoons seasoned salt
½ teaspoon salt

¼ teaspoon pepper
1 teaspoon rosemary
2 pounds Italian style
   tomatoes, undrained
7 pound leg of lamb
Chopped parsley

In 6-quart kettle, combine beans with 6 cups water. Bring to boil and simmer 2 minutes. Let stand 1 hour. Drain beans, saving liquid. Add additional water to reserved liquid to measure 2 quarts. Return beans and liquid to kettle and bring to boil. Reduce heat and cook until beans are tender. Drain.
Preheat oven to 325°. Crush 1 clove garlic. In hot butter in large skillet, sauté onion and garlic until golden. In shallow pan combine beans, onion, seasoned salt, salt, pepper, rosemary, and tomatoes. Mix well. Split remaining clove of garlic and rub over lamb. Sprinkle lamb lightly with seasoned salt and rosemary. Place leg on beans and insert meat thermometer. Roast, uncovered, 3 to 3½ hours.

To serve, remove lamb to serving platter. Turn beans into serving dish and top with chopped parsley. Serves 10.

Mrs. William E. McClellan

MOTHER'S ROGEN JOSH

3 medium onions
1 two-inch piece of ginger or
  1 teaspoon ground ginger
2 tablespoons cooking oil
2 pounds lamb, cubed
1 teaspoon salt
¼ teaspoon garlic powder or 1
  garlic bud, minced

½ teaspoon red chili powder
½ teaspoon turmeric powder
1 teaspoon garam masola
  (cinnamon, cloves, nutmeg)
½ teaspoon coriander, crushed
1 cup yogurt
1 (16 ounce) can tomatoes,
  chopped

Cut the onions and ginger finely. Heat the oil and slowly brown the ginger and onions. The secret of Indian cooking is to brown the spices and onion slowly. Push the onions and ginger to side of pan. Add meat, salt, garlic, turmeric, chili, garam masola, and coriander, and stir for 2 minutes. Add yogurt and the canned tomatoes. Put into a greased casserole. Cook in a 325° oven for 3 hours. Serves 4 to 6. Good served with rice and green peas.

Mrs. John C. Steven

KAPAMA — SPRING LAMB WITH LETTUCE

A Turkish Recipe

Mary Lee Settle, a native of Charleston, is the author of many successful novels, the newest one being **Prisons**. *Research for her next novel was done in Bodrun, Turkey. Miss Settle has been on the faculty of Bard College, Rhinebeck, N.Y., for a number of years. Among her books with West Virginia themes are* **Know Nothing, O Beulah Land, The Kiss of Kin, The Love Eaters,** *and* **Fight Night on a Sweet Saturday.**

1 large bunch green onions
  with tops
1 carrot
4 large heads lettuce (cos or
  garden, but not iceberg)
4 to 5 pounds lamb neck,
  shank, shoulder, bone and
  all

1 lemon
3 tablespoons butter
1 teaspoon sugar
  Salt
1 cup water
1 bunch fresh dill, chopped

Chop the onions with tops and the carrot, and lay across the bottom of a large heavy casserole. Chop the lettuce and layer over the onions and carrot; it will melt down. Cut the lamb into three-inch chunks; rub with a piece of lemon and place over lettuce. Add the rest of the ingredients, except for the dill. Bake at 250° until the meat is tender, about 2 hours. Test for doneness. Add dill and cook five minutes longer. Serve with hot bread. Use only the cheap cuts of lamb for this dish; the leg is too expensive.

Mary Lee Settle

ANISE PORK ROAST

1 pork roast (3 to 5 pounds)
Salt and pepper
3 tablespoons minced parsley
1 or 2 cloves garlic, minced
Flour

1 cup chicken stock, or 2
   chicken bouillon cubes in 1
   cup boiling water
1 tablespoon anise seed
½ cup white wine

Season the roast with salt and pepper, and cut 5 or more deep gashes in it. Fill these with a combination of parsley and minced garlic cloves. Rub well with flour and put into a 350° oven for 30 minutes. During that time, make a baste of the stock, wine, and anise seed. Simmer it all for 15 minutes. At the end of the 30 minutes in the oven, reduce the heat of the oven to 325°, and cook for 40 minutes to the pound, basting every 15 or 20 minutes. If roast begins to become dry in the last hour of cooking, it may be covered with foil.

Mrs. E. Charles Brod

CASSOULET

1 (1 pound) package dried
   white Great Northern
   beans
2 quarts water
4 garlic cloves, divided
4 cups sliced onion, divided
4 parsley sprigs
2 tablespoons salt, divided
4 whole cloves
½ pound sliced bacon, cut into
   1″ pieces

2 pounds lean pork, cut into
   1″ pieces or 2 pounds boned
   chicken cut in large chunks
2 (10½ ounces each) cans condensed beef broth, undiluted
1½ cups tomato pureé
1 teaspoon thyme
3 bay leaves
1 pound Polish sausage
½ cup dry white wine

Bring the water to boiling in a 4-quart kettle and add beans. Return to boiling point and boil for 2 minutes. Remove from heat; let stand 1 hour. Crush 2 of the garlic cloves, and add to the beans along with 2 cups of the onion, parsley sprigs, 1 of the tablespoons of salt, and cloves. Bring to a boil; reduce heat and simmer, covered, for 1½ hours. Drain. Remove cloves and discard.

Meanwhile in a large skillet, sauté bacon until crisp. Remove bacon and set aside; pour off drippings. Return 2 tablespoons of the drippings to the skillet and brown pork or chicken on all sides. Remove and set aside. Crush the remaining 2 garlic cloves; add them with the remaining 2 cups of onion to skillet and sauté until golden, about 5 minutes. Return bacon and pork to skillet. (If using chicken, do not add until the final baking step because it will cook to shreds.) Add 1 tablespoon salt, beef broth, tomato purée, thyme, and bay leaves to meat mixture and bring to a boil. Reduce heat; simmer, covered, for 1½ hours. Remove bay leaves and discard.

While the pork is cooking, make cuts in sausage in several places to prevent curling or cut sausage into 2″ lengths. Cook in boiling water for 30 minutes.

Add drained beans and the wine to meat mixture. Turn into a 3-quart casserole and top with sausage. Bake, uncovered, at 350° for 1 hour. Stir beans before serving. If prepared ahead, refrigerate and heat, covered, at 350° until hot and bubbly, about 1½ hours. Serves 8 to 10.

Mrs. H. L. Snyder, Jr.

CHINESE PORK

1½ pounds lean pork, cut into julienne strips
2 tablespoons oil
2 onions, sliced thin
3 cups chicken broth
1 teaspoon salt
1 cup julienne cut strips green pepper

2 cups shredded Chinese cabbage (sometimes called Chinese celery)
1 cup diagonally sliced celery
1 (1 pound) can bean sprouts, drained
2 tablespoons diced pimiento
3 tablespoons cornstarch
3 tablespoons soy sauce

Brown meat strips in oil in hot (340°) skillet. Add onions; cook 5 minutes. Reduce heat to simmer, add broth and salt. Cover and cook 20 minutes. Add vegetables and bring to boil. Make paste of cornstarch and soy sauce. Add immediately and cook until thick. Serve over rice. Serves 4 to 6.

Mrs. Jon Michael Gaston

COTES DE PORC A LA SAUCE NENETTE

(Pork chops with mustard, cream, and tomato sauce)

6 well-trimmed pork chops
1½ cups whipping cream
¼ teaspoon salt
Pinch of pepper

1 tablespoon dry mustard
2 tablespoons tomato paste
2 tablespoons fresh chopped parsley or 1 teaspoon of dried chervil or basil

While the pork chops are baking at 325° in an uncovered casserole or baking pan, prepare the sauce as follows: simmer the cream, salt, and pepper in a small saucepan for 8 to 10 minutes, or until it has reduced to 1 cup. Beat the mustard and tomato paste together in a small bowl; then beat in the hot cream; set aside.

After removing the chops from the casserole and degreasing the meat juices, pour in the cream mixture and simmer for 3 or 4 minutes. Season to taste; stir in the herbs, and pour the sauce over the chops. Serve on hot plates. Serves 4 to 6.

Mrs. Thomas P. O'Brien

"In my growing up years, we ate Chinese food often and one dish that Mother enjoyed most was:

FRESH FRIED SWEET — SOUR PORK RIBS"

Pearl S. Buck, author of numerous novels and short stories, is one of the outstanding figures in literature of our century. She was born Pearl Sydenstricker in Hillsboro, West Virginia, in 1892. Miss Buck is the only American woman to be awarded both the Pulitzer and Nobel Prizes for literature; **The Good Earth** *won for her the Pulitzer Prize in 1932, and she was presented the Nobel Prize in 1938. As an infant, Miss Buck was taken to China by her missionary parents, and there she spent most of her life until 1933. Living in the Orient provided her with the firsthand experience on which she drew for much of her writing. Today the Pearl Buck Birthplace Museum at Hillsboro commemorates the late author.*

3 pounds pork ribs, 1 inch long	5 tablespoons sugar
5 tablespoons cooking oil	4 tablespoons soy sauce
4 tablespoons vinegar	½ teaspoon salt
2 heaping tablespoons cornstarch	1 cup water

Each bit of rib should have both bone and meat. Heat oil in skillet and fry ribs for 10 minutes. Take out the ribs and pour off the oil except for 1 tablespoonful. Mix the vinegar, cornstarch, sugar, soy sauce, salt, and water in a bowl and pour into skillet. Cook, constantly stirring, until it becomes clear. Then put the ribs back into the skillet with this sauce and simmer on a very low flame for about 10 more minutes. Green or red peppers can be added, or a half can of pineapple tidbits or sweet pickles. Of course, this dish is served with rice and vegetables of one's own choosing.

Mrs. Joseph Lippincott
Daughter of Pearl Buck

LAYERED PORK CHOP CASSEROLE

6 medium pork chops, fat
trimmed
5 tablespoons flour,
seasoned with 1 teaspoon
salt and ¼ teaspoon pepper
1 tablespoon shortening or
butter
½ cup raw rice
6 teaspoons Dijon mustard

2 ripe tomatoes, thinly sliced
1 (10½ ounce) can consommé
½ cup sherry
⅛ teaspoon marjoram
⅛ teaspoon thyme
1 large onion, sliced thin
(optional)
1 small green pepper, cut in
rings (optional)

Dredge chops in seasoned flour and brown in butter. While browning, put rice in bottom of a buttered 8" x 11" baking dish. Layer chops on rice and spread each with a teaspoon of mustard. Top with tomatoes. Add consommé, sherry, marjoram, and thyme. Cover and bake at 350° for 1 hour. Check toward end of baking time, and add a little water, if needed, to make a sauce of good browned juices. Serves 6.

Mrs. G. Thomas Battle

PIG IN THE BLANKET

After performing as an outstanding player for Morris Harvey College in Charleston, West Virginia, and later in professional basketball, George S. King entered the field of coaching. He has led teams at Morris Harvey College, West Virginia University, and Purdue University. Currently, he is the athletic director at Purdue.

Medium head cabbage
½ cup uncooked rice
1 pound pork sausage
Salt and pepper to taste

1 (16 ounce) can sauerkraut
1 (16 ounce) can tomatoes
6 or 7 lean pork chops

Wash and place cabbage leaves in boiling water for 5 minutes and drain. Mix sausage and rice; roll up in cabbage leaves; fasten with toothpick. Place rolls in bottom of large pan in a nest of extra cabbage leaves. Brown pork chops. Pour tomatoes and sauerkraut over cabbage rolls; then add browned pork chops. (Liquid should cover it.) Salt and pepper to taste. Cook 4 hours over low heat, covered tightly. Serves 6.

George S. King

PORK CHOPS AND SPINACH

4 thick pork chops
1 (20 ounce) can tiny new
  potatoes
2 packages fresh or thawed
  frozen spinach, chopped
2 tablespoons butter

2 tablespoons flour
Salt and pepper, to taste
¼ teaspoon nutmeg
1 cup milk
Grated cheese

Sauté the pork chops and new potatoes in the fat from the chops. Mix the potatoes with the chopped spinach in the bottom of a low, buttered casserole. Place pork chops on top. Make a cream sauce by melting the butter, blending in the flour, and adding the seasonings and milk very slowly. Cook and stir until smooth and thickened. Pour over chops and sprinkle grated cheese on top. Bake at 375° for 50 minutes. Serves 4.

Mrs. Henry W. Battle, III

STUFFED PORK CHOPS — BURGUNDY SAUCE

6 double-thick pork chops
3 tablespoons butter
1 tablespoon minced onion
½ cup chopped mushrooms
1 clove garlic, minced
¼ green pepper, chopped
¼ cup shortening

Salt, pepper, paprika,
  cayenne, to taste
8 slices bacon, fried, drained,
  and crumbled
½ cup cooked rice
Paprika

Melt butter in skillet. Add onion, mushrooms, garlic, and green pepper. Cook 5 minutes over low heat. Remove from heat. Add seasonings, bacon, and rice. Mix well. Stuff into pockets which have been slit in chops. Dust chops with paprika. Place in a baking dish. Heat shortening and pour over chops. Bake, uncovered, at 325° for 1½ hours, basting frequently. Serves 4 to 6. Serve with Burgundy sauce.

BURGUNDY SAUCE

2 tablespoons butter
3 tablespoons flour
1½ cups canned beef broth,
  undiluted
¼ cup Burgundy

1 tablespoon sherry
½ teaspoon Worcestershire
1 tablespoon currant jelly
⅛ teaspoon pepper
1 teaspoon Kitchen Bouquet

Melt butter in saucepan. Stir in flour. Slowly add beef broth. Simmer until thickened. Add remaining ingredients; stir well and simmer 5 minutes. Makes about 2 cups.

Mrs. Neil Robinson, II

SUPREME PORK CHOPS

4 lean pork chops, ½ inch thick
¼ teaspoon salt
¼ teaspoon pepper or paprika
1 tablespoon shortening
¾ cup water
½ cup finely cut celery
1 envelope dried onion soup mix
1 (4 ounce) can mushroom stems and pieces
¼ cup flour
1 tablespoon dried parsley flakes
⅔ cup evaporated milk (1 small can)

Sprinkle the chops with salt and pepper. Brown the chops on both sides in shortening in a skillet over medium heat. Drain off the drippings and stir in the water, celery, and onion soup mix. Cover and cook over low heat for 30 minutes, or until the chops are tender. Remove the skillet from heat. Stir together the mushrooms and the flour. Move the chops to one side in the skillet. Stir the flour and mushroom mixture, the parsley flakes, and the evaporated milk into the liquid in the pan. Place over low heat and stir until steaming, but do not boil. Serves 4. Serve with 3 cups of steamed rice or with buttered noodles.

Mrs. Frederick H. Morgan

SWEET AND SOUR PORK

SAUCE

2 slices pineapple, cut in small pieces, or 8 slices sweet pickle, chopped
Cooking oil
¼ teaspoon ginger
2 tablespoons vinegar
5 teaspoons sugar
1 teaspoon catsup
1 teaspoon brandy
1 tablespoon cornstarch
1½ teaspoons soy sauce
1 cup water
¼ cup green onion, shredded lengthwise

Fry pineapple in oil; sprinkle with ginger. Mix vinegar, sugar, catsup, brandy, cornstarch, soy sauce, and water; stir into pineapple and simmer 5 minutes. Pour over deep-fried meat. Garnish with onion and serve over steamed rice. Serves 4. Good also with fried rice.

MEAT

1 pound lean pork shoulder
1 egg, lightly beaten
Salt
Cornstarch
Cooking oil

Cut pork into ¾" cubes. Lightly salt each piece, dip in egg, and then in cornstarch. Let dry 10 minutes. Deep fry in hot oil; cubes sink and then rise when done.

Variation: May add 1 (10 ounce) package frozen pea pods which have been lightly cooked, 2 carrots sliced on the diagonal and cooked until crisp-tender, and 1 (8 ounce) can drained bamboo shoots. Add these ingredients to the meat and pour sauce over. Double the sauce recipe, and prepare ½ to 1 pound more meat when using this variation. Serves 8.

Mrs. G. T. Weaks

BREAKFAST SAUSAGE BALLS

2 tablespoons concentrated
    orange juice
2 tablespoons maple syrup
4 slices of bread

1 egg, slightly beaten
½ pound mild bulk sausage
½ cup finely chopped roasted
    pecans

2 tablespoons parsley flakes

Break up bread in orange juice and maple syrup. Add egg and mix thoroughly. Blend in remaining ingredients. Make into small sausage balls about 1 inch in diameter or into patties. Fry slowly in a skillet or griddle over medium heat until browned.

May be served as a hors d'oeuvre or accompaniment to macaroni for a family supper. Can be made ahead and frozen after cooking. Reheat in a warm oven before serving. Makes 4 to 6 patties or 12 to 16 sausage balls.

Mrs. Steven Thomas, III

SAUSAGE APPLE RING

2 pounds bulk sausage
1½ cups cracker crumbs
2 eggs, slightly beaten

½ cup milk
¼ cup minced onion
1⅓ cups chopped apples

Apricot halves as garnish

Combine all ingredients and mix thoroughly. Press lightly into a greased 6 cup mold, and then unmold into a shallow pan. (Do not cook in the mold.) Bake at 350° for 30 minutes. Drain off fat, and bake 30 minutes longer. This recipe may be partly cooked the preceding day. Serves 10 to 12. Garnish with apricot halves and serve with cheese-scrambled eggs.

Mrs. H. D. Tallman

SAUSAGE DUMPLINGS

1 pound sausage

2 medium onions, chopped

Your favorite recipe
for pie crust

Make sausage into 12 balls and brown; cook thoroughly. Wrap balls in dough made from pie crust. Bake at 400° for 10 minutes. While baking, sauté onions until brown in sausage grease. Add flour and water to make gravy. Pour gravy over dumplings and serve.

Mrs. Carl B. Hall, Jr.

ROGNONS DE VEAU FLAMBES
Veal Kidneys flamed in brandy

3 veal kidneys, peeled and
   trimmed of fat
8 tablespoons butter, divided
⅓ cup cognac
½ cup brown sauce or canned
   beef bouillon
1 teaspoon cornstarch
⅓ cup Madeira

½ pound sliced, fresh
   mushrooms
1 cup whipping cream
1 tablespoon minced shallots
   Salt and pepper
½ tablespoon prepared Dijon
   mustard
½ teaspoon Worcestershire
   sauce

Using a fireproof casserole, cook the kidneys for about 10 minutes or longer in 4 tablespoons hot butter, until done. Pour the cognac over the kidneys and flame. Shake the casserole and baste the kidneys for a few seconds until the flames have subsided. Remove the kidneys to a hot plate and cover them. Mix the brown sauce or bouillon, cornstarch, and the Madeira and pour into the casserole. Boil for a few minutes until reduced and thickened. Sauté the mushrooms and shallots in 2 tablespoons butter. Stir the cream and mushrooms into the kidney sauce and boil a few minutes more. Sauce should be thick enough to coat the spoon lightly. Season to taste with salt and pepper. Blend the mustard, 2 tablespoons butter, and Worcestershire sauce. Off heat, swirl the mustard-butter into the sauce. Rapidly cut the kidneys into crosswise slices ⅛" thick. Season with salt and pepper and put them and their juices into the sauce. Shake and toss the kidneys over low heat for a moment to reheat them without bringing the sauce near the simmer. Serve immediately on hot plates. May be served on a bed of rice. Serves 4.

Mrs. Thomas P. O'Brien

SAUCY VEAL CHOPS

4 to 6 veal chops
½ cup dry bread crumbs or flour
1 teaspoon salt
2 tablespoons butter or margarine
1 cup water, divided

1 package (⅝ ounce) Pillsbury brown gravy mix
1 (5 ounce) can water chestnuts, drained and sliced
1 cup fresh mushrooms or 1 (4 ounce) can mushrooms, drained

Coat chops with bread crumbs and sprinkle with salt. In large fry pan, brown chops in butter until deep brown. Add ½ cup of the water and cover. Reduce heat and simmer for 10 minutes. Combine gravy mix and remaining ½ cup water in measuring cup. Add gravy mixture, mushrooms, and water chestnuts to chops. Continue simmering, covered, for 10 to 15 minutes, until meat is tender. Serve with gravy. Serves 4 to 6.

Miss Jane Mathews

STUFFED BREAST OF VEAL

5 pound breast of veal
1 pound sausage
2 cups chopped apple
4 tablespoons chopped onion
1 teaspoon salt

Dash pepper
1½ cups hot water
2 cups soft bread crumbs
2 cups medium cracker crumbs
Bacon slices

Have the butcher bone and prepare a breast of veal. Sauté sausage; add chopped apples and onion; cook until soft. Season with salt and pepper. Add hot water to bread crumbs and crackers. Mix well and add seasoned sausage, apples, and onion. Use this mixture to stuff the breast of veal. Lay bacon slices over the top. Bake at 325° for 2 hours. Serves 6.

Mrs. Robert W. Lawson, Jr.

VEAL CHOPS IN WINE

4 veal loin chops, 1¼ inches thick (about 2½ pounds)
8 tablespoons butter or margarine, divided
¼ cup flour
1 teaspoon salt
⅛ teaspoon pepper
1 teaspoon tarragon
1 teaspoon snipped chives
1 teaspoon liquid gravy seasoning

¾ cup dry white wine, approximately
1 (10½ ounce) can condensed beef bouillon
½ pound fresh mushrooms, sliced
2 tablespoons lemon juice
½ cup sliced onion
1 clove garlic, crushed

Trim excess fat from chops. If the chops have tails, secure the tails to the chop with a toothpick. Wipe chops with damp paper towel; set aside. Melt 4 tablespoons margarine in medium saucepan; remove from heat. Stir in flour, salt pepper, tarragon, chives, and gravy seasoning. Add enough wine to bouillon to measure 2 cups. Gradually stir into flour mixture. Bring just to boiling, stirring occasionally. Remove from heat and set aside.

Toss mushrooms with lemon juice. Sauté mushrooms in 1 tablespoon margarine for about 5 minutes; set aside.

Heat remaining margarine in a heavy skillet with cover. Brown chops on both sides. Move chops to the side of the skillet. Add onion and garlic; sauté until golden. Add ½ cup wine gravy and the mushrooms to skillet; simmer, covered, 30 minutes or until chops are tender. (More wine gravy may have to be added during cooking.) Place chops on platter and remove wooden picks. Stir any remaining wine gravy into skillet, mixing well; reheat. Spoon mushrooms and some of the gravy over chops. Pass rest of gravy. Makes 4 servings. May be prepared ahead and reheated.

Mrs. Charles G. Moyers, Jr.

VEAL LOAF

1 pound veal round steak	2 to 3 tablespoons
2 to 3 stalks celery	mayonnaise
Water	1 cup veal stock
3 hard cooked eggs,	1 envelope unflavored
chopped finely	gelatin
1 medium onion, or green	Salt and pepper to taste
onions chopped finely	

Cook veal round steak with celery stalks in water until very tender. When done, reserve liquid and grind meat. Add eggs and green onions. Mix all with mayonnaise. Mix 1 cup of reserved stock with gelatin which has been dissolved in cold water. Mix all together. Season with salt and pepper. Mold in a loaf pan and serve chilled, sliced thinly. Serves 8 to 10.

Mrs. Robert W. Lawson, Jr.

VEAL ROMANO

4 (1½ ounces each) slices	Bread crumbs
veal per serving	Butter
Flour	Juice of ½ lemon
1 egg, beaten	Lemon wedges

Dredge the veal in flour; dip in egg and press firmly in bread crumbs until well coated. Sauté over low heat until golden brown and tender. Drain excess butter. Squeeze juice of ½ lemon over veal while hot. Serve at once with lemon wedges.

Ernie's Esquire Supper Club

VEAL STEAK WITH SOUR CREAM

¼ cup flour
1 teaspoon salt
1 teaspoon paprika
½ teaspoon poultry seasoning
¼ teaspoon pepper
1½ to 2½ pounds veal steak,
    cut in serving pieces

2 tablespoons fat
1 cup soft bread crumbs
2 tablespoons butter, melted
½ cup Parmesan cheese
¼ cup sesame seeds, toasted
¼ cup hot water
1 recipe sour cream sauce

Combine first 5 dry ingredients. Dredge meat in flour and seasonings. Brown in hot fat (reserve drippings) and arrange meat in 10" x 6" baking dish. Combine crumbs, butter, cheese, and sesame seeds and spoon over meat. Stir water into meat drippings and pour around the meat. Bake at 350° about 50 minutes. Serve with the following sauce.

SOUR CREAM SAUCE

1 (10½ ounce) can condensed
    cream of chicken soup

½ teaspoon monosodium glutamate
1 cup sour cream

Heat and stir soup. Add monosodium glutamate and blend in sour cream. Pour sauce over meat. Serves 6.

Mrs. Charles Q. Gage

VEAL AND SWEETBREADS

2 pounds veal pieces
Salt

Garlic
Butter

Rub veal with salt and split garlic clove. Sauté in butter for 10 minutes. Place in 300° oven 1 hour to finish cooking. Slice thin and serve with the following sauce.

SAUCE

1 pound sweetbreads
½ pound mushrooms
2 tablespoons butter

2 tablespoons flour
2 cups light cream
¼ cup sherry

Parboil sweetbreads and mushrooms for 30 minutes. Melt butter; add flour and stir until bubbly. Add cream and stir constantly until thickened. Add sweetbreads, mushrooms, and sherry. Pour over veal. Serves 6.

Mrs. Robert W. Lawson, Jr.

BEEF - SLAW SANDWICH

6 (¼ inch thick) slices
   cooked beef
Butter

6 (½ inch thick) slices home-
   made French bread,
   buttered

Place meat on bread and top with slaw (below).
When no cooked beef is on hand, marinate a 1½ inch thick round steak roast in an oil and vinegar dressing for 24 hours; grill the meat, and slice very thinly across the grain. 3 or 4 slices overlapping slightly are then needed.

SLAW

1 cup shredded cabbage
½ cup grated carrot
2 tablespoons chopped onion

¼ cup mayonnaise
¼ teaspoon curry powder
Sliced ripe olives, for garnish

Mix all ingredients well.

Mrs. Ronald A. McKenney

HAM BARBECUE

2 small onions, finely
   chopped
1 small green pepper,
   finely chopped
3 to 4 stalks celery,
   finely chopped

2 tablespoons cooking oil
1 (10½ ounce) can tomato soup
½ cup chili sauce
3 tablespoons brown sugar
Dash Worcestershire sauce
¾ to 1 pound shaved ham

Sauté onion, green pepper, celery in the oil until browned. Drain. Add the remaining ingredients and simmer until heated through. Serve on hamburger buns. Serves 8 to 10.

Mrs. Craig M. Wilson

HAM AND CHEESE BUNS WITH SAUCE

SAUCE

⅓ pound butter or margarine   1 tablespoon poppy seeds
1 small onion, chopped

Melt butter; add poppy seeds and onion.

SANDWICHES

3 seeded hamburger buns   Sliced baked ham
Sliced Swiss cheese

Spread sauce on inside of each bun. Place a layer of ham and cheese on one side of each bun, add more sauce, and top with the other half of the bun. Put more sauce over all, and bake at 350° until hot, about 10 to 15 minutes. Serves 3.

Can be made ahead and wrapped individually in foil, but remember to heat longer.

Mrs. Robert F. Goldsmith

HOT HAM SALAD SANDWICHES

1 cup salad dressing	6 hard-cooked eggs, diced
¼ cup chili sauce	½ cup scallions or green onions
2 cups diced ham	½ cup sliced stuffed olives

Hot dog or hamburger buns

Mix salad dressing and chili sauce, then mix with the rest of the ingredients. Fill buns; wrap each in foil; and bake at 400° for 20 to 30 minutes. Serves 8.

Mrs. Kenneth Underwood

HOT PASTRAMI SANDWICHES

1½ cups sauerkraut	6 slices rye bread, toasted
1 tablespoon caraway seed	1 pound pastrami, salami, or
½ cup mayonnaise	corned beef, sliced and
1 tablespoon horseradish	divided in sixths

6 slices tomato

Simmer sauerkraut and caraway seed for 30 minutes. Drain. Mix mayonnaise and horseradish and spread on toasted bread. Top with pastrami and drained kraut. Place a slice of tomato on this and broil 5 inches from heat for 5 minutes or until tomato is cooked.

Mrs. Ronald A. McKenney

PIMIENTO BURGERS

1½ pounds ground beef	½ cup finely chopped onion
1 (6 ounce) can evaporated milk	1 tablespoon prepared mustard
	1 teaspoon salt
1 egg	¼ teaspoon pepper
½ cup cracker crumbs	1 (5 ounce) jar of pimento
½ cup finely chopped green pepper	cheese spread, at room temperature

Hamburger buns

Mix all ingredients except pimiento cheese spread. Spread the mixture on a piece of waxed paper 12 inches square. Spread the cheese on meat mixture. Roll up like a jelly roll. Cut into 1-inch slices. Broil about 5 minutes on each side or until brown. Serve on warm hamburger buns with mustard or mayonnaise.

Mrs. William C. Payne

BARBECUE SAUCE

¼ cup vinegar
½ cup water
1 tablespoon prepared
   mustard
1 teaspoon sugar
½ teaspoon pepper
1½ teaspoons salt

¼ teaspoon cayenne pepper
1 thick slice of lemon
1 medium onion, sliced
¼ cup margarine
½ cup catsup
2 tablespoons Worcestershire
   sauce

Simmer everything together except the catsup and Worcestershire sauce for 20 minutes. Add the catsup and Worcestershire and boil for 1 minute. May be used to baste chicken or pour over shredded roast beef.

Mrs. Charles M. Love, III

BEEF MARINADE

3 tablespoons oil
¾ cup catsup
¼ cup white vinegar
   Heaping tablespoon salt
5 to 6 tablespoons sugar

1 tablespoon Worcestershire
   sauce
4 tablespoons A-1 sauce
¼ teaspoon Tabasco sauce
¼ teaspoon garlic powder

Mix all ingredients. Soak meat overnight. Grill meat until done, basting with remaining marinade. Good on steaks, shish kabobs, English roast, etc.

Mrs. Fred L. Kellmeyer

FLANK STEAK MARINADE

⅓ cup catsup
⅓ cup chili sauce
½ cup water
⅓ cup lemon juice
1 teaspoon celery seed

2 tablespoons Worcestershire
   sauce
1 bay leaf
½ teaspoon pepper
¼ teaspoon basil

Combine all ingredients. Pour over flank steak. Cover and let stand 6 to 8 hours. Broil flank steak 10 minutes on each side, basting with marinade. Slice steak across grain into thin strips to serve.

Mrs. Craig M. Wilson

HAM DISGUISE

Mustard Sauce for Ham

2 eggs, beaten	1½ tablespoons flour
½ cup dark brown sugar	¼ cup dry mustard
½ cup strong consommé	½ cup cider vinegar

In top of double boiler (no heat), mix beaten eggs, sugar, and consommé. Slowly add flour, mustard, and vinegar. Heat water to boiling and stir constantly until thick and smooth. Serve hot on ham (or dilute with mayonnaise and serve cold). It will keep in refrigerator for a long time. Also a good hot sauce for oriental dishes.

Mrs. Robert W. Lawson, III

LAMB SAUCE

1 heaping tablespoon flour	½ cup tart jelly (currant)
½ cup catsup	½ cup lamb stock drippings
½ cup sherry (regular, not cooking)	

Stir flour into a small amount of catsup; stir in remainder of catsup to form a smooth paste. Add jelly and stock. Heat until jelly is melted, stirring frequently. Before serving, add sherry.

Mrs. Thomas McMillan

MINT SAUCE

½ cup fresh mint leaves, finely chopped	3 tablespoons sugar
	⅔ cup white vinegar

Add sugar and vinegar to chopped mint leaves and let stand until sugar is dissolved. Strain and add a drop of green food coloring, if desired. Place in a cruet and serve with lamb as a meat sauce. May be refrigerated and kept indefinitely.

Mrs. H. O. Melton

SAWMILL GRAVY OR DOUGH SOP

Billy Edd Wheeler, playwright, poet, songwriter, and performer, grew up in the coal mining town of Highcoal, West Virginia, a town he often fictionalizes for the setting of his works. In addition to writing several country music hits such as "Jackson," Mr. Wheeler has had many plays produced. His outdoor musical drama, The Hatfields and the McCoys, which plays at Beckley, West Virginia, is highly acclaimed.
Mr. Wheeler writes that he was "raised on milk gravy. It will stick to your ribs better than anything I know. (Some people who were poor growing up remember this gravy without the milk.) We were poor, but fortunately we had the milk for it. We'd have it several times a week for breakfast, sometimes with fried potatoes. We had eggs only once or maybe twice a week." The method for the milk gravy, he says, was obtained from his grandfather, who made it on the caboose when he worked for the C & O Railway.

Bacon grease	Evaporated milk
Flour	Salt
Water	Lots of pepper
	Biscuits

Leave a good amount of bacon grease in the skillet, along with any brown cracklings from the bacon itself. Let the skillet stay hot as you sprinkle in the flour. Brown the flour until the skillet almost smokes. When you almost think you've burned the flour, keep stirring it in with the grease. It shouldn't be too thin or too thick. Only practice can tell you how much flour to put in.

Then add water, cutting down the heat slightly. Stir vigorously, mixing the water into the browned flour and grease, until it is quite thin. It will take a lot more water than you think. When you've got a pretty good stand of gravy mixed, add the evaporated milk; stir it in well; add some salt and a lot of pepper; then let it simmer until it gets back to the thickness you want. Surprisingly, it doesn't take it but a minute or two.

Pour it on your hot biscuits and stand back. They'll be ripping the pan up to get at it.

Billy Edd Wheeler

AURORA FONDUE SAUCE

8 tablespoons mayonnaise	Pepper
1 tablespoon catsup	Worcestershire sauce
	1 tablespoon cognac

Mix all ingredients and serve cold.

Mrs. Edward L. Sherwood

FONDUE SAUCE ROYALE

1 cup sour cream
1 package dry onion soup
   mix
3 egg yolks

1 teaspoon lemon juice
½ teaspoon Worcestershire
   sauce
Pepper

Salt

Mix sour cream and soup. Add egg yolks, lemon juice,Worcestershire sauce, salt and pepper. Cook over low flame; don't boil. Stir and serve cold.

Mrs. Edward L. Sherwood

BLENDER BEARNAISE SAUCE

2 egg yolks
½ tablespoon lemon juice
½ tablespoon tarragon vinegar
⅛ teaspoon salt

½ teaspoon parsley
½ teaspoon bottled onion juice
Dash of cayenne pepper
½ cup butter

Place all ingredients except butter in blender. Heat butter until very hot but not boiling. With blender on, pour butter very slowly in thin stream into blender. This makes a rather thick sauce. Serves 6. Serve with steaks, egg dishes, broiled fish or broiled chicken.

Mrs. Angus E. Peyton

MAKING SHINGLES

"While the church was being raised, several men had cut down a big shingle oak and split shingles from its straight-grained wood. To make shingles the logs were sawed into blocks about two feet long, which, in turn, were split into halves, quarters and eighths. The heart was split out; then the eighths were again split. A tool called a froe was used to split each piece until it was about three-fourths of an inch thick. This piece was again split with the froe, and by careful bending of the thickest of the two pieces the resulting board was a split shingle. Enough shingles were made in a few days to cover the building. They were nailed on with square cut nails, making a roof that would last for years."

Reprinted by permission of William B. Price, from "Brother Heavener Nizel" in **Tales and Lore of the Mountaineers;** Quest Publishing Company; Salem, West Virginia; 1963. Copyright by William B. Price. Page 25.

Photo by Gerald S. Ratliff

FOWL AND GAME

Turkey Tracks

BREAST OF CHICKEN ALOHA

Nestled in the Appalachian Mountains at White Sulphur Springs, West Virginia, is the world-renowned Greenbrier Hotel. Gourmet dining at its best is an outstanding feature of this luxurious hotel, a vacation spot for many of our Presidents.

2 breasts of chicken
½ teaspoon salt
½ teaspoon allspice
½ teaspoon pepper
½ cup coconut milk, divided
   (see method below)
½ cup shredded coconut

2 eggs
½ cup clarified butter (see
   method below)
2 pineapple rings, sugar-glazed
   for garnish
1 cup cooked wild rice for
   serving

Season chicken with salt, allspice, and freshly ground pepper, then wet it with coconut milk. Let it settle for a few hours. Toast coconut until light brown. One hour before using, make egg batter of 2 eggs and ⅓ cup of coconut milk. Roll chicken in the toasted coconut, then dip in egg batter, and fry in clarified butter in a skillet until golden brown, approximately 25 minutes. Serves 2.

To make coconut milk: Grate the meat from a quarter of a fresh coconut. Pour 1 cup hot milk over it and let stand 1 hour. Strain through 2 thicknesses of cheesecloth and squeeze dry. Makes 1 cup.

To clarify butter: Melt butter in small pan over low heat. Pour off the clear golden liquid and discard the milky sediment remaining in the pan.

SAUCE FOR CHICKEN ALOHA

1 chicken leg and bones from
   chicken breasts
½ tablespoon paprika
2 tablespoons olive oil
½ cup mushroom stems

1 tablespoon flour
½ cup sour cream
½ cup brown gravy
Salt and, pepper
Lemon juice

Cut leg of chicken and breast bones in pieces. Heat oil with paprika in frying pan; add chicken and cook slowly, covered, for 30 minutes, turning once or twice. Add mushroom stems and cook 10 minutes more. Then add flour, smoothing it in to prevent lumps. Add sour cream and cook slowly — do not let it boil — until juices are well-mixed. Add brown gravy, boil, and season with salt, pepper, and lemon juice. Strain and serve with the breasts.

Serve on silver platter topped with a sugar glazed pineapple ring and garnished with wild rice.

The Greenbrier

BUFFET CHICKEN

2 pounds chicken breasts	2 tablespoons flour
Flour	½ cup water
Cooking oil	½ cup sherry
Salt to taste	½ teaspoon paprika
Pepper to taste	½ teaspoon thyme
Butter	1 teaspoon parsley
1 clove garlic, finely diced	½ can pitted ripe olives, sliced
6 green onions, chopped	1 can consommé
½ cup mushrooms	1 cup sour cream

Bone and skin chicken breasts. Flour lightly and brown in oil. Salt and pepper and place in large casserole. Sauté garlic, onions, and mushrooms in butter until tender but not brown. Add this to the chicken. Make a paste of flour, water, and sherry. Pour over the chicken. Then sprinkle on the paprika, thyme, and parsley. Add olives and pour over all the can of consommé. Bake at 350° until tender, about 40 to 60 minutes. Add the sour cream and heat through. This may be made far ahead and even frozen. Just reheat and stir in the sour cream until heated (do not boil), about 10 minutes. Serve in chafing dish. Serves 4.

Mrs. Hugh G. Thompson, Jr.

CHICKEN BREAST CASSEROLE

4 chicken breasts	2 (10¾ ounces each) cans beef
½ pound mushrooms, sliced	bouillon
1 green pepper, diced	½ cup white wine
1 medium onion, diced	¾ cup raw minute rice

Brown chicken breasts in butter and remove. Brown the mushrooms, onion, and pepper in butter. Place everything in casserole with the chicken breasts on top. Bake in the oven, covered, for 2 hours at 350°. Remove the lid for the last 15 minutes. Serves 4.

Mrs. Thomas H. Edelblute, Jr.

CHICKEN BREASTS IN SOUR CREAM

5 chicken breasts
10 strips bacon (uncooked)
1 package chipped beef
  (thin-dried)

1 (10¾ ounce) can cream soup,
  undiluted (mushroom,
  celery, or cream chicken)
½ pint sour cream

Halve chicken breasts and bone the halves. Wrap each half in a bacon strip and secure with toothpick. Line a greased 9" x 13" x 2" casserole with chipped beef. Combine sour cream and cream soup and pour over chicken which has been placed on beef in casserole. Bake covered at 325° for 2½ hours and uncovered for ½ hour longer. Serves 6 to 8. May use 2 cans of soup and 1 pint of sour cream, if more sauce is desired.

Mrs. Carl Agsten

CHICKEN BREASTS PARMESAN

½ cup pancake mix
¼ teaspoon salt
¼ teaspoon pepper
4 small chicken breasts, split

1 (10¾ ounce) can cream of
  mushroom soup
⅓ cup dry onion soup mix
½ cup milk
½ cup grated Parmesan cheese
Parsley

In a bowl, combine pancake mix, salt, and pepper. Roll chicken breasts in the mixture a few at a time to coat well. Place chicken in a shallow 3 quart baking dish, overlapping slightly, if necessary. Combine mushroom soup, onion soup mix, and milk in a small bowl and blend until smooth. Pour over the chicken. Cover dish tightly with aluminum foil. Bake at 375° for 60 minutes. Remove foil and sprinkle cheese on top. Bake uncovered 15 minutes longer. Garnish with parsley. Serves 6.

Mrs. Andrew R. Quenon

SHERRY — SOUR CREAM CHICKEN BREASTS

4 chicken breasts
1 (3 ounce) can sliced
  mushrooms
1 (10¾ ounce) can cream
  of mushroom soup

½ soup can sherry
1 cup sour cream
Paprika

Arrange chicken in a shallow baking dish. Cover with mushrooms. Combine undiluted soup, sherry, and sour cream. Blend. Pour over chicken, completely covering it; dust with paprika. Bake at 350° for 1½ hours. Serves 4.

Mrs. Leslie Hawker

CHICKEN BREASTS WITH ORANGE SAUCE

3 large whole broiler-fryer
  chicken breasts, halved
1 teaspoon salt, divided
¼ cup butter or margarine
2½ tablespoons flour
2 tablespoons sugar

¼ teaspoon dry mustard
¼ teaspoon cinnamon
¼ teaspoon ginger
1½ cups orange juice
3 cups hot cooked rice
  Parsley, as garnish
Orange slices, as garnish

Sprinkle chicken breasts with ½ teaspoon salt. Brown in butter in skillet; remove. Add flour, sugar, spices, and remaining ½ teaspoon salt to drippings in skillet; stir to smooth paste. Gradually stir in orange juice. Cook, stirring constantly, until mixture thickens and comes to boil. Add chicken breasts and cover. Simmer over low heat until chicken is tender, about 30 to 40 minutes. Remove chicken to serving platter. Serve with hot cooked rice and sauce. Garnish with orange slices and parsley. Serves 6.

Mrs. Thomas J. Blair, III

CHICKEN CASSEROLE

12 chicken breasts
½ cup olive oil
1 stick butter
  Salt to taste
1 small onion, finely chopped

1 small bunch parsley, finely
  chopped
2 heaping tablespoons flour
2 cans consommé
¾ cup tomato juice
¾ cup sherry, divided

Skin and brown chicken in olive oil and butter. Salt to taste. Lay pieces in a large baking dish. Add onion and parsley to remaining oil and fry slightly. Add flour, consommé, tomato juice and ½ cup sherry. Pour over chicken. Cover and bake at 275° for 3 hours. Remove bones; place breasts on mound of wild rice. Add ¼ cup sherry to sauce, then spoon on sauce. (If sauce is too thin, add thickening after removing chicken.) Serves 8 to 10.

Mrs. George R. Heath

CHICKEN DIVAN

4 stalks cooked broccoli
  (do not overcook)
2 tablespoons melted butter

6 tablespoons grated Parmesan
  cheese
7 tablespoons sherry
4 large cooked and boned chicken breasts

Put broccoli into baking dish. Sprinkle with butter, 2 tablespoons Parmesan cheese and 3 tablespoons sherry. Lay chicken breasts over broccoli. Sprinkle with 2 tablespoons cheese and 2 tablespoons sherry. Make cream sauce and pour over the chicken. Sprinkle with 2 more tablespoons cheese and 2 tablespoons sherry. Bake at 350° until delicately brown, about 12 minutes. Serves 3 to 4.

CREAM SAUCE

2 tablespoons butter	Salt and pepper to taste
2 tablespoons flour	2 egg yolks, slightly beaten
1 cup half and half	1 tablespoon whipped cream

Melt the butter in a heavy pan. Stir in the flour. Blend well over low heat. Slowly add half and half, stirring constantly, bringing slowly to the boiling point. Cook 2 minutes. Season to taste with salt and pepper. Stir in slightly beaten egg yolks. Fold in whipped cream.

Mrs. F. Thomas Graff, Jr.

QUICK CHICKEN DIVAN

2 whole chicken breasts	1 tablespoon lemon juice
1 package frozen broccoli, spears or chopped	Dash curry powder
	½ cup shredded Cheddar cheese
1 (10¾ ounce) can cream of chicken soup	Bread crumbs or Pepperidge Farm stuffing mix
½ cup Hellman's mayonnaise	

Simmer the chicken breasts in salted water until tender, about 45 minutes. Let cool in broth. Remove meat from bones. In shallow casserole, place frozen broccoli, separated, with chicken on top. Mix together the soup, mayonnaise, lemon juice, curry, and cheese. Pour the mixture over the chicken and broccoli. Top with bread crumbs and bake at 350° uncovered for 45 minutes.

EASY CHICKEN CASSEROLE

1 (10 ounce) package frozen broccoli	1 (10½ ounce) can cream of chicken soup
½ cup chopped onion	1 (10½ ounce) can cream of mushroom soup
½ cup chopped celery	
1 cup wild rice	1 (4 ounce) jar processed cheese spread
4 chicken breasts, cooked and chopped	

Cook broccoli according to package directions, adding onions and celery while cooking. Drain. Cook rice according to package directions. Cook chicken breasts in salted water. Cook, bone, and chop chicken. In a large casserole, place the rice in layer, next the chicken, and then the broccoli. Mix soups together and pour over the chicken. Drop the cheese spread by spoonfuls over the top. Bake at 350° for 40 minutes. Serves 6.

Mrs. K. Paul Davis

MEXICAN CHICKEN CASSEROLE

5 chicken breasts, boned and cut up
1 dozen tortillas
1 (10¾ ounce) can cream of chicken soup
1 (10¾ ounce) can cream of mushroom soup

2 (7 ounces each) cans green chile salsa
1 cup milk
1 onion, chopped
1 pound sharp Cheddar cheese, grated

Cut tortillas in 1″ squares. Combine all other ingredients except cheese. Butter casserole; layer tortillas, chicken, and soup mixture. Top each layer with grated cheese. Let stand in refrigerator for 24 hours. Bake at 300° for 1½ to 2 hours uncovered. Serves 8. Accompany with a tart fruit salad.

Mrs. John L. Sullivan, Jr.

MOO GOO GAI PAN
Stir-Fried Chicken and Mushrooms

The Continental Key Club in Fairmont, West Virginia, is popular for its intimate dining atmosphere and continental cuisine.

8 tablespoons corn oil or peanut oil
2 green onions, sliced
½ pound fresh mushrooms, sliced

2 whole chicken breasts, boned and sliced
2 tablespoons or more soy sauce
1 teaspoon salt

Have all ingredients ready before beginning. Heat 2 tablespoons oil in a frying pan, wok, or electric skillet. When the oil is very hot, stir-fry the onions and mushrooms for 3 minutes. Remove to a bowl, and add 6 tablespoons more oil to the pan. Stir-fry the chicken until no longer pink, about 5 minutes. Return the mushrooms and onions to the skillet, and add soy sauce and salt to taste. Remove to a plate and serve immediately. Serves 4. Note: The chicken pieces may be marinated for 15 to 30 minutes before frying in a mixture of 1 egg white, 2 teaspoons cornstarch, 2 teaspoons medium-dry sherry, and salt and pepper to taste. This tenderizes the chicken and adds flavor. Sliced water chestnuts and snow peas may be stir-fried with the mushrooms.

Joe Sestito
Continental Key Club

PARTY CHICKEN BAKE

1 tablespoon dry Italian salad
   dressing mix
2 tablespoons butter or
   margarine (melted)
3 whole chicken breasts, split
1 (10½ ounce) can
   mushroom soup

3 ounces cream cheese,
   softened
1 tablespoon chopped chives
⅓ cup sauterne
1 cup instant rice

Reserve ½ teaspoon salad dressing mix. In large skillet combine butter and dressing mix; add chicken and brown slowly until golden. Place in 9" x 13" baking dish. Blend soup, cream cheese, chives, and sauterne. Spoon over chicken. Bake uncovered at 325° for 1 hour. Baste with sauce occasionally. Serve over rice which has been cooked in water to which the reserved ½ teaspoon salad dressing mix has been added.

Mrs. J. Eldon Rucker, Jr.

PARTY CHICKEN — CASSEROLE
Crabmeat Casserole

2 (8 ounce) cans crabmeat
1 cup dry Pepperidge Farm
   Dressing
2 chicken breasts, boned
   and split
   Parsley or pimiento
   strips for color

¼ teaspoon salt
¼ teaspoon pepper
1 (10¾ ounce) can mushroom
   soup
¼ teaspoon paprika

Butter 9" x 9" casserole. Bone crabmeat and place on bottom. Make stuffing according to package directions and place on top of crabmeat. Skin chicken breasts and lay over stuffing. Sprinkle on parsley or pimento and salt and pepper. Add one can mushroom soup, undiluted. Sprinkle with paprika. Bake, uncovered, at 325° for 1½ hours. Serves 4.

Mrs. Siegle Parks

ROLLED CHICKEN BREASTS

3 large chicken breasts,
 boned, skinned, and
 halved or 6 small chicken
 breasts, boned and
 skinned
Salt

6 thin slices boiled ham
6 ounces natural Swiss cheese,
 cut in 6 sticks
¼ cup flour
2 tablespoons butter or
 margarine

Place chicken pieces, boned side up, on cutting board. Working from center out, pound chicken lightly with wooden mallet to make cutlets about ¼ inch thick. Sprinkle with salt. Place a ham slice and a cheese stick on each cutlet. Tuck in sides of each, and roll up as for a jelly roll, pressing to seal well. (Sometimes necessary to use less cheese to get to seal well; otherwise, all the cheese melts and runs out.) Skewer or tie securely. Coat rolls with flour; brown in the butter or margarine. Remove chicken to 11" x 7" x 1½" baking pan.

SAUCE

½ cup water
1 teaspoon chicken-flavored
 gravy base
1 (3 ounce) can broiled sliced
 mushrooms, drained (½
 cup)

⅓ cup sauterne
2 tablespoons flour
½ cup cold water
Toasted sliced almonds

In same skillet, combine water, the gravy base, mushrooms, and wine. Heat, stirring to incorporate any crusty bits from the skillet. Pour mixture over chicken in baking pan. Cover and bake at 350° for approximately 1 hour or until tender. Transfer chicken to warm serving platter. Blend the 2 tablespoons flour with ½ cup cold water. Add to sauce in baking pan. Cook and stir till thickened. Pour a little sauce over chicken; garnish with toasted sliced almonds. Pass remaining sauce. Serves 6.

Mrs. Thomas J. Mewbourne

SOUR CREAM CHICKEN

2 whole chicken breasts,
 halved
Salt and pepper
¼ cup butter
¼ cup chopped onion
1 clove garlic, minced
1 teaspoon paprika

1 package frozen broccoli,
 cooked
4 canned peach halves
1 cup dairy sour cream
¼ cup mayonnaise
2 teaspoons poppy seeds
¼ cup grated Parmesan cheese

Season chicken with salt and pepper. In small skillet, melt butter; add onion and garlic and sauté for a few minutes. Add paprika. Dip chicken in this mixture and coat well. Put in shallow baking dish. Bake in 375° preheated oven for 20 minutes. Cover with foil and bake 10 more minutes. Arrange drained hot broccoli around chicken. Put in peaches. Mix sour cream and mayonnaise and spoon over all. Sprinkle with poppy seeds and Parmesan cheese. Broil low in broiler 6 to 8 minutes.

Mrs. Joseph Moriarty

SWEET AND SOUR CHICKEN

4 chicken breasts, halved, boned, and skinned

½ cup flour with salt and pepper
⅓ cup oil or shortening

Shake chicken in flour; brown both sides well in hot oil. Put in 9" x 13" baking pan. Bake at 350° for 20 minutes.

SAUCE

1 (13 ounce) can chopped pineapple
1¼ cups juice (juice from pineapple plus water)
⅔ cup vinegar
¾ cup sugar

¼ teaspoon ginger
1 chicken bouillon cube
2 tablespoons cornstarch
1 tablespoon soy sauce
1 (10 ounce) can mandarin oranges
½ cup maraschino cherries

Mix all ingredients except pineapple, oranges, and cherries. Boil for 2 minutes, stirring. Pour sauce over chicken. Add pineapple, oranges, and cherries. Baste and bake 20 minutes more. Serves 6. Accompany with rice.

Mrs. Joseph Moriarty

BOURBON CHICKEN

3 chicken breasts, halved and skinned, or mixed pieces of chicken

⅓ cup bourbon
⅓ cup salad oil
¼ cup soy sauce

Place washed, skinned chicken in baking dish, meaty side down. Mix the bourbon, salad oil, and soy sauce. Pour mixture over chicken and marinate for several hours for enhanced flavor. Bake at 350° for 50 minutes. Serves 6. Serve with rice.

Mrs. Henry W. Battle, III

CHICKEN CACCIATORE

1 frying chicken, cut into
    pieces or about 8 pieces
    (breasts, legs, thighs)
2 eggs, beaten
¾ cup bread crumbs
¾ cup Parmesan cheese

1 teaspoon salt
½ teaspoon pepper
½ teaspoon monosodium
    glutamate
2 tablespoons chopped parsley
    or parsley flakes

¼ cup olive oil

Dip the chicken in the eggs and then in the crumb mixture (made by mixing crumbs, cheese, salt, pepper, monosodium glutamate, and parsley). Let the chicken pieces stand on wax paper for about 30 minutes after they have been dipped. Brown chicken in olive oil evenly. Place browned chicken in large flat casserole and cover with tomato sauce.

TOMATO SAUCE

1 (1 pound, 12 ounce) can
    tomatoes, mashed, or 3½
    cups mixed in blender
1 (8 ounce) can tomato sauce
1 teaspoon salt
2 teaspoons oregano

½ teaspoon pepper
2 teaspoons chopped parsley
    or parsley flakes
1 (8 ounce) can sliced mush-
    rooms or fresh mushrooms
    sliced and sautéed in butter

Mix tomato sauce ingredients. Pour over chicken. Bake at 325° for 1 hour. A small amount of water may be added, if needed. One-half cup white wine may be added right before baking, if desired.

Mrs. William C. Payne

CHICKEN CORDON BLEU

2 cups thin noodles
6 tablespoons butter
1 cup fresh sliced mushrooms
1 medium onion, sliced

3 tablespoons flour
2 cups milk
⅓ cup brandy
2 cups grated Swiss cheese

4 cups cooked and chopped chicken

Cook noodles according to the directions on the package and drain. Cook mushrooms and onion in butter. Blend in flour. Gradually add milk and brandy and stir until thickened. Fold in cheese, reserving 3 tablespoons. Combine noodles, chicken, and sauce in a large casserole. Sprinkle reserved cheese on top. Bake at 350° for 45 minutes. Serves 8.

Mrs. Craig M. Wilson

CHICKEN CURRY

1 medium-sized chicken
2 tablespoons butter
1 cup diced apples
1 cup diced onions
3 teaspoons curry powder

1 (14½ ounce) can stewed
  tomatoes
1 cup chicken broth
½ teaspoon lemon juice

Boil chicken until tender and reserve liquid. Cut chicken into bite-size pieces and set aside. Melt butter in large frying pan and add apples, onions, tomatoes, broth, lemon juice, and curry powder. Simmer 10 minutes. All steps up to this point may be done a day ahead. Thirty minutes prior to serving, begin simmering sauce again. Add chicken for last 5 minutes. Serve with rice and any of the following: toasted coconut, mandarin oranges, chopped boiled eggs, peanuts, olives, raisins, bacon and/or chutney. Serves 6 to 8.

Mrs. Connie Carrico

CHICKEN HAWAIIAN

1 large green pepper, cut in
  strips
1 clove garlic, minced
2 tablespoons oil
2 (10¾ ounces each) cans
  cream of chicken soup

1 (13 ounce) can pineapple tidbits with juice
2 cups cooked cubed chicken
2 tablespoons soy sauce
2 cups cooked rice
⅓ cup toasted slivered almonds

In large frying pan, cook green pepper with garlic in oil until tender. Blend in soup and pineapple juice from can. Add chicken, pineapple bits, and soy sauce. Simmer about 10 minutes, stirring occasionally. Serve over rice and top with toasted slivered almonds.

To toast almonds, put them in a 350° oven for about 10 minutes with a tablespoon of butter, stirring and watching to see that they do not get too brown. Serves 6.

Mrs. Andrew V. Roderick

CHICKEN INTERNATIONAL

1 cup sauterne or sherry
2 tablespoons brown sugar
4 tablespoons butter
1 teaspoon salt
1 teaspoon freshly ground
  pepper
1 teaspoon seasoning salt

1 teaspoon paprika
1 tablespoon chopped parsley
1 chicken cut into parts
Flour
Mushrooms, optional
Pearl onions, optional
Artichoke hearts, optional

Combine all but chicken, vegetables and flour. Heat until butter is melted. Pour over chicken and marinate at least four hours. Bake, uncovered in 350° oven for 1 to 1½ hours. One-half hour before serving sprinkle lightly with flour and baste with the sauce. Add whole mushrooms (be sure to baste them too, or they will be dry). Serve with wild rice and remaining sauce from the baking.

Mrs. Richard R. Meckfessel

CHICKEN JUBILEE

4 fryers quarterd	½ cup brown sugar
2 teaspoons salt	1 (12 ounce) bottle chili sauce
¼ teaspoon pepper	1 tablespoon Worcestershire
½ cup melted margarine	sauce
1 cup water	1 (16 ounce) can pitted bing
½ cup raisins	cherries, drained

1 cup sherry

Place chickens in shallow pans (skin side up). Season and dribble with margarine. Brown under medium heat of broiler. Combine remaining ingredients except wine and cherries. Mix thoroughly. Pour over chicken and cover entire pans with foil. Bake one hour at 325°; remove foil and add wine and cherries. Bake 15 minutes longer, basting. To serve, pour gravy over chickens on platters.

Mrs. Soul Snyder

CHICKEN A LA KING

4 tablespoons butter	2 egg yolks
4 tablespoons flour	1 tablespoon water
1¼ cups chicken stock	1 tablespoon lemon juice
1¼ cups half and half	2 tablespoons sherry
1 teaspoon salt	2 cups diced, cooked chicken
¼ teaspoon white pepper	2 tablespoons chopped pimiento
½ teaspoon celery salt	1 sweet green pepper for
2 drops onion juice	garnish

6 ripe olives for garnish

Melt butter in saucepan. Add flour and stir until smooth and bubbly. Stir in stock and cream. Cook and stir over low heat until thick and smooth and ready to boil. Season with salt, pepper, celery salt, and onion juice. Beat egg yolks with water, lemon juice, and sherry. Add with chicken and pimiento to cream and cook slowly for a minute or two. Garnish with rings of green pepper and olives cut from pits. Serve with hot crisp toast or over rice. Serves 6.

Mrs. Helen Townsend Ziebold

CREAMED TURKEY

1 (4 ounce) can mushrooms
2 tablespoons chopped onion
¼ cup chopped green pepper
¼ cup butter
¼ cup flour
½ teaspoon salt

⅛ teaspoon pepper
1 cup chicken or turkey broth
  or cream of chicken soup
1 cup half and half
1½ cups diced cooked turkey
¼ cup chopped pimiento

Dash of white wine or sherry, optional

Sauté mushrooms, onion, and green pepper in butter. Blend in flour and seasonings. Remove from heat. Slowly stir in broth and cream. Bring to a boil over low heat, stirring constantly. Boil 1 minute. Add turkey and pimiento. Continue cooking until meat is heated. Serve hot with rice. Serves 4.

Mrs. John Charles Thomas

CHICKEN AND LOBSTER CANTONESE
(or what to do with leftover chicken)

Eleanor Steber, a soprano from Wheeling, is one of America's foremost native born opera singers. She has sung with the Metropolitan Opera Company.

1 tablespoon safflower oil
1 clove garlic, minced, optional
1 green pepper, cut in strips
1 small onion, sliced
1 cup diced celery
½ cup boiling water
1 chicken bouillon cube
1½ cups (7 ounces) leftover chicken or turkey

1 (6½ ounce) can lobster, drained
½ cup (one 6 ounce can) water chestnuts, drained and sliced
2 cups bean sprouts, drained
2 tablespoons soy sauce
½ teaspoon ginger
Pepper

Heat oil in skillet, or wok, tilting pan to coat bottom. Sauté garlic, green pepper, onion, and celery. Dissolve bouillon cube in water and add. Cover and simmer 8 to 10 minutes. Add chicken, lobster, and all remaining ingredients. Simmer an additional 5 minutes. If necessary, add a little more water. Serve on rice or with Chinese noodles. Serves 6.

Miss Eleanor Steber

CHICKEN PIE DELUXE

1¾ cups Pepperidge Farm
    stuffing
½ cup butter (margarine may
    be used for half)
1 (10½ ounce) can cream of
    celery soup

1½ cups boned chicken or
    canned chicken, cut in
    large pieces
½ cup milk
¾ cup cooked peas
1 tablespoon minced onion
Dash of pepper

Mix crumbs and butter and save ¾ cup of crumbs for top. Put butter and crumb mixture in bottom of 2 quart casserole. Mix remaining ingredients and put on top of crumbs. Top with remaining crumbs. Bake at 425° for 15 to 20 minutes or until bubbly. Serves 6.

Mrs. William C. Payne

CHICKEN POT PIE FILLING

2 cups cooked cubed chicken
¼ cup slivered cooked carrots
½ cup cooked green peas
½ cup cubed cooked potatoes

1 (8 ounce) can onions, small or
    cut into halves
1 teaspoon salt
⅛ teaspoon pepper

SAUCE

2 tablespoons butter
2½ tablespoons flour
¼ teaspoon salt

⅛ teaspoon pepper
¾ cup chicken broth
¾ cup milk

Melt butter; blend in flour, salt, and pepper, and cook until smooth. Stir in chicken broth and milk. Bring to a boil and cook 1 minute. Mix filling and sauce. Pour into prepared pie shell. (See "Pies" for recipe.) Cover with top crust and slit. Bake at 425° for about 35 minutes. Serves 6.

Mrs. John Charles Thomas

CHICKEN RAPHAEL

2 (2 pounds each) broiling
    chickens
½ lemon or 1 tablespoon
    lemon juice
Salt and pepper
Flour
¼ cup butter or margarine
3 medium green onions,
    chopped
½ cup sauterne or dry
    white wine

2 tablespoons rich chicken
    broth
4 egg yolks
1½ cups heavy cream
Dash of nutmeg
Cayenne pepper
2 tablespoons minced chives
    (dried can be used)
¼ cup fresh parsley
½ teaspoon lemon juice

Cut chickens into serving-size pieces. Rub with cut lemon or sprinkle with lemon juice. Sprinkle with salt and pepper. Dust with flour. Heat butter in skillet and sauté chicken until golden on all sides. Remove pieces as they brown to make room for the rest. Use more butter, if necessary, to avoid sticking. Cover and cook 10 minutes. Add onions and cook 5 minutes longer. shaking the pan frequently. Pour over wine and simmer 2 minutes. Add chicken broth. Cook covered over low heat about 20 minutes. until fork tender. Shake pan to avoid sticking. Do not boil. Meanwhile, beat egg yolks with heavy cream. Season to taste with nutmeg, cayenne, chives, and parsley. Just before serving, remove chicken pieces to a heated platter. Spoon off fat. Pour cream mixture into the skillet, and cook over very low heat, stirring or shaking until sauce thickens. Add ½ teaspoon lemon juice. Pour sauce over chicken, garnish platter with parsley, and serve at once. Serve this dish with rice cooked with chicken broth. Ladle extra sauce over rice as it is served. Serves 8.

Mrs. William O. McMillan, Jr.

CHICKEN AND RICE BAKE

1 (10½ ounce) can onion soup
1 (10¾ ounce) can cream of
  celery soup
1 (10¾ ounce) can cream of
  mushroom soup

2 soup cans water
1 (3 ounce) can mushroom
  pieces
1 cup uncooked rice
  Salt to taste

1 chicken, cut up

Mix the 3 cans of soup, 2 cans of water, mushrooms, rice, and salt. Place in a 9" x 14" glass baking dish. Lay chicken pieces skin side up on the bed of rice. Cover with foil and bake at 350° for 1 hour. Remove wrap and allow to brown for 15 minutes longer. Serves 4.

Mrs. A. S. Thomas, Jr.

CHICKEN TETRAZZINI

8 ounces thin spaghetti
2 tablespoons butter or
  chicken fat
¼ pound fresh mushrooms,
  sliced
¼ cup butter or chicken fat
¼ cup flour

1¼ teaspoons salt
⅛ teaspoon pepper
2½ cups chicken stock
3 tablespoons sherry
½ cup heavy cream
2 cups diced cooked chicken
½ cup grated Parmesan cheese

Cook spaghetti, drain, and keep hot. Melt 2 tablespoons butter in frying pan. Sauté mushrooms until golden brown. Melt ¼ cup butter in large saucepan; remove from heat. Blend in flour, salt, and pepper. Stir in chicken stock slowly. Cook over low heat, stirring constantly, until sauce thickens and boils 1 minute. Remove from heat. Stir in sherry and cream slowly. Combine sauce, mushrooms, chicken, and spaghetti; spoon into greased 2 quart casserole and sprinkle cheese over top. Bake at 425° for 15 to 20 minutes until bubbly and brown on top. Serves 6 to 8.

Mrs. John F. Ziebold

CHOP SUEY

1 (4 pound) chicken	1 (6 ounce) can bamboo shoots
6 medium onions, sliced	1 (6 ounce) can water chestnuts
Cooking oil	4 tablespoons cornstarch
1 bunch celery, diced	¼ cup cold water
4 cups chicken broth (if not	4 tablespoons sugar
enough, add water)	½ cup molasses
1 (16 ounce) can bean sprouts	2 tablespoons soy sauce
1 (16 ounce) can mixed	1 tablespoon salt
Chinese vegetables	1 green pepper or 1 pimiento

Cook whole chicken until tender. Remove meat from bones. Save broth. Slice onions and sauté in cooking oil or chicken fat for five minutes. Add diced celery and chicken broth; cook 5 minutes. Add chicken meat, bean sprouts, mixed Chinese vegetables, bamboo shoots, and water chestnuts. Heat. Mix cornstarch with water. When dissolved, add sugar, molasses, soy sauce, and salt. Add to chicken mixture and stir over heat until thickened. For added color and taste, put in 1 finely shredded green pepper or thin slices of pimiento. Serve over rice with additional soy sauce. Serves 15 to 20.

Mrs. John Raynes

CHRISTMAS CASSEROLE

1 cup melted butter or	6 cups turkey or chicken stock
margarine	1 pound or more Cheddar or
1¼ cups sifted flour	American cheese, grated
2½ cups milk or light cream	6 to 8 packages frozen aspar-
4 teaspoons salt	agus or broccoli
1 teaspoon onion salt	8 cups or 24 slices turkey or
5⅓ cups instant rice	chicken
½ to 1 cup slivered almonds	

Melt butter; stir in flour and cook until bubbly. Add milk and stir until it thickens. Add 2 teaspoons salt and ½ teaspoon onion salt. Pour equal amounts of instant rice into 2 large (9″ x 13″) shallow casseroles. Pour broth and remaining salts over rice. Sprinkle half of cheese over rice; top with asparagus (or broccoli) and the turkey (or chicken). Pour cream sauce over all and sprinkle with remaining cheese. Bake 20 minutes at 375°. Sprinkle with slivered almonds and toast under broiler. Serves 24.

Mrs. Sidney P. Davis, Jr.

COQ AU VIN

3 to 4 ounces chunk of lean bacon
2 quarts water
2 tablespoons butter
2½ to 3 pound cut-up frying chicken
½ teaspoon salt
⅛ teaspoon pepper
¼ cup cognac (3 stars only)
3 cups full-bodied red wine, such as Burgundy or chianti

1 to 2 cups brown chicken stock or canned beef bouillon
½ tablespoon tomato paste
2 cloves garlic, mashed
¼ teaspoon thyme
1 bay leaf
12 to 24 brown braised onions
½ pound sautéed mushrooms
Parsley for garnish

Remove bacon rind and cut bacon into strips. Simmer for 10 minutes in 2 quarts of water. Rinse in cold water. Dry. In heavy 10″ fireproof casserole or an electric skillet, put 2 tablespoons butter. Sauté the bacon slowly in hot butter until it is very lightly browned. Remove to a side dish. Dry the chicken thoroughly. Brown it in the hot fat in the casserole. Season the chicken thoroughly with salt and pepper. Return the bacon to the casserole with the chicken. Cover and cook slowly for a few minutes. Uncover and pour in the cognac. Averting your face, ignite the cognac with a match. Shake the casserole back and forth for several seconds until the flames subside.

Pour the wine into the casserole. Add just enough stock or bouillon to cover the chicken. Stir in the tomato paste, garlic, and herbs. Bring to a simmer. Cover and simmer slowly for 25 or 30 minutes, or until the chicken is tender and its juices run a clear yellow when the meat is pierced with a fork. Remove the chicken to a side dish. While the chicken is cooking, prepare the onions and mushrooms. Thirty minutes before serving, add onions and mushrooms. Serve on a hot platter. Decorate with parsley. Serves 4.

Mrs. Thomas P. O'Brien

HASTY GOURMET CHICKEN CASSEROLE

Cecil H. Underwood, former Repulican governor of West Virginia from 1958 to 1962, currently is president of Bethany College at Bethany, West Virginia. Mrs. Underwood writes that the recipe she submitted can be done quickly and does not require exact measurements.

Butter
½ cup long grain rice
1¼ cups chicken broth
1 chicken fryer, cut up
¼ cup lemon juice
½ cup white cooking wine (sauterne)
Parsley, minced (dried or fresh)

1 medium onion, thinly sliced
1 teaspoon thyme, marjoram, or rosemary or a combination
Salt and pepper to taste
1 teaspoon paprika
3 tablespoons butter

Butter a shallow casserole which is large enough to hold a cut-up chicken fryer in a single layer. Place rice in casserole; add chicken broth and fryer pieces, skin side up. Sprinkle each piece of chicken generously with lemon juice, sauterne, parsley, and onion slices. Add a light sprinkling of thyme, rosemary or marjoram, salt and pepper to taste, paprika, and a small pat of butter or margarine on each piece of chicken. Bake at 350° about 1 hour, until brown and tender. Serves 4.

Variation: After sprinkling on lemon juice and wine, mix the remaining ingredients with one can of condensed cream of chicken soup or cream of mushroom soup and spoon over chicken. Bake as usual.

Mrs. Cecil Underwood

FRENCH-STYLE BAKED CHICKEN

1 whole 3 pound broiler-fryer chicken
2 teaspoons salt, divided
1 teaspoon Monosodium glutamate
½ teaspoon dried leaf thyme
4 parsley sprigs
2 celery tops with leaves

1 yellow onion
2 tablespoons butter or margarine
12 small white onions, peeled, or 12 whole mushrooms
¼ cup dry sherry, or more
12 small potatoes, pared
Chopped parsley for garnish

Sprinkle inside of chicken with 1 teaspoon salt, monosodium glutamate and thyme. Place parsley, celery, and yellow onion in cavity of chicken. Tie legs together; then tie to tail. Place chicken in a large heavy casserole with lid; dot with butter. Cover and bake at 375° for 30 minutes. Add white onions, sherry, and 1 teaspoon salt, and bake 15 minutes longer. Add potatoes and bake for 15 minutes, or until potatoes are tender. Remove cover; bake until chicken and vegetables are browned and tender, about 30 minutes to 1 hour. Baste frequently with juices in casserole. Sprinkle with chopped parsley. Make a thin gravy with the pan juices. Serves 4.

Note: If using mushrooms in place of onions, add them at the same time as potatoes.

Mr. Charles G. Moyers, Jr.

FILLING FOR CREPES

1 (2 to 3 pound) stewing chicken, cooked and diced
12 (more or less) fresh mushrooms, diced or sliced and sautéed in butter
1 onion, chopped and sautéed in butter with mushrooms
1 to 2 cups medium cream sauce
Hollandaise sauce and sour cream in equal amounts
Slivered almonds

Combine chicken, mushrooms, and onion with medium cream sauce. Cream sauce is good made with butter in which mushrooms and onions have been sautéed, and chicken broth. Amount of sauce depends on amount of chicken, mushroom and onion mixture, about 1 to 2 cups.

Place 1 large tablespoon, more or less, of this mixture in the center of the crêpe. Roll up and line these in oblong glass baking dish. These can be prepared 1 or 2 days ahead of time. Just before heating, pour over the crêpes a mixture of equal parts hollandaise sauce and sour cream and sprinkle top with almonds. Bake at 350° for 20 to 30 minutes.

* See Breads for crêpe recipe.

Mrs. John M. Slack, III

DUTCH OVEN CHICKEN

2½ to 3 pounds whole chicken fryer
Salt and pepper
2 tablespoons cooking oil
1 large carrot, sliced
1 medium onion, thinly sliced
2 bay leaves
2 tablespoons rosemary, crushed if desired
1 cup dry white wine
½ cup water
Flour

Wash and dry chicken, as dry as possible inside and out. Remove neck and giblets. Salt and pepper chicken and brown slowly in oil in a 4 quart Dutch oven. After browning the hen on all sides, pull Dutch oven off heat and add remaining ingredients except flour. Bake covered in a preheated 350° oven for 1 hour longer until bird looks tender. Baste and turn chicken over or change its position if needed to keep from drying out. More wine may be added. At the end of the cooking time, remove bird. Strain out vegetables and spices and use flour or arrowroot to thicken sauce to desired consistency. Serves 4.

Mrs. P. Thomas Denny

ONE DISH CHICKEN DINNER

1 4 to 5 pound roasting chick-
   en or 1 cut up frying
   chicken
1 (10½ ounce) can Golden
   Mushroom soup or
   1 (10½ ounce) can cream
   of chicken soup

4 to 6 potatoes, halved
6 carrots, cut into 1″ pieces
2 small onions or 1 tablespoon
   onion flakes
1½ teaspoons salt
2 teaspoons chopped parsley
   for garnish

Clean and prepare chicken for baking. The whole chicken will be baked 45 minutes longer than the pieces. Place in large pan or Dutch oven and pour undiluted soup over chicken. Cover and bake whole chicken 45 minutes at 375°. If using chicken pieces, proceed to next step without baking. Place remaining ingredients, except parsley, in liquid around the chicken. Cover and bake 1 hour longer. Baste vegetables occasionally. Remove cover; brown for 15 to 20 minutes. Sprinkle with parsley. Serves 4.

Mrs. Otis O'Conner

ORIENTAL CHICKEN OR TURKEY CASSEROLE

2 cups diced celery
½ cup ground onion
4 tablespoons butter
2 cups mushroom soup

½ cup chicken broth
2 cups diced chicken or turkey
½ cup cashew nuts
2 cups Chinese noodles

Brown celery and onions in butter. Dilute soup with broth. Mix all with meat and nuts. Add noodles last, leaving some noodles to sprinkle on top 15 minutes before serving. Bake at 350° for 1 hour. Serves 6.

Mrs. John J. Droppleman

PRESSED CHICKEN

2 whole chicken breasts
4 chicken legs and thighs or
   equivalent amount of other
   chicken pieces
3 stalks celery

2 carrots
4 chicken bouillon cubes
3 slices of hard dry toast
¼ cup water
1 tablespoon flour

Stew chicken, vegetables, and bouillon until done and almost dry. Remove chicken and bone it. Grind chicken, vegetables, and toast in food grinder. Mix ¼ cup water and flour to make a chicken gravy with residue from stewing chicken. Mix with ground chicken until moist. Pat into a loaf dish and press down firm and solid. Place in refrigerator. Slice when cold and serve. Serves 8.

Miss Virginia Kelly

SMOKED TURKEY — 1890 STYLE

6½ to 7 pound turkey
Salt and pepper
4 cloves garlic
1 bay leaf
⅓ cup liquid smoke, divided
1 cup boiling water
6 peppercorns
1 small pod red pepper
1 tablespoon dry mustard

Rub dry turkey cavity and skin with salt and pepper. Cut 1 clove garlic in half and rub cavity. Then leave the split garlic and the bay leaf in the cavity. Rub the skin with the second clove of split garlic and discard. Cut two slits in the skin of breast and insert clove of garlic in each. Brush entire bird, inside and out, with ¼ cup liquid smoke. Let stand overnight in refrigerator. Next day, put turkey in a shallow roasting pan and bake 20 minutes in a preheated 500° oven. Reduce oven to 400°; pour a mixture of 1 cup boiling water, remaining ingredients, and remaining liquid smoke over turkey. Cover and cook according to your own roasting scale, basting frequently. Cool, or serve hot. Serves 6 to 8.

Mrs. Donald Ellsworth

WILD RICE AND CORNISH HENS

2 tablespoons butter
1 package dry onion soup mix
1 package long grain and wild rice mix with seasoning packet
3 Cornish hens, split to make 6 pieces
1 (10¾ ounce) can cream of mushroom soup
1½ cups chicken broth

Melt butter in 9" x 14" glass casserole. Sprinkle with the onion soup mix. Spread uncooked rice over the soup. Spread the seasoning package from the mix over the rice. Place Cornish hen halves on top. Dilute mushroom soup with chicken broth and pour this mixture over all. Cover with foil. Bake in pre-heated 350° oven for 1½ hours. Remove foil for last 15 minutes. Serves 6.

Mrs. P. Thomas Denny

WATERZOOI

A hearty Flemish peasant dish.

2 chicken broiler - fryers	Salt
2 medium onions, chopped	Pepper
2 tablespoons butter	½ to ¾ cup cream
3 leeks	2 tablespoons brandy
4 celery stalks	8 medium potatoes, peeled,
6 carrots	quartered and boiled
1½ cups white wine	2 shakes cayenne
Parsley for garnish	

Remove wings, backs and insides of chicken. Place in kettle with 4 cups water. Add a slice of carrot, a slice of onion and a small piece of celery to make a stock and simmer slowly 1½ to 2 hours. Remove vegetables and scum from surface. Cut rest of chicken into serving pieces and refrigerate. Cut leeks lengthwise in half, then sliced across, in ¾" slices. Sauté onion in butter in large container, add medium-diced carrots, celery, and leeks. Top with chicken pieces; add wine and enough of the stock to cover. Season to taste with salt and pepper. Cover and simmer 35 to 45 minutes or until chicken is tender. Add cream and brandy and simmer 5 minutes longer. Add potatoes to dish, shake cayenne over all and stir gently. Remove to soup tureen and garnish with parsley.

Using shallow bowls, serve each a piece of chicken, a piece of potato, and a generous amount of the broth and chopped vegetables. As this is neither a soup nor a stew; a knife, fork and soup spoon will be needed. Serves 8.

Mrs. Rain Purre

ALICE'S CHICKEN SALAD

1 (5 pound) roasting chicken	1 tablespoon lemon juice
¾ cup diced celery	½ teaspoon salt
1 cup sliced white seedless	¼ teaspoon pepper
grapes	½ teaspoon packaged salad
1 cup mandarin oranges	dressing herbs
½ cup mayonnaise	Toasted almonds
½ cup sour cream	Lettuce leaves
2 tablespoons minced onion	
(optional)	

Steam the chicken until tender. Cut in bite-size pieces. Mix all ingredients except almonds and lettuce. Chill and serve on lettuce, topped with toasted almonds. Serves 8.

Mrs. G. Thomas Battle

CHICKEN SALAD

¼ cup chicken broth
¾ cup Miracle Whip salad dressing
2½ cups cooked diced chicken
1½ cups diced celery

¼ cup broken pecans
¼ cup sliced stuffed olives
¾ teaspoon salt
Dash pepper

Add chicken broth to salad dressing and blend gradually. Mix the chicken, celery, pecans, olives, salt, and pepper. Add salad dressing and chill. Serves 4 to 6. This may be used to stuff into miniature cream puffs for a brunch or luncheon.

Mrs. Alexander J. Ross

HOT CHICKEN SALAD

2 cups cooked cubed chicken
2 cups coarsely chopped
celery
½ cup chopped toasted
almonds
1 cup mayonnaise

2 teaspoons grated onion
½ teaspoon salt
½ teaspoon monosodium
glutamate
2 teaspoons lemon juice
1 cup crushed potato chips

½ cup grated Cheddar cheese

Combine chicken, celery, and almonds with mayonnaise. Add onion, salt, monosodium glutamate, and lemon juice which have been mixed together. Put in a 2 quart casserole. Top with potato chips and Cheddar cheese. Bake 20 minutes at 450°. Serves 6. Can be made ahead of time except put topping on just before placing in the oven.

Mrs. William H. Knight

MARINATED CHICKEN SALAD

1 cup cooked and cut up
chicken
⅓ cup vinegar
⅓ cup oil

⅓ cup sugar
½ cup chopped celery
¼ cup seedless green grapes
⅛ cup toasted sliced almonds

Mayonnaise

Marinate chicken in vinegar, oil, and sugar overnight. Add celery, grapes, and almonds. Mix with a little mayonnaise. Serves 2.

Mrs. Robert F. Goldsmith

DEVONSHIRE SANDWICHES

3 tablespoons butter	2 egg yolks
5 tablespoons flour	Salt to taste
2 cups chicken broth	Pepper to taste
2 tablespoons white wine,	4 slices toasted bread
sherry, or lemon juice	4 thin slices ham
⅔ cup cream	4 slices chicken

Parmesan cheese

Make a white sauce of butter, flour, chicken broth, and wine. Beat cream and egg yolks together and add to sauce. Season with salt and pepper. Top a slice of toast with slices of ham and chicken. Pour sauce over all and sprinkle with Parmesan cheese. Broil until cheese melts. Makes 4 open-faced sandwiches.

Mrs. Craig M. Wilson

HOT BROWNS

CREAM SAUCE

2 tablespoons butter	1 chicken bouillon cube
2 tablespoons flour	1 tablespoon sherry
Salt and cayenne to taste	1 (3½ ounce) can sliced
¼ teaspoon curry powder	mushrooms
1 cup milk	

Melt butter in a small skillet; add flour, salt, cayenne, and curry. Blend well. Remove from heat, and add milk slowly, stirring constantly until smooth. Return to heat, add bouillon cube, and cook slowly until thick. Add mushrooms and sherry last.

OPEN-FACED SANDWICH

4 slices bread, toasted lightly	4 slices bacon, cut in half, very
4 breasts chicken, cooked	slightly cooked
and sliced, or leftover	1 cup grated Cheddar cheese
sliced turkey	

Place toast in baking dish, cover with chicken and cream sauce, and sprinkle with grated cheese. Put bacon on top. Place about 6″ from broiler and broil until bacon is done. Serves 4.

Mrs. J. Holmes Morrison

GAME

Game is not hard to cook, but the meat is extremely lean and has very little fat to self-baste. Either broth or fruit juice must be added, or frequent basting must be done. Add wine, a piece of apple, potato, or onion if you are not fond of the "gamey" taste.

Mrs. Robert M. Chilton

POTTED DOVES

6 doves
6 slices bacon
1 cup catsup
1 small onion

Salt and pepper
3 tablespoons Worcestershire sauce
1 tablespoon butter

Red pepper or hot sauce

Steam birds for 20 minutes on top of the stove with a little water. Add remaining ingredients, laying the bacon on top of the birds. Cook covered for about 1½ hours, or until very tender. Remove cover and brown in oven. Serves 6.

Mrs. William H. Carter

SIMMERED DOVE

1 stick butter
2 doves, cleaned

Salt and pepper to taste
3 cups water

Use black iron skillet with top or electric frying pan with top. Melt butter. Brown doves evenly. Season with salt and pepper. Add water, cover, and simmer slowly about 3 hours, or until done. Serves 3.

Mrs. William H. Carter

GUINEA
First, catch a guinea!

Breast of 1 guinea (may use meat from upper joints) use rest for stock
½ teaspoon salt
1 cup uncooked rice; boiled in stock

Flour to add to frying pan
2 eggs
1 cup cream
½ cup sherry wine
½ cup currants

Cut raw breasts in 4 pieces; sprinkle with salt. Brown in butter on both sides. Place cooked rice in shallow dish; lay breasts on rice. Add flour to frying pan, brown, and add beaten eggs, cream (more milk if necessary), sherry, and currants. Cook until thickened. Pour over meat and rice and bake at 350° until meat is done.

Mrs. Robert Lawson, Jr.

BRUNSWICK STEW

8 quail, dressed and split (½ chicken may be substituted)
3 squirrels, dressed and quartered
Flour
6 tablespoons butter
1 cup chopped scallions
4 medium potatoes, thinly sliced

2 cups Lima beans
3 cups okra, sliced across
1 cup canned tomatoes
1 bay leaf
2 tablespoons chopped fresh parsley
1½ teaspoons salt
2 cups fresh corn, added during the last 10 minutes

Flour the quail and squirrels lightly and brown them in butter; place in a large pot and cover with water. Simmer for 1½ hours. Then add the rest of the ingredients, except the corn, and enough water to again cover. Simmer until the vegetables are tender, stirring often to prevent sticking to the bottom. Add the corn and simmer 10 minutes more. Serve in a flat soup plate. Serves 6.

Mrs. Robert M. Chilton

"GENTLEMAN SPORTSMAN" BRANDIED QUAIL

4 quail
1 stick butter, clarified*, divided

½ cup currant or apricot jelly
Dash of salt
2 tablespoons brandy (or more according to taste)

Cut quail into serving pieces, using breasts only or breasts and legs if you wish. Brown slowly in ½ of butter for about ½ hour. When nicely browned on all sides, push to one side and add currant or apricot jelly to the drippings. Add remainder of butter, a dash of salt, and stir well while the jelly melts. When sauce is well blended, spread the browned pieces of quail out again and baste with the sauce. Cover and let simmer until meat is fork tender. Skim off fat and add brandy to the mixture. Amount depends solely upon taste preference. Stir in brandy just until heated and serve. Serves 2 to 4.

*Clarified butter: melt butter over low heat until it separates. Use clear liquid and discard sediment.

Don Whitlatch

BAKED DEER MEAT

Deer meat, rubbed with 1
  tablespoon salt and ¼ teaspoon pepper
1 to 2 (16 ounce) cans small
  whole carrots
1 to 2 (16 ounce) cans small
  whole onions
Sliced celery stalks
2 halved cloves of garlic
1 tablespoon thyme
1 tablespoon rosemary leaves
2 bay leaves
¼ cup minced parsley
2 whole cloves
1 whole nutmeg or 4 allspice
  berries
5 cups red wine
½ cup brandy or vinegar
½ cup olive oil
Cornstarch

Combine all of the above ingredients except the carrots, onions, and corn starch, in a large container. Stir. Add piece of deer meat and marinate for at least 24 hours, turning occasionally. May be marinated for as much as 48 hours. Bake at 300° to 350° until done. Remove meat from marinade; strain marinade and thicken it with a little cornstarch and water, which have been returned to original cooking container. Add meat, carrots, and onions. Return to oven and heat thoroughly. Arrange on serving platter and serve. This recipe is for a 4 to 8 pound deer loin. It may be used for any size piece of deer meat; adjust amount of marinade accordingly. Cooking time for 8 pounds is about 4½ hours at 300° oven. Extra marinade may be served separately. Meat should be turned or basted once or twice during cooking, but should not be covered during cooking. Do not overcook.

Mrs. Marshall Bond, Jr.

VENISON STEW

2 pounds meat, cubed
  Flour
3 tablespoons fat
4 potatoes, cubed
2 onions, sliced
6 carrots, sliced
1 package peas
4 ribs celery, sliced
  Salt and pepper to taste
2 tablespoons parsley
Monosodium glutamate

Dredge meat in flour, sear in hot fat. Cover with water and boil. Add remaining ingredients and cook until tender, about 1 hour. Thicken with flour mixed with a little liquid and add to pan. Serves 6 to 8.

Mrs. Carl B. Hall, Jr.

RABBIT SAUSAGE

A standard of excellence in the field of wildlife art has been achieved by Don Whitlatch of Parkersburg, West Virginia. Having reproduced his first painting in 1970, many of Mr. Whitlatch's portraits of nature have become collector items. Mr. Whitlatch writes about his recipe for rabbit sausage that it is "a country boy's delight and a treat that every sportsman will relish."

Remove all meat from bones of cleaned rabbit; add equal amount of fresh pork chunks, and coarsely grind together. Add sausage seasoning and mix well. Form into patties.

Slowly fry patties in an iron skillet until done. DO NOT BROWN. Place in layers in a large crock or stoneware jar and slowly pour hot grease over them. Additional lard may be used if enough grease is not available. Cover the jar and place in "cold cellar" or springhouse. It will keep perfectly all winter long.

To serve, simply pry as many patties out of the jar as needed. Heat thoroughly and finish the browning. Sopp'en milk gravy is always made with the drippings and served over hot homemade biscuits. Throw in two fried eggs and enjoy life. Forget cholesterol.

Don Whitlatch

LEAH'S LEMON BUTTER

3 eggs	2 cups sugar
Juice of 3 lemons	2 tablespoons butter
	Pinch of salt

Beat whole eggs until pale yellow Add all other ingredients and cook in top of double boiler until slightly thickened. Do not overcook, as mixture thickens more as it cools. Makes 1½ pints. Delicious with any meat and especially with fowl.

Mrs. L. Douglas Curnutte

THE CLEARING

He set his claim upon the bark
Of corner oaks with lawless mark.
And while the April moon was low
To dry the sprouts which fought to grow,
He banded every tree with doom,
So sun might pry into the gloom
To pull the blades of life from grain.
He'd drop the corn across the plain
When dogwood blossoms curving round
Gave him the sign that mountain ground
Was warm enough to make seed swell
Breaking the hardened golden shell,
Thrusting the green spear which would make
The silk-wrapped ear to grind and bake
In dodger, pone, and johnnie cake.

Reprinted by permission of Louise McNeill, from **Gauley Mountain;**
Harcourt, Brace and Company; New York, New York; 1939; Page 9.

Photo by Gerald S. Ratliff

GRAINS

Dutch Mill

BARLEY AND MUSHROOM CASSEROLE

½ pound mushrooms, sliced
6 tablespoons butter, divided
Salt, pepper, and marjoram, to taste

2 cups barley
1 medium onion, chopped
4 or more cups strong chicken broth

Sauté mushrooms in some of butter; remove from skillet and season with salt, pepper, and marjoram. Brown barley and chopped onion in remaining butter. Add mushrooms to barley and onion mixture and put in a buttered casserole. Cover with chicken broth and bake covered for 2 hours at 300°. Add more chicken broth during baking, as needed; season to taste with salt and pepper. Serves 8 to 10.

Mrs. Harry V. Campbell

BARLEY-PINE NUT CASSEROLE

½ cup pine nuts
½ cup butter, divided
1 cup finely chopped onions
1 cup pearl barley

1 cup finely chopped parsley
1 cup finely chopped chives
2 cups canned beef consommé
1 teaspoon salt and pepper to taste

Sauté pine nuts in butter until golden and set aside. Sauté onion in remaining butter until golden. Add barley and brown lightly. Stirring constantly, add parsley, chives and consommé. Salt and pepper half the pine nuts and pour pine nuts and barley into 2 quart casserole. Bake at 350° for 1 hour, stirring once after 30 minutes. Sprinkle the remaining pine nuts on top and bake 20 minutes more. If it is too dry, add a little more liquid; the barley seems to soak up liquid at different rates from time to time. Serves 6.

Mrs. Frank Baer

CORNMEAL MUSH-FRIED

1 cup stoneground cornmeal
1 teaspoon salt
1 teaspoon sugar
1 cup cold water
2¾ cups boiling water
Bacon drippings

Combine dry ingredients with cold water; gradually add to boiling water, stirring constantly. Cook until mixture thickens, stirring frequently. When thick, cover, turn heat low and cook 20 to 25 minutes. Pour into 7½ inch by 3½ inch pan. Cool and chill. Unmold and cut into ½ inch slices. Dip in extra cornmeal. Fry in hot bacon drippings until brown. Turn and brown other side. Serve with butter and syrup.

Ancil B. Cutlip

GARLIC CHEESE GRITS

4 cups water
¾ teaspoon salt
1 cup quick grits
½ cup margarine (1 stick)
1 (6 ounce) stick garlic cheese, grated
2 eggs
Water
Crumbs (cornflake, cracker, or potato chips)

Bring water and salt to boil; stir in grits and cook 5 to 6 minutes. Remove from heat and stir in margarine and cheese. Beat eggs slightly and add water to make 1 cup; stir into grits. Pour into greased 1½ quart casserole and top with crumbs. Bake at 350° for 45 minutes. Allow to stand a few minutes before serving. Serves 6 to 8. Especially good for breakfast or brunch, or as a vegetable at dinner.

Mrs. H. Herchiel Sims, Jr.

GRANOLA — A CEREAL

7 cups uncooked oats
2 cups coconut
1 cup wheat germ
1 cup sesame seeds
1 cup brown sugar
1 cup oil (peanut, corn, or safflower)
1 tablespoon vanilla
1 teaspoon salt
Slivered almonds or shelled sunflower seeds, optional

Combine the above ingredients. Roast in large shallow pans for 2 hours at 200°, stirring occasionally. Keep in covered jars or cans in a cool place, or refrigerate. Serve with milk as with a dry cereal.

Mrs. Richard R. Meckfessel

FETTUCCINI A'LA CONTINENTAL

1 pound ½" noodles
½ pound salted butter
¾ cup heavy cream

1½ cups grated Parmesan cheese
Freshly grated white pepper

Drop noodles into a large pot of boiling salted water. Melt butter over hot water in double boiler. Drain the boiled noodles well. Pour noodles into hot butter, tossing gently. Add Parmesan cheese and toss until well coated. Add cream and toss until blended. Sprinkle on more cheese and freshly grated white pepper. Serves 4 to 6.

Joe Sestito

HAZEL'S NOODLE PUDDING

1 (8 ounce) package egg
   noodles
4 eggs, separated
1 (15 ounce) carton cottage
   cheese

2 cups milk
¾ cup sugar
Salt to taste
Cinnamon to taste
Sour cream

Cook noodles according to package; drain. Beat egg whites until stiff. Beat yolks well; mix with cheese, milk, salt, sugar, and cooked noodles. Fold in whites. Sprinkle with cinnamon. Bake 1 hour at 350°. Serve with sour cream. Serves 8 to 10 generously. Especially good with ham.

Mrs. A. F. McKenney

ROLL OUT THE LASAGNA

This is intended to be a meatless dish, but it is very good with meat balls which have been seasoned with Italian seasoning.

10 lasagna noodles
1 cup cream style cottage
   cheese
1 (8 ounce) package cream
   cheese
1 large garlic clove, minced
   and divided (or garlic
   powder)

½ teaspoon salt
¼ teaspoon pepper, divided
6 tablespoons Parmesan
   cheese, divided
2 (10½ ounce) cans condensed
   tomato soup
½ cup water
1 teaspoon oregano

Cook noodles according to package directions, and drain. Arrange noodles, overlapping ½ inch in a rectangle. Combine cottage cheese, cream cheese, half the garlic, half the pepper, and half the Parmesan cheese. Spread mixture on noodles. Roll as for jelly roll.

Place roll in a shallow baking dish (10″ x 6″ or 13″ x 9″). Combine soup, water, oregano, and remaining garlic and pepper; pour over noodles. Sprinkle with remaining Parmesan cheese. Bake at 350° for 30 minutes. Serve with additional Parmesan cheese. Serves 4.

Mrs. William C. Payne

MACARONI CHEESE PUFFS

½ cup small elbow macaroni
1½ cups milk, scalded
1 cup soft bread crumbs
2 cups shredded sharp processed American cheese
3 eggs, separated
¼ teaspoon cream of tartar

¼ cup pimiento, diced
3 tablespoons butter or margarine, melted
1 tablespoon chopped parsley
1 tablespoon grated onion
½ teaspoon salt

Cook macaroni in boiling, salted water, until tender. Drain. Pour hot milk over bread crumbs. Reserve, ½ cup cheese, add remaining cheese to milk mixture; cover and let stand until cheese melts. Add macaroni, beaten egg yolks, pimiento, butter, parsley, onion, and salt. Beat egg whites and cream of tartar until stiff, but not dry. Fold into macaroni mixture. Pour into ungreased baking dish. Bake in slow oven, 350°, about 50 minutes, or until set. Top with remaining cheese and return to oven for a few minutes until cheese melts. Serve at once. Serves 6.

Mrs. Richard Repaire

VERY FLUFFY RICE

1 teaspoon salt
2 quarts boiling water
1 cup long grain rice

Add salt to boiling water and gradually stir in rice. Cook for 20 minutes, keeping the water at an even boil. Pour rice into a colander. Run hot water over rice until all of the starch is removed. Place rice, still in colander, in a pot containing an inch or two of water. Place a clean, dry linen cloth over the colander, and cover with lid. Steam for at least ½ hour, or up to 2 hours if you need to hold dinner. Serves 4, and goes well with Rogen Josh.

Mrs. John C. Steven

FRIED RICE

1 teaspoon butter	1 small onion, chopped
1 teaspoon olive oil	2 cups cooked rice
1 small can Spam, cut in ¼	1½ tablespoons soy sauce
to ½" cubes	1 egg

Heat butter and oil in large frying pan. Add Spam and onion and brown. Add rice and soy sauce. Heat thoroughly. Break egg into mixture and stir to mix well. Serves 4.

Variation: Chopped green onion, green pepper, and bean sprouts may be added to this recipe for extra flavor.

Mrs. Robert W. Lawson, III

HOT RICE

1 cup rice, uncooked	1 (10 or 12 ounce) package jack
1 pint sour cream	or sharp Cheddar cheese
1 (4 ounce) can green chile	Salt, pepper, garlic salt to
peppers, diced	taste

Cook rice according to directions on package. Mix with sour cream and chile mixture; season. In 2 quart greased casserole layer half of rice mixture, ½ cheese, sliced, remaining rice mixture, and top with remaining cheese, grated. Bake uncovered for 30 to 35 minutes at 350°. Serves 6. (For a milder flavor, substitute banana peppers for the green chile peppers.)

Mrs. Sydney P. Davis, Jr.

MINTED RICE CASSEROLE

2 teaspoons salt	Dash monosodium glutamate
2 cups water	1 (14 ounce) can (1¾ cups)
1 cup long grain rice,	chicken broth or 2 chicken
uncooked	bouillon cubes, dissolved in
4 tablespoons butter or	1¾ cups hot water
margarine	½ teaspoon dried mint leaves,
Dash garlic salt	crushed
¼ cup slivered almonds, toasted	

Add the salt to the water; bring to a boil and pour over rice. Cover and let stand for 30 minutes. Rinse rice with cold water and drain well. Melt butter in a skillet. Add rice and cook over medium heat, stirring frequently, until butter is almost absorbed, about 5 minutes. Turn rice into a 1-quart casserole; sprinkle with garlic salt and monosodium glutamate. Pour chicken broth over rice. Bake, covered, at 325° for 45 minutes. Add mint and fluff with a fork. Sprinkle almonds over top. Bake, uncovered, for 10 minutes more. Serves 6.

Mrs. P. Thomas Denny

ORIENTAL RICE CASSEROLE

This recipe was brought back from the Orient.

2 cups cooked rice
Margarine or butter
1 medium white onion, diced
½ bell pepper, diced
½ of a 4 ounce jar pimiento, chopped

1 (4 ounce) can sliced mushrooms
1 scrambled egg, mashed with fork
4 to 6 slices bacon, fried crisp and crumbled
1 to 2 tablespoons soy sauce
Pinch of salt

Fry rice lightly in butter. Fry onion, pepper, pimiento, mushrooms, egg, and bacon in butter in a separate skillet. Mix rice and all ingredients and put in buttered casserole. This may be made in advance and refrigerated. To heat, cover casserole top with aluminum foil and then casserole cover. To serve right away, heat in 350° oven for 30 minutes or until hot through. If dinner hour is delayed, the casserole may be placed in a very low oven (200°) for 1 to 3 hours. Serves 6 to 8.

Mrs. W. O. McMillan, Sr.

RICE-BROCCOLI CASSEROLE

2 cups cooked rice (not instant)
1 (10 ounce) package frozen chopped broccoli
¼ cup chopped onion
½ cup chopped celery
3 tablespoons butter or margarine

1 (10½ ounce) can cream of chicken soup
½ cup milk
1 (5 ounce) can water chestnut, cut fine
1 (8 ounce) jar pasteurized process cheese spread, softened

Cook enough rice to yield 2 cups. Thaw broccoli and drain thoroughly. Sauté onion and celery in melted butter. Blend in soup, milk, chestnuts, rice, broccoli, and ⅓ jar of softened cheese spread. Turn into 10" x 7" x 2" glass baking dish. Cover with remaining cheese, which has been softened by setting jar in hot water. Bake at 350° for 40 minutes. Serves 6.

Mrs. Thomas H. Edelblute, Jr.

RICE CASSEROLE

4 tablespoons margarine
1 medium onion, minced
1 medium green pepper, minced
1 garlic clove, minced
1 cup raw rice

2 tablespoons soy sauce
1 teaspoon oregano
1 (12½ ounce) can chicken broth
1 (4 ounce) can mushroom stems and pieces
¾ cup water

Melt butter in skillet. Add onion, garlic, and green pepper, and cook over moderate heat until tender. Stir in rice and cook over moderate heat until lightly browned, stirring occasionally. Add soy sauce and oregano; reduce heat and simmer 20 minutes, stirring occasionally. Pour rice mixture into a buttered 1½ quart casserole; add broth, mushrooms, and water. Cover and bake at 350° for 1¼ hours. Serves 6. This recipe can be done the day before to the prebaking stage; if so, cut baking time in half. Good with chicken, beef or pork.

Mrs. Charles G. Moyers, Jr.

RICE AND MUSHROOMS

½ cup rice
1 (4 ounce) can mushrooms, drained

3 tablespoons butter
1 (10½ ounce) can onion soup
½ soup can of water

Brown rice and mushrooms in butter. Add soup and water. Cover and simmer 20 to 35 minutes, depending on degree of moisture desired. Serves 4 generously. Good with roast beef.

Mrs. Seigle W. Parks

RICE PUDDING

2 cups hot milk
2 tablespoons butter
½ cup grated Cheddar cheese

1 cup cooked rice
½ teaspoon salt
2 eggs
Paprika

Melt butter and cheese in the milk. Add rice and salt. Beat eggs slightly and add to mixture. Mix thoroughly and pour into greased casserole. Sprinkle with paprika. Bake at 350° for 45 minutes or until silver knife comes out clean. Serves 6.

Mrs. John McGarty

RICE RISOTTO

2½ cups chicken broth
3 tablespoons butter, divided
1 teaspoon salt
½ teaspoon sage

½ teaspoon thyme
1 teaspoon parsley
¼ teaspoon curry powder
1 tablespoon minced onion

1 cup rice, long grain

To the broth add seasonings and 1 tablespoon butter and bring to a boil. Add the rice and reduce heat. Simmer 20 minutes covered and without stirring. When cooked, fluff and add the rest of the butter. Serve at once. Serves 6. One cup of chopped mushrooms or celery may be added.

Mrs. William O. McMillan, Jr.

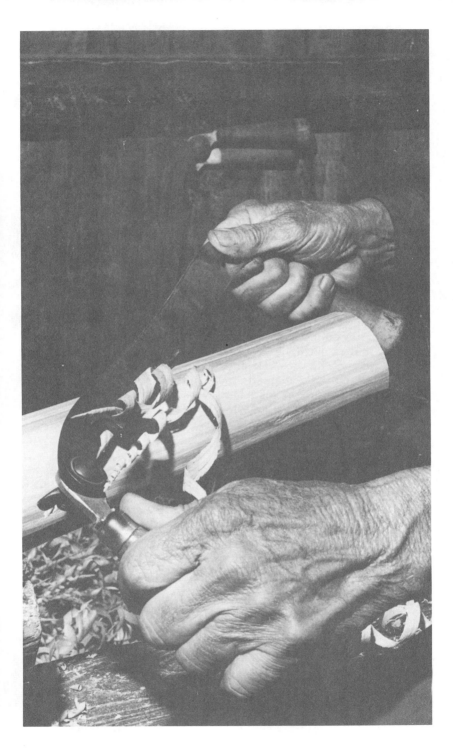

GLEEN HYLTON

He stays close to the land and tills the land,
His flesh is brown, his hands are calloused by
The handles of the plow, the ax and spade.
Gleen Hylton is as rugged as his land,
He sees years come and ripen and roll by,
He does not laugh at them nor does he sigh,
But solemnly he stands as years roll by.
No finer hill farmer has ever made
Furrows in earth than Gleen Hylton has made.
A man of earth, he lives close to the earth,
And such has been Gleen Hylton's heritage.
And he has lived among these hills since birth,
Though young in years hard work has made him age.
Gleen Hylton is as honest as the day,
His metal is as true as native clay.

From Man With A Bull-Tongue Plow by Jesse Stuart. Copyright© 1959 by Jesse Stuart. Reprinted by permission of the publishers, E. P. Dutton and Co., Inc.

Photo by Gerald S. Ratliff

VEGETABLES

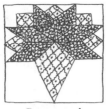

Cornucopia

ASPARAGUS CASSEROLE

¾ cup cracker crumbs
1 cup grated sharp cheese

1 (14½ ounce) can asparagus, drained

Butter a 2 quart casserole and line it with some of the crumbs. Arrange alternate layers of asparagus, cheese, and cracker crumbs, saving ¼ cup cheese for the top.

SAUCE

1 (10½ ounce) can cream of mushroom soup
½ cup milk
1½ teaspoons Worcestershire sauce

½ cup toasted almonds
⅛ teaspoon paprika
⅛ teaspoon nutmeg
Salt and pepper to taste
1 tablespoon butter

Gradually add milk and Worcestershire sauce to mushroom soup. Heat almost to boiling. Add almonds, paprika, nutmeg, salt, and pepper. Pour over casserole ingredients and top with remaining cheese. Dot with butter. Bake at 350° for 45 minutes. Serves 6.

Mrs. Isaac Noyes Smith, Jr.

ASPARAGUS CHEESEWICHES

2 English muffins, halved and toasted
1 (3 ounce) package cream cheese
4 slices tomato

1 (1 pound) can asparagus spears, drained
Dash garlic salt, pepper, minced onion, oregano
4 slices sharp American cheese

4 tablespoons sour cream

Spread muffin halves evenly with cream cheese; place on large cookie sheet. Top each with a tomato slice and 3 asparagus spears. Combine seasonings and sprinkle over asparagus. Cover pan with foil and bake at 375° for 25 minutes. Uncover and top with cheese slices. Return to oven for 2 or 3 minutes to melt cheese. Garnish each with sour cream. Serves 4.

Mrs. John Nesius

MARINATED ASPARAGUS

2 (10 ounces each) packages
    frozen asparagus
1 cup Italian dressing

2 to 4 tablespoons salad oil
¼ cup mild vinegar
Pimiento, as garnish

Cook asparagus according to package directions until tender. Drain completely, being careful not to damage the stalks. Combine dressing, oil, and vinegar. Arrange the asparagus in a large baking dish, and while still hot, pour the dressing mixture over it, making sure each stalk is thoroughly coated. Cover tightly. Chill overnight. Garnish with pimiento strips. Serves 8. Can be used as a vegetable or salad.

Mrs. James L. Surface

SCALLOPED ASPARAGUS AND EGGS

2 (14½ ounces each) cans
    asparagus, drained
5 hard-boiled eggs, sliced

3 cups grated Cheddar cheese
4 cups medium-thick white
    sauce

Grease a 3 quart baking dish. Layer asparagus, eggs, cheese, and white sauce. Repeat. Bake at 350° until heated through, about 20 to 30 minutes. Serves 8.

Mrs. Joe Hereford

BAKED GREEN BEANS

2 (16 ounces each) cans French
    cut green beans
1 cup sliced water chestnuts
1 (16 ounce) can bean sprouts,
    drained
1 medium onion, chopped

¾ cup grated cheese
1 (10½ ounce) can cream of
    mushroom soup
1 (4 ounce) can mushrooms,
    undrained
1 can French fried onion rings,
    crushed

In a 2-quart casserole, layer all ingredients except onion rings, starting with beans. Soup should be diluted with juice from mushrooms. Repeat until all ingredients are used. Bake at 350° for 60 minutes. Sprinkle with crushed onion rings and bake 5 to 10 minutes more until onions are hot. Serves 6 to 8.

Mrs. Robert Hart

BARBECUED BEANS

7 strips bacon, divided
2 medium onions, thinly
  sliced
¼ cup vinegar
½ cup catsup
½ cup brown sugar
1 (16 ounce) can kidney beans,
  drained
1 (16 ounce) can pork and
  beans, drained
1 (16 ounce) can baby limas, drained

Cook 4 slices of bacon and drain; reserve bacon for another use. Sauté onions in bacon grease until limp but not brown, (or use 4 tablespoons bacon grease which you already have). Add vinegar, catsup, and brown sugar. Heat, stirring frequently. Put the beans in large casserole and add sauce. Top with 3 chopped pieces of raw bacon; bake at 350° for 1 hour. Serves 8 to 10.

Mrs. William H. Carter

"GREASY BEANS"

3 pounds fresh green beans
6 slices of bacon, or ½ cup of
  bacon drippings, or a ham
  bone
2 medium onions, quartered
1 teaspoon salt (omit if salt
  cured bacon or country
  ham is used)
¼ teaspoon pepper
¼ cup brown sugar

Wash, string, and snap beans into three pieces. Place in a large pot with water to cover. Add rest of the ingredients, dicing the bacon. Cook for at least 3 or 4 hours, the longer the better. Serves 8.

Mrs. Robert M. Chilton

GREEN BEAN CASSEROLE

1 tablespoon butter
2 tablespoons flour
1 teaspoon salt
2 teaspoons sugar
4 teaspoons grated onion
1 cup sour cream
1 (4 ounce) package grated
  Swiss cheese
2 (10 ounces each) packages
  frozen French cut green
  beans, cooked and drained
Pepperidge Farm dressing
6 tablespoons melted butter

In a double boiler, melt butter; add flour, salt, sugar, onion, sour cream, and Swiss cheese. Cook until cheese melts. Spread cooked and drained green beans in greased 1½ quart casserole. Pour sauce over beans. Sprinkle with Pepperidge Farm dressing. Top with 6 tablespoons melted butter. Bake at 350° for 25 minutes. Serves 6 to 8. May be prepared ahead of time except for dressing and melted butter.

Mrs. Connie Carrico

LEATHER BRITCHES BEANS
(Fodder Beans)

Green beans　　　　　　　　Water
Salt　　　　　　　　　　　　Lard or bacon grease
　　　　　　　　　Pepper

String very full beans as you would for cooking, but do not break them. Thread beans on twine, using just enough beans on each string for one or two meals. Then drop them into a brine of ½ cup coarse salt and one gallon of water for 15 minutes. Drain on newspaper. The brine will keep bugs away from your beans. Hang the strings of beans on wire or rope in a dry place for at least three weeks. Make sure they are completely dry or they will mold.

Prior to cooking the dried beans, pour lots of boiling water over the beans and soak overnight. In the morning, wash the beans well and cover with water in a pan. Cook for 2 hours; then add salt, lard or bacon grease, and pepper. Finish cooking about 2 hours more, adding water as needed.

Mrs. Estil Monk

MARGARET'S GREEN BEANS

1½ cup cornflakes
2 tablespoons butter, melted
2 cups frozen green string-
　beans
5 slices bacon

3 tablespoons bacon drippings
2 tablespoons flour
⅞ cup liquid from beans
½ cup milk
¾ cup (3 ounces) grated extra
　sharp Cheddar cheese

Crush cornflakes and mix with butter. Cook beans over low flame until tender-crisp. Pan broil bacon until crisp; drain bacon well and reserve drippings. To 3 tablespoons drippings add flour which has been mixed with a small amount of the bean liquid. Add flour to the drippings, stir in remaining bean juice, and stir until mixture thickens. Add cheese to sauce, then beans. Place in well-greased 6 cup casserole and sprinkle on cornflakes. Bake at 325° for 20 minutes. Crumble bacon and sprinkle over top a few minutes before removing casserole from oven. Serves 4.

Mrs. Thomas H. Edelblute

STRINGBEANS ARDENNAISE

1 (10 ounce) box frozen green
　beans (French, Italian, or
　whole)
1 tablespoon butter
4 slices Canadian bacon,
　chopped

¼ cup chopped onion, or
1 tablespoon instant minced
　onion
½ teaspoon sweet basil
　Salt, pepper, crushed red
　pepper to taste
　　　¼ cup beef consommé

Melt butter in skillet. Add bacon and onion and cook 5 minutes. Add beans, basil, salt, pepper, and red pepper. Mix together, add consommé, cover, and simmer 30 minutes. Serves 4.

Mrs. Neil Robinson, II

WAX BEANS

2 pounds wax beans
2 cups fresh or canned
  tomatoes

2 tablespoons butter
2 teaspoons flour

Shred beans and parboil until just about tender, 10 to 15 minutes, in salted water. Simmer a can of tomatoes or use fresh ones; strain, reserving liquid. Melt 2 tablespoons butter, add 2 teaspoons flour and the strained juice. Then add beans and finish cooking until tender. Season and serve. Serves 6 to 8.

Mrs. P. Thomas Denny

BARBECUED LIMA BEANS

2 cups dry Lima beans
6 cups water
1 onion, chopped
1 garlic clove, chopped
2 tablespoons bacon fat
1½ teaspoons chili powder
1 (10½ ounce) can tomato soup
8 to 10 slices bacon (fry slightly, drain off fat, and cut up)

2 teaspoons Worcestershire
  sauce
2 teaspoons prepared mustard
¼ cup brown sugar
¼ cup cider vinegar
1 teaspoon salt

Rinse beans and cook in boiling salted water about 1½ hours. Drain beans and save liquid. Sauté chopped onion and garlic in bacon fat. In large casserole combine beans, 1½ cups reserved bean liquid, sautéed onion and garlic, chili powder, tomato soup, Worcestershire sauce, mustard, brown sugar, vinegar, salt, and partially cooked bacon pieces. Cover and bake at 350° for 30 minutes; then uncover and continue baking another 30 minutes, or until beans are tender. Serves 8 to 10.

Mrs. Edward W. Rugeley, Jr.

LIMA BEANS SUPREME

1 (10 ounce) package (2 cups)
    frozen Lima beans
  Salt

2 tablespoons scallions
2 tablespoons pimiento
2 tablespoons butter
½ cup sour cream

Cook frozen Limas in boiling salted water until tender. Drain. Sauté scallions and pimiento in butter. Add to Limas and stir in sour cream. Heat to desired temperature, but do not boil. Serves 4.

Mrs. D. Stephen Walker

LIMA BEAN AND TOMATO CASSEROLE

4 tablespoons chopped onion
3 tablespoons butter
1 (15 ounce) can tomato sauce
Salt and pepper to taste
¼ cup bread crumbs
1 (16 ounce) can Lima beans (or 2 packages frozen baby Limas, cooked and drained)
½ cup Parmesan cheese

Sauté onions in butter. Combine onions, tomato sauce, drained Lima beans, and salt and pepper. Place in buttered casserole and sprinkle Parmesan cheese and bread crumbs on top. Bake at 375° for about 20 minutes, or until top is brown and liquid is bubbling.

Mrs. John Charles Thomas

LOW CALORIE PICKLED BEETS

2½ cups canned beets
Red wine vinegar
1 teaspoon whole pickling spice
½ teaspoon salt
1 teaspoon liquid no calorie sweetener

Drain beet juice, and reserve it, adding enough red wine vinegar to liquid to make ½ cup. Place liquid in small saucepan with spice, salt, and sweetener. Simmer covered for five minutes. Strain and pour over beets. Refrigerate at least 24 hours before using. Serves 4.

Mrs. Samuel W. Channell

BROCCOLI CASSEROLE

2 (10 ounces each) packages frozen chopped broccoli
1 (10¾ ounce) can mushroom soup, undiluted
1 cup mayonnaise
1 small onion, chopped
10 Ritz crackers, crushed

Cook broccoli. Place in 1½ quart casserole with mushroom soup, mayonnaise, and onion. Mix together and top with Ritz crackers. Bake at 325° for 30 minutes. Serves 6 to 8.

Mrs. Joseph Wright

CHEESE BROCCOLI SPECIAL

2 (10 ounces each) packages
  frozen broccoli
1 (10½ ounce) can cream
  of chicken soup

½ cup grated Cheddar cheese
Paprika

Cook broccoli according to directions on package. Place crosswise in a casserole. Pour chicken soup over broccoli. Top with cheese, then sprinkle with paprika. Heat for 30 minutes at 350°. Serves 4.

Mrs. John C. Steven

BROCCOLI-VERMICELLI CASSEROLE

8 ounces vermicelli
2 (10 ounces each) packages
  frozen chopped broccoli
½ teaspoon salt
½ teaspoon pepper
½ teaspoon thyme

½ teaspoon savory
1 bunch green onions
4 tablespoons butter, divided
1 pound processed cheese
½ cup (or more) half and half
Parmesan cheese

Cook vermicelli 4 minutes and drain. Cook broccoli 2 minutes and drain. Sprinkle seasonings on broccoli. Chop onions and saute' in 2 tablespoons butter over low heat. Put vermicelli in buttered casserole; then add half of processed cheese, cut in slices. Pour cream over this and add broccoli, onions, and rest of butter. Top with remaining cheese slices. Sprinkle with Parmesan cheese and dots of butter. Bake at 350° for 30 minutes.

Mrs. William E. McClellan

BRUSSELS SPROUTS IN BOUILLON

1 medium onion, chopped
3 tablespoons butter

1 carton fresh Brussels sprouts
1 cup bouillon

Salt and pepper

Cook onion in butter until soft. Add Brussels sprouts. Add bouillon; cover and simmer 20 minutes or until sprouts are just done. Turn once during cooking. Salt and pepper to taste.

Mrs. Neil Robinson, II

BRUSSELS SPROUTS SOUFFLE

1 (10 ounce) package frozen
  Brussels sprouts
3 tablespoons butter
¼ cup flour
½ teaspoon salt
⅛ teaspoon freshly
  ground pepper

1 cup milk
1 teaspoon grated onion (more
  or less to taste)
4 eggs, separated
1 cup mozzarella cheese,
  grated

Cook sprouts, drain, and chop. Melt butter and add flour, salt, and pepper. Add milk and onion and stir until thickened. Beat egg yolks and add to warm sauce. Add cheese and cook for one minute, stirring constantly. Add sprouts and remove from heat. Beat egg whites until stiff and fold into hot mixture. Turn into ungreased 2-quart soufflé dish. Bake at 300° for 1½ hours and serve immediately. Serves 4 to 6.

Mrs. Isaac Noyes Smith, Jr.

MRS. HOWARD'S BAKED CABBAGE

Mrs. Annetta Howard's Boarding House sits just across the tracks of the Baltimore and Ohio Railroad in Rowlesburg, West Virginia, once an important railroad center. Mrs. Howard came to Rowlesburg with her doctor-husband, who set up practice while she busied herself running the hotel and dining room. She is still there serving home-cooked meals, but appreciates a call in advance, if you are coming.

2 tablespoons butter
2 tablespoons flour
1½ cups milk
4 to 5 cups coarsely cut
  cabbage

1½ teaspoons salt
¼ pound longhorn cheese,
  grated
¼ pound processed cheese,
  grated
½ cup cornflakes

Salt and cook the cabbage with very little water until tender. Drain well. Grease a baking dish. Alternate a layer of cabbage, a layer of grated cheese (a mixture of longhorn and processed), and then a layer of the white sauce. Top with a layer of cheese and sprinkle with cornflake crumbs. Bake at 350° until the ingredients are heated through and the cheese is golden brown. Serves 6.

Make medium white sauce by melting butter over low heat, adding flour, and cooking a few minutes. Add milk and stir constantly until thickened (about 10 minutes).

SCALLOPED CABBAGE

1 large head cabbage
  Water
  Salt
2 teaspoons bacon grease

½ cup cracker crumbs
2 teaspoons sugar
  Butter
  Milk

Shred cabbage and cook in boiling, salted water with bacon grease or a tablespoon of chopped ham fat for 10 minutes. Drain and remove any pieces of fat. Mix with cracker crumbs or bread crumbs and sugar. Place in baking dish. Dot well with butter. Add enough milk to half cover cabbage and cook in oven at 300° for 25 minutes or until milk is absorbed. Serves 8.

Mrs. William L. Cooke

STEAMED CABBAGE

1 tablespoon oil	1 green pepper, chopped
1 onion, chopped	3 cups chopped cabbage
	Salt to taste

Heat oil in skillet. Add onion, pepper, and cabbage and stir constantly until heated through and steaming. Cover and cook 5 minutes, still stirring frequently. Salt to taste. Serves 6. When served, cabbage will be slightly crisp. Tastes like Chinese-cooked vegetables.

Mrs. Mack L. Johnson

SWEET SOUR RED CABBAGE

1 medium red cabbage (1½ to 2 pounds)	¼ cup brown sugar, packed
Salted water	2 tablespoons flour
2 tablespoons vinegar or lemon juice	½ cup water
	¼ cup vinegar
4 slices bacon, diced (can add more if needed, or Bacon Bits or Bacos)	1 teaspoon salt
	⅛ teaspoon pepper
	1 small onion, sliced

Remove the outside leaves and wash the cabbage. Shred to measure 5 cups. In saucepan, heat ½ inch water, salted. (1½ teaspoons salt to 1 cup water), and vinegar or lemon juice to boiling. Add cabbage, cover and heat to boiling, and cook about 5 minutes or until crisp-tender. Drain.

Fry bacon until crisp and drain. Pour off all but 1 tablespoon bacon drippings. Stir brown sugar and flour into drippings in skillet. Add water, ¼ cup vinegar, salt, pepper, and onion. Cook, stirring frequently, until mixture thickens, about 5 minutes. Add bacon and sauce mixture to cabbage, stir together, and heat through. If you wish, garnish with more bacon. Serves 6.

Mrs. Richard Repaire

CAULIFLOWER — CARROT CASSEROLE

1 head cauliflower, broken into large chunks
1 package carrots, cut in half crosswise (if small, leave carrots whole)
Cracker crumbs

Boil cauliflower and carrots separately just until tender. Arrange vegetables in a casserole. Make white sauce and pour over vegetables. Sprinkle top with cracker crumbs. Bake at 350° for ½ hour or until bubbly on top. Serves 8.

WHITE SAUCE

4 tablespoons butter
4 tablespoons flour
½ teaspoon salt

¼ teaspoon pepper
2 cups milk
½ pound processed cheese, grated

Melt butter and add flour, salt, and pepper. Cook, stirring until smooth and bubbly. Add milk and stir constantly. Add cheese and stir until it melts.

Mrs. Kenneth Underwood

BAKED STUFFED CARROTS

A former professor of English at Fairmont State college in Fairmont, West Virginia, Dr. Ruth Ann Musick lived and taught in West Virginia for more than twenty years. During this time she gathered folklore of West Virginia which she published in articles for various journals and in book form. The late Dr. Musick was a long-time editor of **West Virginia Folklore**.

4 large carrots
1 medium onion (or ½ large onion)

½ green or red pepper
Salt and pepper to taste
3 tablespoons butter or margarine, divided

Boil carrots for 30 minutes or until mildly cooked. Cut in halves. Scoop out centers and mash. Chop onion and pepper and add salt, pepper, and 2 tablespoons butter. Add to mashed carrot centers and stuff the eight remaining halves of carrots. Bake in a dish greased with 1 tablespoon butter for about 30 minutes at 350°. Serves 8.

Dr. Ruth Ann Musick

CARROTS AND GREEN GRAPES

6 large carrots
1½ cups green seedless grapes

1 tablespoon butter
1 tablespoon frozen lemonade concentrate

Cut carrots in ½ inch slices and cook in boiling salted water, until done but quite firm. Drain. Just before serving, add grapes (whole, if small, but may be cut in half). Add butter and frozen lemonade concentrate. Toss well and serve. Serves 6.

Miss Julia Newhouse

CARROT RING WITH PEAS

4 cups mashed carrots (20-25 medium carrots)
½ cup sugar
3 eggs, separated
1 teaspoon grated onion
8 tablespoons butter, divided

2 tablespoons flour
½ cup milk
2 cups mushrooms
4 cups peas
1½ teaspoons salt
18 ¼" wide green pepper strips

Cook carrots until tender. Drain under cold water and remove skins and mash. Add sugar, beaten egg yolks, and onion. Reserve.

Melt 4 tablespoons butter; stir in flour and then milk to make thick sauce. Pour into carrot mixture and blend thoroughly. Fold in stiffly beaten egg whites. Pour into well-buttered ring mold. Place mold in pan of hot water and bake at 325° about 45 minutes or until mold shrinks slightly from side of pan. Unmold onto large plate. Fill mold with the following vegetables mixed together; 2 cups mushrooms sautéed until tender in 4 tablespoons butter; 4 cups peas cooked with salt but still bright green. Outside of mold may be garnished with parboiled green pepper strips stood on end. Serves 8 to 10.

Mrs. Howard Barnett

CARROTS BOURGUIGNONNE

1 medium onion, chopped
4 or more tablespoons butter

12 small carrots, peeled and quartered lengthwise
Seasoned flour

1 cup beef broth

Sauté onion in butter until yellow. Coat carrot strips with flour. Add to onions and brown. Turn once. Add broth; cover and simmer 30 minutes or until carrots are soft.

Mrs. Neil Robinson, II

HONEY GLAZED CARROTS

4 cups small cooked carrots
Rind of one orange, grated
3 tablespoons butter
½ cup honey

Carrots can be cooked until tender early in day. When ready to serve, combine all ingredients in skillet and heat. Carrots should be well coated. Serves 8.

Mrs. F. T. Graff, Jr.

ORANGE CARROTS

12 small carrots, washed and peeled
2 tablespoons butter or margarine
¼ cup sugar
1 tablespoon cornstarch
½ teaspoon salt
¼ cup orange juice
1 tablespoon lemon juice

Cook carrots in small amount of salted boiling water until tender. Drain. Melt butter in saucepan. In bowl combine sugar, cornstarch, and salt. Gradually add orange juice and lemon juice. Pour into melted butter and cook over moderate heat, stirring constantly until thickened. Pour sauce over carrots. Serves 4.

Mrs. Thomas J. Blair, III

BRAISED CELERY

Outside celery ribs, 1 per person
Sliced almonds
10 tablespoons butter, divided
1 bouillon cube
½ teaspoon salt
½ cup water
2 tablespoons minced onion (or equivalent in instant flakes)
1 teaspoon monosodium glutamate
2 tablespoons white wine

Cut celery into short diagonal slices. Sauté almonds until golden brown in some of the butter. Sauté cut celery in ½ stick butter. Add bouillon cube, salt, water, and minced onion to the celery. Cook on low flame 10 minutes. Add monosodium glutamate and white wine. Cook 10 minutes more until moist but not too wet. Add almonds, stir, and serve.

Mrs. Kenneth Kleeman

FAR EAST CELERY

4 cups diagonally sliced celery
1 (10 ounce) can cream of celery soup
1 (8 ounce) can water chestnuts, drained and sliced
¼ cup pimiento
¼ cup slivered almonds
1 slice bread, crumbled
Butter

Boil celery in salted water for 8 minutes. Drain. Mix celery, soup, water chestnuts, pimiento, almonds, and crumbled bread. Place in a 1½ quart casserole. Dot with butter. Bake for 30 minutes at 350°. Serves 6.

Mrs. Joseph Wright

CORN PUDDING

4 eggs
2 cups canned cream-style corn
3 tablespoons flour
2 or 3 teaspoons sugar
1 teaspoon salt
¼ teaspoon pepper
1 cup milk
1 tablespoon butter or margarine, melted

Beat eggs until thick and add corn. Combine flour, sugar, salt, and pepper. Stir milk into dry ingredients. Blend in melted butter. Combine with corn mixture. Beat well by hand, rotary beater, or low speed of electric mixer. Pour into greased 1½ quart casserole and bake at 325° for 1 hour and 20 minutes. Pudding is done when knife inserted in middle comes out clean. Serves 5 to 6.

Mrs. Ladd Michael Kochman

CREOLE EGGPLANT

1 medium eggplant
5 tablespoons butter, divided
3 tablespoons flour
2 cups canned tomatoes, chopped
1 small green pepper, chopped
1 small onion, chopped
Salt and pepper to taste
1 tablespoon brown sugar
Bread crumbs
Grated cheese, preferably Parmesan

Peel eggplant, cut up, and boil in salted water about 10 minutes. Drain and place in buttered baking dish. Melt 3 tablespoons butter and stir thoroughly into eggplant; sift flour over it and mix. Mix tomatoes, green pepper, onion, salt, pepper, and sugar and cook for 5 minutes; add to eggplant mixture. Mix well. Top casserole with bread crumbs and dot with butter and cheese. Bake at 350° for 40 minutes.

Mrs. Henry Battle

EGGPLANT AND TOMATOES IN CREAM

1 large eggplant
5 tablespoons butter, divided
4 medium tomatoes, peeled and sliced
½ cup grated Parmesan cheese
½ pint whipping cream
½ teaspoon salt
¼ teaspoon pepper

Slice eggplant into half inch slices. Sauté until tender in 4 tablespoons of butter. Place in buttered 9" square casserole to cover bottom. Place layer of sliced tomatoes and then a layer of half the Parmesan cheese; repeat layers ending with Parmesan cheese. Pour whipping cream over all; dot with butter, salt, and pepper to taste. Bake 30 minutes at 375°. Serves 6.

Mrs. Robert M. Chilton

RATATOUILLE

3 cloves garlic, finely chopped
2 onions, thinly sliced
⅓ cup olive oil
1 green pepper, cut in rounds
2 medium eggplant, diced
1 (20 ounce) can tomatoes or 6 to 8 ripe tomatoes, chopped
1 teaspoon dry basil
1½ teaspoons salt
1 pound mushrooms
Grated Parmesan cheese

Sauté garlic and onion in oil until soft. Add green pepper and eggplant and cook 5 minutes over medium heat shaking pan and stirring well. Add tomatoes, basil, and salt and simmer 30 minutes, half of the time covered. Add mushrooms and simmer until heated. Dust with grated Parmesan cheese.

Variations: add small chunks of zucchini and summer squash. Serves 6 to 8. Serve hot or cold. Best made a day ahead to allow flavors to blend.

Mrs. Ronald A. McKenney

POKE GREENS

Poke greens
Water
Chopped onion
Bacon grease

Pick very young leaves from the poke plant when they first appear in the spring. Wash the leaves and boil them in water to cover until they are tender. Drain the leaves. With two knives, cut the leaves across on a cutting board into small pieces. Sauté them with a little chopped onion in bacon drippings. Serve as a green vegetable with country ham and cornbread.

Mrs. Gladys Harris Hines

CREAMED SPINACH

3 (10 ounces each) packages
   frozen chopped spinach
2 (3 ounces each) packages
   cream cheese
1 (10½ ounce) can cream of
   mushroom soup

Onion salt to taste
Salt and pepper to taste
1 (16 ounce) can artichoke
   hearts
Butter

Cook and drain spinach. Add softened cream cheese to spinach. Mix soup and seasonings and add to spinach. Place in a buttered casserole and bake at 350° for 30 minutes. Top with artichoke hearts which have been drained and sautéed in butter. Serves 8 to 10.

Mrs. F. G. Bannerot, Jr.

SPINACH AU GRATIN

1 bag fresh or 1 box frozen
   chopped spinach
½ cup grated Cheddar cheese
1 cup hot medium white sauce

3 slices crisp cooked bacon
¼ cup bread crumbs
2 tablespoons melted
   margarine

Remove large stems from the spinach leaves and rinse under running cold water. Cook the spinach a few minutes, covered, without any added water. Drain after cooking. Add cheese to hot white sauce and stir until melted. Mix spinach and sauce. Pour into 9" square baking dish. Crumble bacon over the top. Mix the crumbs with the melted margarine enough to moisten and sprinkle over top of casserole. Bake at 350° about 20 minutes or until crumbs are brown. Serves 4.

Mrs. William T. Ziebold

SPINACH ARTICHOKE CASSEROLE

2 (10 ounces each) packages
   frozen chopped spinach
1 (16 ounce) package frozen
   artichokes
½ cup bread crumbs

1 (8 ounce) package cream
   cheese
1 stick butter or margarine
1 tablespoon lemon juice

Cook spinach and artichokes according to directions on packages. Add softened cream cheese, butter, and lemon juice to drained spinach. Place artichokes on bottom of casserole and add spinach. Top with bread crumbs. Bake at 350° for 25 minutes. Serves 6.
   Variation: Add 1 (10½ ounce) can cream of mushroom soup and onion salt to taste instead of margarine and lemon juice.

Mrs. Stanley H. Rose

SPINACH CASSEROLE

2 (10 ounces each) packages
frozen chopped spinach
1 medium onion, chopped
fine
6 tablespoons heavy cream

6 tablespoons Parmesan
cheese
6 tablespoons melted butter,
divided
½ cup soft bread crumbs (1½ to
2 slices)

Cook spinach in very small amount of water and drain thoroughly. Add onions, cream, cheese, and 4 tablespoons melted butter. Mix remaining 2 tablespoons butter with bread crumbs. Place spinach mixture in greased casserole and sprinkle bread crumbs on top. Bake uncovered at 400° for 15 minutes. Serves 4.

Mrs. Bert Bradford, Jr.

SPINACH PIE

1 9″ pie shell, unbaked
1 (10 ounce) box frozen
chopped spinach
3 eggs

1 pound cottage cheese
3 tablespoons flour
½ stick butter
6 slices Old English cheese

⅛ teaspoon garlic salt

Defrost and drain spinach well. Mix eggs with cottage cheese and flour. Add spinach. Melt butter and add cheese and garlic salt. Mix both mixtures together. Fill pie shell. Bake 1 hour at 350°. Cool 10 minutes. Serves 6.

Mrs. Daniel Martin

CUISSON DES CHAMPIGNONS BLANCS
(Boiled Mushrooms)

1 pound fresh mushrooms
1 cup water

1 tablespoon butter
Juice of ½ lemon

Salt and pepper

Wash the mushrooms. Remove caps from stems. Do not peel caps unless the mushrooms are old. Cut off hard tip of stem. Combine the water, butter, and lemon juice. Bring to a boil; add mushrooms (stems and caps). Cover and boil hard for 3 minutes. Season with salt and pepper.

These mushrooms may be served as they are, but they are more often cooked this way in preparation for another dish where the broth of the mushroom is used as part of the sauce.

Mrs. Margaret Blaine Horn

MUSHROOM AND ARTICHOKE HEART SAUTE

Juice of 1½ lemons
3 tablespoons butter
2 cups fresh mushrooms

2 (16 ounce) cans artichoke
    hearts, drained
1 tablespoon dry sherry

Add lemon juice to melted butter, and sauté mushrooms and artichoke hearts 12 to 15 minutes over medium heat. Add sherry and serve immediately. Serves 4 to 5.

Mrs. Thomas Mewbourne

MUSHROOM PIE

4 tablespoons butter
1 pound fresh mushrooms,
    washed and peeled
2 hard-cooked eggs, sliced

½ cup cream
1 teaspoon salt
¼ teaspoon white pepper
Prepared crust for 1 pie
Oysters, optional

Melt butter in saucepan. Add mushrooms and cook gently at simmer for 10 minutes. Add sliced eggs, cream, salt, and pepper. Pour into a greased 1½ quart baking dish and cover top with pie crust. Slash crust for steam vents. Bake at 375° until crust is brown, about 10 minutes. Serve hot. Serves 6 to 8. Especially nice served in individual ramekins as entrée, cutting crust to fit ramekins and baking as above. Broiled or sautéed oysters may be added to the mushroom mixture.

Mrs. Donald Ellsworth

MUSHROOM SOUFFLE

1 pound mushrooms
1 cup cream
½ cup flour
¼ cup butter, softened

1½ teaspoons salt
⅛ teaspoon pepper
5 sprigs parsley
4 eggs, separated

Wash mushrooms in salted water and dry; chop mushrooms well. In blender, put cream, flour, butter, salt, pepper, and parsley. Blend until smooth. Put this mixture in saucepan over medium heat, cooking and stirring until thick. Remove from heat and stir slightly beaten egg yolks in by hand. Add mushrooms and fold in well-beaten egg whites. Put in greased 1½ quart casserole. Set in a pan of warm water and bake at 350° for 1 hour. Serves 4.

FRIED ONION RINGS

2 large Bermuda or Spanish onions
Ice water
1 cup flour
½ teaspoon salt
1 teaspoon baking powder
1 cup milk
1 egg, slightly beaten
Hot deep fat

Peel onions and slice ¼ inch thick. Separate into rings and soak in ice water 2 hours. Drain and dry thoroughly. Dip into batter made by mixing flour, salt, baking powder, milk, and egg. Fry in hot deep fat at 370° until browned. Drain on absorbent paper. Bake at 375° for 10 minutes or until crisp. Serves 4.

Mrs. James E. Seibert

ONIONS AND GREEN PEPPERS

1 or 2 green peppers
2 tablespoons butter
2 tablespoons flour
1 cup milk
1 pound small cooked onions
Salt and pepper

Cut peppers in half and remove seeds and white membrane. Slice and sauté in butter. Stir in flour, add milk and cook until thick. Add onions. Heat slowly and season to taste with salt and pepper. Serves 4 to 6.

Mrs. Gardner M. Stultz

ONION PIE

1½ cups crushed crackers
1 cup melted butter, divided
3½ cups sliced onions
1 cup milk, scalded
3 eggs, slightly beaten
1 teaspoon salt
1 pound Wisconsin sharp Cheddar cheese, grated

Make a pie crust of crushed crackers and ½ cup melted butter. Press this mixture around the bottom and sides of a 10 inch pie plate.

Sauté onions until tender, but not brown, in ½ cup butter. Add the milk, eggs, salt, and grated cheese. Pour this mixture slowly over the crust. Bake 50 to 60 minutes at 300° until the pie is golden brown. Serves 8 to 10.

ONIONS SUPREME

1 quart sliced onions (about 3 pounds)
½ pound mushrooms (more if desired)
½ pound butter, divided
1 (10½ ounce) can tomato soup, undiluted
⅓ cup blanched almonds
1 teaspoon salt
1 teaspoon sugar
⅛ teaspoon pepper
2 cups bread crumbs (or less)

Cook onions in boiling salted water until tender. Drain thoroughly. Cut mushrooms in 2 or 3 pieces. Sauté in half the butter. Combine onions, mushrooms, tomato soup, almonds, salt, sugar, and pepper in a flat 8″ x 12″ baking dish. Melt remaining butter and mix with bread crumbs. Cover mixture with buttered crumbs. Bake 30 minutes at 350°, until crumbs are brown. Serves 12.

Mrs. Ralph J. Jones

RAMPS

Ramps, related to wild leeks, are perhaps the best known of all edible wild plants in West Virginia. This herb is found in great abundance in many of the mountainous counties from April to June, although in some areas it is rapidly becoming scarce due to commercial collectors. Only time will tell whether or not this plant follows ginseng into relative oblivion.

Many people are seemingly offended by the rather strong lingering odor associated with ramp eaters, but a two to three day waiting period is usually sufficient to re-enter society and the taste more than compensates for the inconvenience.

Ramps are excellent raw, although they are usually parboiled and seasoned, or fried in bacon grease.

RAMP SOUP

1 pound stew beef
18 to 20 ramps
4 or 5 stalks celery
2 or 3 carrots
1 pound potatoes
18 to 20 ramps
2 tablespoons butter
Salt and pepper to taste

Boil 1 pound of beef for about 15 minutes in 2 quarts of salted water, skimming off any scum that may form. Then dice and add 18 to 20 ramps, the celery stalks, carrots, and the pound of potatoes to the mixture, and simmer for 2 to 3 hours. Afterwards, fry another 18 to 20 ramps in butter for about 10 minutes or until thoroughly cooked. To these add one large cup of soup, salt and pepper to taste, and simmer for 10 to 15 minutes. Extract the meat (serve separately), combine both mixtures, press through a colander, stir, and reheat.

Ramps can be canned or frozen for winter use.

Mrs. William A. Pugh

WEST VIRGINIA RAMPS

Ramps, cut in 1 inch pieces   Salt and pepper to taste
Bacon pieces   Hard-cooked egg slices

Parboil clean, cut ramps in plain water. While ramps are boiling, fry bacon in large iron frying pan to the point of becoming crisp. Cut bacon into small pieces. Drain parboiled ramps and place in hot bacon fat with bacon pieces. Season with salt and pepper to taste and fry until done. Serve garnished with egg slices.

Mrs. Carl B. Hall, Jr.

BAKED POTATO SALAD

4 baking potatoes   3 tablespoons vinegar
1½ teaspoons salt   6 tablespoons cooking oil
½ teaspoon dry mustard   2 tablespoons grated onion
½ teaspoon paprika   ⅓ cup grated green pepper

Bake potatoes as usual until tender. Scoop out shells and reserve them. Mash potatoes thoroughly. Combine remaining ingredients; add to potatoes and mix well. Fill shells and let stand (this can be done early in the day). When ready to serve, put in 350° oven and heat through, 20 to 30 minutes. Serves 4.

Mrs. Michael T. DeVan

CHEESE POTATOES

12 medium new potatoes   1 stick melted butter or
1 cup grated Cheddar cheese   margarine
8 slices bacon, cooked and   Salt and pepper to taste
   crumbled

Wash and slice potatoes, but do not peel; cook in boiling water until done. In an ovenproof dish, put layer of potatoes, then cheese, bacon, and butter. Repeat. Season to taste. Bake in a 350° oven until hot, about 20 minutes. Serves 8.

Mrs. John G. McGarty

DILLED POTATOES

3 tablespoons chopped onion   1 cup beef consommé
3 tablespoons butter   ⅓ cup chopped fresh dill or 1
½ teaspoon pepper   teaspoon dried
1 teaspoon mustard   6 medium potatoes, peeled,
                                       parboiled and cubed

Sauté onion in butter with pepper and mustard. Add consommé and dill. Alternate this mixture with layers of potatoes in a greased casserole. Bake covered, at 350° for 1 hour. Serves 4 to 6.

Mrs. William C. Payne

GERMAN STYLE HOT POTATO SALAD

12 medium potatoes	1 teaspoon flour
3 hard-boiled eggs	½ cup vinegar
2 slices bacon	½ cup water
	2 to 3 teaspoons sugar

Boil the potatoes in their jackets. When done, let cool slightly; then peel, slice, place in a serving bowl, and keep warm. Slice 2 hard-boiled eggs and add to the potatoes. Cut the bacon in small pieces and fry in a skillet until brown. Add the flour and mix with a fork. Mix the vinegar, a little more than ½ cup water, and the sugar. Add this to the bacon and flour, stir with a fork, and let come to a boil. Pour this over the potatoes, stir gently, and top with 1 sliced hard-boiled egg. Season to taste. Serves 8 to 10.

Variation: Add 1 pound frankfurters sliced on the diagonal and heated through.

Mrs. Charlene Bonsall

HURRY-UP POTATO CASSEROLE

Instant mashed potatoes	½ pint sour cream
for 8	1 cup small cubes processed
½ cup milk, warmed	cheese

Mash instant potatoes with hot milk. Add sour cream and blend thoroughly. Place in a large greased casserole. Top all over with chunks of processed cheese. Bake at 350° for 30 minutes or until cheese is melted and mixture completely heated. Serves 8.

Mrs. Robert F. Goldsmith

PATRICIAN POTATOES

4 cups mashed potatoes,	¾ cup sour cream
leftover or instant	1½ teaspoons minced onion
3 cups cottage cheese	2½ teaspoons salt
	Butter

Mix all the ingredients and place in flat baking dish. Dot with butter. Bake at 350° for ½ hour. Important to let stand 20 minutes before serving. Serves 8 to 10.

Mrs. George Daugherty

SHREDDED POTATO CASSEROLE

1 large bag frozen shredded
  potatoes or hash browns
1 quart half and half cream
8 tablespoons butter

2 heaping tablespoons chives
Salt and pepper
Parmesan cheese
Paprika

Place all ingredients except Parmesan and paprika in a large pot on top of stove. Stir to the consistency of pudding. Place in greased casserole. Cover with Parmesan, sprinkle with paprika, and bake at 350° for 45 minutes. This may be prepared, except for baking, a day ahead.

Mrs. David Haden

SOUR CREAM POTATO SALAD

7 cups diced, cooked potatoes
½ cup chopped green onions
  and tops
1 teaspoon celery seed

1½ teaspoons salt
½ teaspoon pepper
3 hard-boiled eggs
1 sliced cucumber for garnish

Combine potatoes, onions, celery seed, salt, and pepper; toss lightly. Separate whites of eggs from yolks, reserving yolks for dressing; chop whites and add to potato mixture. Chill.

DRESSING

Egg yolks
1 cup sour cream

½ cup mayonnaise
¼ cup vinegar

1 teaspoon prepared mustard

Mash hard-boiled yolks. Add sour cream, mayonnaise, vinegar, and mustard. Mix well. Pour dressing over potatoes and toss lightly. Chill thoroughly. Just before serving, garnish with sliced cucumber. Serves 6 to 8. Flavor improves the second day.

Mrs. John Charles Thomas

COUNTRY SWEET POTATOES

1 (3½ cups) can sweet potatoes
  in heavy syrup
¼ cup milk
2 tablespoons brown sugar or
  maple syrup

3 tablespoons margarine or
  or butter
⅛ teaspoon salt
⅓ cup chopped pecans
10 large marshmallows, cut in
  half

Drain syrup from potatoes. Mash potatoes. Add milk, sugar, butter, and salt, and mix well. Fold in nuts. Put in a shallow greased baking dish. Top with marshmallows. Heat at 375° for 15 minutes or until marshmallows brown on top. Serves 4.

Mrs. Richard R. Meckfessel

SWEET POTATO BALLS

1 can (approximately 2½ cups)   ½ teaspoon cinnamon
     sweet potatoes   1 tablespoon butter
¼ teaspoon salt   2 cups shredded coconut
           Marshmallows (6 to 8)

Cook sweet potatoes until they can be mashed easily, approximately 20 minutes. Mash and combine with salt, cinnamon, and butter. Lay out about 20 inches of waxed paper on which coconut has been thickly sprinkled. Using about a half cup of mashed potatoes, form a ball. Press a marshmallow with thumbs into the center of the ball and compress between hands. Roll ball in coconut. Bake at 350° for 10 to 15 minutes or until browning has begun. Remove and serve. Serves 6 to 8.

Mrs. Leigh Shepherd

SWEET POTATO AND ORANGE CASSEROLE

2 pounds fresh sweet potatoes   1 teaspoon salt
     (4 cups mashed)   1 teaspoon grated orange rind
⅓ cup sugar   ½ cup fresh orange juice
3 tablespoons butter or
     margarine

Cook potatoes in skins; peel and mash while hot. Add remaining ingredients. Beat until fluffy. Turn into a buttered casserole. Bake at 350° for 30 minutes or until brown. Serves 8.

Mrs. Andrew R. Quenon

SWEET POTATO PONE

3 cups peeled and grated raw   1 cup molasses
     sweet potatoes or yams   2 eggs, beaten well
1 cup brown sugar   1 teaspoon cinnamon
        ½ teaspoon nutmeg

Combine all ingredients in order given and mix well. Place in a greased 2-quart casserole. Bake for 1 hour and 15 minutes at 350°. Serves 6 to 8.

Mrs. Ralph C. Dusic, Jr.

SWEET POTATO PUDDING

2 cups or 1 large can cooked
    sweet potatoes
2 eggs, beaten lightly
1 cup brown sugar, packed
1 cup milk or ¾ cup milk and
    ¼ cup bourbon
¼ cup melted butter

1 teaspoon lemon rind
2 teaspoons lemon juice
¼ teaspoon ginger
¼ teaspoon ground clove
½ teaspoon cinnamon
½ teaspoon salt
1 cup coarsely chopped
    walnuts

Put potatoes in mixing bowl, add eggs, and mix well. Gradually beat in the sugar. Stir in milk, butter, lemon rind and juice. Add ginger, cloves, cinnamon, and salt. Mix together thoroughly, adding the nut meats last. Pour into a greased baking dish, not too deep. Bake at 350° for 30 minutes or until set. Serves 6.

Mrs. Latelle M. LaFollette, III

CHOUCROUTE BRAISEE A L'ALSACIENNE
(Braised Sauerkraut)

Braised sauerkraut may be used as a bed for sliced roast pork, pork chops, ham, browned sausages, or with duck or pheasant. The dish is usually accompanied by boiled potatoes and either a chilled Alsatian wine, a white domestic wine, or beer.

2 pounds (about 5 cups) fresh
    sauerkraut (canned raw
    may be used)
½ pound chunk of bacon
½ cup carrots, thinly sliced
1 cup onions, sliced
4 tablespoons rendered fresh
    goose or pork fat, or butter

4 sprigs parsley
1 bay leaf
6 to 10 peppercorns
1 cup dry white wine
2 to 3 cups white wine or brown
    stock, or canned beef or
    chicken bouillon
Salt

Drain the sauerkraut, and soak it in a large basin of cold water for 20 minutes or more, changing the water 3 times. Drain again.

Remove rind and slice bacon into half inch pieces about 2 inches long. Simmer bacon in 2 quarts water for 10 minutes and drain.

Cook bacon, carrots, and onions slowly in fat or butter in 2½ or 3-quart casserole (fireproof and covered) for 10 minutes without browning. Stir in the sauerkraut, and when it is well covered with fat and vegetables, cover and cook slowly for 10 minutes more. Tie parsley, bay leaf, and peppercorns in small piece of cheesecloth and bury it in sauerkraut. Pour in the wine and enough stock or bouillon to cover sauerkraut. Season lightly with salt. Bring to simmer on top of stove. Lay on a round of buttered wax paper cut to fit inside of casserole. Cover and place on middle rack in 325° oven. Regulate heat so sauerkraut bubbles slowly for 4½ to 5 hours, until all liquid has been absorbed by sauerkraut.

Mrs. Thomas P. O'Brien

SAUERKRAUT

2 tablespoons bacon fat
1 medium-sized onion,
   chopped
1 quart sauerkraut
1 raw potato, grated

1 teaspoon caraway seed
Boiling water
1 medium sized apple, peeled
   and chopped (optional)
2 tablespoons brown sugar
   (optional)

Melt the bacon fat and add the chopped onion. Sauté until tender. If using canned sauerkraut, instead of the kind in a glass jar, rinse it. To the sautéed onion add the kraut, grated potato, and caraway seed. The chopped apple or brown sugar may be added, if desired. Cover with boiling water and cook uncovered 30 minutes over slow heat. Then cover and cook 30 minutes longer. Flavor is enhanced the third day. Serves 6 to 8.

Mrs. Alexander J. Ross

BAKED ACORN SQUASH WITH PINEAPPLE

3 medium-size acorn squash
1 (8 ounce) can crushed pineapple
½ cup brown sugar

1 teaspoon mixed spices (cinnamon, nutmeg, allspice)
¼ cup chopped pecans
2 tablespoons soft margarine
½ cup water

Cut squash in half lengthwise; remove seeds. Place squash in baking dish. Drain pineapple and combine with brown sugar, spices, pecans, and margarine. Spoon mixture into cavity of each squash half. Pour water into bottom of dish. Cover. Bake at 375° for 45 minutes. Remove cover. Bake 15 minutes longer, until slightly brown. Serves 6.

Mrs. John L. Sullivan

BAKED SUMMER SQUASH

3 pounds yellow summer
   squash
1 stick butter, divided
½ cup chopped onions
½ cup cracker meal or flavored
   bread crumbs

2 eggs
1 tablespoon sugar
1 teaspoon salt (to taste)
½ teaspoon black pepper (to
   taste)

Wash and cut up squash. Boil until tender; drain thoroughly and mash. Add all ingredients except half the butter to squash. Melt remaining butter. Pour squash mixture in baking dish; then spread melted butter over top and sprinkle with meal or crumbs. Bake at 375° about 1 hour, or until brown on top. This recipe can be cooked ahead, frozen, defrosted, and reheated. Serves 6 to 8.

Mrs. Marsha Pushkin

GOOSENECK SQUASH

3 or 4 squash, peeled and sliced   Salt and pepper
1 large onion, sliced   Buttered crumbs
2 tomatoes, thinly sliced   Parmesan cheese (optional)

Arrange vegetables in alternate layers of squash, onion, and tomato. Salt and pepper each layer. End with layer of tomatoes. Cover with crumbs. Sprinkle on Parmesan cheese, if desired. Bake uncovered at 350° for 1 hour. Serves 4 to 6.

Mrs. Neil Robinson, II

SUMMER SQUASH

3 or 4 yellow squash   Cracker crumbs
4 tablespoons oleo   Salt and pepper
1 medium onion, chopped   Crushed red pepper to taste

Slice squash and cook in salted water to cover till tender. While cooking squash, sauté onion in oleo. Drain squash and add to onion and oleo. Mash squash into mixture. Season with salt, pepper, and red pepper. Put in a casserole and top with buttered cracker crumbs. Bake at 350° for 30 minutes or until crumbs are brown. Serves 4 to 6.

Mrs. Chester P. Smith, Jr.

SUMMER SQUASH CASSEROLE

Summer squash, sliced   Grated cheese (preferably
Grated onion   Cheddar)
Bread crumbs   1 (10¾ ounce) can cream of
                                             mushroom soup

Cook squash in small amount of water until tender. Butter a casserole. Layer squash, grated onion, bread crumbs, and grated cheese; then make another layer of the same. Pour soup over all and cover with more bread crumbs and cheese. Bake at 350° for 30 to 45 minutes. Serves 4.

Mrs. Henry E. Payne, III

YELLOW SQUASH STUFFED
WITH MEAT AND GRUYERE CHEESE

1 pound ground chuck	1½ tablespoons sugar
1½ cups minced onions	¼ cup water
Salt and pepper to taste	¼ pound Gruyère cheese,
1 (6 ounce) can tomato paste	chopped
6 medium yellow straight neck squash	

Brown ground chuck and onions with salt and pepper. Stir in tomato paste, sugar, and water and simmer 10 minutes. Remove from heat and stir in cheese. Cut squash into halves lengthwise; scoop out seeds with spoon and discard. Place squash halves cut side up in 9″ x 13″ baking dish and sprinkle with salt and pepper. Spoon in meat mixture. Cover dish with foil and bake for 35 minutes at 375°. Serves 5 to 6.

Mrs. Frank S. Harkins, Jr.

BAKED ZUCCHINI & MUSHROOMS

2 tablespoons butter	⅛ teaspoon pepper
½ pound fresh mushrooms, sliced	¼ teaspoon oregano
	1 pound zucchini
½ teaspoon salt	¼ cup fresh bread crumbs
⅛ teaspoon garlic powder	¼ cup grated Parmesan cheese
3 eggs	

Sauté mushrooms in butter until lightly browned and most of liquid has evaporated. Stir in seasonings and herbs and set aside. Wash and peel zucchini and grate it coarsely. Combine zucchini with bread crumbs, cheese, and mushroom mixture. Spoon into greased 8″ square baking dish. Beat eggs slightly and pour over zucchini mixture. Stir slightly with fork. Bake uncovered at 325° until set, about 35 minutes. Serves 6 to 8.

Mrs. William E. McClellan

GLORIFIED ZUCCHINI

4 or 5 medium zucchini, sliced 1 inch thick	½ cup white wine
	1 (10½ ounce) can cream of
1 large onion, chopped	mushroom soup
2 tablespoons butter	Salt to taste
2 tablespoons flour	Grated cheese
Bread crumbs	

Cook zucchini slightly and drain. Place in buttered 9″ x 11″ baking dish. Brown onions in butter and stir in flour, wine, soup, and salt to taste. Pour over zucchini. Top with cheese and crumbs. Bake 30 to 40 minutes at 350°. Serves 6 to 8.

Mrs. Stanley H. Rose

SIMPLE ZUCCHINI

½ medium zucchini per person   2 tablespoons Parmesan
   Salt and pepper to taste   cheese per serving
2 tablespoons bread crumbs   1 tablespoon butter per serving
   per serving

Cut off ends of zucchini, halve, and steam until not quite tender. Add pinch of salt and pepper. Remove to serving dish that can be used in broiler. Cover with mixture of bread crumbs, Parmesan cheese, and butter. Broil under medium heat until brown.

Mrs. Harry N. Casto

ZUCCHINI CASSEROLE

1 medium zucchini, sliced ¼"   ¼ cup sour cream
   thick   2 tablespoons butter
¼ cup grated onion   Salt and pepper to taste
         Parmesan cheese

Parboil zucchini and drain well. Butter oven proof dish. Layer zucchini in dish with a little onion, sour cream, and dots of butter, and season with salt and pepper to taste. Continue until all ingredients have been used. Sprinkle with cheese. Bake at 300° for 45 minutes. Serves 6.

ZUCCHINI FLAN

2 tablespoons butter   2 eggs, lightly beaten
3 tablespoons chopped onion   ¼ teaspoon nutmeg
6 firm and unblemished zucc-   Salt and pepper to taste
   hini, thinly sliced   ½ cup Swiss or Gruyère cheese
1 cup heavy cream (may use   grated
   evaporated milk)

Cook onions until transparent in butter. Add sliced zucchini and cook until tender. In buttered casserole, blend cream, eggs, nutmeg, salt, and pepper. Add zucchini to cream mixture and sprinkle top with cheese. Bake at 350° until custard is lightly set, about 30 minutes. Serves 6.

Mrs. Charles Q. Gage

ZUCCHINI AND TOMATO CASSEROLE

Prior to being elected to represent West Virginia in the United States House of Representatives, John M. Slack, Jr., Democrat, held elective offices in Kanawha County government.

1 large zucchini, cut in small pieces
3 tablespoons butter
3 tablespoons flour
3 large tomatoes, peeled and chopped (or 2 cups canned tomatoes)
1 green pepper, chopped
1 small onion, chopped
Cracker crumbs
Grated cheese for topping

Boil zucchini until tender and set aside. Melt butter and blend in flour; then add tomatoes, green pepper, and onion. Season and simmer 5 minutes. Place zucchini in well-buttered casserole. Pour tomato mixture over zucchini, lightly cover with bread or cracker crumbs, and dot with cheese. Bake at 350° for 30 minutes. This recipe can be made ahead. Serves 4.

Congressman John M. Slack

BAKED TOMATOES

1 (26 ounce) can whole tomatoes
Ritz crackers, crumbled
Butter
Oregano (or Italian seasoning)
Grated Parmesan cheese
Onion and/or garlic powder

Drain tomatoes; squeeze some of the juice from each tomato and place in a shallow greased baking dish. Mix remaining ingredients. Make a small dent in the top of each tomato and cover with other ingredients. Bake at 350° until hot and browning, 20 to 30 minutes. Serves 6.

Miss Sallie Jefferds

RICE STUFFED TOMATOES

The fine food presented at The Daniel Boone Hotel has pleased the palates of Charlestonians since the hotel's beginning in 1929. The chefs, some of whom have served the hotel for over forty years, continue the high quality cuisine, which includes ice cream and baked goods made on the premises. Of historical interest is the site of the hotel on Capitol and Washington Streets in Charleston; this was once the location of the "pasteboard capitol," a building that served as a temporary capitol for West Virginians in the 1920's.

8 medium-size tomatoes
¼ pound long grain rice
1 large onion, chopped
1 large green pepper,
   chopped
4 teaspoons unsalted butter
1 teaspoon salt
¼ teaspoon pepper
¼ teaspoon monosodium
   glutamate
Parmesan cheese, grated

Scoop out tomatoes. Cook rice according to directions. Sauté onion and green pepper in unsalted butter and add rice, salt, pepper, and monosodium glutamate. Stuff tomatoes with rice mixture, sprinkle Parmesan cheese on top, and bake at 350° for 30 minutes. Serves 8.

The Daniel Boone Hotel

STUFFED TOMATOES

8 medium tomatoes
8 teaspoons mustard
2 packages frozen corn soufflé,
   thawed
8 slices bacon, cooked crisp
   and crumbled
Parmesan cheese

Cut a thin slice from the top of each tomato and scoop out pulp, leaving shell. Do not peel tomatoes. Drain shells upside down 20 minutes. Spread inside of each shell with 1 teaspoon mustard. Divide corn and bacon into tomatoes. Sprinkle Parmesan cheese over each tomato. Arrange snugly in a baking dish and bake uncovered at 375° for 30 minutes, or until golden brown on top. Serves 8.

Mrs. Andrew A. Payne, Jr.

STUFFED TOMATOES A LA RIVIERA

1 cup (7½ ounce can) king crabmeat, rinsed, drained, and
   separated or use fresh crabmeat
⅓ cup sour cream
¼ cup grated Cheddar cheese
4 teaspoons dry French dressing seasoning blend
4 medium tomatoes, cut almost
   completely through into
   6 sections
1 medium avocado, cut into 24
   wedges

Combine crab, sour cream, cheese and dressing blend; mix well. Spread the cut tomatoes and carefully insert avocado wedges in the spaces of each tomato. Fill centers with crab meat. Serve on Bibb or Boston lettuce. Serves 4.

Mrs. John H. Slack, III

TOMATO PUDDING A LA PALMER

¾ to 1 cup brown sugar
¾ cup boiling water
½ teaspoon salt

1 (10 ounce) can tomato purée
1 cup bread, diced
½ cup melted butter

Combine sugar, water, salt, tomato purée; boil 5 minutes. Place bread squares in casserole; pour butter over top. Add tomato mixture, and cover. Cook 30 minutes at 350°. Serves 4.

Mrs. Edward C. Armbrecht, Jr.

TOMATO SOUFFLE

3 tablespoons butter
4 tablespoons flour
1 teaspoon salt
½ teaspoon onion salt
¼ teaspoon freshly ground
  pepper

1½ cups stewed tomatoes (fresh
  ones in season; otherwise,
  half fresh and half from can
  for flavor)
4 eggs, separated

Melt butter; add flour and seasonings. Add tomatoes and cook for 3 minutes, stirring constantly. Beat egg yolks until thick and add to tomato mixture. Beat whites and fold into tomato mixture. Pour into well-greased 1½ quart baking dish. Bake at 350° for 45 minutes. Serves 4.

Mrs. I. N. Smith, Jr.

TOMATO TOWERS

3 large tomatoes
  Salt
4 ounces processed Swiss
  cheese, shredded (1 cup)

1 (10 ounce) package frozen
  chopped broccoli, cooked
  and drained
¼ cup chopped onion

Cut tomatoes into slices ¾ inch thick. Sprinkle each lightly with salt. Set aside 2 tablespoons of the shredded cheese; combine remaining cheese, the broccoli, and onion. Place tomato slices on baking sheet. Spoon broccoli mixture onto tomatoes. Sprinkle with reserved cheese. Broil 7 to 8 inches from heat for 10 to 12 minutes or till cheese bubbles and tomato slices are hot. Serves 6.
Variation: Before baking place 6 Holland Rusks on the baking sheet. Cover each with a slice of ham. Then place the tomato with the broccoli topping on this. Makes a nice luncheon dish.

Mrs. Thomas Mewbourne

TURNIP SAUTE

Peel and slice turnips. Cook in a little salted water until just tender. Do not overcook which may cause graying. Sauté in butter until golden, about 10 minutes. Sprinkle on a little sugar and cook until sugar melts.

TURNIPS AND HOLLANDAISE

Peel and dice turnips. Cook in a little salted water, until just tender. Do not overcook. Season with a little lemon juice and a little butter, or fold in a little Hollandaise sauce.

CREAMED TURNIPS

Peel and dice turnips. Simmer 20 to 30 minutes until tender. Mash and season with salt, pepper and butter; return to heat a minute to dry. Stir in a little heavy cream. Season with a dash of sherry.

CHEESE VEGETABLE CASSEROLE

¼ cup margarine or butter
¼ cup flour
1½ cups milk, scalded
½ teaspoon salt
¼ teaspoon pepper

¼ pound processed cheese, diced
¼ cup chopped pimiento
1 large package frozen mixed vegetables

1 or 2 cups seasoned croutons

Melt butter; add flour and let bubble 3 to 5 minutes. Add scalded milk, salt, and pepper. Stir in cheese gradually and cook until smooth. Mix in pimiento. Place vegetables in a 2-quart casserole and pour cheese sauce over them. Bake at 350° for 10 minutes; then top with croutons and cook 20 minutes longer. Serves 6 to 8.

Mrs. William C. Payne

MIXED VEGETABLE CASSEROLE

1 (10 ounce) package mixed frozen vegetables
½ cup chopped onion
½ cup chopped celery
2 tablespoons butter or margarine

Salt and pepper to taste
½ teaspoon basil
½ teaspoon marjoram
1 (10½ ounce) can mushroom soup
½ cup stuffing mix

Cook vegetables slightly in water. Sauté onion and celery in butter or margarine. Combine seasonings and soup with all vegetables in casserole. Top with stuffing mix and bake 30 minutes at 350°. Serves 4.

Mrs. Stanley H. Rose

MIXED VEGETABLE CURRY

In India this is traditionally served with rice as a main dish.

1 pound green peas	4 tablespoons butter
¾ pound carrots	3 onions, thinly sliced
2 potatoes	2 teaspoons chopped mint
1 pound string beans	leaves
1 clove garlic	½ cup yoghurt
¾ tablespoon green ginger	¾ tablespoon cummin
(or ¼ teaspoon powdered	1½ tablespoons tomato paste
ginger)	Salt to taste

½ teaspoon black pepper

Shell and wash peas; dice carrots; peel and halve potatoes; add beans. Mix vegetables together and place in a casserole or saucepan of boiling water. Cover and cook until just tender; remove from heat and reserve.

Pound garlic and ginger and mix with ¾ cup water. Heat butter and fry onions; when well browned, add bruised mint leaves. Fry for 1 minute more; then add yoghurt and cummin. Cook very gently for 5 minutes and add drained vegetables; reserve vegetable liquid. Cook vegetables for another 10 minutes; then add ginger-garlic water, tomato paste, salt, and pepper. Cook until liquid is gone; then add 2 cups of water from vegetables. Cook covered (adding more water if necessary) until done. Serves 8.

Mrs. John Charles Thomas

TRIPLE VEGETABLE DISH

6 large potatoes, pared and cut	4 cups milk
in ¾ inch cubes	2 (6 ounces each) cans whole
2 pounds small white onions,	mushrooms
peeled	1 cup soft bread crumbs (2
½ cup margarine	slices)
½ cup flour	1 bunch fresh broccoli, about
2 packages instant chicken	2 pounds
broth	

Cook potatoes and onions, covered, in boiling salted water for 15 minutes or until tender; drain and return to pan. Melt margarine in a large saucepan and stir in flour and chicken broth. Cook, stirring constantly until bubbly. Stir in milk; continue cooking and stirring until sauce thickens and boils for 1 minute. Drain liquid from mushrooms and stir this liquid into sauce. Add mushrooms to potatoes and onions; fold in sauce. Spoon into a 3-quart baking dish and sprinkle bread crumbs in center. Bake at 375° for 30 minutes, until bubbly and crumbs are toasted. While vegetables bake, trim broccoli and cut flowerets from stems. Cook flowerets, covered, in boiling salted water for 8 minutes or until tender. Drain broccoli and arrange in a ring around edge of baking dish. Serves 12.

Mrs. Andrew R. Quenon

VEGETABLES AU GRATIN

1 (16 ounce) can solid pack tomatoes	⅓ cup flour
2 (16 ounces each) cans whole onions	⅔ cup milk
1 (9 ounce) package frozen corn	¾ teaspoon salt
¼ cup butter	⅛ teaspoon basil
1 clove garlic, crushed	⅛ teaspoon pepper
	⅛ teaspoon oregano
	¼ teaspoon sugar
	1 cup grated Cheddar cheese, divided

Drain tomatoes and onions very well. Thaw a package of frozen corn. Melt butter and brown garlic in butter. Stir in flour. Add milk, salt, pepper, basil and oregano. Add sugar. Cook until thick. Stir in ½ cup cheese. Add the well-drained tomatoes to the cheese sauce. Cook until thickened again. Put the corn and onions in a 1½ quart (or 2 quart) casserole. Pour cheese-tomato sauce over vegetables. Top with the other ½ cup grated Cheddar cheese. Bake at 350° for 50 minutes, uncovered. Serves 8.

Mrs. Connie Carrico

WATERCRESS

Watercress	Bacon drippings
Salt and pepper to taste	

There are two kinds of watercress found in West Virginia. Both are good, but the lacy leafed variety is milder. It is usually found in bottom land near streams of water. Pick it early in the spring before flower buds form. Wash and cook the cress until tender in a small amount of water. Season with bacon drippings, and salt and pepper to taste.

Mrs. John S. Faber

CHEESE AND CHIVES SAUCE

¾ cup large curd cottage cheese	1 to 2 tablespoons chopped chives or green onion tops
¼ cup sour cream	

Beat cheese until smooth. Stir in sour cream and chives. Serve with baked potatoes. Makes 1 cup.

Mrs. Ancil B. Cutlip

EASY HOLLANDAISE SAUCE

½ stick butter   1 egg yolk
Juice of ½ lemon

Cut up butter in several pieces and place in top of double boiler with other ingredients, over slightly simmering water. Stir constantly with wire whisk for 2 or 3 minutes, until thickened. Do not overcook. Transfer sauce to small bowl and leave at back of stove until ready to serve. Serves 4.

Mrs. Angus E. Peyton

SESAME SAUCE FOR BROCCOLI

1 tablespoon salad oil   1 tablespoon soy sauce
1 tablespoon vinegar   4 teaspoons sugar
1 tablespoon toasted sesame seeds

Combine ingredients and heat to boiling. Serve over cooked broccoli. Makes approximately ½ cup, or enough for one small bunch broccoli.

Mrs. Robert McEldowney, III

275

MARTHA MacELMAIN

" . . . While passing by her woodpile roofed with snow,
She thought by now her hearth-fire guttered low,
And kneeling just outside the cabin door,
Gathered some bark strips edged with frozen clay
And bundled them into her apron sack.
Then quavering a psalm, went in the shack
To poke the embers up and wait for day."

Reprinted by permission of Louise McNeill, from **Gauley Mountain;**
Harcourt, Brace and Company; New York, New York; 1939; Page 22.

Photo by Commerce Photography

FRUITS

Melon Patch

SCALLOPED APPLES

4 cooking apples, pared and
    sliced
1 teaspoon cinnamon

1½ tablespoons flour
3 tablespoons sugar
1 tablespoon butter

Sprinkle cinnamon, flour, and sugar over apples and gently mix. Pour into a greased casserole, and put butter on top of apple mixture. Bake covered for 50-55 minutes at 350°. Serves 4.

Especially good for breakfast, brunch, or served as an accompaniment to chicken or pork for dinner.

Mrs. Charles G. Moyers, Jr.

MOTHER'S OLD FASHIONED APPLESAUCE

4¾ quarts apples
2½ cups water

1¼ cups sugar
1 teaspoon cinnamon
½ teaspoon nutmeg

Core and quarter apples; no need to peel. Add water and cook over low heat until soft, about 30 minutes. Strain through food mill. Add sugar and spices to taste. Return to heat to dissolve sugar. Makes 5 to 6 quarts.

Mrs. Robert F. Goldsmith

CANTALOUPE WITH FRUIT AND GRAND MARNIER

Mandarin oranges
Grapes

Strawberries
Grand Marnier

Cantaloupe

Marinate mandarin oranges (fresh or canned), grapes, and strawberries in Grand Marnier for at least 1½ hours. Use 2 or 3 pieces of each type of fruit for each serving of cantaloupe. Cut cantaloupe in half, scoop out cavity, and fill with fruit mixture. This can be served as either an appetizer or a dessert.

Mrs. John D. Amos

GLAZED ORANGES

4 oranges sliced ¼ inch thick
2 cups sugar
½ cup vinegar
¼ cup water
5 cloves
1 stick cinnamon

Simmer the oranges 30 minutes in water to cover in open pan. Drain and rinse. Mix the remaining ingredients, and add to orange slices. Simmer one hour uncovered. Chill.

Mrs. Paul F. Saylor

BAKED MINCEMEAT PEARS

1 (28 oz.) can pear halves
1 tablespoon cornstarch
1 teaspoon nutmeg
1 cup syrup, drained from pears
2 tablespoons butter or margarine
2 tablespoons lemon juice
½ cup mincemeat

Drain pear halves, reserving 1 cup syrup. Combine cornstarch and nutmeg in saucepan, add syrup. Boil for 1 minute, stirring constantly. Stir in butter or margarine and lemon juice. Place pear halves, cut side up, in baking dish; fill centers with mincemeat. Pour nutmeg sauce over all. Bake for 15 minutes at 350°. Serve warm. Serves 4 to 6.

Miss Mary Blaine McLaughlin

ESCALLOPED PINEAPPLE

1½ cups sugar
¼ pound butter
2 eggs
½ cup milk
5 slices bread, cubed (1 quart)
2¼ cups pineapple cubes & juice

Cream sugar and butter. Add eggs, milk, bread cubes, and pineapple cubes and juice. Toss together. Bake one hour at 350° in one large oblong flat pan or two small square ones. Can be doubled easily. May be served with ham, or as a dessert. Serves 6 to 8.

Mrs. Joseph R. Goodwin

PINEAPPLE SURPRISE

6 ounces cream cheese
1 (8 ounce) can crushed
   pineapple
⅔ of a (16 ounce) bag of miniature marshmallows

1 envelope of whipped topping,
   prepared in advance
2 tablespoons mayonnaise
Maraschino cherries as
   garnish

Cream the cream cheese. Add crushed pineapple including juice with the marshmallows, mayonnaise, and the topping. Mix all of this together and pour into two 8 inch cake pans. Place in freezer 24 hours before needed. Remove from freezer 10 minutes before serving and cut in wedges to serve. Garnish with a cherry. Serves 14.

Mrs. Charlene Bonsall

CHATEAU LA SALLE COMPOTE

1 apple
1 pear
1 orange
1 banana
½ cup fresh strawberries
1 (16 ounce) can apricots,
   drained

¼ cup orange juice
1 tablespoon lemon juice
Less than ¼ cup sugar, to
   taste
½ cup Chateau LaSalle white
   sweet wine

Grate the pear and apple; dice the rest of the fruit. Combine in a large bowl. Sprinkle with orange and lemon juice. Add sugar and wine. Mix lightly and keep at room temperature 2 hours. Chill. Serves 6.

Serve the rest of the wine with this fresh fruit compote as a dessert.

Mrs. William O. McMillan, Jr.

CURRIED FRUIT

1 (16 ounce) can apricot halves
1 (16 ounce) can peach halves
1 (16 ounce) can pear halves
1 (15 ounce) can pineapple
   chunks

1 cup golden raisins
¾ cup brown sugar
½ cup melted butter
3 teaspoons curry powder
3 tablespoons lemon juice

Drain all fruit and place in 2 quart oven-proof casserole. Mix last four ingredients and pour over fruit. Bake 1 hour at 325°. Cover and chill. Reheat following day. Serves 10 to 12. Especially good with salty meats.

Mrs. Quin Morton

HOT FRUIT COMPOTE

1 lemon
1 orange
½ cup light brown sugar (packed)
1 (16 ounce) can apricot halves

1 (16 ounce) can pineapple chunks
1 (16 ounce) can peach slices
1 (16 ounce) can pitted bing cherries
Nutmeg
1 cup dairy sour cream

Grate rind of lemon and orange into sugar. Thinly slice lemon and orange, removing seeds.

Drain canned fruits. Spread fruit in layers (including orange and lemon slices) in 2 quart baking dish. Sprinkle each layer with sugar/rind mixture and a light dusting of nutmeg. Bake in a 400° oven for 30 minutes, until very hot and bubbly.

Serve hot; top each serving with sour cream sprinkled with nutmeg, or pass sour cream. Serves 10 to 12.

Mrs. Jon Michael Gaston

SHERRIED FRUIT CASSEROLE

1 (16 ounce) can sliced pineapple
1 (8 ounce) jar apple rings
1 (16 ounce) can peach halves
1 (16 ounce) can pear halves

1 (16 ounce) can apricot halves
8 tablespoons butter or margarine
½ cup brown sugar
2 tablespoons flour
¾ to 1 cup sherry

Drain all fruit. Cut pineapple and apple slices in half; peach halves, if they are large, may also be cut. Arrange fruit in alternate layers in a medium-deep casserole. In top of a double boiler, combine butter, sugar, flour, and sherry. Cook over hot water, stirring until smooth and thick. Pour over fruit in casserole. Cover casserole and refrigerate overnight. Before serving, heat in 350° oven until hot and bubbly, about 20 to 25 minutes. Keeps well for several days. Serves 12.

Mrs. Charles G. Moyers, Jr.

LIGHT FRUIT DESSERT

1 (8 ounce) can cubed pineapple (in own juice, not syrup)
Sections of 4 grapefruits (or 2 cans sectioned citrus fruit)

Sections of 6 oranges (or 1 can mandarin oranges)
1 small container whipped topping (or whipped cream)
Brandy to taste

Put fruit sections in individual dishes. Top with whipped cream mixed with brandy. Serves 8.

Mrs. G. M. M. Ragland

RUMTOPF

A fruit dessert, served as is, or as a sauce for ice cream or pound cake. May also be used for salads.

Starting in the spring with fresh strawberries, thoroughly wash and pick over the berries so that only the best, fully ripened berries are used. In a glazed stoneware crock, place a layer of strawberries and an equal amount of sugar. Cover with rum.

As each fruit comes in season, add a layer to the crock and an equal amount of sugar, and always keep rum so that it covers the fruit. (You may add other liquid, but you must use at least ½ rum.) Do not use apples, black currants, or blackberries. Keep jar airtight by keeping a piece of plastic wrap stretched over the top. The fruit is ready to use 6 weeks after the last layer is added. You may substitute honey for sugar.

Mrs. Robert M. Chilton

SPINNING

"The wool from sheep was first washed to free it from oil. It was then picked free of burrs and other trash. Then it was carded. A wool card had thousands of short steel bristles or teeth set at an angle. Bits of wool were placed on a card and another card was raked over it matting the wool in rolls. These rolls were then spun on a spinning wheel. After a spool was filled with the twisted yarn it was doubled and twisted again. This doubling and twisting caused the yarn to stay twisted together."

Reprinted by permission of William B. Price, from "Pioneer Life" in **Tales and Lore of the Mountaineers;** Quest Publishing Company; Salem, West Virginia; 1963. Copyright by William B. Price. Page 160.

"We were put to tasks very early. When I was as young as five, I did my stint of the winter knitting, and I could turn the big spinning wheel to fill a spindle as evenly as my mother before I was ten. I learned to weave, to help with the stock, to work in the garden patch, and to take my portion of the care of the house, all at a very tender age. I count it excellent training for any woman."

Reprinted by permission of Janice Holt Giles, from **The Believers;** Paperback Library, Inc.; New York, New York. Copyright by Janice Holt Giles. Pages 7 and 8.

Photo by Gerald S. Ratliff

CAKES, PIES AND COOKIES

Flower Basket

CHEESECAKE

CRUST

2 cups graham cracker
   crumbs

½ cup sugar
½ cup melted butter

Mix ingredients well and press into the bottom of a 9″ spring form pan.

FILLING

4 (8 ounces each) packages
   cream cheese
6 tablespoons lemon juice
   (juice of 4 lemons)
⅔ cup half and half cream

8 eggs, well beaten
1½ cups sugar
1 tablespoon flour
Strawberry preserves or fresh
   fruit for topping

Have ingredients at room temperature. Beat cream cheese and lemon juice. Add cream and eggs to cream cheese and lemon juice. Combine sugar and flour and add to the cream cheese mixture. Beat until all ingredients are well blended. Pour into spring form pan lined with graham cracker crust. Bake at 350° for 1½ hours or until top is lightly browned. Serves 16. Top with homemade strawberry preserves or any fresh fruit topping.

Mrs. William W. Smith

CHOCOLATE CHEESECAKE

CRUST

1½ cups crushed chocolate
   wafers

½ cup melted margarine

Combine and press into the bottom of 9″ spring pan. Bake at 325° for 10 minutes.

FILLING

1 (8 ounce) package cream
    cheese, softened
¼ cup sugar
1 teaspoon vanilla
2 egg yolks, beaten

1 (6 ounce) package chocolate
    bits (melted and cooled)
2 egg whites
¼ cup sugar
1 cup heavy cream, whipped

¾ cup finely chopped nuts
Whipped cream for garnish (optional)

Combine cream cheese, sugar, and vanilla, mixing until well blended. Stir in egg yolks and melted chocolate bits. Beat egg whites and sugar. Fold in egg white mixture, whipped cream, and nuts. Pour over crumbs and freeze. Serve with whipped cream, if desired.

Mrs. J. Douglas Machesney

COMPANY CHEESECAKE

*Dr. George H. Crumb, formerly of Charleston, West Virginia, is a composer and a professor at Temple University. He is the first and only West Virginian to receive a Pulitzer Prize for music: his **Echoes of Time and the River** won for him the Pulitzer Prize in 1968. Additionally, Dr. Crumb, who composes for a variety of instruments, has been the recipient of many awards and grants.*

GRAHAM NUT CRUST

1¾ cups fine graham cracker
    crumbs
¼ cup finely chopped walnuts

½ teaspoon cinnamon
½ cup melted butter

Mix all ingredients; reserve 3 tablespoons to decorate top. Press 2½ inches up the sides and on bottom of a 9 inch spring form pan.

CAKE

3 eggs, well beaten
8 ounces cream cheese,
    softened
1 cup sugar

¼ teaspoon salt
2 teaspoons vanilla
½ teaspoon almond extract
3 cups sour cream

Combine eggs, cheese, sugar, salt, and extracts; beat until smooth. Blend in sour cream, pour into crust, trim with reserved crumbs. Bake 35 minutes at 350°. Chill well, 4 to 5 hours; filling will be soft. Serves 10.

Mrs. George Crumb

CHOCOLATE CAKE

4 ounces unsweetened
   chocolate
1 stick margarine
1 cup boiling water
2 cups sugar
2 eggs

2 cups flour
Dash of salt
1½ teaspoons baking soda
½ cup sour milk
1 teaspoon vanilla
Red food coloring

Melt chocolate and margarine in the boiling water over low heat. Cool slightly. Blend sugar and eggs together. Sift dry ingredients; add alternately with milk to the sugar mixture. Add chocolate mixture, vanilla, and a few drops of red food coloring to make a thin batter. Bake in an ungreased tube pan at 325° for 50 minutes or until cake pulls away from side of pan and leaves no thumbprint when pressed lightly. Glaze cake if desired.

Mrs. John G. Mueller

NO EGG CANADIAN CHOCOLATE CAKE

3 cups flour
6 tablespoons cocoa
2 teaspoons soda
2 cups sugar
1 teaspoon salt

¾ cup cooking oil, divided
6 tablespoons white vinegar,
   divided
6 teaspoons vanilla, divided
2 cups cold water

Sift together the flour, cocoa, soda, sugar, and salt. Make 3 holes in the dry ingredients. In each hole pour ¼ cup oil, 2 tablespoons white vinegar, and 2 teaspoons vanilla. Pour cold water over all. Stir just until well mixed. Pour in an ungreased 9" x 12" pan. Bake at 350° for 35 to 40 minutes.

ICING

½ cup butter
½ cup cocoa

7 tablespoons milk
1 pound powdered sugar

1 teaspoon vanilla

Melt butter; add cocoa, and heat for 1 minute. Pour in a bowl and add sugar and milk alternately. Then add vanilla and spread thoroughly over cooled cake. (Try using jellies and preserves between the layers if you make this cake in 2-8" round pans.)

Mrs. J. Holmes Morrison

WHITE CHOCOLATE CAKE

½ pound white chocolate
1 cup butter
2 cups sugar
4 eggs, separated
2½ cups flour

1 teaspoon baking powder
½ teaspoon salt
1 cup buttermilk
1 cup chopped pecans
1 cup flaked coconut

1 teaspoon vanilla

Melt chocolate over hot water. Cream butter and sugar. Add egg yolks, beat. Add chocolate to creamed mixture. Sift flour, baking powder, and salt together. Add alternately with buttermilk to above mixture. Add pecans, coconut, and vanilla. Beat egg whites until stiff and fold into batter. Pour into ungreased tube pan. Bake at 350° one hour and ten minutes.

Mrs. William E. Hamb

GRASSHOPPER CAKE

4 squares (4 ounces) unsweet-
    ened chocolate, melted
½ cup boiling water
¼ cup sugar
2¼ cups sifted cake flour
1½ cups sugar
3 teaspoons baking powder

1 teaspoon salt
½ cup cooking oil
7 egg yolks
¾ cup cold water
1 teaspoon vanilla
7 egg whites
½ teaspoon cream of tartar

Thoroughly blend melted chocolate, boiling water, and ¼ cup sugar; cool. In large bowl, sift together flour, 1½ cups sugar, baking powder, and salt. Make a well in the center of the dry ingredients and add oil, egg yolks, cold water, and vanilla in the order given. Beat until very smooth. Stir the chocolate mixture into the egg yolk mixture. In large mixer bowl, beat egg whites with cream of tartar until very stiff peaks form. Pour chocolate batter in thin stream over entire surface of egg whites, gently folding to blend. Turn batter into an ungreased 10″ tube pan. Bake at 325° for 1 hour and 5 minutes or until cake tests done. Invert pan; cool thoroughly. Split cake into three layers. Fill cake with the following filling, and also spread the top with the filling. (The sides should not be frosted.) Serves 14.

GRASSHOPPER FILLING

1 envelope (1 tablespoon)
    unflavored gelatin
¼ cup cold water

⅓ cup white crème de cacao
½ cup green crème de menthe
2 cups whipping cream

Soften gelatin in the cold water. Heat together crème de cacao and crème de menthe. Add softened gelatin; stir until gelatin is dissolved. Cool. Whip cream; fold in gelatin mixture. Refrigerate 15 minutes.

Mrs. Charles G. Moyers, Jr.

BANANA CAKE

2 cups sifted flour	1 stick margarine
1 teaspoon baking powder	½ cup milk
1 teaspoon baking soda	1½ cups sliced banana
½ teaspoon salt	2 eggs
1 cup sugar	1 teaspoon vanilla

Grease and flour two 8" cake pans or 20 cups. In a large bowl sift together flour, baking powder, baking soda, and salt. Put into a blender the sugar, margarine, milk, banana, eggs, and vanilla, and mix well. Pour the mixture into a bowl with the other ingredients and mix well. Pour everything into prepared pans and bake at 350° for 35 to 40 minutes. When cake is cool, frost with icing.

ICING

½ cup butter or margarine	2 egg yolks
2 cups powdered sugar	2 tablespoons mashed banana
	Lemon juice

Blend butter or margarine with sugar and egg yolks. Add mashed banana and lemon juice. Mix well. Put the cream between layers and frost the cake.

Mrs. V. Courtlandt Smith, II

BLACKBERRY CAKE

Wylene Dial is West Virginia University's area extension specialist on aging who has made a hobby of researching regional dialects on which she frequently lectures.

4 eggs	1 cup blackberry preserves
1 cup sugar	3 cups sifted flour
1 teaspoon soda	1 tablespoon nutmeg
1 cup buttermilk	2 tablespoons cinnamon
1 cup butter, softened	2 tablespoons allspice

Cream eggs and sugar. Dissolve soda in buttermilk. Add butter, preserves, flour, spices and buttermilk to creamed mixture. Mix well. Bake in four greased and floured 9" layers at 325° for 25 minutes or until done. Cool. Ice with Butter Icing. Serves 16.

BUTTER ICING

1½ cups sugar	½ cup butter
	½ cup heavy cream

Combine ingredients and cook to soft ball stage.

Mrs. Wylene P. Dial

CARROT CAKE

2 cups sugar
1½ cups cooking oil
4 eggs
3 cups finely grated raw carrots
1 teaspoon cinnamon, or more, if desired

1 teaspoon black walnut flavoring
1 teaspoon vanilla
2 cups self-rising flour
1 cup chopped black walnuts or pecans

By hand mix sugar, oil, and eggs. Add carrots, cinnamon, extracts, flour, and walnuts. Bake for 1½ hours at 350° in a tube pan, or a Bundt pan which has been lightly greased. Place a cookie sheet under cake for the baking process. Omit walnut flavoring, if not using black walnuts.

If self-rising flour is not used, add 2 teaspoons soda and 1 teaspoon salt.

GLAZE

⅓ cup buttermilk
1 cup sugar

½ teaspoon baking soda
1 teaspoon light corn syrup

Mix all ingredients and bring to a boil. Spoon over hot cake.

Mrs. Charles G. Moyers, Jr.

OATMEAL CAKE

1¼ cups boiling water
1 cup quick oats
1 stick margarine
1 cup brown sugar
1 cup white sugar

2 beaten egg whites
1 teaspoon vanilla
1½ cups flour
1 teaspoon soda
½ teaspoon salt

Pour boiling water over oats. Let stand for 20 minutes. Cream margarine, brown sugar, and white sugar. Add egg whites and vanilla. Add oatmeal to creamed mixture, alternating with flour, soda and salt. Bake in 9" x 13" pan at 350° for 30 minutes. Spread on topping while hot.

TOPPING

⅔ cup brown sugar
2 egg yolks
2 tablespoons margarine, softened

1 cup shredded coconut
1 cup chopped nuts
Whipped topping for garnish

Mix brown sugar, egg yolks, margarine, coconut, and nuts. Sprinkle evenly over cake. Bake 15 more minutes at 350°. Serve with whipped topping.

Mrs. Robert F. Goldsmith

BROILED ORANGE CAKE

1 stick butter or margarine	¼ teaspoon salt
1 cup sugar	1 cup buttermilk
1 egg	1 cup ground white raisins
2 cups sifted flour	Rind of 1 orange, grated
1 teaspoon soda	½ cup chopped nuts, optional

Cream butter, add sugar, and blend. Add unbeaten egg and beat well. Sift dry ingredients together and add alternately with buttermilk. Blend in raisins, orange rind, and nuts, if desired. Pour into 8" x 11" x 2" pan and start in cold oven set at 325°. Bake until well done, about 1 hour. Test for doneness with toothpick; cake is done when toothpick comes out clean.

TOPPING

Juice of 1 orange	1 cup sugar
Juice of 1 lemon	1 tablespoon melted butter
Whipped cream, as garnish	

Combine orange and lemon juices with sugar and melted butter. Pour over cake. Place under broiler until topping browns slightly, but watch carefully not to burn. Serve warm or cold with whipped cream. Keep cake in pan to retain moisture.

Mrs. T. A. Galyean

ORANGE CUPCAKES

1 stick butter	2 cups flour
1 cup sugar	1 teaspoon baking powder
2 eggs, separated	⅔ cup milk
Vanilla or lemon extract flavoring	

Cream butter and sugar; add egg yolks. Combine flour with baking powder and add alternately with milk. Fold in flavoring and beaten egg whites. Fill small greased muffin tins half full and bake at 350° for 15 minutes. Ice before cooling.

ICING

1 orange, grated and juiced	Juice of another orange
1 lemon, grated and juiced	1¼ cups sugar

Combine rinds and juices. Dip muffins in juice while hot, then in sugar. Put on wax paper to cool. Makes 2 or 3 dozen small muffins.

Mrs. Chapman Revercomb

FRESH PEACH CAKE

1 stick margarine
1½ cups brown sugar, firmly
    packed
1 egg
2 cups flour

1 teaspoon soda
Dash of salt
1 cup buttermilk
4 peaches, peeled and diced
¼ cup sugar
1 teaspoon cinnamon

Cream margarine and brown sugar until light. Add egg. Sift together flour, soda, and salt and add alternately with buttermilk. Stir in peaches. Pour into greased 9" x 13" pan. Sprinkle mixture of sugar and cinnamon on top. Bake at 350° for 30 to 35 minutes. Serves 10 to 12.

Mrs. Thomas H. Edelblute, Jr.

APPLE CAKE

1½ cups cooking oil
2 cups sugar
3 eggs, beaten
3 cups flour
1 teaspoon soda
1 teaspoon baking powder
1 teaspoon salt

1 teaspoon cinnamon
1 teaspoon nutmeg
1 cup chopped nuts
3 cups chopped, peeled apples
1 cup raisins or chopped dates
¾ cup coconut, optional
2 teaspoons vanilla

Cream together oil and sugar. Add eggs and beat well. Sift together the dry ingredients and add to creamed mixture, blending well. The batter will be very heavy. Stir in apples, nuts, raisins, and vanilla. Pour into a well-greased and floured tube pan. Bake at 325° for 1 to 1½ hours or until a toothpick inserted in center of batter comes out clean. Let age one day before cutting.

Mrs. Charles B. Watkins

TEENS FRUITY APPLESAUCE CAKE

1 cup seedless raisins
1 cup sliced dates
1 cup halved pecans
1½ cups candied cherries and
    pineapple, green and red
3½ to 4 cups flour sifted with:
    2 teaspoons cinnamon
    and 1 teaspoon each:
    salt, cloves, nutmeg

1 stick each butter and
    margarine
2 cups sugar
1 teaspoon rum (optional)
1 teaspoon almond flavoring
    (optional)
3 eggs, well beaten
2 cups unsweetened
    applesauce
2 teaspoons baking soda

Mix raisins, dates, nuts, and candied fruit and let stand, covered, overnight. Sift together flour, salt, and spices. Put fruit-nut mixture on waxed paper. Sift ½ cup flour-spice mixture over fruit and mix until coated with flour. Cream butter, margarine, and sugar thoroughly. Add rum and almond flavoring. Add beaten eggs. Heat applesauce, add baking soda, and blend well. Add flour and spices and applesauce alternately, mixing well. Pour in greased and floured tube pan. Bake at 275° for about 2 hours or until done.

Mrs. John Raynes

DANISH CHRISTMAS CAKE

1 cup shortening
1⅓ cups sugar
3 eggs
1½ teaspoons soda
1 teaspoon salt
3 cups sifted flour
1 tablespoon orange juice

1 pound dates, chopped
2 cups chopped nuts
1 (10 ounce) bottle maraschino
    cherries, chopped
1 tablespoon grated orange
    rind
1 cup buttermilk

Combine shortening, sugar, and eggs. Sift soda, salt, and flour together and add to shortening mixture. Add orange juice. Fold in remaining ingredients. Bake in one large tube pan that has been well greased or in 2 loaf pans. Bake at 325° for 1 hour and 20 minutes for tube pan and 60 to 70 minutes for loaf pans. Make sauce while cake is cooking and pour it on the hot cake. Let cake cool in pan for about 30 minutes. Turn out onto foil, seal tightly, and keep in refrigerator or freezer.

SAUCE

1 cup sugar
1 cup orange juice

1 orange rind, grated
1 cup coconut

Heat sugar and orange juice. Add grated rind and coconut. Mix well; remove from heat, and allow to rest and cool while cake bakes. Add extra coconut to the top after sauce is poured over cake.

Mrs. E. Garfield Atkins

CRANBERRY CAKE

A good ending for a Christmas or Thanksgiving dinner.

2½ cups flour
1 cup sugar
1 teaspoon salt
1 teaspoon soda
1 teaspoon baking powder
1 cup chopped pecans
1 cup chopped dates

2 cups whole cranberries
Grated rind of 2 oranges
2 eggs
1 cup buttermilk
¾ cup cooking oil
Whipped cream as garnish

Sift flour and measure; sift with sugar, salt, soda, and baking powder. Stir in nuts, dates, cranberries, and orange rind. Combine beaten eggs with buttermilk and oil; add to fruit mixture. Bake in a well-greased tube pan for 1 hour at 325°.

GLAZE

¾ cup orange juice   ¾ cup sugar

Heat juice and sugar until sugar is dissolved; do not boil. Pour over hot cake and let stand 30 minutes. Remove from pan, cool, and serve. Serve with whipped cream. Serves 12.

Mrs. William H. Knight

FIG CAKE

2 cups sugar	1 teaspoon allspice
¾ cup butter	1 teaspoon soda
4 eggs	1 cup buttermilk
3 cups flour	1 pint jar of figs
½ teaspoon salt	1 cup chopped nuts
1 teaspoon cinnamon	1 teaspoon vanilla

Cream sugar with butter; add eggs one at a time beating well. Sift flour, salt, cinnamon, and allspice together. Stir soda into buttermilk. Add flour and buttermilk alternately to the butter mixture. Chop figs with their liquid in a blender and add to batter, combining thoroughly. Add nuts and vanilla. Mix well. Bake at 325° for 75 to 90 minutes. Do not open door until 75 minutes.

Mrs. Melville Hyatt

DATE CAKE

1 (8 ounce) package of dates	1 cup sugar
1 teaspoon soda	1 egg
1 cup boiling water	½ cup chopped walnuts
1 tablespoon vegetable short-ening or margarine	1 teaspoon vanilla
	1½ cups flour
	¼ teaspoon salt

Stone the dates and cut them into small pieces. Sprinkle with soda and cover with the cup of boiling water. Let the mixture cool.

Cream the shortening and sugar together; add the egg, walnuts, and vanilla, and beat. Add the date mixture and mix well. Add the flour sifted with the salt. Bake in a 9" x 5" loaf pan at 325° for 45 to 50 minutes.

Dr. Ruth Ann Musick

QUEEN ELIZABETH CAKE

1 cup boiling water	1 teaspoon baking powder
1 cup dates, chopped	1 cup sugar
1 teaspoon soda	¼ cup margarine
1½ cups flour	1 egg, beaten
⅓ teaspoon salt	1 teaspoon vanilla

Mix water, dates, and soda and let stand. Sift flour, salt, and baking powder and combine with remaining ingredients, adding vanilla last. Bake at 350° for 30 minutes in greased 9″ x 12″ pan.

TOPPING

5 tablespoons brown sugar	2 tablespoons butter
5 tablespoons cream	¾ cup shredded coconut
½ cup pecans, chopped	

Boil sugar, cream and butter 4 minutes. Spread on warm cake and sprinkle with coconut and pecans.

Mrs. Dana B. Pitchford, Jr.

PRUNE CAKE

1½ cups sugar	1 teaspoon allspice
1 cup cooking oil	½ teaspoon salt
3 eggs, beaten	1 cup sour milk
2 cups flour	1 cup chopped nuts
1 teaspoon soda	1 cup cooked prunes, seeded
1 teaspoon cinnamon	and finely chopped
1 teaspoon nutmeg	1 teaspoon vanilla

Blend sugar and oil. Add beaten eggs and beat well. Sift dry ingredients together three times and add alternately with sour milk, beating well after each addition. Add nuts, chopped prunes, and vanilla; stir to distribute evenly through batter. Pour batter into buttered 9″ x 13″ x 2″ pan and bake at 300° for 1 hour. While cake is baking, prepare sauce and pour it over cake while it is still hot. Leave cake in pan.

SAUCE

1 cup sugar	½ teaspoon soda
½ cup buttermilk	2 teaspoons vanilla
¼ to ½ cup butter	

Combine all ingredients in saucepan. Boil for 1 minute without beating. Pour immediately over cake while it is still hot.

RAISIN CAKE

1 cup raisins
2 cups water
½ cup shortening
1 cup sugar
1 teaspoon soda
1 egg

1½ cups flour
1 teaspoon cocoa
1 teaspoon cinnamon
Pinch of salt
1 teaspoon vanilla
½ teaspoon ground cloves

Boil raisins in 2 cups water for 15 minutes; drain, reserving juice. Set aside to cool. Combine shortening and sugar until creamed. Dissolve soda in 1 cup raisin juice and add to creamed mixture. Add remaining ingredients until mixed well to a thin batter. Bake in greased sheet cake pan at 400° for 45 minutes.

TOPPING

3 tablespoons sugar

Juice of 1 lemon

Mix sugar and lemon juice and pour over warm cake.

Mrs. Craig M. Wilson

ALMOND CAKE

5 eggs, separated
1 cup sugar
¼ teaspoon salt

2 cups finely chopped
  unblanched almonds
Almond flavored butter and
  sugar glaze for topping

Beat egg yolks until creamy. Add sugar and salt and beat until light in color. Combine this mixture with chopped almonds (will be very stiff.) Beat egg whites until stiff and fold in. Bake in a greased 9″ square or round cake pan at 350° for 25 to 30 minutes. Top with almond-flavored butter and sugar glaze.

GLAZE

2 tablespoons margarine
2 cups powdered sugar

½ teaspoon almond flavoring
2 to 3 tablespoons milk

Cream all ingredients until smooth.

Mrs. T. Harvey McMillan

BLACK WALNUT CAKE
(or Hickory Nut)

Mary Helen Cutlip is a lecturer, a demonstrator, and a teacher of the craft of spinning. She and her family have an active interest in the pioneer family, its foods, crafts, and skills. The research for the Preface to Mountain Measures was provided by Mrs. Cutlip.

1 cup shortening	3 teaspoons baking powder
2 cups sugar	1 cup milk
4 eggs, separated	1 teaspoon vanilla
3 cups sifted cake flour	1 cup ground black walnuts or
¼ teaspoon salt	hickory nuts

Cream shortening and sugar until light and fluffy. Add egg yolks one at a time, beating thoroughly after each addition. Sift dry ingredients together. Add alternately with milk and vanilla, beating smooth after each addition. Fold in nuts, then the stiffly beaten egg whites. Pour into greased and floured 10" tube pan or bundt pan. Bake at 350° for 60 minutes or until done. Remove from pan to wire rack and drizzle glaze over hot cake.

GLAZE

3 tablespoons white corn syrup   3 tablespoons margarine

Combine corn syrup and margarine in small saucepan and boil 3 minutes.

Mrs. Ancil B. Cutlip

HICKORY NUT CAKE

1 cup butter	3¼ teaspoons baking powder
2 cups sugar	Pinch of salt
4 eggs	1 cup milk
3 cups flour	2 cups broken hickory nuts

Cream butter and sugar. Add eggs and beat. Sift flour before measuring; then sift flour, baking powder, and salt together. Add dry ingredients alternately with milk. Stir in nuts. Bake in a greased tube pan about 1 hour at 350°. Do not let crust brown too much. Cake is done when toothpick comes out clean.

Mrs. Richard Currence

RAINBOW SHERBET CAKE

½ gallon vanilla ice cream
½ cup chopped nuts
½ cup chocolate chips (the
   mini-chips work best)
1 quart each lime, orange, and
   raspberry sherbet

1 pint whipping cream
⅓ cup powdered sugar
Green food coloring
Fresh strawberries for
   garnish

Soften vanilla ice cream and stir in nuts and chocolate chips. Put ½ of this mixture in an angel food cake pan. Add alternating scoops of sherbets until all are used or pan is nearly full. Then add other ½ of vanilla ice cream mixture. Freeze for at least 24 hours. Shortly before serving, whip cream and sweeten with powdered sugar. Tint whipped cream pale green. Dip angel food pan in hot water to rim, and run a knife around edges to loosen. Invert "cake" on large chilled serving plate; frost with whipped cream; and garnish with fresh strawberries (leave stems on.) Good with coconut macaroons and lemonade or coffee and tea. Serves 20 to 24.

Mrs. Joseph Wright

APPLE BUTTER SPICE CAKE

2¼ cups sifted flour
1 teaspoon baking powder
1 teaspoon soda
½ teaspoon salt
1 cup sugar

½ cup butter
2 eggs
¾ cup apple butter
1 teaspoon vanilla extract
1 cup sour cream

Grease and flour bottom of 13" x 9" pan. Sift flour with baking powder, soda, and salt. Gradually add sugar to butter in a large mixing bowl; cream at high speed of mixer until light and fluffy. At medium speed, add eggs, beating well after each addition. Blend in apple butter and vanilla extract. At low speed, add sifted dry ingredients alternately with sour cream, beginning and ending with dry ingredients. Blend well after each addition.

TOPPING AND FILLING

½ cup firmly packed brown
   sugar
1 teaspoon cinnamon

½ teaspoon nutmeg
½ cup chopped nuts
Whipped cream for garnish,
   optional

Combine topping ingredients. Pour half of cake batter into pan. Sprinkle half of topping mixture over batter. Spoon remaining batter into pan; spread evenly. Sprinkle with remaining brown sugar mixture. Bake at 350° for 40 to 45 minutes until cake springs back when lightly touched in center. Serve warm or cold with whipped cream, if desired.

APRICOT SPICE CAKE

2 cups flour
2 cups sugar
¼ teaspoon salt
1 teaspoon soda
1 teaspoon cinnamon
1 teaspoon nutmeg
½ teaspoon baking powder

1 cup Crisco oil (do not
    substitute)
2 small jars or 1 cup apricot
    baby food (or banana or
    applesauce)
1 cup chopped nuts (optional)
3 eggs

Mix together dry ingredients. Add oil, baby food, nuts, and eggs. Beat by hand. Do not overbeat. Bake in tube pan at 350° for 30 minutes and lower to 300° for 20 minutes. Do not allow to get too brown.

ICING

½ cup brown sugar
½ cup margarine

¼ cup milk
Powdered sugar
1 teaspoon vanilla

Boil brown sugar and margarine. Add milk and bring to boil again. Remove from heat and add powdered sugar to spreading consistency. Add vanilla.

Mrs. Cinda Lively

GLORIFIED GINGERBREAD

2 cups flour
1 cup sugar
½ cup solid shortening
1 egg
1 teaspoon ginger

2 tablespoons dark molasses
1 cup buttermilk
1 teaspoon soda
¼ teaspoon salt
Whipping cream for garnish

Mix flour, sugar, and shortening until texture of cornmeal; set aside ½ cup. Make hole in the remainder, and add egg, ginger, molasses, buttermilk, soda, and salt. Mix and don't mind the lumps. Pour in a greased 9" x 9" cake pan and sprinkle ½ cup of reserved mixture on top. Bake 30 minutes at 350°. Serve with whipped cream. Serves 9.

Mrs. C. K. Payne, III

PUMPKIN CAKE

1 package spice cake mix   3 eggs
2 cups pumpkin   ½ cup oil
          2 teaspoons baking soda

Follow directions on back of cake mix box for mixing and baking.

ICING

1 (3 ounce) package vanilla   ¾ cup milk
   instant pudding, dry   1 teaspoon vanilla
1 envelope whipped
   topping mix

Whip all ingredients together and spread on cooled cake.

Mrs. David H. Wallace

SOUR MILK SPICE CAKE

1 cup shortening   1 teaspoon baking powder
2 cups brown sugar   ½ teaspoon salt
2 eggs plus 2 yolks   1 teaspoon cloves
2⅔ cups flour, sifted   1½ teaspoons cinnamon
1 teaspoon soda   1 cup sour milk

Cream shortening. Add sugar gradually. Beat eggs and yolks well into creamed mixture. Sift together flour, soda, baking powder, salt, and spices. Add alternately with sour milk to cream mixture. Pour into a greased 9″ x 13″ sheet cake pan.

TOPPING

2 egg whites   1 cup brown sugar
      ½ cup broken pecans

Beat egg whites until firm. Beat in brown sugar. Spread on top of cake batter. Sprinkle with nuts. Bake at 325° for 45 minutes.

Mrs. Frederick H. Belden, Jr.

CHERRY DELICIOUS CAKE

1 package 2-layer chocolate
cake mix, preferably red
devil's food
1 (8 ounce) package cream
cheese, softened
4 tablespoons sugar,
divided

2 tablespoons milk
1 pint whipping cream
1 (16 ounce) can dark,
sweet cherries with
syrup
2 tablespoons cornstarch
¼ cup water

¼ cup kirsch

Prepare cake mix as directed. Pour into a well-greased 10″ bundt pan. Bake at 350° for 45 minutes or until cake tests done. Cool in pan for 10 minutes; remove to cooling rack.

Beat together cream cheese, 2 tablespoons sugar, and the milk until fluffy. In another bowl beat whipping cream until fluffy and fold into cream cheese mixture. Chill. Drain cherries, reserving syrup. In small saucepan, combine cornstarch and remaining sugar. Mix well. Gradually stir in cherry syrup and water. Cook and stir over medium heat until thickened and bubbly. Stir in cherries; heat through. Remove from heat; stir in kirsch. Spoon cheese mixture into center of cake. Top with some of the warm cherry sauce. Slice cake; pass additional cherry sauce for individual use.

Mrs. E. Garfield Atkins

COTTAGE PUDDING

3 tablespoons butter
¾ cup sugar
1 egg
1¼ cups flour

2 teaspoons baking powder
Salt
½ cup hot water
½ teaspoon vanilla

Cream butter, add sugar, beat well, and add beaten egg. Mix and sift together flour, baking powder and salt. Add to first mixture and mix. Add hot water and beat until smooth. Add vanilla. Pour into shallow greased 9″ pan. Bake 25 minutes at 350°. Cut in squares and serve warm with the following sauce. Serves 6 to 8.

SAUCE

4 tablespoons butter
¾ cup powdered sugar, sifted
½ cup whipping cream, whipped

¼ teaspoon vanilla
1 cup strawberries

Cream butter, add sugar, and beat until creamy. Add vanilla and strawberries. Fold in whipped cream. Do not make sauce until ready to use.

Mrs. Helen Townsend Ziebold

ITALIAN CREAM CAKE

½ cup margarine
½ cup cooking oil
2 cups sugar
5 egg yolks
2 cups sifted flour

1 cup buttermilk
1 teaspoon vanilla
1 cup coconut
1 cup chopped pecans
5 egg whites, beaten stiff

In mixer blend margarine and oil. Add sugar, and then egg yolks one at a time, until creamy. Alternately add flour with buttermilk to egg mixture. Add vanilla, coconut, and pecans. Slowly fold in egg whites. Bake in greased and floured 9″ x 13″ pan at 350° or until cake is done, 30 to 35 minutes.

FROSTING

¼ cup margarine
1 (8 ounce) package
cream cheese

1 pound powdered
sugar
1 teaspoon vanilla

Blend margarine and cream cheese. Add powdered sugar and vanilla. Frost cake. Refrigerate.

Mrs. V. Courtlandt Smith, II

"DUMP" CAKE

1 large can crushed
pineapple
1 large can cherry pie filling
2 sticks margarine, cut in squares

1 large box yellow
cake mix
½ cup chopped nuts

Grease 9″ x 13″ cake pan. Dump in the pineapple and spread around the pan. Spread the cherries on top of that, then sprinkle the cake mix over the fruits. Add the nuts and place squares of margarine on top. Bake at 350° for one hour. Serve with whipped cream or ice cream. Serves 8 to 12.

Mrs. Charles B. Gates, Jr.

LANE CAKE

1 cup butter (butter only)
2 cups granulated sugar
1 teaspoon vanilla
3¼ cups flour

3½ teaspoons baking powder
¾ teaspoon salt
1 cup milk
8 egg whites

Grease and line bottom of four 9″ pans with waxed paper. Cream butter until fluffy; gradually add sugar, one cup at a time, beating after each addition until fluffy. Add vanilla and beat until mixture is as light as whipped cream. Add flour, sifted with baking powder and salt, alternating with milk in small amounts, beating each time. Beat egg whites stiff (soft peaks), but not dry, and fold into batter using a large spoon. Evenly divide batter in pans and bake at 375° about 15 minutes or until cake leaves side of pan. Let pans cool on cake racks for 5 minutes. Turn layers upside down on racks. Cool. Frost with the following frosting:

FROSTING

12 egg yolks	1½ cups coarsely chopped
1¾ cups granulated sugar	pecans
½ teaspoon salt	1½ cups seedless raisins
¾ cup butter (butter only)	1½ cups shredded fresh
½ cup rye or bourbon	coconut
1½ cups quartered candied cherries	

Put egg yolks in top of double boiler and beat slightly with rotary beater or electric beater at medium speed. Add sugar, salt, and butter. Cook over simmering water, stirring constantly until mixture is slightly thickened. Do not overcook. Remove from heat; add rye or bourbon. Beat 1 minute. Add pecans, raisins, coconut, and candied cherries. Cool. Spread frosting between layers and on top and sides. Cover with cake cover or loosely with foil, and store to ripen several days in cool place. Will keep well for several weeks. If frozen, wrap in vapor proof wrapping; store in freezer.

This is a very rich cake — and delicious. It is a specialty in eastern North Carolina.

Mrs. J. Vann Carroll

DR. JOHN C. NORMAN'S MOTHER'S NO FAIL PLAIN CAKE

Formerly on the staff of Harvard Medical School, Dr. John C. Norman is presently an associate of the renowned Dr. Denton Cooley of the Texas Heart Institute in Houston, Texas. At the Institute Dr. Norman is Director of the Cardiovascular Research Laboratory. His mother, Mrs. John C. Norman, Sr., of Charleston, provided the cake recipe which is one of her son's favorites.

2 sticks butter	3 cups cake flour
1 stick margarine	3 tablespoons milk
1 box powdered sugar	2 teaspoons vanilla (or
6 eggs	desired flavoring)
Pinch of salt	

Cream butter and margarine until light and fluffy. Gradually add sugar. Add alternately 2 eggs at a time, one cup of flour, one tablespoon milk, and the flavoring. Repeat 3 times. Do not overbeat. Bake in a greased 10" tube pan at 350° for one hour. Cool in pan, not inverted.

BLACK WALNUT POUND CAKE

¾ pound softened butter   1 pound flour (4 cups)
1 pound box powdered sugar   ½ cup water
6 eggs   2 teaspoons vanilla
       4 ounces black walnuts, chopped

Grease and lightly flour a 9″ tube pan. Cream butter until light and fluffy; then gradually add sugar. Add eggs one at a time, beating until light and creamy. Add flour alternately with water and vanilla, beating until smooth and light. Fold in walnuts. Pour in pan and bake at 350° one hour or until tester comes out clean. Do not over-bake, or it will be dry. Serves 12 to 16.

Mrs. Ronald A. McKenney

POUND CAKE

Harley O. Staggers, Democrat, represents West Virginia in the United States House of Representatives. He has been a teacher and a coach and has worked in local government.

½ pound sweet butter   1 teaspoon almond flavoring
½ cup shortening (or one stick   (or vanilla)
   margarine)   3 cups flour (sifted once with
3 cups sugar   ½ teaspoon baking powder and
1 cup milk   ¼ teaspoon salt)
1 teaspoon rum flavoring (or   5 eggs
   vanilla)

Cream shortening and butter and add sugar gradually. Add the two flavorings to the milk and put half of the milk mixture in the creamed shortening. Then, starting with about 3 tablespoons of flour and one egg, add these alternately until all the flour mixture and all the eggs have been used, beating after each addition. Then add remainder of milk. Blend well. Pour into a greased tube pan and bake 1½ hours at 350°.

Rep. Harley O. Staggers

MOUNTAIN POUND CAKE

3 sticks butter   3 cups cake flour, sifted
5 eggs   1 teaspoon coconut flavoring
1 pound box powdered sugar   ½ teaspoon almond flavoring

Cream butter until light. Add eggs one at a time, beating be-tween each addition. Blend in sugar well. Add flour and flavorings and beat until smooth. Bake in greased and floured tube pan for one hour at 350°. Cool 30 minutes and remove from pan.

Mrs. Helen Forren, Mountain Artisans Seamstress
Hinton, W. Va.

7-UP POUND CAKE

2 sticks butter	3 cups sifted flour
½ cup solid shortening	1 teaspoon vanilla
3 cups sugar	1 teaspoon lemon flavoring
5 eggs	1 small bottle 7-Up (a scant cup)

Cream well the butter, shortening, and sugar. Add eggs and continue beating. Add sifted flour gradually. Add vanilla and lemon flavoring and then slowly add 7-Up (do not substitute). Pour into large tube pan lined with greased and floured brown paper. Bake at 325° for 1 hour and 10 minutes.

Mrs. John C. Thomas

RUM CAKE

1 package yellow cake mix	4 eggs
1 (3 ounce) package instant vanilla pudding mix	½ cup salad oil
	½ cup rum
½ cup chopped nuts	

Mix the above ingredients except nuts for about 2 minutes. Combine well. Sprinkle chopped nuts on bottom of greased and lightly floured bundt pan (an angel food cake pan can be used.) Pour in batter and bake at 325° for about 1 hour. Remove from oven and thoroughly pierce top of cake with toothpick. Immediately pour glaze over cake while it is in the pan. Cool completely before removing from pan.

GLAZE

1 stick butter	½ cup water
1 cup sugar	1 ounce rum

Boil first three ingredients for 1 minute; then add rum. For alternate version omit rum and chopped nuts and replace with sherry wine.

Mrs. Richard Repaire

CHOCOLATE SHEATH CAKE

2 cups sugar	½ cup buttermilk (or 1 table-
2 cups flour	spoon vinegar and enough
½ cup margarine	sweet milk to make ½ cup)
½ cup solid shortening	2 eggs, slightly beaten
¼ cup cocoa	1 teaspoon soda
1 cup water	1 teaspoon cinnamon
1 teaspoon vanilla	

Sift together the sugar and the flour. In a saucepan melt the margarine, shortening, cocoa, and water. Bring to a rapid boil and pour over the flour and sugar. Stir well. Add the buttermilk, slightly beaten eggs, soda, cinnamon, and vanilla. Pour into a greased 9" x 13" sheet pan and bake 20 minutes at 400°. About 10 minutes before the cake is done, make the icing to pour over cake as soon as it comes out of the oven.

ICING

½ cup margarine	1 box sifted powdered sugar
¼ cup cocoa	1 teaspoon vanilla
6 tablespoons sweet milk or buttermilk	1 cup nuts

Melt together the margarine, cocoa, and milk. Bring to a boil and add the powdered sugar, vanilla, and nuts.

Mrs. John Prince Harris

GRANDMOTHER'S APPLESAUCE STACK CAKE

2 cups sugar	2 teaspoons vanilla
1 cup buttermilk	2 teaspoons soda
¾ pound solid shortening	1 teaspoon salt
2 eggs	8 cups flour

2 quarts cold homemade applesauce
(Grimes Golden apples best)

Mix with hands all ingredients but flour and applesauce in large bowl. Add the flour a small amount at a time; it has to be stiff.

Pinch out into 16 balls of the same size. There are 8 layers to a cake. Roll each ball of dough out thin, like pie crust, almost as large as the cake pans; finish pressing with hand to fit pan. Bake at 450° 8 to 12 minutes until brown. Three cake pans at a time may be used. While hot stack each layer and spread with applesauce. Store in refrigerator overnight for enhanced flavor. Makes 2 cakes.

Mrs. Estil Monk

APPLE BUTTER STACK CAKE

For more than fifteen years, Delmer Robinson has given the Charleston area outstanding recipes and cooking tips through his **Charleston Gazette** *column, "Man, That's Cooking!" Mr. Robinson, who has attended the Cordon Bleu school of cooking in Paris, frequently lectures and conducts demonstrations with his wife, Ann.*

⅔ cup butter
1 cup sugar
4 eggs
1 teaspoon vanilla

2½ cups sifted all-purpose
flour
1 teaspoon ammonium
carbonate*
1½ pounds apple butter

Cream butter and sugar at least 10 minutes by hand, or 5 minutes in electric mixer. The mixture should be thick and white. Add eggs one at a time, beating well after each addition. Stir in vanilla. If the ammonium carbonate is in granular form, crush it to a powder with a rolling pin or a bottle. Sift flour and ammonium carbonate together. Stir flour into egg mixture and blend thoroughly. Dough will be soft. Chill for at least 30 minutes.

Cut 6 to 8 — 8″ rounds from waxed paper. Spread the dough thinly and evenly on paper rounds, leaving about a half-inch margin to allow for expansion during baking.

Place two or three rounds (whatever it will hold) on a baking sheet. Bake at 400° 8 to 10 minutes, until golden brown on edges. Remove at once from cookie sheet, but do not remove paper until you are ready to assemble cake. Assemble by placing well-spiced apple butter between each layer. Leave top unadorned.

The ammonium carbonate (hartshorn or baker's ammonia) may be bought at drugstores or 3¾ teaspoons of baking powder may be substituted for the ammonium carbonate.

Mr. Delmer Robinson

SUNSHINE CAKE

6 egg whites (at room
temperature)
Pinch of salt
¼ teaspoon cream of tartar
6 egg yolks (at room
temperature)

½ cup water
1½ cups sugar
1 cup sifted cake flour
1 teaspoon vanilla

Beat egg whites until very stiff. Add salt and cream of tartar to egg whites and beat just to blend. Beat egg yolks until lemon-colored in separate bowl. Heat sugar and water in saucepan until bubbly and mixture reaches the "string" point on a candy thermometer. (This mixture should string as for boiled icing.) Slowly pour sugar-water mixture over egg whites while beating constantly with electric mixer at medium speed. Add to beaten egg yolks slowly, continuing to beat. Fold sifted cake flour into mixture a little at a time. Add vanilla and fold several times to blend. Bake batter in an ungreased angel food cake pan at 325° for 40 to 50 minutes. Cake is done when light brown on top. Remove from oven and cool upside down on rack or bottle before removing from pan.

This cake should be treated exactly like angel food cake. No frosting is needed, but a light dusting with sifted powdered sugar or super-fine granulated sugar will make it look prettier. (This recipe has been passed down for about 200 or more years. It has been adjusted for hearth, wood-burning, and electric ovens over the years. Failure to rise may result from too small eggs or over-beating egg whites.) Serves 12.

Mrs. Ladd M. Kochman

CHOCOLATE TORTE

MERINGUE

6 egg whites
¼ teaspoon cream of tartar
1½ cups sugar

Beat egg whites until foamy. Sprinkle in the cream of tartar. Beat until soft peaks form; then fold in sugar by sprinkling over whites. Spread on *three* 8" greased brown paper rounds placed on cookie sheet, and bake 1 hour at 250°. Leave in oven, turned off, for at least another hour to dry out well. Remove and cool.

CUSTARD

1 (6 ounce) package of chocolate bits
16 marshmallows
⅔ cup canned milk
1 cup whipping cream, whipped
½ cup chopped nuts

Combine chocolate bits, marshmallows, and milk and cook in top of double boiler until melted and blended. Cool, then refrigerate until thick. Fold whipped cream into chocolate custard. Spread on meringue layers, sprinkling each layer with chopped nuts. Stack layers like cake. Chill well before cutting. Serves 8 to 10.

Mrs. John M. Slack, III

FORGOTTEN TORTE

5 egg whites
½ teaspoon cream of tartar
1½ cups sugar
1 teaspoon vanilla
¼ teaspoon salt

Beat egg whites, cream of tartar, salt, and vanilla at highest speed for meringue, adding sugar 2 tablespoons at a time. Pour into well-buttered 9" springform pan. Place in pre-heated 450° oven. Turn off the heat immediately and *do not open the oven door*. Bake overnight with stored-up heat. Remove the next morning. Serve with ice cream and crushed strawberries, raspberries, or fresh peaches.

Mrs. John P. Killoran

HOUGENOT TORTE

4 eggs
2 cups sugar
½ cup flour
5 teaspoons baking powder
½ teaspoon salt

2 cups peeled and chopped tart apples
2 cups chopped pecans or English walnuts
2 teaspoons vanilla

Ice cream and additional nuts for topping, optional

Beat eggs until frothy and add sugar. Sift together the flour, baking powder, and salt, and add them to the egg-sugar mixture. Beat in the remaining ingredients in the order they are listed, mixing after each addition. Pour into a greased 10" x 16" pan. Bake 45 minutes at 325°. To serve, top with ice cream and nuts, if desired. Makes about 15 squares.

Mrs. Alexander J. Ross

HUNGARIAN ALMOND TORTE

7 eggs, separated
⅔ cup sugar
½ pound ground almonds (If possible, use half almonds with skins and half without.)

5 tablespoons ground dry bread crumbs
1 teaspoon almond extract
1 pint whipping cream (If desired, sweeten to taste.)

Grease the bottoms of two 9" cake pans. Beat the egg yolks; add the sugar and beat well. Add the almonds, crumbs, and flavoring. Beat the egg whites until stiff, and fold into mixture. Pour into pans, and bake 25 to 30 minutes at 350°. Cool in pans for 10 minutes, and then remove. When cooled, slice each layer horizontally if a four-layer torte is preferred. Stack layers with whipped cream between layers and on top of cake. This torte may be made early in the day before serving.

Mrs. Charles A. Gray

MOCHA TORTE

1 pound marshmallows
2 tablespoons instant coffee
½ cup boiling water

1½ to 2 pints whipping cream, divided
2 dozen lady fingers

Chocolate curls or grated chocolate

Melt marshmallows in top of double boiler. Dissolve coffee in water, blend into marshmallows. Chill. Line bottom and sides of a 9" springform pan with lady fingers. Whip one pint of whipping cream and fold in coffee mixture. Spoon a layer of filling into pan, place a layer of lady fingers on filling and continue alternating filling and lady fingers until pan is filled. Chill overnight. Remove outside ring of pan. Whip remaining cream and ice the mold. Garnish with chocolate curls or grated chocolate. Serves 10 to 12.

STRAWBERRY CREAM TORTE

1 package two-layer yellow
   cake mix
2 sticks butter or margarine
1¼ cups sugar
1 egg
3 tablespoons strong coffee
2 tablespoons rum

1 (4 ounce) package crushed
   almonds
1 pint whipping cream
1 jar strawberry jelly
Fresh or frozen
   strawberries, sliced

Bake cake according to directions. Cut each layer in half horizontally. Combine butter and sugar and add egg. Beat in coffee, rum, and almonds. Whip cream; then fold into butter mixture. Fill each layer with a thin layer of strawberry jelly, slices of fresh or frozen strawberries, and the cream mixture. Stack layers.

Mrs. Charles Bibbee

CHOCOLATE CREME DAVIS

CAKE OR TORTE FILLING

2½ cups evaporated milk
1½ squares unsweetened
   chocolate
1 cup granulated sugar

5 tablespoons flour
3 egg yolks, beaten well
2 tablespoons butter, melted

¼ teaspoon almond or rum extract

Heat milk and chocolate in double boiler. Mix sugar and flour; then add to chocolate mixture. Cook until very thick. Add small amount of hot mixture to well-beaten egg yolks. Add blended egg mixture to chocolate mixture and cook 2 minutes. Remove from heat and add butter and extract. Cool filling well before putting between layers.

Mrs. W. Gaston Caperton, III

CHOCOLATE ICING FOR 2 LAYER CAKE

2 cups sugar
2 (1 ounce each) squares
   unsweetened chocolate

1 stick margarine
¼ cup white corn syrup
½ cup milk

½ teaspoon vanilla

Combine all ingredients except vanilla and place over medium heat. Stir until it comes to full boil; boil one minute, not stirring. Add vanilla and beat in mixer until thick enough to spread.

Mrs. John M. Slack, III

MARY SUTTON'S SPONGE CAKE FILLING

Sponge cake or angel food   1 cup sugar
  cake, purchased or home   4 eggs, separated
  baked   Juice and rind of 1 lemon
½ cup butter   1 pint whipping cream

Cream butter, sugar, and egg yolks. Add lemon juice and rind. Beat egg whites until stiff. Fold into yolk mixture. Slice cake into 4 layers and spread with filling. Refrigerate overnight. Before serving, ice with whipped cream.

EASY PENUCHI ICING

½ cup butter   ¼ cup milk
1 cup light brown sugar   1¾ cups powdered sugar,
                                  sifted

Melt butter. Add brown sugar; boil 2 minutes, stirring well. Add milk and bring to boil. Cool to lukewarm and add powdered sugar, beating until creamy. Spread at once. Ices 20 cupcakes.

Mrs. Frank A. Thomas, Sr.

WHISKEY SAUCE FOR CAKE

1 cup butter   1 egg yolk, beaten
2 cups sugar   ½ cup whipping cream
                    Bourbon

Cream together butter and sugar. Add egg yolk and whipping cream. Cook in a double boiler. Add bourbon to taste. Serve over fruit cake or pound cake.

Mrs. David H. Wallace

ANGEL PIE
MERINGUE SHELL

2 egg whites   ½ cup sugar
⅛ teaspoon salt   ½ cup finely chopped walnuts or
⅛ teaspoon cream of tartar   pecans (optional)
              ½ teaspoon vanilla

Beat egg whites, salt, and cream of tartar until foamy. Beat in sugar, 2 tablespoons at a time until mixture is in stiff peaks. Fold in nuts and vanilla. Spoon into a lightly greased 8" pie pan. Bake at 300° for 50 to 55 minutes. Cool to room temperature. (Shell may be made the day before.)

CHOCOLATE FILLING

¼ pound German sweet
    chocolate
3 tablespoons water

1 teaspoon vanilla
1 cup whipping cream,
    whipped

Place chocolate and water over low heat to melt. Cool until thickened. Add vanilla. Fold chocolate mixture into whipped cream. Pile into meringue shell and chill 2 hours before serving. This pie may be frozen. Serves 6 to 8.

Mrs. William S. Gravely, Jr.

1850 BLACKBERRY PIE

1 unbaked 10" pie shell
1 quart blackberries

1 cup flour
2 cups granulated sugar
1 cup milk

Fill shell with berries. Mix flour, sugar, and milk. Pour mixture over berries. Bake at 350° for 45 to 50 minutes until center is set. If desired, brown under broiler. Serves 8.

Mrs. Charles G. Moyers, Jr.

CHUCK HOWLEY'S CHERRY PIE

Chuck Howley, a seven-time All-Pro linebacker for the Dallas Cowboys and former collegiate star at West Virginia University, prepares this cherry pie frequently for his family. He obtained the recipe from his mother, formerly of Wheeling, West Virginia.

2 cans (16 ounces each) red
    tart, pitted cherries,
    drained
6 tablespoons tapioca

1½ cups sugar
    Juice of 1 lemon
2 tablespoons butter
    Pastry for a double
      pie crust

Combine all but butter; allow to stand 5 to 10 minutes. Pour filling into pie shell; top with pats of butter; add lattice top crust. Bake at 450° for 15 minutes; reduce heat to 375° and bake about 45 minutes longer, or until crust has browned and filling is bubbly.

Chuck Howley

CHOCOLATE BAVARIAN CREAM PIE

1½ cups (about 20) chocolate
    wafers, crushed
½ cup butter, melted
1 tablespoon gelatin
¼ cup cold water
3 egg yolks, slightly beaten
½ cup sugar
¼ teaspoon salt
1 cup milk, scalded
3 egg whites, stiffly beaten
1 cup whipped cream
1 teaspoon vanilla
Additional crushed chocolate wafers for garnish

Mix crushed wafers and butter together and pat into a buttered 8" x 11" cake pan. Chill.

Soften gelatin in cold water and set aside. In top of double boiler combine egg yolks, sugar, salt, and milk. Add custard to gelatin mixture and cool. Fold stiffly beaten egg whites, whipped cream, and vanilla into gelatin-custard mixture. Pour into crust. May be garnished with additional cookie crumbs. Chill for several hours before serving.

Mrs. David J. Christensen

GERMAN CHOCOLATE PIE

1 (4 ounce) package
    German sweet chocolate
¼ cup butter
1 (14½ ounce) can
    evaporated milk
1½ cups sugar
3 tablespoons cornstarch
⅛ teaspoon salt
2 eggs
1 teaspoon vanilla
1⅓ cups coconut flakes
½ cup chopped pecans
2 unbaked 8" pie shells
Whipped cream, optional

Melt butter with chocolate in a double boiler, stirring often. Remove from heat and gradually stir in milk. Mix sugar, cornstarch, and salt; beat these with eggs and vanilla. Gradually blend in the chocolate mixture. Pour into pie shells. Mix coconut and pecans and sprinkle over filling. Bake at 375° for 45 minutes.

Filling will be soft, but it sets while cooling. Cool at least 4 hours before cutting. This is a very rich pie and especially good topped with whipping cream. Serves 12.

Mrs. William W. Smith

CHOCOLATE PIE FILLING

1 (6 ounce) package chocolate
    chips
1 egg
2 egg yolks, beaten
2 egg whites
1 pint whipping cream,
    whipped
1 teaspoon vanilla
1 baked pie shell

Melt 1 package chocolate chips with 1 beaten egg. Remove from the heat and add egg yolks. Beat two egg whites in another bowl and add to the whipped cream and vanilla; fold this into first mixture. Fill pie shell. Chill. Serves 6.

Mrs. John G. Hutchinson

CHOCOLATE MINT PIE

⅔ cup butter or margarine
1 cup sugar
3 eggs, well beaten
2 (1 ounce each) squares un-
    sweetened baking
    chocolate

⅓ cup chocolate chips
½ teaspoon vanilla extract
½ pint whipping cream
⅓ cup finely crushed pep-
    permint stick candy
1 graham cracker pie shell,
    chilled

Whipping cream and additional peppermint candy for topping, optional

Cream butter and sugar together. Add well-beaten eggs. Melt together baking chocolate and chocolate chips. Cool chocolate mixture slightly before adding to creamed butter, sugar, and eggs. Add vanilla. Beat by hand until all ingredients are thoroughly mixed. Put in well-chilled graham cracker pie shell. Chill in refrigerator for several hours, preferably overnight, until chocolate pie mixture is fairly firm. Just before serving, top with whipped cream and crushed peppermint stick candy. Serves 6.

Mrs. John F. Nelson, Jr.

COCONUT CREAM PIE

⅓ cup flour
⅔ cup sugar
¼ teaspoon salt
2 cups milk
3 or 4 egg yolks, slightly
    beaten

2 tablespoons butter
½ teaspoon vanilla
1 cup grated coconut
1 baked pie shell

Mix flour, sugar, and salt. Gradually add milk. Cook in double boiler until thick, stirring constantly for about 20 minutes. Remove from heat and add small amount to beaten egg yolks. Stir in whole amount. Return to double boiler. Cook 2 more minutes. Add butter and vanilla. Stir in coconut. When cool put in baked pie crust. Top with meringue.

Mrs. Robert F. Goldsmith

MERINGUE

3 egg whites   ¼ teaspoon cream of tartar
6 tablespoons sugar

Beat egg whites till foamy and add cream of tartar. Add sugar gradually and continue beating until it forms stiff peaks. Spoon carefully on cooled pies. Bake at 400° for 10 to 12 minutes until lightly browned.

Mrs. William C. Payne

IMPOSSIBLE COCONUT PIE

4 eggs
1¼ cups sugar
½ cup self-rising flour
1 teaspoon vanilla

¼ cup butter, melted
1 (7 ounce) package flaked coconut
2 cups milk

Beat eggs. Blend together sugar and flour, and then stir into eggs. Add remaining ingredients in order listed. Turn into 2 greased 9" pie pans. Bake at 350° for 30 to 40 minutes or until coconut is nicely browned. Makes its own crust.

Mrs. Carl B. Hall, Jr.

COFFEE CHIFFON PIE

1 merigue shell
½ cup water
2 tablespoons instant coffee

2½ cups miniature marshmallows, divided
1 cup whipping cream

Whipped cream and chocolate curls for garnish

Cook water, coffee, and 2 cups marshmallows over low heat until melted. Chill till firm without stirring. Then whip until fluffy. Fold in 1 cup whipped cream and ½ cup miniature marshmallows. Pile into shell and refrigerate at least 2 hours before serving. Garnish with additional whipped cream and chocolate curls.
For meringue shell recipe, see Angel Pie recipe.

Mrs. Susan B. Allen

COGNAC PIE

5 egg yolks
¾ cup sugar
1 envelope gelatin
¼ cup water

½ cup cognac, divided
1 cup heavy cream, whipped
1 10-inch graham cracker crust, baked and cooled

2 tablespoons shaved chocolate, or additional whipping cream for garnish

Beat egg yolks until thick and lemon colored. Gradually beat in sugar. Soften the gelatin in the water and add ¼ cup cognac. Heat over boiling water until gelatin dissolves. Pour the gelatin mixture into the yolks, stirring briskly. Stir in remaining ¼ cup cognac. Chill until this mixture will mound slightly, and then fold in the whipped cream. Pour the filling into the shell and chill. Before serving, garnish with shaved chocolate or whipping cream.

Mrs. William T. Brotherton, Jr.

THE COLONIAL INNKEEPER'S PIE

1 cup flour	⅓ cup butter or margarine
¾ cup sugar	½ cup milk
1 teaspoon baking powder	½ teaspoon vanilla
½ teaspoon salt	2 eggs
1 unbaked pie shell in glass pie pan	

Sift together flour, sugar, baking powder, and salt. Combine the butter, milk and vanilla and add dry ingredients to this. Beat 2 minutes. Add the eggs and beat 2 minutes longer. Pour into unbaked pie shell.

SAUCE

2 (1 ounce each) squares unsweetened chocolate	⅓ cup butter or margarine
	2 teaspoons vanilla
¾ cup boiling water	½ cup chopped nutmeats
1 cup sugar	Chocolate shavings, as garnish
Whipped cream or vanilla ice cream, as garnish	

Melt chocolate in boiling water. Add sugar and bring to a boil. Remove from heat and add butter and vanilla. Pour sauce over pie batter; sprinkle nutmeats over the top. Bake 55 to 60 minutes or until done at 350°. Garnish with whipped cream or vanilla ice cream and shavings of chocolate.

Mrs. William E. Hamb

BLUEBERRY CHEESE PIE

CRUST

20 graham crackers, crushed	3 tablespoons sugar
⅓ cup butter, melted	

Mix crumbs, sugar, and butter. Form into a 9″ pie pan. Bake at 350° for 10 minutes. Cool shell.

FILLING

1 or 2 (8 ounces each) packages
    cream cheese (whether
    you use 1 or 2 depends
    upon how rich and heavy
    you want the pie)

⅔ cup sugar
3 eggs
1 teaspoon vanilla

Soften cream cheese to room temperature. In mixer or by hand blend cheese with sugar, and add one egg at a time. Beat in vanilla. Pour filling into shell and bake 30 minutes at 350°. Turn oven off; open door; and allow pie to cool.

SOUR CREAM TOPPING

½ pint sour cream
               1 teaspoon vanilla
3 tablespoons sugar

Fold sugar and vanilla into sour cream. Spread on top of cooled pie and bake 5 minutes in 450° oven. Chill the pie until the top is very firm. This must be done, or blueberries will sink through.

BLUEBERRY TOPPING

1 (16 ounce) can blueberries
1½ tablespoons flour

2 tablespoons sugar
Pinch of salt

Drain juice from blueberries. To the juice add flour, sugar, and salt. Cook until juice is thickened. Let cool before folding in blueberries. Spread on pie and chill before serving.
This is a very rich dessert so serve in small pieces.

Mrs. Frederick M. Staunton

FRUIT CREAM CHEESE PIE

1 baked 9 inch pastry shell,
    cooled
1 (1⅓ cups) can sweetened
    condensed milk
¼ cup lemon juice
1 (3 ounce) package cream
    cheese

2 egg yolks
*1 cup drained crushed
    pineapple
2 egg whites
¼ teaspoon cream of tartar, if
    desired
4 tablespoons sugar

Put sweetened condensed milk and lemon juice into mixing bowl; stir until mixture thickens. Beat cream cheese, softened at room temperature, until smooth. Add one egg yolk at a time, beating well after each addition. Add fruit and mix well. Fold the cheese-fruit mixture into sweetened condensed milk mixture. Put into baked, cooled pastry shell.

Add cream of tartar to egg whites; beat until almost stiff enough to hold a peak. Add sugar gradually, beating until whites are stiff and glossy but not dry. Pile egg whites lightly on pie filling. Bake at 325° until lightly browned, about 15 minutes. Cool.

*Any one of these fruits may be used instead of the pineapple:
   1 cup sliced strawberries
   1 cup fresh raspberries
   1½ cups (No. 2 can) red sour pitted cherries, drained
   2 medium bananas, sliced

FUDGE PIE

½ cup butter
3 (1 ounce each) squares
   unsweetened chocolate
4 eggs, lightly beaten
3 tablespoons light corn syrup

1½ cups sugar
¼ teaspoon salt
1 teaspoon vanilla
1 unbaked 9″ pie shell

Ice cream or whipping cream for topping, optional

Melt butter and chocolate together and cool. Beat syrup, sugar, salt, and vanilla into eggs. Add chocolate and butter. Beat until well blended, and pour into unbaked shell. Bake at 350° for 25 to 30 minutes until top is crusty and set; mixture will shake like custard. This may be topped with ice cream or whipping cream. This filling may also be used to make thirty 1½ inch tarts.

Mrs. Miller C. Porterfield, Jr.

GRAHAM CRACKER PIE

CRUST

1½ cups graham cracker crumbs
   (approximately 16 crackers)
1 teaspoon flour

½ cup sugar
1 teaspoon cinnamon
½ cup melted butter or
   margarine

Mix dry ingredients together. Add the melted shortening and stir together. Use half of this mixture to line an 8 or 9 inch pie pan, pressing mixture to bottom and sides with fingers. Save the other half of mixture for topping.

FILLING

3 egg yolks
2 cups milk

¼ cup sugar
2 tablespoons cornstarch

1 teaspoon vanilla

Mix egg yolks and milk in top of a double boiler. Mix sugar and cornstarch and add to egg mixture. Cook until mixture coats a spoon, stirring constantly. Add vanilla. Cool slightly and pour into pie crust. Top with meringue (see meringue recipe.) Sprinkle with reserved crumb mixture. Bake at 400° until meringue is slightly browned, about 5 to 10 minutes. Cool several hours (at least 2) to allow filling to set before serving. Serves 6 to 8.

Mrs. Alexander J. Ross

GRASSHOPPER PIE

Faraway Hills, located near Beverly, south of Elkins, has been well known to West Virginians for many years as an elegant experience in fine dining, amid the charm and comfort of an "Old South" setting.

24 marshmallows
⅔ cup milk
1½ ounces crème de menthe
1½ ounces crème de cacao
½ pint whipping cream, whipped
6 tablespoons butter or margarine, melted
1½ cups crushed chocolate wafers

Melt marshmallows in milk in top of double boiler. Cool; then add liqueurs and whipped cream. Mix melted butter with wafer crumbs and line a 9" pie plate with the crumbs. Pour in cream mixture. Place in freezer until frozen firm. Remove from freezer and let stand at room temperature about 10 minutes. Serves 6.
OPTIONAL: Save a few wafer crumbs to sprinkle on top before serving.

Faraway Hills Inn

LEMON VELVET

2½ cups graham cracker crumbs
⅔ cup margarine, melted
2 (8 ounces each) packages cream cheese
1 cup sugar
¼ cup milk
2 tablespoons grated lemon rind
1 cup chopped walnuts
2 cups heavy cream, whipped

Combine crumbs and margarine. Press onto bottom of 13" by 9" pan. In mixing bowl, combine softened cream cheese, sugar, milk, and lemon rind and mix until smooth. Fold in nuts and whipped cream. Spread mixture on crust. Freeze. Cut into squares and garnish with lemon slices and graham cracker crumbs. Makes 16 to 20 servings.

Variation; substitute 2 tablespoons orange rind for lemon rind, and use 7 tablespoons Grand Marnier liqueur in place of the nuts.

Miss Sheila Sandy and Mrs. Robert Q. Jones

SHAKER LEMON PIE

For true lemon lovers only — quite tart and lemony:

2 lemons sliced paper thin —
    rind and all — only omit
    seeds and the very ends

2 cups sugar
4 eggs, beaten
Pastry for 2 crust pie

Mix lemons and sugar; let stand at least 2 hours until sugar and lemons become juicy. Blend eggs and lemon mixture thoroughly. Line 9″ plate with pastry. Pour lemon mixture into the shell. Cover with top crust and crimp edges. Cut decorative steam vents (easier and more effective if done before placing on pie.) Bake at 450° for 15 minutes; reduce heat to 350° for 30 minutes until knife comes out clean from center.

Mrs. Ronald A. McKenney

EASY LEMON CHESS PIE

3 eggs
1½ cups sugar
Pinch of salt
2 teaspoons flour

2 tablespoons lemon juice
    (fresh or bottled)
Grated rind from 1 lemon
    (optional)

6 tablespoons melted butter
1 unbaked pie shell

Beat eggs until smooth. Add sugar, salt, flour, juice, rind and butter. Beat well and pour into crust. Bake at 375° until brown, 25 to 30 minutes. A graham cracker crust may be used, if desired.

Mrs. Betty Scott Cowden

LEMON MERINGUE PIE

1½ cups sugar
4 tablespoons cornstarch
4 tablespoons flour
2 cups boiling water

2 teaspoons butter
4 egg yolks
Grated rind of 2 lemons
6 tablespoons lemon juice

Mix sugar, cornstarch, and flour. Add boiling water, stirring constantly. Stir until mixture boils, and cook 20 minutes in double boiler. Add butter, egg yolks, rind, and juice of lemons. Fill baked pie shell, spread with meringue, and bake until meringue is delicately browned in 300° oven. Serves 8.

MERINGUE

4 egg whites   ¼ teaspoon cream of tartar
7 tablespoons sugar

Beat egg whites with cream of tartar until frothy. Gradually beat in sugar, one tablespoon at a time.

Mrs. John Raynes

ORCHARD MINCE PIE

1 (9″) unbaked pie shell
2 cups (2 to 3 medium) peeled and finely chopped apples
1 cup prepared mincemeat
½ cup chopped nuts
¾ cup light cream
¾ cup firmly packed brown sugar
¼ teaspoon salt

In large mixing bowl, combine apples, mincemeat, cream, brown sugar and salt. Blend well. Pour into an unbaked pastry shell; sprinkle with nuts. Bake at 375° for 40 to 50 minutes until crust is golden brown.

Mrs. Frederick H. Morgan

HASTY MINCE PIE

½ stick butter
1 cup sugar
2 egg yolks
¼ cup buttermilk
1 tablespoon cider vinegar
½ teaspoon cloves
½ teaspoon cinnamon
½ teaspoon allspice
½ teaspoon nutmeg
½ teaspoon vanilla
Pinch of salt
1 cup raisins
1½ cups chopped apples
1- 9 inch pie shell
Whipped cream

Cream butter and sugar. Add egg yolks, buttermilk, vinegar, spices, salt, and vanilla. Then add raisins and apples. Bake at 350° for 35 to 40 minutes. Top with whipped cream if desired. Serves 6 (or more).

EASY MOCHA CREAM PIE

CRUST

2 cups well-crumbled vanilla sugar cookies
½ cup sugar
1 stick margarine or butter, melted

Mix cookie crumbs with sugar. Using a fork, mix in melted butter a little at a time. Be sure to dampen all crumbs. Using spoon or fingers, pat a *thin* layer of mixture on bottom then up sides of 13 inch springform pan without center. If mixture is too crumbly, add a little more butter. Cool in refrigerator until ready to use.

FILLING

4 (3 ounces each) packages instant chocolate pudding mix
3 cups cold milk
2 (9 ounces each) containers of whipped topping

2 tablespoons instant coffee (dissolved and cooled in ¼ cup hot water)
1 (1 ounce square) semi-sweet chocolate

Dissolve pudding mix with cold milk. It will begin to thicken immediately. With electric mixer, beat in 1 container of whipped topping; add coffee mixture. Pour into crust and top with remaining container of whipped topping. Grate or shave semi-sweet chocolate on top. Cover and cool in refrigerator at least 2 hours. Serves 20 to 25 people.

Mrs. Stephen Thomas, III

PAPAW PIE OR PARFAIT

½ cup brown sugar
1 envelope unflavored gelatin
½ teaspoon salt
¼ cup sugar

⅔ cup milk
3 eggs, separated
1 cup strained papaw pulp

In a saucepan, mix together brown sugar, gelatin, and salt. Stir in milk and slightly beaten egg yolks. Cool and stir until mixture comes to a boil. Remove from fire and stir in papaw pulp. Chill until it mounds slightly when spooned (20 to 30 minutes in refrigerator). Shortly before the mixture is sufficiently set, beat egg whites until they form soft peaks; then gradually add sugar, beating until stiff peaks form. Fold the partly set papaw mixture thoroughly into egg whites. Pour into a 9 inch graham cracker crust or into parfait glasses and chill until firm. "Then lock the doors to keep the neighbors out."

Euell Gibbons

PECAN PIE

3 tablespoons butter
⅔ cup light brown sugar, packed
¼ teaspoon salt
3 eggs

¾ cup light corn syrup
½ cup cream
¾ teaspoon vanilla
1 cup chopped pecans or pecan halves
1 unbaked pie shell

Cream butter; beat in sugar and salt. Add eggs one at a time; after each addition beat briskly. Add remaining ingredients and blend entire mixture. Pour into pie shell. Bake 10 minutes at 450°. Remove from oven and cover top with pecans. Reduce heat to 350° until custard sets — about 30 minutes. If nuts begin to get too brown, put foil on top of pie and continue baking.

Mrs. Estil Monk

MERINGUE PECAN PIE

3 egg whites	1 teaspoon vanilla
1 cup sugar	20 Ritz crackers
½ teaspoon baking powder	½ cup chopped pecans
Ice cream or fresh fruit and whipping cream for topping, optional	

Beat egg whites until very stiff; slowly add sugar, baking powder, and vanilla. Break the crackers into pieces about the size of a pea, and stir by hand into the meringue mixture. Add the pecans. Pour into a well-buttered 9" pie pan. Be sure to butter the edge and rim of the pie pan. Bake at 350° for 25 minutes. Serve with ice crear or fresh fruit and whipped cream. Serves 5 to 6.

Mrs. Thomas H. Edelblute, Jr.

PEANUT BUTTER PIE

1 baked pie shell	¾ cup powdered sugar
½ cup peanut butter	1 (3 to 4 ounce) box vanilla
1 envelope whipped topping	instant pudding mix,
mix, prepared according to	prepared according to
package directions	package directions

Blend peanut butter and powdered sugar with a pastry blender. Sprinkle ½ of this mixture into a baked pie shell. Pour the prepared pudding on top of the peanut butter and powdered sugar mixture, and follow with the prepared whipped topping. Top with the remainder of the crumbly mixture. Chill.

It is best to make this pie early in day or even the night before for enhanced flavor. Serves 6 to 8.

Mrs. John J. Droppleman

PINEAPPLE PIE

⅓ cup butter
⅔ cup sugar
2 eggs, separated

1½ cups crushed pineapple, drained
2 teaspoons cornstarch
⅔ cup cream
1-9" unbaked pie shell

Beat the butter, sugar, and egg yolks. Add pineapple. Dissolve cornstarch in cream and add to the pineapple mixture. Beat egg whites until stiff and fold in. Bake in 9" unbaked pie shell at 425° for 10 minutes; reduce heat to 350° and continue baking for 35 minutes more. Test for doneness as in a custard pie.

Mrs. Carl B. Hall, Jr.

PINEAPPLE CHEESE CHIFFON PIE

9" graham cracker pie shell
1 (9 ounce) can crushed pine-apple, drained, reserving syrup
1 (3 ounce) package lemon gelatin

1 (8 ounce) package cream cheese, softened
¾ cup sugar
1 cup evaporated milk, chilled
2 tablespoons lemon juice

Chill the pie shell. Add enough water to the pineapple syrup to make 1 cup liquid. Heat liquid to boiling, remove from heat, and stir in gelatin. Let stand.

Combine cream cheese, sugar, and pineapple in large mixing bowl. Beat at medium speed until creamy. Beat in gelatin at low speed. Chill until thickened.

Chill small mixing bowl and beaters. Pour milk into cold bowl and beat at high speed until fluffy. Add lemon juice and beat until stiff. Add to chilled gelatin and mix at low speed. Chill until mixture will mound and spoon into crust. Chill 2 to 3 hours until firm. Serves 8.

Mrs. Richard Morgan

NUTTY PUMPKIN NOG PIE

CRUST

1 cup graham cracker crumbs
½ cup very finely chopped pecans

3 tablespoons sugar
6 tablespoons butter or margarine, melted

In a small mixing bowl, combine cracker crumbs, pecans, sugar, and butter. Press firmly into a 9 inch pie plate Bake at 375° for 6 to 8 minutes. Remove and cool.

FILLING

1 envelope unflavored gelatin	Dash of ground nutmeg
½ cup brown sugar	1 cup dairy eggnog
½ teaspoon salt	3 eggs, separated
½ teaspoon ground cinnamon	1 cup canned pumpkin
¼ teaspoon ground ginger	¼ cup granulated sugar

In saucepan, combine the unflavored gelatin, brown sugar, salt, cinnamon, ginger and nutmeg. Stir in eggnog, beaten egg yolks and canned pumpkin. Cook and stir over medium heat until gelatin dissolves and mixture thickens slightly. Remove mixture from heat. Chill until partially set. Beat egg whites until soft peaks form. Gradually add the granulated sugar, beating until stiff peaks form. Fold into mixture. Pile into crust. Chill until firm, at least 4 hours. Garnish with whipped cream and pecan halves.

Mrs. Bert Bradford, III

SULLY'S PUMPKIN PIE

1- 10″ pie shell, baked	1 teaspoon cinnamon
1 pint vanilla ice cream (softened)	½ teaspoon ginger
	¼ teaspoon cloves
1 (16 ounce) can pumpkin, or 2 cups	1 teaspoon vanilla
	1½ cups whipping cream
1½ cups sugar	1 cup slivered almonds
½ teaspoon salt	¼ cup sugar

Spread ice cream in cooled pie shell. Place in freezer.

Mix pumpkin with sugar, salt, spices, and vanilla. Whip 1 cup of the whipping cream until stiff and fold into pumpkin mixture. Pour this over ice cream; cover with foil; and return to freezer for 4 hours.

Put almonds and ¼ cup of sugar in skillet. Stir over low heat until nuts are caramelized. Put almonds on a greased cookie sheet. When they are cool, break apart. Before serving whip rest of cream, and spread on top of pie. Garnish with almonds.

Good especially after a heavy Thanksgiving dinner.

Mrs. John D. Amos

RHUBARB PIE

1 high fluted 9-inch unbaked pie shell	1¾ cups sugar
	1 teaspoon cinnamon
2 eggs, well beaten	½ teaspoon nutmeg
2 tablespoons melted butter	¼ teaspoon salt
3½ cups finely chopped rhubarb	⅓ cup flour

Mix eggs, butter, and rhubarb. Combine dry ingredients thoroughly and blend into rhubarb. Fill shell. Bake at 375° for 45 to 50 minutes until set. Serves 8.

Mrs. Ronald A. McKenney

RUM CREAM PIE

CRUST

36 oreo cookies   1 stick margarine or butter, melted

Roll cookies fine and mix well with melted butter. Press into 2 9" pie plates and freeze.

FILLING

6 egg yolks   ½ cup cold water
1 cup sugar   1 pint whipped cream
1 tablespoon gelatin   ½ cup rum
Shaved chocolate

Beat egg yolks well. Add the sugar and beat until thick and creamy. Soak the gelatin in cold water. Place over a low flame and bring to a boil. Pour the gelatin over the egg mixture stirring briskly. Whip the cream until stiff. Fold into pie mixture and stir in the rum. Pour into 2 frozen pie shells. Sprinkle with shaved chocolate. Freeze until firm. Each pie serves 8.

Mrs. Richard R. Meckfessel

AUNT MINNIE'S SHOO-FLY PIE

A popular old Pennsylvania Dutch specialty.

1 8" or 9" unbaked pie shell   2 tablespoons butter or
½ cup brown sugar   margarine
1¾ cups flour   ½ cup hot water
2 tablespoons solid   ½ teaspoon soda
    shortening   ½ cup dark molasses
½ teaspoon salt

Blend brown sugar, flour, shortening, and butter together with a pastry blender. Put aside ½ cup of this mixture. In another bowl, mix the hot water and soda. Then add the molasses and salt. Add the dry ingredients to the wet ones and mix thoroughly. Pour into the pie shell or pour into a 8" or 9" greased pie pan or 8" square pan. Sprinkle top with ½ cup mixture that was set aside. Bake at 350° for 45 minutes.

Mrs. J. Vann Carroll

STRAWBERRY PARFAIT PIE

1 cup boiling water
1 (3 ounce) package lemon
　gelatin
1 · pint vanilla ice cream

1 cup of strawberries (fresh or
　frozen), sliced (other fruit
　may be substituted,
　peaches, blackberries, etc.)
1 baked graham cracker pie shell

Heat one cup of water to boiling in a two-quart pan; remove from heat; add one package of lemon gelatin. Stir in one pint of vanilla ice cream; stir until melted. Chill this mixture until it thickens (about 20 minutes). Fold in strawberries.

Turn into a cooled graham cracker pie shell. Pie will be ready in half an hour. Must keep refrigerated.

Mrs. James L. Cabell

FRESH STRAWBERRY PIE

1 baked (8″) pie shell
1 quart fresh strawberries
1 cup sugar
　Water

⅓ cup cornstarch
1 tablespoon lemon juice
Few drops red food coloring
Whipped cream for topping

Wash and clean strawberries. Add sugar and let stand covered for 2 hours. Drain off juice and add enough water to make 1¾ cups liquid. Blend in cornstarch with about ¼ of the liquid in the top of a double boiler. Add the rest of the liquid and cook over direct heat with constant stirring until sauce boils and is clear. Place over boiling water, cover and cook for 15 minutes. Remove from heat, add lemon juice, and food coloring, and fold in strawberries. Cool to lukewarm before pouring into pie shell. Top with whipped cream. Makes 5 servings.

Miss Katherine Potterfield

FLAKY NO-FAIL PIE CRUST

1 cup lard
½ cup boiling water

1 teaspoon salt
3 cups all-purpose flour

Pour boiling water over lard. Stir well until white and creamy. Add salt and flour all at once. Mix with fork 25 to 30 turns, or until moist. Shape into a ball and chill.

This crust will keep for several days. It should be taken from the refrigerator an hour or so before use so it will be manageable. Makes 3 — 8″ or 9″ crusts.

Mrs. Edwin M. Bartrug, Jr.

PIE CRUST

2 cups flour
1 teaspoon salt

⅔ cup shortening
6 tablespoons cold water

Sift flour and salt. Cut in the shortening. Sprinkle cold water over mixture gradually while stirring. Form into 2 balls. Chill ½ hour before using. Makes one 2-crust pie.

Mrs. John Charles Thomas

CRUMB TOPPING FOR FRUIT PIE

¾ cup flour
½ cup sugar

⅓ cup margarine
Pinch of salt

Mix flour and sugar together with salt. Cut in margarine with a pastry blender. Sprinkle over the top of fruit pie and bake according to pie directions. When using this topping, no thickening is needed in peach pie. Makes topping for one pie.

Mrs. Alexander J. Ross

ALMOND BARS

1 cup butter
2 tablespoons sugar
1 teaspoon almond extract
2½ cups flour

1 egg white
1 tablespoon water
½ cup blanched, shredded
   almonds

½ cup sugar

Cream butter and 2 tablespoons sugar; add extract and flour. Shape in long rolls ½ inch in diameter. Cut into 2 inch lengths and brush with egg white mixed with water. Roll in mixture of almonds and ½ cup sugar. Bake in well-greased pan at 350° about 12 minutes. Remove from pan at once. Makes 5 to 6 dozen.

Mrs. Ronald McKenney

"BLONDIES"

½ cup margarine
½ cup dark brown sugar,
   firmly packed
½ cup granulated sugar
2 eggs

1 cup flour
¼ teaspoon salt
½ teaspoon baking powder
½ cup chopped nut meats
½ teaspoon vanilla
Powdered sugar

Thoroughly cream margarine with brown sugar and granulated sugar. Add eggs. Beat well. Sift together flour, salt and baking powder. Mix into creamed mixture. Stir in nuts and vanilla. Spoon mixture into greased 8″ square pan. Bake at 350° for 30 to 35 minutes. Cut into squares and sprinkle with powdered sugar.

Mrs. George V. Hamrick

BOURBON BALLS

¼ pound butter
Pinch of salt

1 pound powdered sugar
¼ cup bourbon
2 cups chopped pecans

Cream butter and salt together. Add sugar and bourbon alternately. Beat into a cream and add nuts. Put in refrigerator to harden. Remove and roll into small balls. Place on tray lined with waxed paper and return to refrigerator. Dip in the following chocolate mixture.

DIP

2½ squares unsweetened
   chocolate

1½ squares paraffin (size of
chocolate squares)
1 (6 ounce) package semi-sweet chocolate bits

Combine all ingredients and stir until melted in double boiler. Remove a few balls at a time, dip into chocolate mixture, and return to refrigerator. Store in airtight container in refrigerator.

Mrs. Isaac Noyes Smith, Jr.

BROWNIES

1 stick butter
2 (1 ounce each) squares
   unsweetened chocolate
1 cup sugar
2 eggs

½ cup flour
½ teaspoon salt
2 teaspoons vanilla
¼ cup chopped nuts
Powdered sugar, as garnish

Melt butter, chocolate, and sugar in saucepan over low heat. Beat and cool. Add eggs one at a time, beating each well into mixture. Sift flour and salt into mix. Add vanilla and nuts. Pour into greased 7" x 11" pan and bake at 350° for 20 minutes. Sift powdered sugar over top when done and cut into squares immediately. Makes 24 brownies.

Mrs. Howard B. Johnson

ICED BROWNIES

½ cup margarine or butter
1 cup sugar
1 (16 ounce) can chocolate
  syrup

4 eggs
1 cup flour
1 cup chopped nuts

Cream butter and sugar well. Slowly add syrup. Add eggs, one at a time, beating well. Add flour and then chopped nuts. Bake in well-greased 9" x 13" pan at 350° for 25 minutes. Cool. Makes 30.

TOPPING

1 cup margarine
1½ cups sugar

⅓ cup evaporated milk
½ cup chocolate chips
1 teaspoon vanilla

Bring margarine, sugar, and milk to boil and boil 3 minutes. Remove from heat and add chocolate chips. Stir until melted, then add vanilla, and spread on cooled brownies.

Mrs. Charles B. Gates, Jr.

DOUBLE GOOD BROWNIES

½ cup butter
1 (1 ounce) square
  unsweetened chocolate
1 cup sugar
⅔ cup self-rising flour

1½ teaspoons baking powder
1 teaspoon vanilla
¾ cup chopped pecans
2 eggs
1½ cups miniature marshmallows

Grease the bottom of a 9" square pan and lightly dust with flour. Melt butter and chocolate in saucepan. Remove from heat and stir in all ingredients except eggs and marshmallows. Add eggs and beat well. Pour into pan and bake at 350° for 30 minutes. Remove from oven and cover with marshmallows. Return to oven long enough for marshmallows to melt. Have icing ready to spread while brownies are still hot. Makes 16.

ICING

3 tablespoons butter
½ square unsweetened
   chocolate

3 tablespoons hot water
2½ cups powdered sugar
1 teaspoon vanilla

Melt butter and chocolate. Add hot water. Stir in sugar and vanilla. Spread on hot brownies and cool before cutting.

Mrs. George R. Heath

BUTTER COOKIES

1 pound butter (not margarine)
1½ cups sugar
4 egg yolks

2 teaspoons vanilla
4 cups or more flour
Slivered almonds, as garnish

Cream together butter, sugar, and egg yolks. Add vanilla and flour. Chill dough 45 minutes. Roll in small balls (size of a large grape); make indentation in top and put in slivered almond. Place on greased cookie sheets and bake at 325° for 12 to 15 minutes. Watch! Bottom edges get slightly brown; tops never get too brown. Cool on rack. Makes 12 dozen.

Mrs. John Prince Harris

CHEESECAKE COOKIES

⅓ cup butter
⅓ cup brown sugar, firmly
   packed

1 cup flour
½ cup finely chopped
   walnuts

Cream butter with brown sugar in small bowl. Add flour and nuts. Mix until crumbly. Reserve 1 cup of this mixture for topping. Press remainder into bottom of 8" square pan. Bake at 350° for 12 to 15 minutes.

FILLING

¼ cup sugar
1 (8 ounce) package cream
   cheese

1 egg
2 tablespoons milk
2 tablespoons lemon juice

½ teaspoon vanilla

Blend sugar and cream cheese until smooth. Add egg, milk, lemon juice, and vanilla and beat well. Spread over baked crust and sprinkle with reserved crumbs. Bake at 350° for 25 minutes. Cool and cut into 2" squares. Makes 16 squares.

Mrs. William E. Hamb

CHOCOLATE BUD COOKIES

3 (1 ounce each) squares
    unsweetened chocolate
4 eggs
½ cup cooking oil

2 cups sugar
2 teaspoons vanilla
2 cups flour, sifted
2 teaspoons baking powder
    Powdered sugar

Melt chocolate. Beat eggs; add oil, sugar, vanilla, and melted chocolate. Add flour and baking powder to egg mixture and beat well. Cover and place in refrigerator for several hours or overnight, if necessary. Roll in balls the size of small walnuts. Shake in bag with powdered sugar (shake about four at a time). Bake on ungreased baking sheet 10 to 12 minutes at 325°.

Mrs. Meredith K. Rice

CHOCOLATE MINT STICKS

2 (1 ounce each) squares
    unsweetened chocolate
½ cup butter
2 eggs
1 cup sugar

1 teaspoon vanilla
½ cup flour
¼ teaspoon baking powder
¼ teaspoon salt
½ cup chopped nuts

Melt chocolate and butter together. Cool. Add eggs, sugar, vanilla, flour, baking powder, and salt. Mix well. Add nuts. Pour into greased 9" x 13" pan and bake at 350° for 15 minutes. Cool and frost with the following icing.

ICING

3 tablespoons butter, divided
1 tablespoon cream

1 cup powdered sugar
¾ teaspoon peppermint extract
1 (1 ounce) square unsweetened chocolate

Combine 2 tablespoons butter, cream, sugar, and peppermint extract and frost brownies. Chill until firm. Then melt chocolate with 1 tablespoon butter and drizzle over white frosting. Cut into 1" x 3" sticks. Makes 36.

Mrs. J. Douglas Machesney

COCONUT COOKIES

1 cup shortening
2 cups brown sugar
2 eggs
2 cups flour
½ teaspoon soda

1 teaspoon baking powder
1 teaspoon salt
2 cups oatmeal (quick)
1½ cups coconut
½ cup chopped nuts
1 teaspoon vanilla

Cream shortening and sugar. Add eggs and beat well. Sift together flour, soda, baking powder, and salt, and add to creamed mixture. Add oatmeal, coconut, nuts, and vanilla. (These last items might have to be mixed in with a spoon, as it is a heavy batter.) Drop by spoonfuls on a greased cookie sheet. Bake at 375° for about 10 to 12 minutes. Makes about 8 dozen cookies.

Mrs. Meredith K. Rice

COOKIES WHILE YOU SLEEP

2 egg whites	½ teaspoon almond extract
Pinch salt	1 teaspoon vanilla extract
⅔ cup sugar	1 cup chocolate chips
	1 cup finely chopped nuts

Beat egg whites until frothy. Add salt and continue beating until stiff. Gradually add sugar. Beat until very thick. Add almond extract and vanilla extract. Fold in chocolate chips and nuts. Line cookie sheet with aluminum foil and drop mixture onto sheet by teaspoons. Put cookies in 350° oven, close door tightly, and turn off heat. GO TO SLEEP FOR THE NIGHT. Makes about 3 dozen.

Mrs. William T. Brotherton, Jr.

CONGO BARS

⅔ cup solid shortening	2½ teaspoons baking powder
1 pound brown sugar	½ teaspoon salt
3 eggs	1 teaspoon vanilla
2¾ cups flour	1 cup chopped pecans
	1 (6 ounce) package chocolate chips

Mix shortening, sugar, and eggs; beat. Add dry ingredients, vanilla, nuts, and chocolate chips. Bake 30 minutes at 350° in 13" x 9" greased pan. Cool before cutting.

Mrs. Philip W. Wooten

GINGER COOKIES

1½ cups flour
½ teaspoon salt
1 teaspoon ginger
1 teaspoon allspice
1 teaspoon baking soda (level)
1 teaspoon baking powder
 (rounded)
1 teaspoon nutmeg

1 teaspoon cinnamon
1 large tablespoon solid
 shortening
6 tablespoons butter
1 cup sugar
1 egg (or 2, if small)
½ cup molasses
Additional sugar, as garnish

Sift together dry ingredients including spices. Cream shortening and butter until fluffy. Add sugar slowly, then egg and molasses, and beat thoroughly. Stir in dry ingredients all at once. Shape dough into 1 inch balls (size of English walnut) and roll into sugar spread on waxed paper. Place 2 inches apart on cookie sheets, flatten with fingers, and sprinkle more sugar on tops of cookies. Bake at 325° for 7 minutes. Let stand a minute before removing from sheets.

Mrs. Frederick M. Staunton

GRIZZLENUCKLES

1 can sweetened condensed
 milk
2 cups graham cracker crumbs

1 cup coconut
1 (6 ounce) package chocolate
 chips
Powdered sugar

Mix all ingredients. Pour in a 9" x 13" greased pan. Bake at 350° for 20 minutes. Sprinkle with powdered sugar. Cool and cut.

Mrs. Charles M. Love, III

HALFWAY COOKIES

1 cup butter, softened
½ cup granulated sugar
1½ cups light brown sugar,
 divided
2 eggs, separated
1 tablespoon water
2 cups sifted flour

1 teaspoon vanilla
¼ teaspoon salt
¼ teaspoon soda
1 teaspoon baking powder
1 (12 ounce) package chocolate
 bits

Mix butter, granulated sugar, ½ cup brown sugar, beaten egg yolks, water, flour, vanilla, salt, soda, and baking powder. Spread in greased oblong pan and sprinkle chocolate bits on top of this mixture. Beat egg whites and mix with 1 cup brown sugar. Spread thinly on top of chocolate bits and cover completely with waxed paper, having it touch the egg-white mixture. Bake at 350° for 20 to 25 minutes. Cut into squares when cool.

Mrs. Frank S. Harkins, Jr.

"K" COOKIES

¾ stick butter or margarine	½ teaspoon soda
¾ cup light brown sugar, firmly packed	¼ teaspoon salt
	1 teaspoon vanilla
¼ cup granulated sugar	2 cups "Special K" cereal
1 egg	¼ cup chopped nuts
1 cup flour	½ to ¾ cup shredded coconut

Cream butter and all sugar until fluffy. Add egg and continue to beat. Sift flour, soda, and salt together and add to mixture. Beat only until well-mixed. Fold in vanilla, cereal, nuts, and coconut. Drop by spoonfuls onto ungreased cookie sheet. Bake at 350° for about 10 minutes. Remove from hot cookie sheet immediately, and leave upside down to cool so they will not stick together. Makes 50 cookies.

Mrs. T. A Galyean

LEMON BARS DELUXE

2 cups sifted flour	2 cups granulated sugar
½ cup sifted powdered sugar	⅓ cup lemon juice
1 cup butter	¼ cup flour
4 beaten eggs	½ teaspoon baking powder
Powdered sugar	

Sift together the flour and powdered sugar. Cut in the butter until the mixture clings together. Press in a 13" x 9" x 2" baking dish. Bake at 350° for 20 to 25 minutes or until lightly browned. Beat together eggs, granulated sugar, and lemon juice. Sift together ¼ cup flour and baking powder; stir in egg mixture and pour over baked crust. Bake at 350° for 25 minutes longer. Sprinkle with powdered sugar. Cool. Cut into bars 1 to 1½ inch in size. Makes 30 bars.

Miss Julia Newhouse

MACAROONS

1 pound fine granulated sugar	6½ fluid ounces egg whites, divided

1 pound almond paste

Add 3 fluid ounces egg whites to sugar and mix well. Cut paste into small pieces and add. Mix well, gradually adding remaining egg whites until batter is completely smooth. Drop macaroons on double paper-lined tins. Bake at 320° to 330° for 18 minutes. Leave oven door open slightly for first 5 minutes, until macaroons rise and "crack." Close door and finish baking.

The Greenbrier

MINCEMEAT COOKIES

½ cup butter	2 eggs
½ cup solid shortening	1 teaspoon vanilla
1 cup sugar	3 cups sifted flour
½ cup brown sugar	1 teaspoon soda

1 cup brandied mincemeat, drained

Cream butter, shortening, and sugars. Add eggs and vanilla. Beat well. Sift flour and soda together and add to creamed mixture. Chill dough at least 2 hours. Form dough into small balls and place on greased cookie sheets 2 to 3 inches apart to allow for spreading. Make a depression in each ball with thumb or a round (teaspoon size) measuring spoon dipped in sugar and fill with mincemeat. Be sure mincemeat is drained! Bake at 375° for 12 to 15 minutes. Remove from sheets to rack immediately to cool. These cookies break easily, so handle gently. Makes 36 cookies.

PEANUT BUTTER COOKIES

½ cup margarine	1 egg
½ cup peanut butter	1¼ cups flour
½ cup brown sugar	¾ teaspoon soda
½ cup granulated sugar	¼ teaspoon salt

½ teaspoon baking powder

Cream margarine and peanut butter together. Add all sugar and cream well. Add well-beaten egg. Sift flour with soda, salt, and baking powder and add to creamed mixture. Chill well and form into walnut-sized balls. Place on lightly greased pan. Flatten balls with fork dipped into flour, making a crisscross pattern. Bake at 375° for 10 to 12 minutes. Makes 48 cookies.

Mrs. Andrew R. Quenon

POLKA-DATES

1 (8 ounce) package dates,
  chopped
1 cup hot water
2 eggs
1¼ cups sugar
1 cup butter

1¾ cups flour
1½ teaspoons soda
1 teaspoon vanilla
1 cup chocolate chips,
  divided
½ cup chopped nuts

Mix dates and hot water. Set aside to cool. Beat eggs, sugar, and butter until creamy. Add flour and soda. Stir in undrained dates and vanilla. Add ½ cup chocolate chips. Spread in a greased and floured 9" x 13" pan. Top with nuts and remaining ½ cup chocolate chips Bake at 350° for 30 minutes. Cut into squares.

Mrs. Carol Fletcher

POTATO CHIP COOKIES

1½ cups sugar
1 pound butter or margarine
2 teaspoons vanilla

3½ cups sifted flour
1 cup crushed potato chips
Powdered sugar

Mix ingredients except powdered sugar and drop onto greased cookie sheet. Bake at 350° for 15 to 20 minutes. When cookies are completely cool, sprinkle with powdered sugar.

Mrs. John M. Slack, III

POTATO FLOUR COOKIES

1 cup butter
½ cup sugar
½ cup potato flour or cornstarch
Sliced almonds

1½ cups all-purpose flour
1 teaspoon vanilla
Powdered sugar

Combine softened butter and sugar with mixer. Slowly add all flour and vanilla. Shape into 1 or 2 logs about the size of a half dollar in diameter. Chill overnight. Slice thin and bake on lightly greased cookie sheet at 350° about 12 minutes, until light golden brown. Remove from oven; sprinkle with powdered sugar and place a sliced almond or two in the center.

Mrs. Susan B. Allen

AUNT LOUISE ANNA'S RAISIN NUT COOKIES

2 cups raisins	1 teaspoon baking powder
1 cup water	1 teaspoon soda
1 cup shortening	2 teaspoons salt
2 cups sugar	1½ teaspoons cinnamon
3 eggs	¼ teaspoon nutmeg
1 teaspoon vanilla	¼ teaspoon allspice
4 cups flour	1 cup chopped pecans or walnuts

Plump raisins by boiling with water for 5 minutes uncovered. Cool. Cream shortening and sugar. Add eggs and beat well. Add vanilla and the cooled raisin mixture. Sift together the flour, baking powder, soda, salt, cinnamon, nutmeg, and allspice. Add sifted mixture to raisin mixture and blend well. Mix in chopped pecans or walnuts. Chill for 2 hours. Drop by tablespoons on greased baking sheet. Bake at 325° for 12 to 15 minutes. Cool completely on rack. These cookies keep for weeks.

Mrs. H. L. Snyder, Jr.

RUM BALLS

3 cups crushed vanilla wafers	1½ tablespoons cocoa
1 cup powdered sugar	2 tablespoons white corn syrup
1½ cups finely chopped pecans	¾ cup light rum
Powdered sugar	

Mix ingredients thoroughly and roll into small balls, about 1 heaping teaspoon each. Roll in powdered sugar and store in tin box with wax paper between layers. May be frozen. Makes 4 dozen.

Mrs. Samuel W. Channell

SAND TART COOKIES

1 cup margarine	1 cup chopped walnuts
1½ cups powdered sugar, divided	2 cups flour
1 teaspoon vanilla	1½ teaspoons water

Cream margarine. Add 3 heaping tablespoons powdered sugar, vanilla, nuts, flour, and water. Mix and work well together. Shape into oblong finger pieces (about the size of small dates) or roll into balls half the size of a golf ball. Bake on ungreased cookie sheets at 300° for 25 to 30 minutes until delicately browned. Roll in remaining powdered sugar immediately and allow to cool uncovered. Seal in airtight container. Makes 8 dozen.

Mrs. Ladd M. Kochman

ENGLISH SHORTBREAD

Lucy Quarrier, a member of a pioneer West Virginia family, is a teacher of the cloth crafts of weaving and vegetable dying. She attended Penland School to perfect her skills and is a founder of the annual Arts and Crafts Fair at Cedar Lakes.

1 pound of butter (not margarine)	1 pound sugar
	1 to 1¼ pounds flour

Warm the bowl to make creaming easier. Cream butter thoroughly; add sugar a little at a time, beating between each addition. Add flour a little at a time, using mixer as long as possible. Reserve a little flour for rolling out. Roll out enough dough at a time to make 3 medium cookies, and roll ¼ inch thick. Place on cookie sheet, 12 to a sheet, as they spread in baking. If working alone, bake at 300°; with help it is quicker at 350°.

Before putting in oven, mark with a *silver* thimble to keep out the witches. Three overlapping marks are pretty. Bake until the edge of the first cookie begins to turn brown. Take out and look at it. If sugar granules show, it is not done. Cool and store in tight box. They keep well. Makes 5½ to 6 dozen cookies.

Miss Lucy Quarrier

STIR-N- DROP COOKIES

2 eggs	¾ cup sugar
⅔ cup cooking oil	2 cups flour
2 teaspoons vanilla	2 teaspoon baking powder
1 teaspoon grated lemon rind	½ teaspoon salt
1 cup raisins or nuts	

Beat eggs. Stir in oil, vanilla, and lemon rind. Blend in sugar until mixture thickens. Sift together flour, baking powder, and salt. Add to egg mixture. (Batter will be soft.) Add raisins or nuts. Drop by teaspoons about 2 inches apart on ungreased cookie sheet. Stamp each cookie flat with bottom of glass dipped in sugar (lightly oil glass, then dip in sugar.) Continue dipping in sugar to keep bottom of glass completely covered. Bake at 400° for 8 to 10 minutes. Remove immediately from cookie sheet and cool on rack. Makes 3 dozen cookies 3″ in diameter.

Mrs. John C. Thomas

SUGAR COOKIES

1½ sticks butter, divided	½ teaspoon soda, dissolved in 1 tablespoon warm water
1 cup sugar	⅛ teaspoon nutmeg
1 egg	1¾ cups sifted self-rising flour
1 teaspoon vanilla	
Colored sugar (optional)	

Cream 1 stick butter and sugar. Add egg, vanilla, dissolved soda, and nutmeg. Slowly add flour. Cool in the refrigerator. Use ½ teaspoon of batter for each cookie and roll in small balls. Place a fork in ice water and then press down each cookie, spreading with soft butter and sprinkling with colored sugar. Bake at 325° for 7 to 10 minutes, just letting edges brown. Makes 72 cookies.

Variation: Roll dough out with rolling pin on cloth towel with powdered sugar and plastic wrap on top. Cut out with fancy cutters. Bake as directed.

Mrs. Robert E. O'Connor

TOFFEE BARS

½ cup butter   ½ cup brown sugar
                    1 cup flour

Cream butter, sugar, and flour. Press in a greased 8″ or 9″ square cake pan. Bake at 350° for 10 minutes. Cool.

FILLING

2 eggs   Pinch of salt
1 cup brown sugar   1 cup coconut
½ teaspoon vanilla   1 cup chopped walnuts or
2 tablespoons flour   pecans
1 teaspoon baking powder   Powdered sugar

Beat eggs and add brown sugar, vanilla, flour, baking powder, and salt. Beat. Add coconut and nuts. Spread on crust and bake at 350° for 25 minutes. Cut in squares and dip in or dust with powdered sugar.

This is a very rich cookie-bar, a favorite at Christmas. The recipe can be doubled, tripled, or quadrupled. Use 9″ x 13″ pan if doubled; use 9″ x 13″ pan and a small cake pan if tripled; use 2-9″ x 13″ pans if quadrupled.

Mrs. C. K. Payne, III

VANILLA REFRIGERATOR COOKIES

1 cup shortening (½ cup of   4 cups sifted flour
    this should be butter)   3 teaspoons baking powder
2 cups sugar   ¼ teaspoon salt
½ cup brown sugar   1 cup nuts
2 eggs, beaten   1 tablespoon vanilla

Cream shortening and sugars. Add eggs and beat until light. Sift together flour, baking powder, and salt. Add to the creamed mixture and mix well. Add nuts and vanilla. Shape into rolls about 2" in diameter and refrigerate overnight. Slice ¼" thick and bake on greased cookie sheet about 8 minutes at 425°.

Mrs. William C. Payne

LINZER TARTS

1 pound butter	1½ teaspoons cinnamon
1 cup sugar	3 cups flour
2 eggs, well beaten	¼ teaspoon baking powder
1 tablespoon brandy	½ pound pecans, coarsely
2 teaspoons salt	ground or chopped

1 large jar red raspberry jam

Cream butter and sugar. Add eggs and brandy. Sift dry ingredients together and add with pecans. Mix well and chill thoroughly. Save a portion of dough for lattice top crust. Pat remainder of dough into two 9 inch pie pans, making it come up ½ inch along the sides of the pan. Spoon jam smoothly over dough; place strips of dough over top. (Rolling dough between sheets of waxed paper makes it more manageable.) Bake at 300° for 1 hour. Cut into small triangular pieces. Makes two 9 inch pies.

Mrs. Chapman Revercomb

GARDEN MOMENT

Forty years I lived,
Never saw before
What I saw this morning,
And if forty more —
Though I watch forever,
Straining patient eyes —
Shall I see such other
Miracle arise:
See the brown earth cracking —
Rupture of the night —
And the seed, the flower,
Rising to the light.

Reprinted by permission from Louise McNeill, in **Paradox Hill: From Appalachia to Lunar Shore;** West Virginia University Library; Morgantown, West Virginia; 1972; Page 35.

Photo by Commerce Photography

DESSERTS

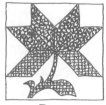

Peony

APPLE DUMPLINGS

6 to 8 medium-sized tart apples, peeled and sliced or chopped

4 tablespoons butter

PASTRY

Pastry:
2¼ cups flour
¾ teaspoon salt

¾ cup shortening
7 or 8 tablespoons water

Mix flour and salt; cut in shortening with pastry blender; add water until all flour is moistened. This should be exactly like pie crust.

SUGAR MIXTURE

Sugar mixture:
1 cup sugar

1½ teaspoon cinnamon
1 teaspoon nutmeg

SYRUP

Syrup:
½ cup sugar
½ teaspoon cinnamon

4 tablespoons butter
2 cups water

Mix syrup ingredients together and cook until butter is melted and sugar is dissolved. Divide pastry into eight equal portions. Roll out each dumpling crust thin and round as if for pie. Place chopped apples on each dumpling, ⅔ or ¾ cup on each. Divide sugar mixture equally on each. Place ½ tablespoon butter on each. Wrap pastry around each and seal shut. It is easier if pastry is moistened around the edges. Place dumplings in a baking dish, 13" x 9". Pour syrup over all. Bake at 500° for 5 minutes, then at 350° for 30 minutes. Serves 8.

These can be served with ice cream or American cheese, but they are especially good served with lemon sauce.

LEMON SAUCE

Lemon sauce:
1½ cups milk
3 tablespoons flour
Juice of 1 lemon

1½ to 2 teaspoons lemon rind
¼ cup sugar
Yellow food coloring

Mix milk and flour in a jar and shake well. Pour into a saucepan; add remaining ingredients and a couple of drops of yellow food coloring. More milk may be added for a thinner sauce. Cook until sugar is dissolved, and serve warm over dumplings.

Mrs. William C. Payne

APPLE PECAN COBBLER

½ cup sugar	1 cup sugar
½ teaspoon cinnamon	1 teaspoon baking powder
¾ cup coarsely chopped	¼ teaspoon salt
pecans, divided	1 egg, well beaten
4 cups thinly sliced, pared,	½ cup evaporated milk
tart apples	⅓ cup butter or margarine,
1 cup sifted flour	melted

Whipped cream or ice cream as garnish

Mix sugar, cinnamon and ½ cup pecans. Place apples in bottom of a greased 8¼" x 1¾" round baking dish. Sprinkle with the cinnamon mixture. Sift together the dry ingredients. Combine egg, milk, and butter; add dry ingredients, all at once, and mix until smooth. Pour over apples; sprinkle with remaining pecans. Bake at 325° about 55 minutes or until done. Spoon warm cobbler onto dessert plates; top with cinnamon-flavored whipped cream or ice cream. Serves 8.

Mrs. Frederick H. Morgan

BLUEBERRY FRITTERS WITH SHERRY SAUCE

1 cup flour	½ cup milk
2 tablespoons sugar	2 eggs, separated
1 tablespoon baking powder	¾ cup blueberries
¼ teaspoon salt	Hot fat

Powdered sugar

Sift together flour, sugar, baking powder, and salt. Add milk and well-beaten egg yolks. Beat until smooth. Fold in egg whites, stiffly beaten, and blueberries. Drop by spoonfuls into hot fat. Fry until brown. Drain and dust with powdered sugar. Serve with sherry sauce.

SHERRY SAUCE

⅓ cup butter, softened	2 egg yolks
⅓ cup powdered sugar	¾ cup sherry

1 egg white, beaten stiff

Combine softened butter and powdered sugar. Beat until fluffy. Drop in egg yolks, one at a time. Beat well after each. Pour in sherry. Cook in top of double boiler, stirring constantly, until thick. Fold in egg white, stiffly beaten. Blend. Serve immediately.

Mrs. Connie Carrico

CHARLOTTE RUSSE

2 egg whites
½ cup sugar, sifted
1 tablespoon unflavored
  gelatin
½ cup milk

2 teaspoons vanilla
2 dessert spoons of sherry
1 pint whipping cream
Ladyfingers (optional, but
  traditional)

Beat egg whites until stiff, add sugar slowly and mix well. Soften gelatin in milk and place on very low heat for a few minutes until gelatin is thoroughly dissolved. Cool gelatin and milk mixture a little, and pour this over the egg whites and sugar mixture, mixing well. Add vanilla and sherry. Then fold in cream which has been whipped, and pour Charlotte into a decorative serving bowl. Chill. Ladyfingers may be placed in the bowl first, around the sides, before pouring in the Charlotte. May be prepared the day before. Serves 6.

Mrs. David A. Faber

CHOCOLATE ROULADE

5 eggs, separated
½ cup powdered sugar, sifted
1 teaspoon vanilla
2 tablespoons flour, sifted

4 tablespoons cocoa, sifted
⅛ teaspoon salt
½ teaspoon cream of tartar

Beat egg yolks until creamy. Add powdered sugar gradually and continue beating until smooth. Add vanilla, flour, cocoa, and salt. Whip egg whites with cream of tartar until stiff but not dry. Fold lightly into cake batter. Line shallow 8″ x 12″ pan with greased heavy paper and spread dough to a thickness of about ¼ inch. Bake in a 325° oven for about 25 minutes. Let cool in pan for 5 minutes.

Reverse pan onto a clean towel that has been dusted with powdered sugar. Peel off paper. Trim off crust edges. Roll cake and towel. When cool, unroll cake and spread with filling; then reroll.

CHOCOLATE FILLING

2 (1 ounce each) squares unsweetened chocolate
1½ cups milk, scalded
½ cup sugar

4 eggs
¼ cup flour
½ teaspoon vanilla
Powdered sugar for garnish

Grate chocolate and add to milk so that it melts while milk is scalding. Cream sugar and eggs until light. Add flour to this mixture, stirring gently. Add scalded milk gradually, stirring constantly. Cook and stir until it reaches boiling point, but do not let it boil. Add vanilla; strain and cool. Spread on cooled cake and reroll. Dust roll with powdered sugar; slice, and serve. Serves 8 to 10.

Mrs. John M. Slack, III

CLAFOUTI (CHERRY FLAN)

1¼ cups milk
⅓ cup granulated sugar
3 eggs
1 tablespoon vanilla extract
⅛ teaspoon salt
⅔ cup sifted flour

3 cups pitted black cherries (Use fresh black, sweet cherries in season. Otherwise, use drained, canned, pitted bing cherries)
⅓ cup granulated sugar

Powdered sugar for garnish

Place milk, sugar, eggs, vanilla, salt, and flour in blender. Cover and blend at top speed for 1 minute. Butter a 2-quart fireproof baking dish, 1½ inches deep. Pour a ¼ inch layer of batter in the baking dish. Set over moderate heat for a minute or two until a film of batter has set in the bottom of the dish. Remove from heat. Spread the cherries over the batter and sprinkle on the sugar. Pour on the rest of the batter and smooth the surface with the back of a spoon. Place in middle position of preheated 350° oven and bake for about 55 minutes or 1 hour. The Clafouti is done when it has puffed and browned, and a needle or knife plunged into its center comes out clean. Sprinkle top with powdered sugar just before bringing it to the table. Serves 6 to 8. (The Clafouti need not be served hot, but should still be warm. It will sink down slightly as it cools.)

Mrs. Thomas P. O'Brien

CREAM PUFF SHELL

½ cup margarine
1 cup boiling water

1 cup flour
¼ teaspoon salt

4 eggs

Put margarine and water in small saucepan. Add salt to flour. Sift if necessary. Bring margarine and water to a boil. Add flour mixture all at once. Beat vigorously until smooth and dough comes away from the edge of the pan. Drop in eggs, one at a time, and beat thoroughly after each addition. Drop from teaspoon onto greased pan. Bake at 400° for 30 minutes. Reduce heat to 350° for 5 to 7 minutes. Cool and fill with cream filling or custard for dessert. May also be filled with chicken, crab, or egg salad for luncheons or hors d'oeuvres. Make cream puffs smaller for cocktail or coffee use.

Mrs. Robert E. O'Connor

FRENCH MERINGUES

2 egg whites   ⅔ cup sifted granulated sugar
½ teaspoon almond extract or 1 teaspoon vanilla extract or
pure maple syrup

Beat egg whites until stiff; then add sugar in small amounts, beating until very stiff. Add flavoring, keeping egg whites stiff by extra beating after adding flavoring. For small meringues, grease a cookie sheet. Dust it with flour. Drop by spoonfuls as to size desired. Bake 15 minutes in a preheated oven at 300°; open door for a minute or two; then reduce heat to 200° and bake for an hour or more. Meringues cannot be too dry. Store in a tin canister. To make one 9 inch pie shell grease and flour pie pan, line generously with stiff egg whites, and bake the same. Fill with ice cream and serve with various sauces over ice cream. Disposable pie pans work well. After cooling, bend rims very gently and work loose. Store in pan.

Mrs. Margaret Blaine Horn

FRUIT COCKTAIL DESSERT

2 eggs   1 (28 ounce) can fruit cocktail,
1 cup sugar   drained
1 cup flour   1 teaspoon almond flavoring
1 teaspoon soda   ½ cup brown sugar
   Pinch of salt   ½ cup chopped pecans
                Whipped cream

Combine eggs and sugar well. Add flour, soda, and salt and mix well. Then add fruit cocktail and almond flavoring. Mix by hand with spoon. Spread in greased pan, 11" x 7" or 9" x 9". On top sprinkle brown sugar and pecans. Bake 1 hour and 20 minutes at 250°. Serve either hot or cold with whipped cream. Serves 8 to 10.

Mrs. Harry Thayer

GRAPEFRUIT ALASKA

3 grapefruit, halved   1 pint vanilla ice cream
                ½ cup sugar

Remove sections from grapefruit halves with a spoon or knife. Take fiber from shells. Add sugar to grapefruit sections. When ready to serve, put a dipper of vanilla ice cream in each shell, cover with grapefruit, then top completely with meringue. Put under broiler until meringue is brown.

MERINGUE

3 egg whites, room
   temperature
1 teaspoon vinegar

1 teaspoon cold water
⅛ teaspoon salt
½ teaspoon baking powder
1 cup sugar

Put egg whites, vinegar, water, salt, and baking powder into small bowl of electric mixer. Beat until very stiff, adding sugar at the last very gradually. This meringue can be made at least 30 minutes before serving if kept in the refrigerator. Serves 6.

Mrs. Seigle W. Parks

HIPPO'S "HEAVEN"

1 box vanilla wafers
½ pound butter
1 pound powdered sugar
4 eggs

1 pint whipping cream
1 (16 ounce) can crushed pineapple, drained
1 cup chopped pecans

Crush vanilla wafers and place half in a square pan. Cream butter and sugar and beat in eggs. Place layer on vanilla wafers. Whip cream; fold drained pineapple and nuts into it. Layer on butter mixture. Place remaining crushed wafers on top. Set in refrigerator overnight. Serves 10.

Mrs. Charles W. Yeager

LEMON BISQUE

1 (13 ounce) can evaporated
   milk
3 tablespoons butter
   Graham cracker crumbs

1 (6 ounce) box lemon gelatin
2 cups boiling water
¾ cup sugar
   Juice of one lemon

Refrigerate evaporated milk 24 hours before starting. Melt butter in bottom of 13" x 9" flat cake pan. Add enough graham crackers to cover bottom of pan and press them in firmly. Dissolve gelatin in boiling water. Add sugar and juice of lemon. After gelatin is congealed, beat until fluffy. Beat evaporated milk until thick. Fold the two mixtures together and pour over crumbs. Sprinkle crumbs on top and refrigerate overnight. Cut in squares. Serves 12.

Mrs. John Casto

LEMON SOUFFLE

1 envelope unflavored gelatin
¼ cup cold water
5 eggs, separated
¾ cup fresh lemon juice
2 teaspoons grated lemon rind
1½ cups sugar, divided
1 cup heavy cream, whipped

Sprinkle gelatin over cold water to soften. Put yolks in top of a double boiler. Mix yolks with lemon juice, rind, and ¾ cup sugar. Place over boiling water and cook, stirring constantly, until lemon mixture is slightly thick, about 8 minutes. Remove from heat and stir in gelatin until dissolved. Chill until mixture molds slightly when small amount is dropped from a spoon. Beat egg whites until they start to hold shape. Then add remaining ¾ cup sugar, about 1 tablespoon at a time, until sugar is used and egg whites are stiff. Transfer chilled lemon mixture to a large bowl. Add egg whites and cream and gently fold into lemon until no white streaks remain. Pour into a 2-quart soufflé dish and chill at least 4 hours or until firm. Serves 8 to 10.

Mrs. Angus E. Peyton

MAPLE MOUSSE

¾ cup maple syrup
2 egg whites, beaten stiff
1 cup whipped cream
¼ cup chopped pecans
1 teaspoon vanilla
Lady fingers

Boil syrup for 1 minute; pour slowly into beaten egg whites. Beat for 3 minutes after all syrup is added. Set aside to cool. Fold in whipped cream. Add nuts and vanilla. Place in ice tray or shallow pan. Put in freezer and chill 4 to 5 hours. Serve in parfait glasses with lady fingers. Serves 4.

Mrs. Helen Townsend Ziebold

MOCHA MOUSSE

Since coming to our state as a bride in 1967, Sharon Rockefeller has actively promoted West Virginia crafts and she currently serves on the board of Mountain Artisans. She is the daughter of Illinois Senator Charles Percy and her husband is President of West Virginia Wesleyan College.

4 egg yolks
2 cups light cream
1 envelope unflavored gelatin
½ cup sugar
¼ teaspoon salt
2 squares unsweetened chocolate
1 tablespoon instant coffee
¼ cup brandy
1 cup heavy whipping cream, whipped
Chocolate curls and additional whipping cream as garnish

Beat egg yolks and light cream together until well mixed. Stir gelatin, sugar, and salt together in top of double boiler. Stir in the yolk and cream mixture. Put the pan over boiling water and stir in the chocolate and coffee. Stir constantly until chocolate is melted and coffee is dissolved. Cook, stirring frequently, until mixture thickens, about 25 to 30 minutes. Remove from stove and add the brandy. Beat with rotary beater until well blended. Chill, stirring occasionally, until mixture begins to thicken. Fold in whipped cream and chill for another few hours. Serve in sherbet glasses with a dab of whipped cream and chocolate curls. Serves 8.

Mrs. John D. Rockefeller, IV

PEACH CREAM ROYALE

1½ cups chocolate wafer crumbs	2 tablespoons orange juice
1½ cups vanilla wafer crumbs	2 cups (1 pound 14 ounce can)
2 cups graham cracker crumbs	drained and diced freestone
½ cup butter, melted	peaches
½ pound marshmallows	½ pint whipping cream

Mix crumbs and butter. Press ⅓ crumb mixture firmly in bottom of 9″ x 9″ dish. In a saucepan over low heat, cook marshmallows with orange juice until melted. Cool. Stir in peaches. Whip cream until almost stiff; fold peach-marshmallow mixture into it. Pour half of this mixture into pan. Cover with ⅓ of crumb mixture. Pour remainder of cream mixture over this and cover with remaining crumb mixture. Chill at least 2 hours. Serves 9.

Mrs. William C. Payne

PINEAPPLE FRITTERS

2 cups flour	½ teaspoon salt
3 teaspoons baking powder	1 egg
½ cup sugar	¾ cup milk
1¼ cups crushed pineapple, reserving juice	

Sift flour, baking powder, sugar, and salt. Beat egg, add milk, and add mixture to dry ingredients. Add pineapple, beating rapidly. Drop small amounts into hot fat but cook slowly, turning frequently. Serve at once with sauce. Serves 8 to 10.

SAUCE

1 tablespoon cornstarch	½ cup water
½ cup sugar	3 teaspoons lemon juice
¼ teaspoon salt	2 teaspoons butter
Juice from crushed pineapple	

Mix cornstarch, sugar, and salt. Blend with water. Cook, stirring constantly, until it boils. Add remaining ingredients and remove from fire. Serve over hot fritters.

Mrs. Bert Bradford, Jr.

PUMPKIN MOUSSE WITH VANILLA SAUCE

1 tablespoon gelatin	1¼ cups pumpkin
2 tablespoons cold water	1 teaspoon cinnamon
3 egg yolks	1 teaspoon nutmeg
⅓ cup and 1 tablespoon sugar	1 teaspoon allspice

1 cup heavy cream, whipped

In a small bowl, sprinkle gelatin over cold water. Place bowl in simmering water and stir until gelatin is dissolved. Beat egg yolks with sugar. Stir in pumpkin, cinnamon, nutmeg, allspice, and dissolved gelatin. Fold whipped cream gently into pumpkin mixture. Pour mousse in mold or bowl and chill thoroughly. Serve with vanilla sauce. Serves 8.

VANILLA SAUCE

1 cup milk	4 egg yolks
1 cup light cream	½ cup sugar
½ teaspoon vanilla	Pinch salt

Scald milk and light cream with vanilla. In double boiler, beat egg yolks with sugar and a pinch of salt. Gradually beat in hot milk mixture. Cook sauce over hot water, stirring constantly until it thickens and coats a spoon. (If it does not thicken, add a little flour.) Strain sauce to remove lumps. Chill.

Mrs. John B. Carrico

SHERRY-CHOCOLATE FONDUE

4 (1 ounce each) squares unsweetened chocolate (cut in small pieces)	¾ cup sherry, heated almost to boiling
1 cup granulated sugar	1 teaspoon vanilla extract
	⅛ teaspoon salt

Blend the chocolate pieces, sugar, sherry, vanilla, and salt until smooth, using an electric blender at high speed. Pour into fondue pot; heat and keep warm over low heat. Sauce thickens as it stands. Makes 1½ cups. Use cut-up fresh fruit for dipping: pineapple, pears, strawberries, cherries, etc., or serve it with chunks of pound cake, doughnuts, or marshmallows.

Mrs. Thomas J. Blair, III

STRAWBERRY FONDUE

2 (10 ounces each) packages ½ cup water
   frozen strawberries, thawed 1 (4 ounce) container whipped
¼ cup cornstarch   cream cheese
2 tablespoons sugar Pound cake

In saucepan, crush strawberries slightly. Blend cornstarch, sugar, and water. Add to berries. Cook and stir until thickened and bubbly. Add cream cheese, and stir until melted. Cool in refrigerator. Serve with squares of pound cake. Use butter knives to spread. Makes 3 cups.

Mrs. John M. Slack, III

STRAWBERRY SURPRISE

TOPPING
½ cup butter, softened 1 cup flour
¼ cup brown sugar, packed ½ cup chopped nuts

Mix lightly and put in oblong pan. Bake at 400°, stirring occasionally, about 15 minutes until golden brown. When brown, press half of mixture in bottom of 3-quart ovenproof baking dish, reserving half for top of dessert.

FILLING

1 package frozen strawberries 1 tablespoon lemon juice
2 egg whites 1 teaspoon vanilla
1 cup sugar ½ pint whipping cream,
   whipped

Place all but whipped cream in large mixing bowl. Beat 20 minutes. Fold in whipped cream; pour into baking dish; top with crumbs. Freeze overnight. Cut into squares. Serves 12.

Mrs. Hugh G. Thompson, Jr.

MY MOTHER'S WINE JELLY RECIPE

2 envelopes unflavored gelatin 3 tablespoons brandy
½ cup cold water 1 cup sugar
1 cup boiling water ⅓ cup orange juice
1⅔ cups sherry 3 tablespoons lemon juice
   Sweetened whipped cream or boiled custard for serving

Soften gelatin in cold water. Dissolve in boiling water. Add sherry, brandy, sugar, orange juice, and lemon juice. Pour in mold and chill until set. Serve with sweetened whipped cream, flavored with sherry or brandy, or boiled custard. Serves 6 to 8.

Mrs. Chapman Revercomb

WHITE GRAPE DESSERT

1 cup sour cream   3 tablespoons Drambuie
3 teaspoons lemon juice   ⅓ cup honey
        4 cups juicy, plump, white seedless grapes

Combine first 4 ingredients to make a sauce. Pour sauce over the grapes; stir and refrigerate. Serve in bowls or sherbets with cookies or brownies. Serves 6.

Joe Peck

BLENDER PEACH SHERBET

6 ripe peaches, peeled and   Juice from 1 lemon
    pitted   Pinch of salt
½ cup sugar   ½ teaspoon almond extract
        1 pint whipping cream

Place peaches, sugar, lemon juice, salt, and almond extract in blender. Blend 2 seconds. Whip cream and put all together in ice trays in freezer. Beat with whisk when frozen one inch from side. Takes 2 hours to freeze. Serves about 8.

Mrs. Howard B. Johnson

COFFEE TORTONI

A farmhouse of the Civil War era is the setting for Country Road Inn. Located at Zela, near Summersville, West Virginia, the inn is owned and operated by Mrs. E. L. Jarroll, who lives there with her family. Mrs. Jarroll specializes mostly in Italian cuisine and delights her guests with homemade pasta and a fine assortment of antipasto delectables.

2 tablespoons coconut   ½ cup plus 2 teaspoons sugar
2 tablespoons chopped   1 cup whipping cream
    almonds   1 teaspoon vanilla extract
1 egg white   ⅛ teaspoon almond extract
1 heaping teaspoon instant
    coffee

Toast coconut and chopped almonds. Whip egg white with coffee; gradually add 2 teaspoons sugar. Whip cream; add remaining sugar, vanilla, and almond extract. Fold cream into egg mixture; add coconut and almonds. Pour into fluted paper baking cups. Sprinkle with additional coconut, if desired. Freeze 2 hours or more. Serves 6.

Mrs. E. L. Jarroll
Country Road Inn

FREEZER ICE CREAM, VANILLA

2 cups milk
2 eggs, separated
¾ cup sugar

1 tablespoon vanilla
¼ teaspoon salt
1 cup heavy whipping cream

Make a soft custard of milk, egg yolks, and sugar by cooking in double boiler over boiling water about 6 minutes or longer, stirring often. Beat egg whites until stiff and pour the hot custard over them, mixing well. Add vanilla and salt, and when the mixture is chilled, put in the cream. Pour in freezer and crank until ready. Add 2 cups chopped fresh peaches for variation.

Mrs. John Charles Thomas

FROZEN STRAWBERRY DESSERT

1 (10 ounce) package frozen
  strawberries

1 cup sugar
1 pint sour cream

Thaw berries thoroughly. Combine all ingredients. Freeze in ice tray, stirring 3 times at 25 minute intervals. Serves 6 to 8.

Mrs. Brooks F. McCabe

LEMON MILK SHERBET

1 quart milk
1½ cups sugar

Grated rind of 1 lemon
Juice of 2 lemons

Stir milk and sugar until sugar is dissolved. Freeze until it begins to thicken. Add rind and juice. Freeze, stirring often. Serves 6 to 8.

Mrs. Hugh G. Thompson, Jr.

LIME DELIGHT

1 (14½ ounce) can evaporated
  milk
1 (3 ounce) package lime
  gelatin
1¾ cups hot water

1 cup sugar
¼ cup lime juice
2 teaspoons lemon juice
2 cups chocolate wafer crumbs
½ cup melted margarine

Shaved chocolate, as garnish

Chill evaporated milk in freezer. Dissolve gelatin in hot water, and chill until partially set. Whip gelatin until fluffy; stir in sugar and juices. Whip chilled milk, and fold into gelatin mixture. Combine crumbs and melted margarine, pressing into a 9" x 13" pan. Pour lime liquid over crumbs. Shave chocolate over top. Freeze. Cut into squares. Can be kept for several weeks frozen. Serves 10 to 12.

Mrs. J. Crawford Goldman

ORANGE ICE — FOR CHILDREN

2 cups sugar	2 cups orange juice
4 cups water	¼ cup lemon juice

Cook sugar and water. Boil 5 minutes, cool and add juices. Freeze in pan in freezer until solid. Remove from freezer and put in blender and blend until soft and slushy. Put in plastic or paper cups with saran wrap over each top and freeze. This is like a lemon — orange sherbet. Makes 21 — 3 ounce cups.

Mrs. H. Herchiel Sims, Jr.

PUMPKIN-ICE CREAM SQUARES

1½ cups graham cracker crumbs	½ teaspoon salt
¼ cup sugar	1 teaspoon cinnamon
¼ cup melted butter	¼ teaspoon ginger
1 (16 ounce) can solid pack	⅛ teaspoon cloves
pumpkin	1 quart vanilla ice cream,
½ cup brown sugar	softened

Whipped cream and pecans, as garnish

Mix crumbs with sugar and butter. Press into bottom of 9 inch square pan. Combine pumpkin with brown sugar, salt, and spices. Fold in ice cream. Pour into crumb-lined pan. Cover and freeze until firm. Cut into 3 inch squares about 20 minutes before serving. Top with whipped cream and pecans. Serves 9.

Mrs. Frederick H. Morgan

STRAWBERRY ICE

2 cups sugar	3 packages frozen strawberries
1 quart water	Juice of 4 lemons

Bring sugar and water to boil. Add strawberries which have been puréed in the blender. Add lemon juice. Freeze until mushy; whip and refreeze. Serves 12.

THREE FRUIT SHERBET

1 ripe banana	1 teaspoon lemon rind
Juice of 1 orange	1 cup sugar
Juice of 1 lemon	1 cup water
1 teaspoon orange rind	1 egg white, beaten stiff

Mash the banana and pour over it the juice and rind of the orange and lemon. Add sugar and stir to dissolve. Add water and blend well. Pour into refrigerator tray and freeze until mushy. Turn out into cold bowl and beat until smooth to break up ice crystals. Fold in stiffly beaten egg white, by hand, until completely blended. Pour mixture back into tray and freeze. Serves 6 to 8.

Mrs. Edward W. Rugeley, Jr.

YOGHURT POPSICLES

1 pint homemade yoghurt	1 (6 ounce) can frozen orange or
	grape juice
2 teaspoons vanilla	

Stir the ingredients together and pour into popsicle molds or paper cups. Put an ice cream stick in the center of each. Freeze and serve.

Mrs. Henry W. Battle, III

BAKED DEVIL'S FLOAT

DOUGH

1 cup flour	1 (1 ounce) square unsweet-
½ teaspoon salt	ened chocolate, melted
2 teaspoons baking powder	½ cup milk
¾ cup granulated sugar	1 teaspoon vanilla
½ cup chopped pecans	

Sift together flour, salt, baking powder, and sugar. Add milk and chocolate and mix well. Add vanilla and nuts. Put in greased 9 inch baking pan.

TOPPING

½ cup granulated sugar	½ cup brown sugar
2 tablespoons cocoa	1 cup boiling water
Vanilla ice cream or whipped cream, as garnish	

Sift dry ingredients together and sprinkle over dough in pan. Pour 1 cup boiling water over top and bake at 350° for 45 minutes until crust forms on top. Serve with vanilla ice cream or whipped cream on top. Serves 6 to 8.

Mrs. William T. Ziebold

DATE PUDDING

SYRUP

2 cups brown sugar   2 cups water
2½ tablespoons butter

Put the ingredients in a pan and boil.

PUDDING

2 cups flour   1 teaspoon vanilla
4 teaspoons baking powder   1 cup sweet milk
2 tablespoons butter   Dash of salt
1 cup brown sugar   1 cup chopped dates
1 cup chopped walnuts

Combine flour, baking powder, butter, brown sugar, vanilla, milk and salt. Add the dates and walnuts. Pour syrup mixture into a 13" x 9" x 2" pan. Drop batter mixture by large spoonfuls on top. Bake at 350° for 30 to 35 minutes until cake part is done and bubbling; do not overbake. Spoon syrup generously over each serving. Serves 10 to 12.

Mrs. Miller C. Porterfield, Jr.

DROMEDARY PUDDING

2 eggs   1 tablespoon flour
1 cup sugar   1 teaspoon baking powder
Pinch of salt   1 cup chopped nuts
1 cup stoned and cut dates

Stir together eggs, sugar, salt, flour, and baking powder; then add nuts and dates. Thoroughly grease and flour an 8" square pan. Bake dessert at 300° for 45 minutes. Serve with whipped cream or vanilla sauce. Serves 6 to 8.

VANILLA SAUCE

1 cup sugar   4 tablespoons margarine or
2 tablespoons cornstarch   butter
2 cups water   2 teaspoons vanilla
Dash nutmeg, optional

Mix sugar and cornstarch in saucepan. Gradually stir in water. Bring to a boil and boil one minute, stirring constantly. Stir in margarine, vanilla, and nutmeg. Makes two cups.

Mrs. F. G. Bannerot, Jr.

FLOATING ISLAND

MERINGUE

4 egg whites, stiffly beaten	2 tablespoons arrowroot
2 teaspoons vanilla	Pinch salt
½ cup sugar	1¾ cups boiling water

Toasted almonds, for garnish

Beat egg whites until stiff, and flavor with vanilla. Mix together sugar, arrowroot, and salt, and stir into the boiling water. Cook mixture, stirring constantly, until clear and thickened. Fold in egg whites. Rinse 8 individual molds in ice water. Fill with mixture and refrigerate. Spoon 4 to 5 tablespoons custard into individual dishes. Unmold "island" into center. Sprinkle with toasted almonds. Serves 8.

CUSTARD

2½ cups milk	4 egg yolks
1 cup sugar	2 teaspoons lemon or vanilla
3 tablespoons cornstarch	extract, or 1 teaspoon rose-
½ teaspoon salt	water and 1 teaspoon
	almond extract

Heat milk in double boiler. Mix together sugar, cornstarch, and salt; add this to milk and cook until mixture coats the spoon. Beat egg yolks. Add 3 to 4 tablespoons of custard to yolks, and stir all together. Remove from heat and add flavoring. Strain through sieve. Cover and chill.

Mrs. Helen Townsend Ziebold

GRASSHOPPER PARFAITS

Author of numerous articles in journals and encyclopedias, Dr. James G. Harlow took office as president of West Virginia University at Morgantown in 1967.

20 large marshmallows	3 tablespoons crème de cacao
½ cup milk	(white)
1 cup whipping cream	Green food coloring, optional
3 tablespoons crème de	18 chocolate cookies,
menthe (green)	crushed (1⅓ cups)

Melt marshmallows over low heat with the milk and allow to cool. In chilled glass bowl, whip cream until stiff and combine with crème de menthe and crème de cacao. (Add few drops of green food coloring, if desired.) Fold marshmallow-milk mixture into whipped cream mixture. Alternate this mixture with cookie crumbs in 6 chilled parfait (or wine) glasses. Top with cookie crumbs. Chill.

Variation:
This can be made into a pie. Combine cookie crumbs with ⅓ cup melted butter, and pat into a 9″ pie pan. Chill crust before adding the marshmallow-milk mixture. Garnish with additional cookie crumbs.

Mrs. James Harlow

OPAL'S APPLE PUDDING

¼ cup shortening
⅔ cup white sugar
½ cup brown sugar
2 cups peeled, chopped, raw apples
¼ cup chopped nuts

1 egg
1 cup flour
1 teaspoon baking soda
½ teaspoon nutmeg
½ teaspoon cinnamon
Whipped topping, as garnish

Cream together the shortening and the sugars. Add apples, nuts, and egg. Mix well. Mix the flour, baking soda, nutmeg, and cinnamon; add to the apple mixture. Bake in a greased pan for 30 minutes at 350°. Serve warm with whipped topping. Serves 6 to 8.

Mrs. John Raynes

EASY POTS DE CREME DESSERT

1 (6 ounce) package chocolate chips
2 tablespoons water
6 egg yolks

½ teaspoon salt
1 teaspoon vanilla
6 egg whites, beaten until stiff

Combine chocolate and water. Melt over hot water or low heat until smooth, stirring. Remove from heat and add yolks, one at a time, beating in each one. Add salt and vanilla. Fold in beaten egg whites. Spoon pot de crème into cups, or something similar. Chill 3 hours or overnight. Serves 8.

Mrs. Andrew A. Payne, Jr.

POTS DE CREME LEOPARDO

1 pound ricotta cheese
¼ cup sugar
3 tablespoons orange-flavored liqueur

2 tablespoons heavy cream
2 ounces semi-sweet chocolate, chopped (tiny chocolate chips may be used)

In a bowl combine well ricotta cheese, sugar, liqueur, heavy cream, and chocolate. Fill 12 small ramekins half full.

SECOND LAYER

6 ounces semi-sweet chocolate pieces	2 egg yolks
	Dash of salt
1¼ cups light cream	Toasted almonds

In a heavy saucepan combine chocolate pieces and light cream. Stir over low heat until blended satin smooth. Mixture should be fairly thick, but keep it from boiling. Beat egg yolks with a dash of salt until thick. Gradually stir the chocolate mixture into the eggs. Spoon on top of the ricotta mixture. Chill at least 4 hours. Garnish with toasted almonds. Serves 12.

Dr. Susan Hartman

RICE IMPERATRICE PUDDING FOR 12 TO 15

½ (3 ounce) box red gelatin	4 envelopes unflavored gelatin
1 cup boiling water	¾ cup cold water
¾ cup rice	2 cups whipping cream
2 cups water	¾ to 1 teaspoon lemon oil or
4 cups milk	rind
⅞ cup sugar	1 teaspoon vanilla extract

Dissolve red gelatin in boiling water. Pour into custard cups or 3 quart shallow dish. Let set partially. Cook rice and water until dry. Add milk to rice and cook until thick, about 1 hour. Stir sugar into rice. Soften unflavored gelatin in cold water; stir into rice. Let rice cool. Whip cream and fold whipped cream and flavorings into rice. Carefully spoon onto partially set red gelatin. Refrigerate until set, about 3 hours. Serve with Melba Sauce which is traditional, brandied fruit, Rumtopf, or any other fruit-type sauce.

MELBA SAUCE

3 cups raspberries, strained to remove seeds	1 tablespoon cornstarch, (optional)
¾ cup sugar	¼ cup water, (optional)

Combine berries and sugar; cook for 10 minutes over low heat. For a slightly thicker sauce, soften cornstarch in water and add to sugar-berry mixture, cooking until sauce is thickened and clear.

The Greenbrier

SIMPLE, SPEEDY, TASTY CUSTARD

Phyllis Curtin, born in Clarksburg, West Virginia, has performed as a soprano soloist with leading symphony orchestras in the United States and foreign countries. Miss Curtin made her Metropolitan Opera debut in 1961 and her debut with La Scala Opera in 1962. The recipe for custard is especially enjoyed by Miss Curtin be-

cause, as her husband writes, it supplies "good solid energy" which keeps "the singing machinery in shape."

1 quart milk, approximately	Nutmeg and/or cinnamon
4 or 5 eggs	2 tablespoons sugar

Beat eggs into milk and sugar; a blender gives a smooth mixture. Add sprinkling of nutmeg; cinnamon is optional. Place mixture in top of double boiler with water already boiling. Cover, and let cook for 13 to 15 minutes. When done, a knife stuck into custard should come out quite clean.

For people who like raisins, these may be sprinkled in after custard has been cooking for 10 minutes or so. They can even be dropped in while mixture is being beaten. Also grated lemon peel can be beaten into mixture to add interesting flavor. We prefer the flavor of honey instead of sugar and sometimes substitute this, or even use part sugar, part honey for the sweetening.

Miss Phyllis Curtin

VELVET PUDDING

Miss Wilson is a member of the well-known Greenbrier County family and resides at "Valley View Farm." The residence, originally the "Tuckwiller Tavern," is well documented in Ruth Woods Dayton's book about Greenbrier Valley homes.

4 eggs	4 tablespoons cornstarch
4 cups milk	Pinch salt
1 cup sugar, divided	1 teaspoon vanilla

Separate eggs; beat yolks well and mix with milk. Combine ¾ cup sugar, cornstarch, and salt. Add milk and egg yolks to sugar mixture. Cook in double boiler until thick, stirring often. Remove from heat; add vanilla. Beat egg whites and ¼ cup sugar until stiff. Put pudding in a baking dish and spread egg whites over the top of the pudding. Brown the meringue in a 350° oven until desired brown. Serves 10. The pudding is also delicious if the egg whites are folded into the pudding while it is hot.

Miss Mary J. Wilson

BLACK WALNUT CANDY

1 cup sugar	1 cup shelled black walnuts
1 cup water	½ teaspoon rum extract,
1 teaspoon salt	optional

Cook sugar and water until it barely threads (235°) and let stand until bubbles leave. Add 1 teaspoon salt and beat until cloudy. Add walnuts and rum extract and beat until fairly stiff. Pour onto board, let set, and break into pieces.

Mrs. Carl B. Hall, Jr.

BUTTERCREAMS

1 pound powdered sugar	½ to ¾ teaspoon vanilla
1 stick margarine	1 square inch paraffin
2 tablespoons evaporated milk	4 squares semi-sweet chocolate
	2 tablespoons butter

Cream sugar, margarine, milk, and vanilla; form into 1" balls using hands if necessary. Put in freezer for ½ hour. Melt chocolate, paraffin, and butter in a small heatproof dish over low heat. Dip balls in chocolate. Keep in covered tin in refrigerator. Makes 4 dozen.

To dip: spear chilled candy on toothpick and quickly dip and swirl to cover completely; push off with second toothpick and drop a chocolate drop from tip of pick to cover hole in candy.

Suggestions: at Easter, form into egg shapes and vary the flavoring: Cherry — substitute maraschino cherry juice for milk and add 3 tablespoons finely chopped cherries. Peanut Butter — add 3 tablespoons peanut butter and decrease butter by 2 tablespoons. Coconut — add 3 tablespoons finely chopped coconut. Chocolate — add 2 tablespoons instant cocoa.

ICING

2 cups powdered sugar	4 tablespoons shortening
Milk enough to make a firm but usable icing.	

Mix all ingredients. Food coloring, optional.

Mrs. Jerry L. Frazier

BUTTERMILK PRALINES

2 cups white sugar	1½ tablespoons butter or
1 cup buttermilk	margarine
1 teaspoon soda	1 teaspoon vanilla
⅛ teaspoon salt	2 cups broken pecans

Mix sugar, buttermilk, soda, and salt in a heavy 3-quart saucepan, and cook over medium heat to soft-ball stage. Cool. Beat in butter and vanilla and stir in pecans. Drop by tablespoons onto wax paper to cool. Work fast. If it starts to harden in the pan, add a few drops of buttermilk, reheat, and stir well.

Mrs. Samuel W. Channell

CANDIED GRAPEFRUIT PEEL

2 grapefruit shells	1 quart water
1 cup salt	1 cup sugar
	¼ cup water

Take lining off peel. Use only the yellow part. Cut into strips. Soak a day or 2 in brine, made by mixing salt and 1 quart of water.

Drain and wash. Put in cold water. Boil thoroughly 5 times, changing water each time. Drain well in colander. Boil sugar and ¼ cup water to make a thick syrup. Drop strips into syrup. Baste and simmer till all syrup is absorbed; don't stir. Let cool in pan. When almost cool, roll in granulated sugar.

Miss Ann Hunter

CHOCOLATE NUGGETS

1 cup (6 ounce package) semi-sweet chocolate pieces
½ cup cola beverage
3 tablespoons light corn syrup
1 tablespoon rum extract
2½ cups (7¼ ounce package) finely crushed vanilla wafers
2 cups powdered sugar, sifted
1 cup finely chopped nuts
Chocolate decorating candies

Melt chocolate in double boiler over hot water; remove from heat. Blend in cola, corn syrup, and rum extract. Stir in crumbs, sugar, and nuts, mixing thoroughly (will be sticky and stiff). Cover and chill about 2 hours or until easy to handle. Form into small balls (about 1 rounded teaspoon) by rolling in palms of hands. Roll in decorating candies to coat. Place in single layer on wax paper in shallow pan, and cover loosely. Chill overnight to firm up and to mellow flavors. Makes about 3 dozen.

Mrs. Charles G. Moyers, Jr.

FUDGE CANDY

4 cups sugar
1 (13 ounce) can evaporated milk
½ pound butter
2½ cups chocolate chips
1 jar marshmallow cream
2 cups nuts

Boil sugar and milk for 5 minutes. Add butter and boil for 7 more minutes. Add chocolate chips, marshmallow cream, and nuts. Pour into shallow pan and chill until set.

Mrs. Carroll Dorsey

PEANUT LOG

1 box powdered sugar
1 cup shredded coconut
1 cup chopped nuts
1 cup graham cracker crumbs
1 teaspoon vanilla
½ cup peanut butter
1 cup margarine or butter, melted
1 (6 ounce) package chocolate chips
½ block paraffin

Mix first 6 ingredients. Pour melted butter over mixture and roll mixture into logs or balls. Melt chocolate chips and paraffin over boiling water. Dip logs in chocolate. Lift out with fork. Will keep a long time if stored in tin container in refrigerator.

Miss Betty Cook

SEA FOAM CANDY

3 cups light brown sugar	¾ cup water
¼ teaspoon salt	2 egg whites, beaten
	1 teaspoon vanilla

Dissolve sugar and salt in water. Cook without stirring until mixture reaches 255⁰ or hard ball stage. Remove from heat and pour gradually over beaten egg whites in a large bowl, beating constantly. Add vanilla and continue to beat until cool enough to handle and mixture holds its shape. Drop by spoonfuls on waxed paper. (At this point it would help to have 2 people working to prevent loss of gloss.) Allow candy to harden.

Mrs. H. C. Melton

WALNUT CHRISTMAS TOFFEE

1 cup butter	3 tablespoons water
1 cup sugar	1½ cups chopped walnuts
1 tablespoon white corn syrup	4 plain Hershey bars

Butter a 9″ square pan. Melt butter in 2 quart saucepan; gradually stir in sugar. Add syrup and water. Cook over moderate heat, stirring occasionally, until mixture reaches 290° on candy thermometer. Add 1 cup walnuts, and cook 3 minutes more, stirring occasionally. Pour into pan. When it is set, but not cool, crumble 2 Hershey bars on top and spread them to cover. Sprinkle with ¼ cup finely chopped nuts. Turn onto waxed paper and repeat procedure with remaining 2 Hershey bars and ¼ cup nuts. When cold, break into small pieces.

If toffee gets too cold to melt Hersheys, melt them over warm water, but it works best if chocolate is melted right on toffee.

Mrs. Kenneth Underwood

BUTTERSCOTCH SAUCE

1 cup white or brown sugar	½ cup cream
1 cup blue label corn syrup	1 tablespoon butter

Put ingredients together in double boiler and cook slowly a couple of hours. Serve with toasted almonds or vanilla ice cream.

Mrs. Frederick Staunton

BRANDIED DATE WALNUT SAUCE

2 cups light brown sugar
1 cup water
¼ cup brandy

1 package (8 ounce) pitted
    dates, cubed
1 cup walnut halves

In medium saucepan combine brown sugar and water. Cook, stirring occasionally over medium heat for 20 minutes. Add brandy, dates and nuts. Stir until combined. Serve hot or cooled over vanilla ice cream. If desired, heat another ¼ cup brandy, ignite and pour over ice cream and sauce for Date Walnut Sauce Flambé. Makes 3 cups.

Mrs. W. Gaston Caperton, III

OLD FASHIONED FUDGE SAUCE

1 cup sugar
4 heaping tablespoon cocoa
1 heaping tablespoon flour
1 teaspoon vanilla

½ cup milk
2 tablespoons butter
Pinch of salt

Mix first six ingredients and boil for two minutes, stirring constantly. Remove from heat and add vanilla. Serves 8. Serve over ice cream or pound cake.

Mrs. Henry E. Payne, III

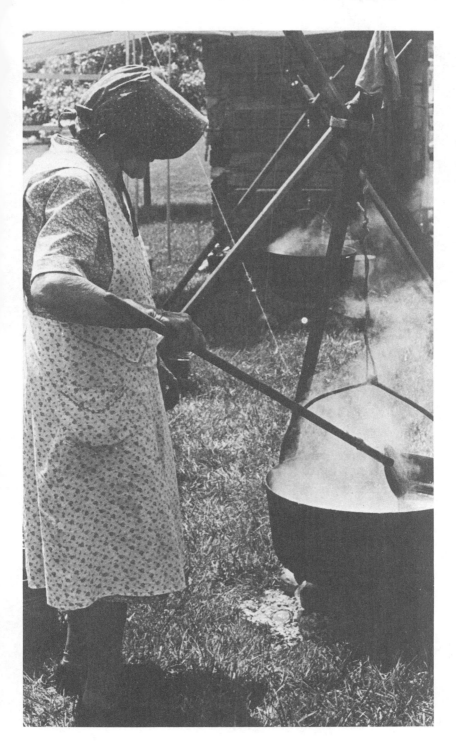

GRANNY SAUNDERS

Her ministration was to heal
With pungent herb and bitter peel.
Up in the drying loft she hung
Horehound and sage and blacksnake-tongue,
Wild cherry, spice bush, "penny rorrel,"
Blue monkshood, ginseng, sour sorrel,
Thin twisted stalks, sharp jimson weeds,
Bloody percoons, hot mustard seeds,
And meadow docks — both broad and narrow,
Rough bone-set, golden thread, and yarrow,
Field balsam, catnip, dittany,
All to be simmered down to tea.

All to be brewed for aches and ills —
Red pepper pods for croup and chills;
Spearmint for phthisic; flax for pain;
Horseradish roots for bruise or sprain;
And for certain maladies
The northwest bark of dogwood trees.

Reprinted by permission of Louise McNeill, from **Gauley Mountain;**
Harcourt, Brace and Company; New York, New York; 1939; Page 18.

Photo by Gerald S. Ratliff

BEVERAGES

Double T

JERRY'S AFTER DINNER COFFEE

1 cup hot strong instant coffee ½ ounce Kahlua or Tia Maria
½ ounce crème de cacao   1 teaspoon brandy
    1 spoonful whipped cream or frozen whipped topping

Mix coffee, crème de cacoa, and Kahlua. Float brandy on top. Add a spoonful whipped cream and serve. This coffee is better if each cup is prepared individually.

H. Jarrett Walker

PINA COLADA

½ (8¾ ounce) can cream of   ¾ cup white rum
    coconut   Ice, to fill blender
1 cup pineapple juice,   Fresh pineapple
    unsweetened

Put all ingredients in blender; blend thoroughly, and serve with garnish of shaft of fresh pineapple. Serves 4.

E. Charles Brod, Jr.

BOURBON SLUSH

4 tea bags   1 (12 ounce) can frozen orange
2 cups boiling water   juice, thawed
2 cups sugar   1 (6 ounce) can frozen
                                   lemonade, thawed
                               1 cup bourbon
                    7 cups water

Steep tea in boiling water for 3 minutes. Stir in sugar. Add remaining ingredients and stir until sugar dissolves. Freeze in cube trays or other shallow pan. Remove 10 minutes before serving. Spoon into cocktail glasses or blend in blender. Garnish with lemon wedges and cherries. Serves 20.

Mrs. William Morrelles

CRANBERRY CORDIAL

1 pound cranberries   1 pound sugar
1 fifth of gin

Wash and discard any unsound berries, but add enough until there is one pound. Dry and punch two holes in each berry. Put berries, sugar, and gin in half-gallon sterile canning jar. Seal and give jar a shake each day for six weeks. Strain and put in decanter with a tight-fitting stopper. Delicious plain, or mixed with ice and 7-Up, ginger ale, etc. Makes great Christmas gifts if you start soon enough.

Mrs. William H. Knight

HOMEGROWN COFFEE LIQUEUR

6 cups sugar   2 ounces instant coffee
2 quarts water, divided   2 ounces *pure* vanilla
1 quart 190 proof grain alcohol

Dissolve sugar in 1 quart boiling water and set aside to cool. Dissolve coffee in 1 quart boiling water and set aside to cool. Pour into gallon jar; add vanilla and grain alcohol. Set aside for 5 minutes. Pour into fifth bottles. Makes 5 fifths.

Mrs. Don R. Richardson

HOT BUTTERED RUM

1 pound butter   Rum
2 pounds dark brown sugar   Boiling water
1 gallon vanilla ice cream   Nutmeg

Melt butter and stir in the sugar. When blended, slowly beat in the ice cream and mix well. Put in a large container and place in the freezer for at least 24 hours. To serve, put 1 jigger of rum and ½ cup boiling water in each pottery mug and top with a generous amount of frozen mixture (about ¼ cup). Sprinkle with a dash of nutmeg and serve immediately.

Mrs. Kenneth E. Underwood

QUICK GRAPE JUICE

1 to 1½ cups ripe Concord   ½ cup sugar
   grapes

Wash grapes and put in sterilized quart jar. Add ½ cup sugar and fill with boiling water. Seal. Process in water bath 30 minutes at simmering temperature (180°). Let stand 6 months.

Mrs. Frank A. Thomas, Sr.

ROOT BEER

4 pounds sugar
5 gallons water, lukewarm

1 bottle root beer extract
½ to 1 package compressed
   yeast (more in cold weather)

Dissolve sugar in lukewarm water. Add root beer extract and compressed yeast. Mix and bottle; cork or seal tightly. Set in warm place. Root beer is ready for use in 10 to 12 hours. It is better if allowed to stand for several days. Store in a cool place.

Mrs. Carl B. Hall, Jr.

SASSAFRAS TEA

½ cup sassafras root, fresh or
   dried

4 to 6 cups water
Honey or sugar to taste

If using freshly dug sassafras root, chop or scrape it into small pieces. Put sassafras and water in kettle and boil until the water turns red. Sweeten to taste. Pour through strainer before serving. The sassafras can be used to make tea at least two more times. Serve iced or hot.

Mrs. John P. Killoran

SPICED TEA

6 cups water
1 tablespoon whole cloves
1 inch cinnamon stick

2½ tablespoons tea leaves
2 tablespoons lemon juice
¾ cup orange juice

½ cup sugar

Boil water; add cloves, cinnamon, and tea leaves. Remove from heat and steep for 5 minutes. Strain. Heat lemon juice, orange juice, and sugar until boiling and add to hot tea. If too strong, add more boiling water. Serves 6 to 8.

Mrs. John Casto

HOT SPICED PERCOLATOR PUNCH

3 cups water
3 cups canned pineapple juice
1 tablespoon whole cloves
½ tablespoon whole allspice

3 sticks cinnamon, broken
¼ teaspoon salt
½ cup brown sugar, packed
   (light or dark)

¼ teaspoon salt

Put pineapple juice and water in bottom part of 8-cup percolator. Put other ingredients in basket and percolate as for coffee. Serve hot in mugs or punch cups. Recipe may be tripled or quadrupled and prepared in large (30 to 35 cup) percolator.

Mrs. Jon Michael Gaston

HOT SPICED CIDER

2 quarts apple cider
¼ cup sugar (more if desired)
⅛ teaspoon salt

8 whole cloves
8 whole allspice
8 sticks cinnamon (2 inches each)

Vodka (optional)

Combine all ingredients except vodka in a large saucepan and bring to a boil. Reduce heat to low and simmer for 5 minutes. Strain out spices before serving. If desired, place a jigger of vodka into each cup and pour the hot cider mixture over this. Serve in mugs with a cinnamon stick stirrer. Serves 8.

Mrs. Charles G. Moyers, Jr.

HOT CHOCOLATE MIX

1 (11 ounce) jar coffee cream substitute
1 (2 pound) box instant chocolate flavor

4 cups powdered sugar
14 or 16 quart box powdered milk

Mix all the ingredients together. Store in 6 quart size jars. To serve, place ½ cup of mix in a teacup and stir in ½ cup boiling water.

Mrs. L. Douglas Curnutte

SUPERB HOT CHOCOLATE

2 squares Baker's chocolate
½ cup water
¾ cup sugar

Pinch of salt
½ cup cream, whipped
1 quart milk

Boil chocolate in water 4 minutes, stirring constantly. Add sugar and salt. Cook 4 minutes, stirring constantly. Cool. When thoroughly cold, fold into whipped cream. Heat milk to boiling point and pour over 1 tablespoon chocolate mixture in each cup when serving. Serves 6.

Mrs. H. H. Smallridge

EGGNOG

5 eggs, separated
5 heaping teaspoons sugar
½ pint whiskey

2 teaspoons rum
1 pint whipping cream
Nutmeg

Beat together the egg yolks and sugar. Slowly stir in the whiskey, then the rum. Add cream. Beat the egg whites until stiff, and then add to the cream and whiskey mixture, stirring well. Grate nutmeg on top to taste. If mixture is too thick, add milk to thin. Serves 7 to 8.

Miss Libby Beury

SYLLABUB

1 quart heavy cream   ½ cup sugar
1 cup Madeira or scuppernong   Nutmeg
     wine or sherry

Whip cream until thick and sweeten with sugar. Gradually pour in 1 cup wine (or to taste). Sprinkle nutmeg on top. Serves approximately 15. Use punch bowl and cups.

Mrs. Otis L. O'Conner

CHRISTMAS PUNCH

1 (12 ounce) can frozen   2 cups water
     lemonade   Strawberries (optional
1 (6 ounce) can frozen orange   quantity)
     juice   1 quart ginger ale
1 quart cranberry juice   Vodka (optional)
2 cups strong tea

If desired, the lemonade, orange juice, cranberry juice, and tea may be mixed ahead. At serving time, add the water, strawberries, and ginger ale. Vodka may also be added at serving time. Serves 16 to 20.

Mrs. L. Douglas Curnutte

COFFEE PUNCH

2 quarts strong coffee   2 quarts milk
     2 quarts vanilla ice cream

Mix the above ingredients. Makes 50 servings.

Miss Mary Blaine McLaughlin

FRUIT SLUSH

3 large bananas, crushed   3 cups pineapple juice
1 (6 ounce) can orange juice   2½ cups sugar
1 (3 ounce) can lemon juice   5 cups water
     2 (32 ounces each) bottles ginger ale

Purée banana in blender with orange juice and lemon juice. Transfer to large container and add pineapple juice, sugar, and water. Pour into 2 large, shallow pans and freeze. Twenty minutes before serving, partially thaw and mix in punch bowl with the 2 bottles of ginger ale. Serves 15 to 20.

Miss Jane Mathews

P.T.A. PUNCH

1 (46 ounce) can pineapple
    juice
1 (46 ounce) can grapefruit
    juice

2 cans (12 ounces each) frozen
    orange juice
2 large bottles ginger ale

Mix juices. Pour half over crushed ice in a bowl. Add one bottle of ginger ale. Add remaining fruit juice with second bottle of ginger ale. Serves 50.

Mrs. Soul Snyder

SANGRIA (A Spanish Punch)

½ gallon California red wine
1 cup gin or brandy (depending
    on flavor preference)
1½ to 2 cups sugar

Juice of 3 oranges
Juice of 2 lemons
1 each: lemon, lime, orange,
    and apple, unpeeled and cut
    in large slices

Mix all ingredients except fruit. Drop fruit into liquors. This is better made the night before so that fruit and liquor flavors will blend. Place in refrigerator overnight and cover to prevent evaporation. This recipe can be easily doubled or tripled.

Miss Sara Ziebold

SUMMER PUNCH

2 cups boiling water
2 teaspoons tea leaves
1 cup extra-fine, powdered
    sugar
2 cups grape juice

Juice of 3 to 4 lemons
2¼ cups pineapple juice
1 quart ginger ale
Lime slices or mint sprigs
Gin or vodka, optional

Pour boiling water over tea; cover and steep for 3 minutes; then strain. Combine tea, sugar, and fruit juices and chill. Add ginger ale just before serving. Serve with cracked ice or ice cubes. Garnish with slices of lime or mint sprigs. Mades 10 large glasses. A jigger of gin or vodka may be added to each serving.

Mrs. Helen Townsend Ziebold

WEDDING PUNCH

5 cases Sauterne wine   1 case California brandy
10 quarts orange ice

Mix all ingredients. Serves 100. To make enough for one punch bowl, mix the following proportions:

12 bottles Sauterne wine   2 bottles California brandy
2 quarts orange ice

Mrs. C. K. Payne, III

WINE PUNCH

1 cup bar syrup   1 cup strong black tea
1 cup dry sherry   1 pint freshly squeezed lemon
1 cup brandy   juice
3 (1/5) bottles Rhine wine
1 quart chilled soda water

Combine syrup, sherry, brandy, and tea, and chill thoroughly. When ready to serve, put in large punch bowl with lemon juice and Rhine wine. Mix. Add block of ice and soda water. Serves 10 to 15.

BAR SYRUP
1 cup water   3 cups sugar

Boil water and sugar for 2 minutes and chill immediately to prevent crystallization.

Ronald McKenney

INDEX

(please print)

JUNIOR LEAGUE OF CHARLESTON, WEST VIRGINIA
MOUNTAIN MEASURES
Post Office Box 1924
Charleston, West Virginia 25327

Please send _____ copies of **MOUNTAIN MEASURES**
at $9.95 plus $1.50 per copy for postage and handling.
West Virginia residents, please include sales tax of 50¢.

Enclosed is $ _____   ☐ check ☐ money order
Send to: _____
_____
_____

(All copies will be sent to same address unless otherwise specified. If
you wish to enclose your own gift card with book, please write name of
recipient on outside of envelope, enclose with order, and we will include
it with your gift.)

Allow four weeks for delivery

Gift wrapping available — Add 50¢ to total price of order.

(please print)

JUNIOR LEAGUE OF CHARLESTON, WEST VIRGINIA
MOUNTAIN MEASURES
Post Office Box 1924
Charleston, West Virginia 25327

Please send _____ copies of **MOUNTAIN MEASURES**
at $9.95 plus $1.50 per copy for postage and handling.
West Virginia residents, please include sales tax of 50¢.

Enclosed is $ _____   ☐ check ☐ money order
Send to: _____
_____
_____

(All copies will be sent to same address unless otherwise specified. If
you wish to enclose your own gift card with book, please write name of
recipient on outside of envelope, enclose with order, and we will include
it with your gift.)

Allow four weeks for delivery

Gift wrapping available — Add 50¢ to total price of order.